Reading Rants

A guide to books that rock!

Jennifer Hubert

Neal-Schuman Publishers, Inc.

New York   London

To my mom, Judith MacIver,
who always believed I could write a book,
and my husband, Philip Swan,
who very patiently coached me through it

Published by Neal-Schuman Publishers, Inc.
100 William Street, Suite 2004
New York, NY 10038–4512

Printed and bound in the United States of America.

The paper used in this publication meets the minimum requirements of American
National Standard for Information Sciences — Permanence of Paper for Printed
Library Materials, ANSI Z39.48-1992.
ISBN-13: 978-1-55570-587-9
ISBN-10: 1-55570-587-1

Library of Congress Cataloging-in-Publication Data

Hubert, Jennifer, 1973–
    Reading rants : a guide to books that rock! / Jennifer Hubert.
        p. cm. — (Teens @ the library series)
    Includes bibliographical references and index.
    ISBN-13: 978-1-55570-587-9 (alk. paper)
    ISBN-10: 1-55570-587-1 (alk. paper)
    1. Teenagers—Books and reading—Bibliography. 2. Young adults' libraries—Book
lists. 3. Young adult literature—Bibliography. 4. Libraries and teenagers. I. Title.
    Z1037.H865 2007
    011.62—dc22

                                                                    2006102711

TABLE OF CONTENTS

Complete List of Recommended Titles v

Series Editor's Foreword ix

Preface xi

Acknowledgments xiii

1. Boy Meets Book: Realistic Reads for Male Teens 1

2. Righteous Riot Grrl Reads 21

3. The Closet Club: Fiction for GLBTQ Teens and Their Friends 47

4. The Terrible Tweens: 10–13 Going on 30 75

5. True Grit: The Most Challenging (and Possibly Challenged) Titles 101

6. Graphic Fantastic: Graphic Novels with Teen Appeal 119

7. Historical Fiction for Hipsters 145

8. Nail-biters: Teen Tales of Mystery and Suspense 175

9. Dystopian Dreams: Teen Sci-Fi 203

10. Graduating Hogwarts: Post–Harry Potter Fantasy for Teens 233

Title Index 261

Author Index 263

About the Author 265

COMPLETE LIST OF RECOMMENDED TITLES

1. **Boy Meets Book: Realistic Reads for Male Teens**
   Auseon, Andrew   *Funny Little Monkey* 2
   Curtis, Christopher Paul   *Bucking the Sarge* 3
   Green, John   *Looking for Alaska* 5
   Hautman, Pete   *Godless* 7
   Jenkins, A.M.   *Out of Order* 9
   Nelson, Blake   *Rock Star Superstar* 10
   Powell, Randy   *Three Clams and an Oyster* 12
   Slade, Arthur   *Tribes* 14
   Weaver, Will   *Full Service* 15
   Yoo, David   *Girls for Breakfast* 18

2. **Righteous Riot Grrl Reads**
   Dessen, Sarah   *This Lullaby* 22
   Flake, Sharon G.   *Who Am I without Him?: Short Stories
                                 about Girls and the Boys in Their Lives* 24
   Frank, Hilary   *Better Than Running at Night* 27
   Lockhart, E.   *The Boyfriend List* 29
   Mackler, Carolyn   *The Earth, My Butt, and Other Big Round Things* ... 31
   Marchetta, Melina   *Saving Francesca* 33
   Moriarty, Jaclyn   *The Year of Secret Assignments* 36
   Sones, Sonya   *One of Those Hideous Books
                                 Where the Mother Dies* 38
   Stone, Tanya Lee   *A Bad Boy Can Be Good for a Girl* 41
   Vance, Susanna   *Deep* 43

3. **The Closet Club: Fiction for GLBTQ Teens and Their Friends**
   Ferris, Jean   *Eight Seconds* 48
   Freymann-Weyr, Garrett   *My Heartbeat* 50
   Hartinger, Brent   *Geography Club* 53
   Hyde, Catherine Ryan   *Becoming Chloe* 55
   Johnson, Maureen   *The Bermudez Triangle* 58
   Larochelle, David   *Absolutely, Positively, Not...* 61
   Levithan, David   *Boy Meets Boy* 63

Myracle, Lauren	*Kissing Kate*	66
Ryan, Sara	*Empress of the World*	68
Wittlinger, Elllen	*Hard Love*	71

4. The Terrible Tweens: 10–13 Going on 30

Boyce, Frank Cottrell	*Millions*	76
Broach, Elise	*Shakespeare's Secret*	78
Choldenko, Gennifer	*Al Capone Does My Shirts*	80
Clements, Andrew	*Things Not Seen*	83
Jocelyn, Marthe	*Mabel Riley: A Reliable Record of Humdrum, Peril, and Romance*	85
Nelson, Blake	*Gender Blender*	87
Nickerson, Sara	*How to Disappear Completely and Never Be Found*	89
Shusterman, Neal	*The Schwa Was Here*	92
Weeks, Sarah	*So B. It*	94
Winerip, Michael	*Adam Canfield of the Slash*	97

5. True Grit: The Most Challenging (and Possibly Challenged) Titles

Burgess, Melvin	*Doing It*	102
Crutcher, Chris	*Whale Talk*	104
Frank, E. R.	*America: A Novel*	105
Hopkins, Ellen	*Crank*	106
Jacobson, Jennifer Richard	*Stained*	108
Johnson, Kathleen Jeffrie	*Target*	110
Nolan, Han	*Born Blue*	111
Paulsen, Gary	*The Beet Fields: Memories of a Sixteenth Summer*	113
Rapp, Adam	*33 Snowfish*	114
Williams-Garcia, Rita	*No Laughter Here*	116

6. Graphic Fantastic: Graphic Novels with Teen Appeal

Cooke, Darwyn	*Catwoman: Selina's Big Score*	120
Clugston-Major, Chynna	*Queen Bee*	122
Loeb, Jeph, and Tim Sale	*Spider-Man: Blue*	124
Niles, Steve, and Ben Templesmith	*30 Days of Night*	127
Parker, Jeff	*The Interman*	129
Smith, Jeff, and Charles Vess	*Rose*	131
Vaughan, Brian K., and Adrian Alphona	*Runaways: Pride and Joy*	134
Vaughan, Brian K., and Pia Guerra	*Y: The Last Man—Unmanned*	136
Whedon, Joss; Karl Moline; and Andy Owens	*Fray*	138
Willingham, Bill, et al.	*Fables: Legends in Exile*	141

7. Historical Fiction for Hipsters

Carbone, Elisa	*Last Dance on Holladay Street*	146
Donnelly, Jennifer	*A Northern Light*	148
Hearn, Julie	*The Minister's Daughter*	151
McCaughrean, Geraldine	*The Kite Rider*	154
Meyer, L. A.	*Bloody Jack: Being an Account of the Curious Adventures of Mary "Jacky" Faber, Ship's Boy*	157
Morpungo, Michael	*Private Peaceful*	159
Napoli, Donna Jo	*Breath*	162
Salisbury, Graham	*Eyes of the Emperor*	165
Spinelli, Jerry	*Milkweed*	168
Updale, Eleanor	*Montmorency: Thief, Liar, Gentleman?*	171

8. Nail-biters: Teen Tales of Mystery and Suspense

Cormier, Robert	*The Rag and Bone Shop*	176
Flinn, Alex	*Nothing to Lose*	178
Giles, Gail	*Shattering Glass*	181
Klass, David	*You Don't Know Me*	183
Lynch, Chris	*Inexcusable*	186
McNamee, Graham	*Acceleration*	189
Morgenroth, Kate	*Jude*	191
Springer, Nancy	*The Case of the Missing Marquess: An Enola Holmes Mystery*	194
Trueman, Terry	*Inside Out*	197
Werlin, Nancy	*The Rules of Survival*	199

9. Dystopian Dreams: Teen Sci-Fi

Adlington, L. J.	*The Diary of Pelly D.*	204
Anderson, M. T.	*Feed*	206
Halam, Ann	*Siberia: A Novel*	209
Hautman, Pete	*Rash*	212
Lanagan, Margo	*Black Juice*	215
Oppel, Kenneth	*Airborn*	218
Pfeffer, Susan Beth	*Life as We Knew It*	221
Reeve, Philip	*Mortal Engines*	224
Westerfeld, Scott	*Uglies*	226
Zahn, Timothy	*Dragon and Thief*	229

10. Graduating Hogwarts: Post–Harry Potter Fantasy for Teens

Barker, Clive	*Abarat*	234
Bray, Libba	*A Great and Terrible Beauty*	236
Delaney, Joseph	*The Last Apprentice, Book 1: Revenge of the Witch*	239
Fisher, Catherine	*The Oracle Prophecies, Book 1: The Oracle Betrayed*	241
Horowitz, Anthony	*Raven's Gate*	244
Pattou, Edith	*East*	246

Pratchett, Terry   *The Wee Free Men* 249
Shinn, Sharon   *The Safe-Keeper's Secret* 252
Stroud, Jonathan   *The Bartimaeus Trilogy, Book 1:*
                       The Amulet of Samarkand 254
Wooding, Chris   *Poison* 257

SERIES EDITOR'S FOREWORD

I work hard to stay up-to-date with the literature written for teens. When I served on the Best Books for Young Adults (BBYA) committee for the Young Adult Library Services Association (YALSA) in the early 1990s, I challenged myself to read an average of one young adult book every day. I have continued this routine ever since. Although I sometimes fall short, I bet I read more than 300 titles per year. Guess what? I still can't read them all! Recommendations from teen readers, teachers, newspapers, magazines, journals, radio, television, and Web sites all constantly alert me to books I have missed.

That's why I look forward to putting *Reading Rants: A Guide to Books That Rock!* to work. Jennifer Hubert has a broad and deep knowledge of contemporary YA literature, developed through a lifetime of reading and her own stint on the BBYA committee. At her incredible Reading Rants Web site, available at *http://tln.lib.mi.us/~amutch/jen*, she demonstrates her signature wit and in-depth understanding of both teens and the books written for them. She has also published hundreds of evaluative reviews on other Web sites and in-print publications. Combine all this with her perspective as a school librarian in New York City and you may conclude, as I did, that she is the perfect person to write *Reading Rants: A Guide to Books That Rock!*

In this volume you will find in-depth synopses of 100 recently published, highly regarded, bound-to-be-popular books for teens. Each summary is like having a conversation with Jen herself. Her summaries for titles you have already read will refresh your memory on plot points and deliver new insights into character, motivation, and theme. You will also be inspired to read those books you've missed. *Reading Rants* will increase your expertise and bolster your confidence in readers' advisory.

Jen provides much more than insightful, cogent, detailed summaries of these great reads. For each title, she includes the following elements:

- "The Message" pinpoints themes
- "Who's It For?" gives the most likely reader's grade level and gender
- "Why It Rocks" highlights particular strengths and appeal
- "Hook It Up With" lists at least one other title that a reader of the book might also enjoy
- "Read More about It" provides citations of published professional reviews.

These carefully considered elements make *Reading Rants: A Guide to Books That Rock!* a truly outstanding reference tool for reading guidance. Jennifer's summaries will motivate you to start reading more. You will find yourself actively looking for opportunities to share these titles with your teen customers. After all, don't they deserve to read the best? *Reading Rants: A Guide to Books That Rock* can help you provide just that—the best readers' advisory service to your teens.

I trust you will enjoy your conversation with Jen as much as I did. Happy reading!

Joel Shoemaker
Teens@ the Library Series Editor

PREFACE

Greetings, fellow young adult librarians, middle and high school teachers, booksellers, and all other technologically savvy and pop-culturally astute mavens of adolescent book style! I hope you'll find that *Reading Rants: A Guide to Books That Rock!* will help you connect with the teen tribe in your school, public library, or local bookstore.

How do we get teens to power down their iPods and Playstation Portables and crack open a book? We do this by learning what their interests are and matching those interests to the growing body of fantastic young adult literature that would be available to them if they just knew about it. *Reading Rants* showcases 100 of the latest, greatest young adult titles. These detailed summaries will help you make selection decisions, identify books for your own reading, and recommend and booktalk titles to your teens.

Reading Rants springs from a need I identified on my Web site, also named Reading Rants (if you haven't heard of it, please check it out: Reading Rants! Out of the Ordinary Booklists for Teens, http://tln.lib.mi.us/~amutch/jen). My informal book review Web site is written to and for teenagers, so I was surprised by how many adult librarians, teachers, and parents enthusiastically responded to the reviews and e-mailed me their questions and suggestions. But the Reading Rants Web site is written for teenagers, not grown-ups. With *Reading Rants: A Guide to Books That Rock*, I have tried to combine my Web site's fun and informal tone with age recommendations, alerts about tough content, and even a little bit of literary criticism for you former English majors.

Librarians, teachers, and book buyers, unlike teens, need to know the *whole* story about a particular title, warts and all, in order to make selection and booktalk decisions. Many of the list topics come directly from my Web site and range from "Boy Meets Book" (reads for guys) and "The Closet Club" (books for GLBTQ [gay, lesbian, bisexual, transgender, questioning] teens) to "Graphic Fantastic" (graphic novels) and "Historical Fiction for Hipsters." Here, you will find the stuff you need to make informed decisions about which current young adult titles you will buy or booktalk, arranged in teen-friendly subject categories that can be used as bookmark bibliographies or display ideas.

How to Use *Reading Rants*

Reading Rants covers 100 books divided among ten topics, with ten titles for each topic. Each chapter focuses on one topic and includes a title list organized alphabetically by the author's last name. I provide full bibliographic information for each title on the list (and by the way, those page numbers are for original hardcovers), followed by six categories: **The Story, The Message, Who's It For? Why It Rocks, Hook It Up With,** and **Read More about It.**

• **The Story** summarizes the full story, including the ending. Expect some spoilers! While I can't mention every plot point, I do include the high points and offer as many details and subplots as space allows. These summaries are intended both to provide you with a working knowledge of a title in order to make collection development decisions and to remind you of certain plot points and characters if you haven't read the book in a while and need a quick refresher before you booktalk it. If you are planning on booktalking a title or recommending it to an individual teen, you should always read it first.

• **The Message** includes the prominent themes of the book.

• **Who's It For?** indicates grade-level recommendations and, if relevant, the presence of strong language, sexual situations, or violent scenes. The grade recommendations are meant as general guidelines only. Teenagers develop, both physically and mentally, at wildly different rates. In my experience, teenagers are amazing self-selectors; they innately know what books they are ready for and which ones are too sexy, too scary, or just too hard to understand. Each librarian knows what will fly in his or her individual community.

• **Why It Rocks** explains why I chose to include this book as one of the one hundred titles. My choices are based on literary merit, originality of topic or unusual execution, and, to a lesser degree, teen appeal. Popularity is subjective and fleeting, and you know what works for your teens in your library. I also tried to highlight some really interesting titles that seemed to fly under the radar when they were first published.

• **Hook It Up With** gives you some similar titles to recommend or display with the book.

• **Read More about It** lists where the book was reviewed in professional journals.

So what are you waiting for? Let's get rockin' with some of the latest, greatest YA lit!

ACKNOWLEDGMENTS

Thanks to my innovative Reading Rants Webmaster and friend Andrew Mutch, who had the vision and technological smarts to suggest the creation of the Reading Rants Web site and who continues to update, design, and keep it cutting-edge to this day.

Thanks to the excellent librarian department at Little Red School House and Elisabeth Irwin High School (LREI)—Stacy Dillon, Jesse Karp, and Karyn Silverman, who all provided me with editorial assistance and continuous encouragement.

Thanks to my LREI Middle School colleagues, who kept me sane: Michelle Boehm, Lynne Cattafi, and Ana Fox Chaney, and to my long-distance librarian support group, who helped me maintain my sense of humor: Angelina Benedetti, Cindy Dobrez, Dorie Freebury, and Lynn Rutan.

Thanks to LREI Middle School principal Mark Silberberg and LREI director Philip Kassen for always supporting me professionally and giving me "personal" days when I had a deadline.

Finally, thanks to all the past, present, and future middle school students of LREI and the teen patrons of the Queens Borough Central Library for teaching me everything I know about YA literature.

CHAPTER 1

BOY MEETS BOOK: REALISTIC READS FOR MALE TEENS

Well, here we are at the beginning, starting with the books for boys. My, my, my, how the pendulum does swing. It wasn't that long ago that we were reviving Ophelia, spurred by psychologists warning that girls were getting short shrift in school, cutting and starving themselves, and falling into despondency over failing to conform to society's unrealistic images of femininity. Soon, a rash of girl-power bibliographies appeared on the market, meant to combat those insidious societal influences that were keeping girls down, including such tomes as *Great Books for Girls* by Kathleen Odean and *Let's Hear It for the Girls* by Erica Bauermeister and Holly Smith.

Enter the girl-power backlash. Suddenly, the boy proponents fought back, and the media were awash with *boy*-power titles, like the books by family therapist Michael Gurian, claiming that traditional school practices address the learning style of girls' brains better than that of boys' brains. Youth books author Jon Scieszka joined the fray with his Guys Read movement, which includes a Web site (www.guysread.com) and paperback anthology. Scieszka's mission is to raise awareness of these biological learning differences and to point out that while some boys may pass over literary fiction, they will happily read humor, nonfiction, comics, and graphic novels.

I think you can see where I'm going with this. Regardless of where society is on the boy-versus-girl continuum, young adult librarians obviously need to be able to recommend reading at all levels and in multiple formats to patrons of both genders. It is an unfortunate fact that boys *are* more likely than girls to drop out of school, and that they often score lower on reading tests than their female counterparts. With that in mind, let's help them find books that speak to the universal concerns of boys, whether these concerns are girls, sex, school, or life in general. The following titles are all literary fiction, which Scieszka contends (and I concur) are not always a boy's first genre of choice. But I know boys who will vouch for these titles, and if you're ever in or around New York City, swing by and I'll introduce you to some; however, if you're dealing with boys who absolutely will not open anything shelved under "fiction," I give you my resigned but sympathetic permission to skip ahead to the chapters on nail-biters or graphic novels.

Auseon, Andrew. 2005. *Funny Little Monkey*. New York: Harcourt. 298p.

The Story: Fourteen-year-old Arty Moore is only four feet two inches tall. He suffers from Growth Hormone Deficiency, and his short stature is even more exaggerated by the fact that his fraternal twin, Kurt, is a muscular giant. Bitter and resentful of his situation, brutally intelligent Arty often takes his anger out on Kurt in the form of sarcastic personal insults. Kurt, who is not as quick-witted as his brother, usually responds with physical violence. He has occasionally stuffed and locked Arty into small dark places, resulting in Arty's fear of the dark.

The two boys live with their mother in a small Ohio quarry town, which they moved to a year ago after their grandfather died and willed their mother his house. Arty's father, a small-time criminal, left the family when the teen was diagnosed and hasn't been heard from since. Arty's mom, a paralegal addicted to workouts on her stationary bike, seems oblivious to Arty's unhappiness and the level to which her sons' feuding has risen.

Arty feels alienated and alone most of the time, until he strikes up an unlikely friendship with Leslie Dermott, an Amazonian beauty who seems to be a member of every single club at school. Arty is mystified as to why she has chosen him but finally decides to just enjoy the attention. After Kurt stuffs Arty in the dryer one time too many, Arty decides he's had enough and enlists the aid of Kerouac, a shady auto shop kid who is the leader of an underground organization of outcasts called The Affront, to help him get revenge. The group helps Arty plan a two-pronged attack on his brother, which involves, first, a series of forged love letters supposedly from Kurt's crush object and, then, a more serious implication of Kurt in the theft and destruction of the school's mascot, Millie, the giant cement box turtle, which was recently stolen and dropped into the local quarry, where it shattered into pieces. When the principal confronts Kurt about Millie, he runs away from home and goes into hiding.

Meanwhile, Leslie has asked Arty to the school dance, which is also a costume party. When she arrives at his house with their handmade costumes, a chicken (hers) and an egg (his), Arty finally understands that Leslie's only interest in him is his unusual condition and how his height draws more attention to her when they are together. He walks away from her without a backward glance. At an end-of-school party, Arty learns that Kurt has decided to skip town to avoid facing criminal charges over the vandalism of Millie. He ends up chasing his motorcycle-riding brother in a borrowed car to his hideout, a shack on the grounds of a run-down factory. There, Arty discovers that the brother he thought was so brutish and stupid had been studying to get into a military academy to escape Arty's razor-sharp insults and their dead-end town. But now his chance is ruined, since he will most likely be expelled for an act of vandalism he didn't commit.

Arty realizes that he is at least partly responsible for the breakdown in the relationship with his brother. So he decides to make restitution for his crimes against Kurt by spinning an elaborate confession to school officials, accepting whatever punishment they decide to mete out. Having completed a surrealistic journey that taught him about both himself and his twin, Arty's story closes with the pleasant discovery that he is now four feet *three* inches tall.

The Message: Appearances can be deceiving. Life isn't fair. Bad things can happen to good people. You need to have peace about the things in life that you can't control, because there will be many situations that are out of your hands.

Who's It For?: 9th–12th grade. This is a sophisticated story and voice that won't be of much interest to middle school students in general, but keep an eye out for mature eighth graders who might appreciate it. "Gothy" high school boys who own DVDs of *Twin Peaks*, worship David Sedaris, and read *The Onion* will probably relate to Arty's self-deprecating, darkly humorous voice the most.

Why It Rocks:
• **Voice:** Auseon infuses Arty's smart, angry first-person narrative with observations that are laugh-out-loud funny because they are so true, like this one about Leslie: "Every school has one like her—the girl with the handcrafted porcelain face and the body that forces you to readjust your sitting position to make room for renovations."
• **Plot:** Pretty nervy and awfully original. It is politically incorrect on so many levels that it's sort of amazing Auseon managed to get away with incorporating a short, angry teenager, giant cement turtle mascot, and diabolical high school revenge machine into one story.
• **Pacing:** Although the narrative sequence is occasionally muddy, the observations are so sharp and witty that it doesn't really matter.
• **Characterization:** Arty is an unforgettable character who is always compelling, even if he's not always likable. His triumphant one-inch height gain by book's end serves as a perfect metaphor for his incredible growth, both mentally and emotionally.

Hook It Up With: *You Don't Know Me* by David Klass and *The Black Book: Diary of a Teenage Stud* series by Jonas Black.

Read More about It:
Booklist: 04/15/05
Horn Book: 10/01/05
Kirkus Reviews: 06/01/05
School Library Journal: 06/01/05
Publishers Weekly, starred: 07/11/05
V.O.Y.A. (Voice of Youth Advocates): 06/01/05

Curtis, Christopher Paul. 2004. *Bucking the Sarge*. New York: Random House. 259p.

The Story: Fifteen-year-old self-proclaimed philosopher Luther T. Farrell wants a lot of out of life. Not only would he like to "three-peat" as first-place winner of the statewide science fair, but also he would like to get up the nerve to ask out his secret crush and top science project competitor, Shayla Patrick, and, perhaps most important, save up enough money to blow out of the depressed factory town of Flint, Michigan, forever and never look back. There's only one thing standing in the way of all these dreams: Luther's tight-fisted, tough-talking mother, the Sarge.

The Sarge owns and operates a series of illegal housing projects and shady halfway houses, as well as serving as the local loan shark. Coldhearted and calculating, the Sarge recognizes the free labor she has in Luther and exploits it to the utmost by having him act as professional chauffeur (she has a phony driver's license made up for him) and live-in caregiver to several old men living in one of her nursing homes. Luther tries to rationalize away his mother's moral bankruptcy by taking the best care he can of the men he affectionately dubs his "Crew" and focusing on doing well at school. His grim situation is eased somewhat by the comical actions of his best friend, Sparky, whose life revolves around get-rich-quick schemes that involve staging "accidents" on public property in order to sue the owners. Luther also appreciates the philosophical musings of Chester X, one of his mother's nursing home "clients" whom she hopes to bilk of all his savings when he dies.

The uneasy truce between mother and son continues until she learns the subject of his first-prize-winning project: the toxic effects of lead paint. Luther appears on local television, and the mayor of Flint promises to step up her campaign to eliminate lead paint from the city's housing projects. The Sarge is furious because she uses discontinued lead-based paint to refinish her slumlord apartments. She gives Luther four days to move out and then leaves for a business trip, telling him he'd better be gone when she returns. In those four days, Luther hatches an ingenious plan to hit the Sarge where it will hurt her most—in the wallet.

Only intending to take what's his, Luther discovers while making a routine deposit of his mother's ill-earned cash that the money she claimed to have been saving for his college education doesn't exist. Luther, who has learned a few tricks from the Sarge over the years, sells the group home van for cash, bribes Sparky with Armani suits to care for the Crew, bids a bittersweet farewell to Shayla's family, packs up one of his mother's new cars, and hightails it to Florida with his new "grandfather," Chester X, to begin again, Sarge-free and guilt-free.

The Message: Be true to yourself. Do the best you can with what you have. Adults can't always be trusted and don't always have the best interest of the teenagers in their lives. Humor goes a long way toward healing hurt. Viewing the world through a "big picture" lens can often bring your own situation into perspective.

Who's It For?: 8th–12th grade. Fans of former Curtis novels be warned: this is no *Watsons Go to Birmingham*. The Sarge's sometimes boyfriend, Darnell Dixon, is a particularly nasty character who enjoys acting as the Sarge's enforcer. Luther is often forced to join him on eviction missions, and these scenes are bound to be upsetting to young *Bud, Not Buddy* fans. On a lighter, but still PG-13 note, Luther considers the difficulty of masturbating while having to share a room with Chester X, and he makes reference to his constant companion Chauncy, the world's oldest condom, who lives in his wallet waiting for love.

Why It Rocks:

• **Voice:** Luther's first-person narrative is occasionally convoluted as he recalls stories from the past and melds them into the present text, with transitions that can be abrupt and are not always clear. This rambling interior monologue is a style choice that overall works in the book, but it could be confusing for less sophisticated readers.

• **Plot:** At turns riotously funny and achingly sad, this is Curtis's most edgy novel to date. *Bucking the Sarge* probably garnered the least acclaim of all of Curtis's books, and I have to wonder if it's because *Sarge* is aimed at a far older audience than his previous titles.

• **Pacing:** Some tangential wanderings, but readers will be quickly flipping pages to discover whether or not Luther will be able to escape the long arm of the Sarge.

• **Characterization:** In creating the characters in this book, Curtis didn't shy away from or deny the existence of negative African American stereotypes. Instead, he fearlessly and often comically uses them to highlight the honest and intrepid Luther's intelligence, strong morals, and good nature. Meanwhile, he takes one of the most revered symbols of modern African American culture—the sacrificing single mother—and turns it on its head with the character of the Sarge, who is anything but.

Hook It Up With: *Jake, Reinvented* by Gordon Korman and *The Gospel according to Larry* by Janet Tashjian.

Read More about It:
Booklist, starred: 07/01/04
Horn Book: Sept./Oct. 2004
Kirkus Reviews, starred: 08/01/04
Publishers Weekly, starred: 07/19/04
School Library Journal, starred: 09/01/04
V.O.Y.A. (Voice of Youth Advocates): 10/01/04

Green, John. 2005. *Looking for Alaska.* New York: Penguin Group. 221p.

The Story: High school junior Miles Halter is a studious loner who enjoys reading biographies of famous literati and memorizing their last words. Having decided he'll never be able to understand the "Great Perhaps" mentioned by dying poet François Rabelais unless he leaves the stagnant atmosphere of his small Florida town, Miles enrolls in his dad's Alabama alma mater, Culver Creek boarding school.

Miles is assigned to room with Chip "Colonel" Martin, who can recite the countries of the world in alphabetical order and is best friends with the alluring Alaska Young. Alaska is a beautiful, brilliant, reckless scholarship student who is addicted to reading and staging elaborate practical jokes. At their first meeting, she flirtatiously promises Miles that if he helps her figure out the meaning behind Simon

Bolivar's last words, "How will I ever get out of this labyrinth?" she will help him get laid. Miles is immediately smitten, despite the fact that Alaska has an older boyfriend.

Alaska, the Colonel, and Takumi, an easygoing Japanese rapper, quickly initiate Miles into their close-knit clique. Soon they are studying pre-calc over french fries, having a quick cigarette in the smoking hole, or planning pranks under the nose of the dean of students, the formidable Mr. Starnes, a.k.a. "the Eagle." The homework is hard and plentiful, but Miles is up to the challenge and is especially pleased with the intelligent content of the lectures of his religion teacher, Dr. Hyde. He also begins to fall more in love with Alaska, and their relationship deepens when the two spend the Thanksgiving holiday alone on campus together, swilling cheap wine and gleefully breaking into the deserted rooms of other students.

Alaska reveals a secret that draws Miles even closer one weekend when the group is camping surreptitiously in the woods, after lying to the Eagle about their weekend destinations in order to plan a complicated prank. In a drinking game of "Best Day/Worst Day," Alaska tells the story of witnessing her mother's collapse and death from an aneurysm when she was eight years old. Miles decides then and there that Bolivar's labyrinth is human suffering. Only a few nights later, Alaska gets drunk and makes out with Miles, who thinks he has died and gone to heaven. But later that night, she receives a phone call, becomes very upset, and insists that Miles and the Colonel distract the Eagle so she can drive off campus. The boys set off firecrackers to mask the sound of Alaska's car, then go back to sleep. They are awakened the next morning by the Eagle, who informs them Alaska died in a car accident.

In their extreme grief, Miles and the Colonel become obsessed with finding out why Alaska had become so upset that night. They feel responsible for allowing her to drive while drunk. They discover that the phone call came from her boyfriend, who was reminding her of their eight-month anniversary, and who also has no idea what made her so upset. It is Takumi who puts the pieces of the puzzle together when he reminds the others that the date Alaska died was also the anniversary of her mother's death. They hypothesize that Alaska grew distraught over forgetting the date and rushed off to her mother's grave.

Meanwhile, they have planned the prank-to-end-all-pranks in her honor when they hire a male stripper in place of an academic speaker for a school assembly. For a final exam, Dr. Hyde assigns the entire class to contemplate Alaska's last essay, which paraphrased Bolivar's quote: How will you ever get out of this labyrinth of suffering? The book ends with Miles's answer, in which he emphasizes his belief that Alaska still exists somewhere, outside the labyrinth.

The Message: Love hurts. Change is inevitable. Open yourself to new people and experiences. Nobody ever gained anything worth having without taking a risk. Life is a package deal—you have to take the good with the bad and learn what you can from both.

Who's It For?: 9th–12th grade. There is some strong language, lots of underage drinking and smoking, and a blow-by-blow (sorry, couldn't resist) description of Miles's first oral sex experience. Miles's and Alaska's contemplations of the labyrinth and the possibility of an afterlife will be far better understood and appreciated by high school rather than middle school students.

Why It Rocks:
• **Voice:** This autobiographical, first-person story is spare and introspective. Green captures the giddiness and sincerity of Miles's teenage milestones (first love, first smoke, first experience with death) with unadorned prose and realistic dialogue that honor and validate the difficulty of the adolescent journey.
• **Plot:** The unusual structure of *Looking for Alaska* heightens the tension of the inevitable climax and emphasizes the role time plays in the healing process. The opening of each chapter starts with a countdown of days until Alaska's death, then counts up again as Miles begins the long, slow journey back to himself.
• **Pacing:** The measured stillness of this smart, articulate book shouldn't be confused with simplicity. It moves at a deliberate pace that allows the reader to experience Miles's epiphanies as he does, with a slow, thoughtful recognition.
• **Characterization:** Miles is an every-teen, a sponge who goes out determined to soak up every experience he can out of his new boarding school life. Although not every reader may be able to relate to Alaska's vulnerable and extreme personality, most will be able to walk in Miles's shoes.

Hook It Up With: *Lovesick* by Jake Coburn and *The Catcher in the Rye* by J. D. Salinger.

Read More about It:
Horn Book: 03/01/05
Kirkus Reviews, starred: 03/01/05
School Library Journal: 02/01/05
Publishers Weekly: 02/07/05
V.O.Y.A. (Voice of Youth Advocates): 04/01/05

———————————

Hautman, Pete. 2004. *Godless*. New York: Simon & Schuster. 208p.

The Story: Sixteen-year-old agnostic Jason Bock is getting fairly annoyed with the Teen Power Outreach sessions his father makes him attend at their Catholic church—especially when the TPO Coordinator, a used-car salesman named Al, insists on referring to Jesus as "one cool dude." So Jason decides to create his own religion called The Church of the Ten-Legged God, whose arbitrary object of worship will be his town's ten-legged water tower. His disciples are called Chutengodians and include his friends Shin, Dan, Magda, and Henry. Together, they decide that Tuesday will be their Sabbath and that Chutengodians discriminate against morons, terrorists, and intelligent fish.

Their practice includes pilgrimages to the top of the water tower, where they almost lose Henry when he accidentally slides over and onto the guardrail, breaking a leg. Luckily, the police show up just in time to help Henry and arrest everyone else for climbing the tower and swimming in the town's water supply. Jason is grounded for six weeks and given assigned religious reading by his father. As for the rest of his crew, Magda and Dan are grounded indefinitely; Henry revolts and creates his own version of Chutengodianism called the Choots, while Shin becomes a radical water tower worshipper.

Jason discovers not only that has Shin been compiling a book of Chutengodian mythology, but also that he actually believes every word. Left out of the last pilgrimage owing to his crippling fear of heights, Shin attempts to climb the tower on his own during a thunderstorm and has to be dragged down against his will by the police. With all his disciples scattered or grounded, Jason, unrepentant and unbelieving, is left wondering how everyone could have taken his lighthearted riff on religion quite so seriously.

The Message: Everyone must develop his or her own individual beliefs. Questioning of parental and other adult authority is necessary for personal growth. Understand that there are consequences to every decision, and know that in life you will be held accountable for the decisions you make.

Who's It For?: 9th–12th grade. There are no sexual or violent-content issues beyond Jason's mild sexual fantasies about Magda and Henry's bullying of the physically smaller Shin, but the themes expressed are complex enough that the book will probably be most enjoyed by older teens. Some devoutly religious teens or parents may be offended by Jason's perceived mockery of religion and his ultimate rejection of Catholicism.

Why It Rocks:
•   **Voice:** Jason's first-person narration is funny, wise, and irreverent, and his struggle to control what he calls "Mr. Mouth" will resound with sympathetic teen readers everywhere.
•   **Plot:** Hautman has taken a big idea and written a short, humorous, accessible book that opens doors to all other sorts of soulful ponderings. Jason asks all the spiritual questions of himself and his friends that real teens struggle with. Does God exist? And if He does, why couldn't He just as easily be symbolized by a water tower as a wooden cross or a stained-glass window?
•   **Pacing:** Quick. Suspense builds as readers realize that what started as a joke is going to have serious consequences for some of the characters, and they want to find out who!
•   **Characterization:** While Jason doesn't end up changing his mind about religion by book's end, he has learned that he is responsible for his own religious creation and what his "disciples" do in the name of Chutengodianism. His father's calmly delivered religious rebuttals and the paths his friends take after Chutengodianism falls apart provide a good counterbalance to Jason's self-assured, and occasionally arrogant first-person narration.

Hook It Up With: *Asylum for Nightface* by Bruce Brooks and *The Last Safe Place on Earth* by Richard Peck.

Read More about It:
Booklist, starred: 06/01/04

Horn Book: 10/01/04
Kirkus Reviews, starred: 05/01/04
Publishers Weekly: 06/28/04
School Library Journal: 08/01/04
Voice of Youth Advocates (V.O.Y.A.): 10/01/04

Jenkins, A. M. 2003. *Out of Order.* New York: HarperCollins. 247p.

The Story: It's six weeks until the end of the marking period, and popular, brash sophomore baseball phenom Colt Trammel is failing almost all his classes. His mom has told him he can forget about playing ball unless his grades come up, so his schoolwork over the next few weeks will determine his fate on the field come spring. Up until now, Colt has always coasted by on his charm and good looks. He understands the order of the high school social hierarchy very well, and he knows his place within it. But besides his undiagnosed, unnamed learning disability, Colt has also been distracted from his studies by three women in his life who are each completely maddening in their own unique way.

First, there's Grace, his steady since seventh grade. Grace is beautiful, intellectual, and completely lacking in humor. She writes earnest poetry that Colt doesn't understand and ponders big questions of the universe that he couldn't care less about. Still, he's completely obsessed with her because he thinks her presence in his life proves he's not as stupid as he believes himself to be. Plus, he's sure that if he keeps appealing to her baser nature, she'll help him relieve himself of his unwanted virginity. Second, there's Corinne, or Chlorophyll as Colt calls her, because of her dyed-green hair. Corinne is a punk rock princess with a college boyfriend and a serious reading habit. She is caustic, rude, and incredibly smart. She deems Colt a waste of space, but reluctantly agrees to tutor him in English when he throws himself on her mercy. Finally, there's Dori, a vulnerable girl with a bad reputation who repeatedly calls Colt "just to talk." Every conversation eventually turns into a dissection of Dori's brief affair with a senior teammate named Jordan Palmer, who dumped her after sex. Colt is often stymied by the mysterious actions of all three. Then one fateful day near the end of the six weeks, each girl becomes a link in a chain of events that provide Colt with a new understanding about himself as a student and friend.

First, Grace dumps Colt after hearing about his part in a cruel prank that involved a freezer and a live cat. It turns out she'd rather date soulful, sweet-talker Jordan Palmer. In his anger and pain, Colt decides to lose his virginity with Dori, which he convinces himself she wants. Dori accepts his clumsy advances with little enthusiasm, and Colt backs away, ashamed of himself. Finally, Corinne notices what a bad day he is having and calls him up to invite him on a "just friends" date. The book ends with a copy of the essay Colt wrote, with Corinne's help, about the Romantic poets and a poem Corinne wrote about Colt, which emphasizes his physical prowess and confidence.

The Message: Sometimes you have to rise above other people's expectations to become a better person. A personal façade is difficult to maintain, especially when life isn't going smoothly. Often the easiest choice isn't the right one.

Who's It For?: 8th–12th grade. Other than some steamy fantasies about Grace and a few make-out sessions that get to the heavy-breathing stage, there are no explicit sexual references. There is some bullying and the cruelty of putting the cat in the freezer, but no one gets beat up, and the cat escapes unharmed. Booktalk it as a sports novel to those boys who you think may relate to conflicted Colt and watch how quickly they take to this richly written, well-rounded character study.

Why It Rocks:
• **Voice:** Jenkins nimbly contrasts Colt's true inner frustrations with his false exterior confidence, using his limited first-person vocabulary in well-written passages that bring his conflicted character to messy, immediate life.
• **Plot:** Thoughtful and character-driven. In this age of increasingly complicated sexual politics and changing gender roles, we need a book like this that helps boys understand and properly manage their feelings for the opposite sex.
• **Pacing:** Considered and slow, although livened up by the occasional cat in the freezer!
• **Characterization:** The realistic, finely tuned dialogue between Colt and the female secondary characters, especially Corinne, reveals and rounds them out as well. By not labeling or defining Colt's learning disability (it seems to be dyslexia), Jenkins ensures that any teen who struggles academically will identify with him. Colt's hard-won understanding of the opposite sex by book's end is that girls are smart, complex, complicated beings in their own right and not just a means to a sexual end.

Hook It Up With: *Prep* by Jake Coburn and *Home of the Braves* by David Klass.

Read More about It:
Booklist: 09/01/03
Horn Book: Nov./Dec. 2003
Kirkus Reviews: 08/01/03
Publishers Weekly: 09/08/03
School Library Journal: 09/01/03
Voice of Youth Advocates (V.O.Y.A.): 10/01/03

Nelson, Blake. 2004. *Rock Star Superstar.* New York: Penguin Group. 229p.

The Story: Seventeen-year-old Pete has always been a straight arrow. He's an accomplished bass player, but he prefers sheet music to improvisation. His borderline alcoholic, largely absent father was big in the 1980s Seattle music scene, and his mom would have been, if she hadn't died of cancer. Pete plays in a cover band called Mad

Skillz that is happy just playing the occasional school dance or bar mitzvah. So when Kevin from a jazz band asks Pete at the end of sophomore year if he would be interested in playing bass in the band with him and the Carlisle brothers, Pete's first reaction is "Hell no." Nick and Billy Carlisle are loud, emotional amateurs, and their overwrought music has no place in Pete's polished, precise world. Still, Kevin persuades him to try out, and Pete is moved by the sheer rawness of the sound, even though Billy Carlisle, whom Pete hates on sight, doesn't even know the names of the chords he's playing.

Meanwhile, Pete's first romance with Margaret, a "punk librarian" hipster, begins to heat up. Pete initially found her, with her black overcoat and vintage clothes, a little weird, but he begins to consider her girlfriend material after a few dates and after hearing his friend Robert describe her as the type of girl who would date a musician. At Margaret's urging, Pete reluctantly agrees to play bass for the Carlisle's band, The Tiny Masters of Today, at their first all-ages club show. He is completely unprepared for how much he loves it—so much so that later that summer before junior year, he is furious when he hears a rumor that Billy plans on replacing him with an old friend from California. He angrily attacks Billy at a party and quits the band before they can fire him. The Carlisle brothers ask Pete back when Billy's friend flakes out, and Pete gratefully accepts.

As junior year begins, Pete is totally committed to The Tiny Masters, while Margaret begins to pull away as her focus turns to grades and college applications. Soon Pete is playing almost every night and weekend—and sleepwalking through school. The band plays a showcase for a record company in Seattle but is disappointed when they are not signed. Still, Pete is thrilled to be living the life of a bona fide musician, complete with late-night shows and local groupies. Margaret tells Pete she wants to break up, and this causes him to tack even more importance on the success of the band. They book studio time and begin to record their first demo.

As the summer before senior year begins, Pete starts to date Allison, a popular girl from school whose beauty is rivaled only by her shallowness. She is attracted to Pete's local fame as a rocker, and soon they are having sex almost every day; yet, Pete has never felt more alone. He learns Margaret is seeing someone else and is surprised at how sad it makes him feel. In late August, The Tiny Masters play another showcase, this time in L.A., for a music agency. Pete and Kevin are devastated when the Carlisle brothers dump them in order to sign with the agency, which wants to hook them up with older, more experienced musicians. Pete is down, but he's not out. He is left on the brink of his senior year hopeful of not only starting his own band but also starting over with Margaret.

The Message: Passion can trump precision. Looks can be deceiving in both life and relationships. You can trust your intuition, but it helps to have talent to fall back on if your gut is wrong.

Who's It For?: 9th–12th grade. Pete's dad drinks a great deal, which is often a point of friction between him and Pete's extended family. The reader definitely gets the idea that Pete's straight-laced manner is a direct result of his father's functional alcoholism. In addition, there are many references to sex and underage drinking, which is not to be unexpected in a novel about teenagers breaking into the music biz.

Seventh and eigth graders will want to read it, but it may not be the best choice for a group booktalk in conservative districts.

Why It Rocks:
- **Voice:** The story is told in limited omniscient third person (from Pete's point of view), with most of the characters' thoughts and feelings revealed through spot-on, realistic teenspeak. Nelson captures loads of low-key details of high school life and adolescent relationships with his trademark stripped-down, dialogue-rich prose.
- **Plot:** The action gradually builds chronologically during the course of Pete's sophomore to senior year in high school, with the question of whether or not The Tiny Masters will secure a record deal driving the story.
- **Pacing:** Thoughtful and straightforward, but not particularly slow. Nelson moves in real time, with no extended flashbacks or multiple subplots. Pete's relationship with Margaret works in a parallel plot with Pete's development as a musician.
- **Characterization:** Pete develops enormously as a character, moving from a tightly wound, technical musician to a passionate rocker who craves the adrenaline of playing live, and his first love affair with the equally well-developed Margaret is clumsy, tender, and heartbreakingly realistic. Pete's many epiphanies about life, love, and rock and roll are incredibly well wrought and will be instantly recognized and embraced by alterna-rock boys and the girls who love them.

Hook It Up With: *Heavy Metal and You* by Christopher Krovatin and *Tribute to Another Dead Rock Star* by Randy Powell.

Read More about It:
Booklist: 11/01/04
Horn Book: 04/01/05
Kirkus Review: 08/01/04
Publishers Weekly, starred: 09/20/04
School Library Journal: 10/01/04
V.O.Y.A. (Voice of Youth Advocates): 10/01/04

Powell, Randy. 2002. *Three Clams and an Oyster*. New York: Farrar, Straus & Giroux. 224p.

The Story: Seventeen-year-old Flint McCallister, Dwight Deshutis, and Rick Beaterson are screwed: the final deadline for their four-man flag intramural football team roster is coming up, and they still haven't been able to get a fourth man to commit. Their usual guy, Cade Savage, has turned into a total partyier this summer, and when he does manage to show up to practices, he's usually drunk or fighting a hangover. The Three Clams and an Oyster, as the team is known, needs another shellfish, and fast.

So they spend a weekend auditioning candidates. There's Thor Hupf, who's an awesome player but smokes a little too much weed to be dependable. Then there's Tim Goon, whose unfortunate last name matches his penchant for silk shirts and disco. He's not really a very good player, but his family owns a cool ski cabin that they might let the Clams use on weekends. Finally, there's the incomparable Rachel Summerfield. She's a great player, with intelligence and dependability to match, but she's a girl, and this team has always been an all-boys club. Finally, during this weekend of stressful choices, beer, and hormones, the boys are also forced to deal with an issue they have painfully ignored for far too long: the untimely death of their original fourth man, a guy they were all best friends with and still can't forget.

Glen Como was the first Oyster, and he died after hitting his head on a rock while wrestling around with Cade in the woods on a camping trip. Since then Cade has felt responsible, even though no one blames him for the accident. After avoiding Flint, Dwight, and Rick all weekend, Cade throws the party-to-end-all-parties. Rumor is that even the old junior high PE teacher who was fired for smoking pot was there. Flint heads over to his house to confront Cade and officially kick him off the team. Dwight and Rick, who come to help clean up the party mess, later join him. Cade tries to weasel back into their good graces by playing the victim, talking about how "haunted" he is by Glen's ghost and how guilty he feels every day. Rick and Dwight fall for it, but Flint knows better and calls Cade's bluff for the last time. He also calls Rachel Summerfield as fast as he can to see if she'll still agree to be on the team. She does, and the Three Clams and an Oyster start the season with a 4–0 lead, and they haven't even yet played their archrivals, Marty's Texaco! It seems that Rachel has found a team, and the Oysters their pearl.

The Message: Sometimes you will have to make tough choices and learn how to live with the consequences. Learning how to manage difficult relationships is a skill. Sometimes we outgrow friends or they outgrow us, and that is okay.

Who's It For?: 9th–12th grade. There is underage drinking, strong language, and some very funny but extremely frank conversations about sex that are typical of 17-year-old boys. This is probably not the best selection for a read-aloud—trust me: I speak from experience.

Why It Rocks:
*   **Voice:** Flint's engaging first-person narration is peppered with dialogue that is immature, often scatological, and occasionally heartrending. These are the types of blunt, gross conversations you would hear only if you were sitting alone with these guys, and to read them on the page is like getting a secret peek into Teenage Guy World. Hee-larious.
*   **Plot:** A character-driven novel in every way, *Three Clams* doesn't offer up much in the way of plot. After all, the entire book takes place over just three days. But the sports angle will tempt readers of Chris Crutcher's books, and before they realize that this isn't exactly a book about football, they will already be hooked by the realistic, riotously funny conversations
*   **Pacing:** Thoughtful and dialogue-heavy, which can move some readers along or slow others down to hear the words in their head.
*   **Characterization:** These are wonderfully real, rounded characters, and Flint's

epiphany at the end when he realizes Cade is just a big martyr is a joy to read as you see him mature right before your eyes. Everyone learns some sort of lesson about life, love, or friendship by book's end, except for Rachel, who had her head on straight from the beginning and was just waiting for the guys to catch up!

Hook It Up With: *Run If You Dare* by Randy Powell and *Rats Saw God* by Rob Thomas.

Read More about It:
Horn Book: July/August 2002
Kirkus Reviews: 03/15/02
Publishers Weekly: 03/11/02
School Library Journal: 03/01/02
V.O.Y.A. (Voice of Youth Advocates): 08/01/02

Slade, Arthur. 2002. *Tribes.* New York: Random House. 134p.

The Story: Percy Montmount is a high school senior in Saskatchewan, Canada, who views the world in a detached, scientific way. His father, a famous anthropologist, died in the field from a tsetse fly bite when Percy was 14. Since then, Percy has adopted his father's anthropological manner of studying his environment as a way of coping with his grief. He keeps a thick notebook entitled "The Origin of the Species Revisited," in which he obsessively records his daily observations of that mysterious tribe, Grade 12.

Percy and his best friend, Elissa, consider themselves an exclusive tribe of two whose job is to observe and comment on their subdivided classmates. There exist the usual Jock, Logo, and Lipstick/Hairspray tribes, which can be found on almost any high school campus, but there is also the Busybody tribe (gossips), the "Gee-the-Seventies-Were-Great" tribe (retro-fashion worshippers), and the Digerati tribe (computer and electronic geeks), among many others. Besides Elissa, Percy's only other real friend was Willard, who committed suicide a year ago after falling in love with a member of the Lipstick/Hairspray tribe who didn't return his affections. Whenever Percy begins to sense his feelings of grief about his father's and Willard's deaths rising to the surface, he makes cuts on his chest using straight pins, which he calls "ritual scarring." In this way, he uses physical pain to distance himself from the deep emotional pain he refuses to allow himself to feel.

Now it is a week before the grandest ritual of all, Graduation, and Elissa wants Percy to be her date for all the pregraduation parties. Percy, who has always been attracted to Elissa (especially to her webbed foot, which utterly fascinates him as a sign of her link to their ocean-dwelling ancestors), is secretly pleased by this but careful to keep his analytical mask firmly in place. Elissa pleads with him to talk to her in "his real voice" and end the long-running tribe joke, but to Percy it is no joke, and he stubbornly clings to his Darwinian observations. At the last party before graduation, Percy and Elissa share a kiss, but she leaves the bonfire in a huff after he whispers oh so romantically in her ear, "So this is what the female mammae feel like."

Percy gets drunk, suffers a terrible hangover the next day, and decides to shave his head for graduation as a sign of his passage into a new stage of life. His mother, a New Age psychic, warns him that his father will be at graduation, and Percy believes she means in the spiritual sense. Percy makes it to graduation, and the entire history of humankind flashes before his eyes as he steps forward to accept his diploma. He looks toward the audience, where he thinks he sees his father's face, and then topples off the stage in a dead faint. The next day his mother orders him into one of her sweat lodges to meditate on a fact he's been trying to repress for three long years—that his father didn't die in the field but left Percy's mother for his much younger research assistant.

Percy's father, who *was* present at graduation, comes into the sweat lodge to apologize for being gone so long and pledges to stay in better touch after he returns to his home in Chicago. Percy spends the summer shedding the distant, scholarly persona he had cultivated for so long, forging a new bond with Elissa, and relearning how to be a participant instead of an observer in his own life.

The Message: Grief must be dealt with or it poisons a person from the inside. Appearances are deceiving; people are often very different inside from how they appear on the outside.

Who's It For?: 9th–12th grade. The sexual content is mild, and death is handled sensitively in a realistic manner, but the sophistication of the extended anthropological conceit and vocabulary calls for an older, more mature reader.

Why It Rocks:
• **Voice:** This highly underrated book contains one of the most original voices in YA fiction ever penned. Percy is a complex, absurd, unreliable first-person narrator whom the reader realizes cannot be trusted as clues from other characters hint at his father's continued good health.
• **Plot:** Although other authors have likened high school cliques to warring tribes, none to my knowledge has carried the metaphor to such hilarious lengths as has Slade. Infused with anthropological vernacular and full of facts about Darwin, evolution, and animal behavior, this novel is not for every teen, but it is a monstrously clever book that should be shared with every intellectual teen loner you know.
• **Pacing:** Somewhat slow, with lots of internal musings on Percy's part. This is a character-driven novel that isn't exactly a page-turner, but the short length and unusual subject matter may tempt a smart, reluctant reader.
• **Characterization:** Percy's coping mechanism of keeping a "field guide" of adolescent behavior to hold the truth about his father at bay is a particularly unusual and interesting way of looking at grief management, and it helps demonstrate how Percy's inner turmoil has ended when he takes a good look at the stuffed journal after graduation and can't even feel a connection with the person who wrote it.

Hook It Up With: *The Unthinkable Thoughts of Jacob Green* by Joshua Braff and *Catalyst* by Laurie Halse Anderson.

Read More about It:
Booklist: 10/15/02
Horn Book: 01/01/03
Kirkus Reviews: 07/01/02
Publishers Weekly: 09/23/02
School Library Journal: 10/01/02
V.O.Y.A. (Voice of Youth Advocates): 02/01/03

Weaver, Will. 2005. *Full Service.* New York: Farrar, Straus & Giroux. 232p.

The Story: It is the summer of 1965 in the small town of Hawk Bend, Minnesota, and 16-year-old Paul Sutton's mother has decided it is time for him to "meet the public." Paul and his family belong to a nondenominational Christian religious group that meets in its members' living rooms (usually Paul's) and emphasizes shared work and family values. His mother, despite her devotion to their religious community, believes that it is important for Paul to experience life outside of their rural farm and neighborhood. So she convinces Paul's father to allow the teen to work in town at the local Shell gas station.

Paul begins to "meet the public" immediately, and the somewhat sheltered farm boy is quickly clued in to the small town's major personalities and the secrets they keep. At the station, there is Mr. Davies, the owner, who drinks a little too much and informs him of the secret company campaign in which he could win $1,000 if he provides excellent service to the anonymous Mr. Shell. Then there is Kirk, the bullying young manager who has a wife and two children but pays an awful lot of afternoon "service calls" to the town's single women. But Paul is mostly fascinated by two sets of customers who require his help: love-struck Dale Bender and Peggy Leikvold and the affable Harry Blomenfeld and his driver, Angelo. Peggy is dating privileged banker's son Stephen Knutson but is secretly in love with blue-collar, Vietnam-draftee, Dale. Paul passes messages between them and arranges clandestine meetings at the garage now and then. Harry is rumored to be a former Chicago mobster on the lam, and Angelo is his crabby driver and friend. Harry takes a liking to Paul's manners, and Angelo is won over by Paul's knowledge of how to carefully change the oil on his prized car. Kirk leaves off bullying Paul once he sees how the ex-cons have taken to him.

At home, relations between Paul and his father are strained because Paul is having a hard time keeping up with his job, farm chores, and Bible study. His father is also conflicted about the family of hippies he has invited to camp on the farm while their broken-down van is being serviced. He feels duty bound to help them but doesn't appreciate their values and isn't pleased with Paul's growing involvement with the oldest girl, Janet. Paul is spending more and more time making out with Janet and less time studying his Bible. He is also beginning to question his parents' religion and the authenticity of the Scriptures.

The day after a long night spent drinking and kissing Janet, Paul awakens to his father's anger, a terrible hangover, and the fact that the hippie van has finally moved on, taking Janet with it. After that, Paul is so disheartened that he begins committing small acts of petty thievery at the gas station, lifting cigarettes and skimming cash out of the register, because he feels like nothing much matters anymore. His spirit is briefly revived at the annual church camp, which involves five days of sermons, potluck meals, and dormitory living. While Paul is attracted to the notion of getting baptized and ridding himself of the sins he feels he's committed, in the end he decides that to do so would be a step back and would fly in the face of everything he had learned and experienced this summer.

On his last day of work, he is visited by the mysterious Mr. Shell but denied the cash prize because of his failure to notice a broken brake light. On the way home, Paul has the presence and grace to laugh at his near miss and goes into the house to thank his mother for sending him out into the not-so-small world of Hawk Bend to meet his public.

The Message: People are rarely ever all good or all bad. Your beliefs will be challenged; be ready to defend or rethink them. Once you have defined your beliefs, practice what you preach. Change is inevitable, and it's useless to fight it. Learn to accept what you can't change about your situation and focus on what you can.

Who's It For?: 7th–12th grade. From a distance, Paul witnesses Dale and Peggy having sex and sees the hippie mom naked. There is also some underage drinking and smoking, but nothing is graphically described, and any questionable content is mostly offset by the kind actions and well-intentioned message of Paul's religious community. This is an incredibly well-balanced book that showcases the complexity of human nature in that no one is all good or bad but often an uneasy mixture of both.

Why It Rocks:
• **Voice:** Paul's first-person narration is clean and direct. Occasionally, it smacks of adult sensibility, but that can be forgiven, since each carefully chosen word rings true, every exchange of dialogue sincere and realistic.
• **Plot:** This is not a flashy book, nor a loud one. It is merely a series of episodic, well-written teenage epiphanies about human behavior, the desires of the human heart, and the nature of secrets. Each episode interlocks into a stairway that Paul climbs to maturity.
• **Pacing:** Chronological and solid, neither too slow nor too fast.
• **Characterization:** Weaver obeys the first rule of writing (Show, don't tell) exceedingly well in this novel; most of what the reader learns about Paul and his situation is revealed through other characters' thoughts and actions. An especially endearing character who is mentioned relatively little but features prominently is Paul's brave mother; she is wise enough to understand that Paul's growth is contingent on getting to know and understand people other than the ones he was raised with.

Hook It Up With: *A Day No Pigs Would Die* by Robert Newton Peck and *Tex* by S. E. Hinton.

Read More about It:
Booklist: 09/01/05
Horn Book: 11/01/05
Kirkus Reviews, starred: 09/15/05
Publishers Weekly: 11/07/05
School Library Journal: 11/01/05
V.O.Y.A. (Voice of Youth Advocates) 10/01/05

————————

Yoo, David. 2005. *Girls for Breakfast*. New York: Random House. 294p.

The Story: Ever since he serendipitously discovered centerfolds in third grade, Nick Park has loved and lusted after those most mysterious and complicated of beings: girls. Now it's the morning before graduation, and Nick is reviewing his past, grade by grade, trying to understand why girls have never taken to him the same way he has to them.

Nick's problems started when he was eight and his family moved to the upscale suburb of Renfield, Connecticut. Nick was the only Asian child in his class, and after accidentally killing the class hamster, he becomes the class outcast as well. This lasts until spring, when in desperation to make friends, he tells his neighbors Paul, Mitch, and Will that he is a deadly kung fu master, and if they want, he can teach them hundreds of ways to kill a man. Paul, grateful for Nick's expertise, invites him for a sleepover in his swank suburban mansion. Nick makes the mistake of bringing what he considers the perfect gift for a host: *Playboy* magazines. The other boys are titillated by the centerfolds, then bored, but Nick is entranced and stays up all night gazing at, even licking, the picture of Miss January. When the boys go to the mall the next day, Paul's mother, a devout Catholic, discovers the porn and sends Nick home in disgrace. Nick looks around his modest home and his traditional, Korean-speaking parents, both of whom suffer in comparison with Paul's palatial house and worldly parents; and his dissatisfaction with his life takes root.

Nick spends the rest of his middle and high school career pursuing both girls and popularity. Each year at school is hallmarked by some incident where he is either spotlighted or shunned for his ethnicity, but it's not until sixth grade that the truth becomes clear to him. He looks through his room one day trying to discover the secret to popularity that everyone else seems to know. He decides that his friendship with Will, whom the other kids have labeled a loser, must be the problem. But after being dragged to a Korean church youth group by his parents, Nick understands that it's not Will who's holding him back—it's his ethnicity. When one of the girls at church notices his disdain for all things Korean and calls him a "banana"—white on the inside, yellow on the outside—he suddenly realizes that the way he looks at all the nerdy Korean kids who only talk about grades, church, and band is the same way his white friends see him. The thing that frightens him most of all is that there is absolutely nothing he can do to change the fact that he is Korean.

In high school Nick scorns playing an instrument or getting good grades, since these are Korean stereotypes. He plays tournament tennis and letters in soccer but is still dateless and is never invited to any parties. As a senior, he is finally a member of the popular jock set, and no longer a virgin, yet he is still strangely dissatisfied. He had had sex the summer before with a girl who wasn't very popular, then ignored her, ashamed of himself. Now he is annoyed that his friends won't pursue the easy freshman girls he considers their due as seniors.

When he starts dating a pretty blond freshman, his friends shun him, and the leader of the pack, Kagis, publicly humiliates him at a party, telling him to date his own kind. Nick, who has dealt with subtle racial slurs before, is shocked and devastated to have his most personal fear made public, and he finds himself an outcast again. But this time, it isn't an invented kung fu talent that saves him, but a girl. And not just any girl—Maggie Shaughnessy, the smartest, cutest girl in the senior class. They have the sort of easy, close relationship Nick has always dreamed of—until Maggie asks him to the senior prom. He is forced to sit with his ex-friends, including Kagis. Nick's jealously over Maggie's connection with this group comes to a head, and he accuses her of flirting. This leads to a fistfight with Kagis and the prom ending in utter ruin.

Which finally brings Nick to the present, musing over his past as he gazes down from the town water tower at the graduation rehearsal that he is missing. He realizes now that he only wanted a girl as proof that he belonged to a club that wouldn't have him just as he was. It was never about getting the girl. It was about his own hatred of who and what he is. As soon as graduation is over, Nick finds Maggie and envelops her in a hug, asking for her forgiveness and thanking her for being the only one who never saw him as anything other than Nick, her friend.

The Message: Learn to accept yourself. Understand that you have to love yourself before others can love you. It is important to come to terms with both your strengths and your faults.

Who's It For?: 9th–12th grade. Nick's first-person narration is frank and explicit when discussing the opposite sex. For example, he claims to have started masturbating at age ten, and he goes into great detail about the period in fourth grade when his obsession with *Playboy* leads to a strange mental problem—he can't stop visualizing his elderly female bus driver and fourth-grade teacher naked. In high school he describes different sexual encounters he experiences, and there is some strong language. Nick also encounters racial slurs throughout the story, which may offend or upset some readers.

Why It Rocks:
- **Voice:** Clearly, Nick Park is David Yoo, and David is Nick. This episodic, immediate book is ripe with the sort of excruciating detail that must be autobiographical, because David Yoo writes about these settings and people as if they have been burned onto his corneas.
- **Plot:** Outrageously funny, poignantly sad, and occasionally crossing the line into vulgar. Though it is obviously set in the 1980s, Yoo's exploration of adolescent feelings of suburban alienation, paralyzing humiliation, and embarrassment over parental units is timeless.
- **Pacing:** Yoo's flimsy frame story (Nick flashes back to key scenes from his

childhood as he contemplates his classmates in the present gathering for graduation) is the weakest element of *Girls*. It interrupts the story's chronological flashbacks and may be unnecessarily confusing to some readers.

• **Characterization:** Nick's deep-seated discomfort with his own ethnicity is explored subtly and in tandem with his immerging sexuality, and the results are both intelligent and humorous. Secondary characters seem as if they have been fully lifted from Yoo's memories and experiences, which helps explain their depth and roundness.

Hook It Up With: *Youth in Revolt: The Journals of Nick Twisp* by C. D. Payne and *Doing It* by Melvin Burgess.

Read More about It:
Kirkus Reviews: 05/01/05
Publishers Weekly: 06/27/05
School Library Journal: 05/01/05
V.O.Y.A. (Voice of Youth Advocates): 06/01/05

CHAPTER 2

RIGHTEOUS RIOT GRRL READS

I don't know about you, but if I see one more hot pink cover with silvery embossed letters called something like "Hot Girl," "It Girl," "Gotta Get It Girl," or "How I Became an 8th-Grade Hottie in 10 Easy Steps," this girl is gonna lose her lunch. Seriously, it was cute when Bridget Jones did it, and when Georgia Nicholson and her thong came along, I was still feeling the chick lit vibe. But enough already! Publishing marketers have finally figured out what we librarians have known for a long time—girls read. If you'll allow me a gross generalization, girls tend to read early, they read a lot, and they read fiction. They read what their friends are reading, they read their mom's Oprah books, and they love to read about relationships—friendships, romances, parent problems—in all their messy, emotional permutations. Publishers are taking advantage of that fact by drowning bookstore shelves in candy-colored, fluffy covers that contain even fluffier stories. Don't get me wrong, fluff has its place. But when all of these stories begin to run together and I can't keep Stacy from this clique straight from Cindy in that country club, then I know I've hit the chick-lit wall. It's over, I can't stomach one more cutesy, clever, sarcastic, knowing, sexy, gossipy, confessional, tell-all, weepy, feel-good, feel-bad girl book. I just can't.

So I'm going to dish up some great girlie reads by smart authors who give the chick-lit genre a little twist and shout, who tell honest stories about girls, their lives and both types of BFs (boyfriends and best friends). These books may have hot pink covers, but it is there that the slickness ends. Let's give girls books that show them standing up for themselves, figuring themselves out, and not taking No for an answer. In other words, let's lose the Gossip Girl and bring out the Riot Grrl that secretly lives in the heart of every female teen with these girls-rule reads!

Dessen, Sarah. 2002. *This Lullaby.* **New York: Penguin Group. 352p.**

The Story: Eighteen-year-old Remy Starr doesn't believe in love. While she is a serial dater, she has steadfastly refused to fall for any one boy. Her distrust of relationships stems from her romance novel-writer mother's inability to stay married (she's planning her fourth wedding) and the fact that her biological father, a long-dead pop singer, penned a one-hit wonder, "This Lullaby," whose lyrics describe a wayward father who already knows he is going to disappoint his baby girl.

It is the summer after senior year, and Remy can't wait to escape to college. She has been accepted at Stanford, across the country from her mother's chaotic lifestyle and helpless nature, and she plans on having one last, great summer with her close girlfriends while keeping a firm hold on her heart. Enter Dexter, a cute, messy, goofy musician. He and his friends are renting a house for the summer as they try to get their band, Truth Squad, a record deal. His band plays at her mom's latest wedding, and after meeting her, Dexter declares to Remy that they have a mystical connection and are meant to be together. Remy quickly dismisses him, because he doesn't even come close to being her type: tall, rich, good looking, and not interested in anything permanent. Dexter scores a day job at a photo-developing booth in the same strip mall where Remy works as a receptionist in a beauty salon.

One day Dexter cajoles Remy into giving him a ride home, then realizes that he's locked himself out of his house. Exasperated, Remy uses a credit card to pop the lock, which Dexter sees as a sign of love. Remy is doubtful. After a difficult dinner that same day with her elder brother, Chris, and his long-time, conservative girlfriend, Jennifer Anne, she goes on a drinking binge at the local bar with her trusty fake I.D., reminding her of the time she lost her virginity as a sophomore at a upperclassman party. Remy was so wasted that she had sex with a senior she barely knew that bordered on date rape, and she has since hardened her heart. Dexter shows up at the bar and takes her back to his house to sleep it off. Although nothing happens between them, she wakes up the next morning and sneaks away, mortified that Dexter saw her lose control. But when she sees him the next day, she finally gives in to the feelings she has begun having for him and kisses him.

After that first kiss, they fall into an easy summer routine of work and band gigs, and Remy is surprised at how comfortable she is with Dexter after only a few weeks. Yet she firmly believes that at the end of the summer, she will leave Dexter just as easily as she has left all the others. When a record company executive shows up at one of Dexter's band's shows, they play "This Lullaby" as part of their set. Remy gets angry because Dexter knows the story of her father and what that song means to her. They have an argument in the parking lot after the set, and Remy realizes that they are breaking up. She is somewhat relieved to feel in control of her feelings again.

At home, Remy's new stepdad, Don, is making a lot of new rules, and Remy is surprised at how easily her mother agrees to them. When Remy talks to her mom about it, her mom is shocked that Remy sees her multiple marriages as a weakness—she doesn't regret any of them because she knows she has loved and been loved. She cautions Remy against denying herself love, because it makes one only weaker when one refuses to take risks out of fear. Remy immerses herself in a new relationship with a shallow, attractive boy and begins packing for college as she tries to forget her mom's words and Dexter.

Ironically, her mother discovers later that Don has been cheating on her, but she refuses to be bitter about it. Remy is touched by her mother's resolve and by the fact that her mother is determined to take care of herself this time, instead of relying on Remy. In light of all that has happened and all that she's learned about the nature of love, Remy finally decides to allow herself to fall in love with Dexter. The story ends with Remy at Stanford, but still dating Dexter, as she plays his band's first single, "This Lullaby," which she has just received from him in the mail.

The Message: Denying yourself love only hurts you. "It's better to have loved and lost than never to have loved at all." If you never take a risk, you'll never change or grow. "Nothing ventured, nothing gained."

Who's It For?: 8th–12th grade. Remy and Dexter do not engage in intercourse, and Remy's sophomore date rape is not explained in detail. There is some strong language and underage drinking, and Remy's mother's multiple marriages may be a problem for some readers.

Why It Rocks:
• **Voice:** Remy's first-person narration is caustic and cynical but not without hope. Readers will be able to see how much she longs for love under the thin veneer of her tough words.
• **Plot:** Original and disquieting. We always see the girl looking for love in typical chick lit, never the girl avoiding love at all costs. Teens will be intrigued by this girl who has sworn off love at such a young age for such complicated and realistic reasons.
• **Pacing:** Arranged by the month, "June, July, August," with an epilogue of "November," Dessen's book captures the bittersweetness of a fleeting summer, and teens will hasten through the pages, wondering if Remy will make good on her promise to can the effervescent Dexter.
• **Characterization:** Surprising and true to theme. Dessen rounds out her characters nicely, making the story feel like it has come full circle, with Remy learning to accept love from a musician who sings her father's song, her mother learning to stand on her own two feet after spending a lifetime looking for someone to support her, and the irascible Dexter holding fast to his belief that love will find a way.

Hook It Up With: *My Heartbeat* by Garrett Freymann-Weyr and *The Key to the Golden Firebird* by Maureen Johnson.

Read More about It:
Booklist: 04/01/02
Horn Book: 07/01/02
Kirkus Reviews: 04/15/02
Publishers Weekly, starred: 05/20/02
School Library Journal: 04/01/02
V.O.Y.A. (Voice of Youth Advocates): 06/01/02

Flake, Sharon G. 2004. *Who Am I without Him?: Short Stories about Girls and the Boys in Their Lives.* **New York: Hyperion. 168p.**

The Stories: These ten short stories feature African American girls negotiating relationships with the men and boys in their lives, primarily boyfriends but fathers and brothers as well. The unnamed high school–aged narrator in "So I Ain't No Good Girl" scorns the neatly dressed, teacher's pet girls who wait with her at the bus stop, "so plain and pitiful, boys don't even look their way or ask their names." She, on the other hand, is dating Raheem, the cutest boy in school. She will do anything to keep him, though he has a wandering eye and sometimes hits her. When she witnesses him making out with one of those "good girls" from the bus stop, she resolves to keep her mouth shut, because "Who I'm gonna be without him?"

In "The Ugly One," high school freshman Asia has been forced to transfer schools seven times because she has been relentlessly bullied for the disfiguring acne on her face. The only place she ever feels safe is in her room, where she dances with a fantasy boyfriend named Ramon who tells her she is beautiful. Alone in her room with Ramon she is always happy "because in here, we make the rules."

In "Wanted: A Thug," 15-year-old Melody writes a letter to "Girl with All the Answers" at *Teen Queen* magazine. In the letter, she reveals that she is in love with her best friend's boyfriend, Rowl-D. Melody is attracted to Rowl-D because he is a "thug," a tough-talking boy who wears plenty of bling, has been kicked out of his house, and loves girls. Despite the disrespectful way h e treats Melody's friend Katherine, Melody is sure that "he's gonna be different with me." Girl with All the Answers writes back that she is an 11th grader at Melody's school and actually knows who Melody is. She herself has been in a similar situation where she started dating her best friend's thug boyfriend, and she ended up being in a nasty six-month feud with her former friend because of it. In a surprise twist, Rowl-D's current girlfriend happens to be the teen columnist's little sister. And if Melody decides to go after Rowl-D, Girl with All the Answers isn't above doing to Melody what was done to her!

An unnamed 16-year-old dead girl narrates "I Know a Stupid Boy When I See One." The narrator meets mentally challenged Willie Greentea when she moves into a home for unwed teenage mothers. Willie lives next door, and the narrator recognizes the potential for manipulation. Using her good looks, the narrator persuades Willie to sneak her money and jewelry, but once when she refuses to kiss him on the lips, he nearly strangles her. Frightened, she stays away from Willie for a while, but after her boyfriend writes from jail that he needs money, she determines to meet with Willie one last time. During that conversation, Willie mistakenly becomes convinced that when the narrator's baby is born, it will belong to him because of the money he's given her. He is furious when he visits the narrator in the hospital after the birth and she tells him that the baby is going to live with someone else. He strangles her, this time succeeding, and the girl leaves this world wishing she'd left Willie alone and hoping that God will accept a 16-year-old unwed mother as an angel.

"Mookie in Love" features an attractive young man who can't call his dating life his own because of his bossy aunts. Mookie is the only boy in a family of all women. As a result, "Mookie got a way with females." But when he sets eyes on his cousin's friend Shanna, 17-year-old Mookie finally understands what it has been like for all the girls who have fallen for him. There's only one problem: his mom and aunts keep trying to break them up. They succeed for a short time, until Shanna hits on the perfect solution: she brings over the baby boy of her cousin's boyfriend's sister; the infant keeps being shuffled from house to house, with no one caring for him permanently. Mookie's mom and aunts completely fall for the new baby, leaving Mookie a bit crestfallen at being replaced so easily but happy at being able to pursue his romance in peace.

"Don't Be Disrespecting Me" is about a love from the wrong side of the tracks. E is poor and from a part of town known as "Death Row." He and his friend Noodles never have enough of anything, though Noodles is good at charming girls into buying him food and clothes. E is in love with Ona, a wealthy girl from the suburbs, and she with him. He asks her to the homecoming dance even though he has no money for tickets or clothes. Noodles talks him into robbing some of the houses in Ona's neighborhood, where the doors are never locked. After a few big scores, E is able to pay for the dance, but Ona's father tells her he doesn't approve of E and that she can't date him. Undeterred, E dresses for the dance and plans on meeting Ona there. When he arrives, he hears that her house was robbed and her bedroom trashed. He knows who did it, and his only regret in calling the police on Noodles is that he knows Noodles will implicate him as well and he will never get a chance to dance with Ona now.

In "I Like White Boys," ninth grader Erika gets in trouble with other black kids at school because she tells them they don't speak correctly. She hates to sit with them at lunch because they are so loud and the white kids call their table "Little Africa." Erika has a crush on blond, blue-eyed Johnny, who looks like her light-skinned cousin, the first boy she ever liked. Her best friend, Winter, tells her that Chet Richards, a wealthy, good-looking black boy likes her, but she wonders why she "only gets to like boys who look like me," when white girls, like Johnny's girlfriend, Wendy, can pick any boy they choose. She knows that Johnny will never ask her out, yet when Chet asks her to the school carnival, she blows him off on the slim hope that maybe Johnny will change his mind.

Mr. Jacobs tries to teach Brandon and his friends about male/female relationships in "Jacobs' Rules." Mr. Jacobs pairs up several tenth graders in his communications elective and challenges them to work on managing a working relationship over the course of a month. Each pair will have a "recorder," a person who observes the relationship and grants or deducts points based on behavior. Each couple must work on a common goal, like buying a house or researching an adoption, while maintaining a civil tone. For Brandon and his friends, used to dating, then ditching, this is a tall order. Brandon is paired with Marimba, a big, loud, athletic girl he's never liked, when in reality, he'd like to be dating their recorder, Kenya, who is pretty and soft-spoken. But when Jacobs orders each couple to change one thing for the other person for one week, Brandon's head is turned when tomboy Marimba shows up in a skirt, heels, and long permed hair, per his request. Her request that he be nicer to her, by opening doors and pulling out chairs, pays off when other girls notice his manners. By the end of the experiment, Brandon doesn't necessarily like Marimba any more than he did before, but the whole experience has made him rethink how he treats girls.

In "Hunting for Boys," ten 14-year-old girls who have grown up together in the

Calvary Church of God's Blessed Example decide that they are tired of missing out on all the fun their secular peers get to experience. They determine that they are going to meet boys if it kills them, so they take a bus together to a neighborhood where they know there is a popular hoop court. They quickly discover that it's easy to attract the basketball players' attention, but what they didn't count on was attracting the attention of the girls who hang out regularly on the court. When the "bad girls" threaten them, they turn tail and run to the nearest pay phone, where they call Pastor to come and pick them up. Later, sadder and wiser after their ill-fated adventure, as they are cleaning the church as punishment, they plan a door-to-door fundraising campaign—where they just might run into some boys.

Finally, in "A Letter to My Daughter," a father who left home long ago writes some advice to his 15-year-old daughter about boys because he has nothing else to leave her. He tells her that a boy needs to be more than nice—he needs to be respectful—and that she should make a list of all the qualities she wants in a man and never settle for less. He tells her not to give up her power too quickly to get a boy to like her, but also to support a boy who has shown himself worthy of her. He concludes with the reminder that "boys is nice," but "if you ain't got a boyfriend, remember you still got you . . . your dreams, your talent, your smarts."

The Message: Boys and girls both deserve respect in love relationships. Anything worth having is worth working for, and nothing is more valuable than self-esteem. You can't judge yourself based on what others think of you. Love comes in all shapes, sizes, classes, and races. Be open to it.

Who's It For?: 7th–12th grade. Flake is a master at conveying authentic feeling and dialogue without the use of profanity, so these stories could easily be recommended to upper-middle-school students. Although there is frank discussion of murder, vandalism, bullying, fistfights, and violence against women, there are no graphic or gratuitous descriptions.

Why It Rocks:
• **Voice:** These mostly first-person narratives are authentic and raw, outstanding examples of realistic and unromanticized teenspeak (without the cursing).
• **Plot:** Going from the sheltered ("Hunting for Boys") to the seen-too-much ("The Ugly One"), Flake's stories are tightly written, each one with an edifying message tucked neatly between the lines.
• **Pacing:** Flake is careful to balance stories that are hard to read ("I Know a Stupid Boy When I See One") with ones that give a chuckle, if not an outright guffaw ("Mookie in Love," "Jacobs' Rules"), giving this collection a very evenhanded tone.
• **Characterization:** These are students in your class, kids in your neighborhood or church. They couldn't be more real, and their stories will feel that way to the teen readers who meet them within the pages.

Hook It Up With: *Jason and Kyra* by Dana Davidson, *Emako Blue* by Brenda Woods, and *The First Part Last* by Angela Johnson.

Read More about It:
Booklist, starred: 04/15/04
Horn Book: 10/01/04
Kirkus Reviews, starred: 04/15/04
Publishers Weekly: 07/05/04
School Library Journal: 05/01/04
V.O.Y.A. (Voice of Youth Advocates): 06/01/04

Frank, Hilary. 2002. *Better Than Running at Night.* Boston: Houghton Mifflin. 263p.

The Story: Ellie Yelinsky has decided to reinvent herself. A Gothy, angsty high school artist whose oil paintings of severed heads disturb her hippie parents, Ellie is starting over as a freshman at the New England College of Art and Design. After seeing a copy of Ilya Repin's *Ivan the Terrible and His Son Ivan,* which depicts the anguished ruler cradling his son's body after accidentally murdering him, Ellie knows, "My figures looked like cartoon characters in comparison. Ivan got your empathy; my paintings did nothing except beg for attention."

Ellie decides she's done with melodrama. From now on she will be a calm, cool, serious art student. That's why when good-looking, smooth-talking sophomore Nate Finerman ("As in: You Never Met a . . . ") starts paying attention to Ellie, she resolves to keep her composure, even though she's never had a serious boyfriend before. She also convinces herself that losing her virginity to him is no big deal, even after meeting his girlfriend, Clarissa, with whom he claims to have an "open" relationship.

Meanwhile, Ellie is frustrated by the basic drawing concepts her freshman Foundations I professor, Ed Gilloggley, is making the class cover. Ellie thought she'd be producing monumental artworks; instead, overly enthusiastic Ed is making his small class start with blocks, still lifes, and color values, things Ellie feels she already understands. Her relationship with Nate has fallen into a pattern of commitmentless sexual encounters. She rarely stays over at his place, preferring instead "the thrill of running [back to my apartment] at night, knowing that someone in the place I just left was wanting me." Nate, whose specialty is painting the nude female form, begins a series of paintings of a busty classmate that cumulates in a depiction of Nate and the girl lying naked together. Ellie tries to pretend it doesn't matter, but when she finds a D cup-sized black bra in Nate's bathroom, she wonders if she isn't being naive.

Right before the semester break in February, Ed tells Ellie he thinks she is one of the more talented students he's worked with and that she should keep at it. Ellie is pleased, especially because she is beginning to see the results of Ed's emphasis on basics in her work, which is getting better and better. The professor shows the class some of his own drawings, quiet, beautiful charcoal nudes that are the complete opposite of his arm-waving personality, and Ellie realizes that she has underestimated her teacher.

Ellie and Nate get into a big fight, right before she goes home to New York for the semester break, about his inability to stop flirting with other girls. But though she is worried about Nate, Ellie spends the long weekend struggling over an old issue with her dad—that they both don't know how to address the unspoken fact that he isn't her biological father and that the identity of that man is unknown by her mother, an active participant in the free love movement of the 1960s.

When Ellie returns to school, Nate calls to tell her he's missed her terribly, even though Clarissa is over at his apartment. She realizes he's never going to give up other girls. He makes a few more attempts to convince her that they should continue dating, but Ellie is through with him, though she does miss the physical closeness of sex. She has begun her Foundations II class with a pretentious performance-art professor named Gregg Cramroy, who has a nonattendance policy and thinks anything that has to do with the craft of creating art is "old school." Ellie quickly takes his nonattendance policy to heart and instead starts taking her new work back to Ed, who is delighted to act as her mentor. She goes to a senior art show that is full of paintings resembling her high school phase and realizes how much she has matured and that she doesn't even want to resume painting until her drawing skills are as good as they can be. Ellie is on her way to becoming a real artist and has learned a serious life lesson about relationships in the process.

A subplot concerning a mild flirtation with one of the boys in her Foundations I class also helps her see that there are boys out there who are not as self-centered as Nate.

The Message: Trust yourself. Be open to new experiences. It's never too late to start over. Keep your goals in mind and always remember your priorities. First impressions don't always hold true over the long term.

Who's It For?: 9th–12th grade. There is a movement in the field of young adult literature to change the upper-age range of young adult to as high as 21 or 22, and that is really the perfect audience for this book, although it can certainly be enjoyed by high school teens. Nate's sexual indiscretions are discussed, though not in great detail; Ellie and Nate have sex; and there is an art student party where several of the girls get topless, but that is the extent of the situation. There is underage drinking mentioned and references to Ellie's parents' hippie days, when they named her "Ladybug" after a mutual LSD hallucination (shortened to "L.B.," and finally, "Ellie").

Why It Rocks:
- **Voice:** The excruciatingly funny and oh-so-affected grad-school-speak in this novel will have you poring over old yearbook inscriptions and laughing your head off.
- **Plot:** Frank has an MFA in drawing from the New York Academy of Art, so her skillful skewering of the pretentiousness of the art school world must have some basis in reality. One performance-art student performs "Art Piñata," where he drops a bag of candy down to a crowd of students, followed by a bag of roadkill. Arts education is a topic not often explored in the field of YA literature, and Frank delves into it in a way that is thought provoking and accessible to teens.
- **Pacing:** The dialogue-heavy, short episodic chapters, adorned with quirky drawings in the margins, belie the seriousness of some of the book's themes and will draw reluctant readers in.
- **Characterization:** Ellie matures as both an artist and an adult, with each path mirroring the other and creating a fully rounded portrait of a young woman in

transition. Some secondary characters are stereotypical (like Ellie's hippie parents), while others shine (Ed the Professor is especially wonderful).

Hook It Up With: *The Perks of Being a Wallflower* by Stephen Chobsky and *Are You Experienced?* by William Sutcliffe.

Read More about It:
Booklist, starred: 10/01/02
Horn Book: Spring 2003
Publishers Weekly: 08/05/02
School Library Journal: 01/01/03
V.O.Y.A. (Voice of Youth Advocates): 02/01/03

Lockhart, E. 2005. *The Boyfriend List.* New York: Random House. 229p.

The Story: Fifteen-year-old Ruby Oliver's life is falling apart. In the past ten days, she has lost her boyfriend, Jackson; her three best friends, Kim, Nora, and Cricket; and her reputation. On top of that, she's started having heart-pounding panic attacks that leave her breathless and terrified; so, she begins seeing a shrink named Dr. Z to try to figure out how to make the attacks stop.

On the outside, Ruby's life seems fairly stable. She lives in Seattle on a houseboat with her mom, who's a performance artist, and her dad, who runs a container-gardening business from their boat deck. Ruby attends Tate Prep, an exclusive private school, on scholarship, and has a tight group of "reasonably popular" best girlfriends with whom she has been writing "The Boy Book: A Study of Habits and Behaviors" since eighth grade. To get at the root of her panic attacks, Dr. Z suggests that Ruby create a "Boyfriend List" to includes every boy she's ever dated, liked, or even had a crush on, as Ruby's first attack happened after Jackson broke up with her. As they discuss each boy, some from Ruby's past, others from the present, she slowly begins to come to some understandings about herself, and Dr. Z hears the real story behind Ruby's panic attacks.

It all started when Jackson (#13 on the list) broke up with her. But he didn't just break up with her—he broke up with her to go out with her best friend, Kim. Although they both claimed to care about her friendship, that didn't stop them from getting together, and Ruby didn't tell either of them how terrible she felt about the whole situation. So when Jackson offers to take her to the Spring Fling (with Kim's permission because she is going to be out of town), Ruby jumps at the chance to go because she's still in love with him. Except . . . she already told Angelo (#10), a cute boy from another school, that she'd take him. She calls and cancels but invites Angelo to the after party she's having at her houseboat.

The evening starts promisingly enough when Jackson kisses her at the restaurant; but he pushes her away when one of Kim's friends spots them and keeps his distance the rest of the night. To console herself, Ruby holds hands with Noel (#14), a boy she knows from art class, once she gets to her house. Jackson shows up again just in time to witness Angelo give Ruby a kiss along with some flowers he brought to her party, after which he storms off. Then Meghan, a neighbor Ruby carpools to school with, arrives and wants to know why she wasn't invited. Ruby is too ashamed to admit she never thought to invite Meghan because Meghan has a senior boyfriend and is so confident in her sexuality that all the other girls are jealous of her. After everyone leaves, Ruby has another attack.

The next day at school, the situation worsens. Someone had found an old copy of Ruby's Boyfriend List, which she had thrown in the garbage, and photocopied it, putting a copy in everyone's student mailbox. All of her old friends are ostracizing her, except Noel, who tries to console her about the increasing amount of "slut" graffiti that's appearing about her in the bathrooms. Now at the very bottom of the social scale, Ruby has nowhere to go but up. She realizes through her sessions with Dr. Z that in order to stop the attacks, she must learn to confront and question others when they behave in a way that hurts her or that she doesn't understand.

So, Ruby confronts Kim about turning on her just when she needed her the most, and Kim admits to photocopying the Boyfriend List, but isn't sorry. Ruby realizes that she and Kim will probably never be good friends again, which makes her begin to rethink her relationship with Meghan. Being called a slut when she knows she isn't one makes Ruby realize that just because other girls are threatened by Meghan and call her a slut doesn't mean that she is one either. She discovers that she needs more than just physical attraction when she agrees to go on a date with popular jock Cabbie (#15). He feels her up during the movie, which feels good, but his dinner conversation is so boring that she knows she can't continue dating him. She also begins to realize that there is more to life than the "Tate Universe" when her ex-friend Nora's older brother Gideon (#4) returns from a year of travel and shares with her how much bigger the world is that exists outside of high school. When school ends, Ruby decides to pursue deeper relationships with Meghan and Noel and to join her mom on tour in California in an attempt to experience life outside the expectations of the "Tate Universe."

The Message: Be honest with yourself and others. Tell the truth, even if it hurts. Stifling your true emotions hurts not only you but also those around you.

Who's It For?: 8th–12th grade. Ruby's funny, first-person narrative is hilarious but also very frank. Ruby talks realistically and honestly about boobs, penises, and sex. Although she hasn't had sex herself, she and her friends speculate about who has and how far some girls have gone. There are no surprises here for Meg Cabot or Louise Rennison readers, but it's probably not the best choice for younger middle school students who still fall into fits of giggles if they hear the word *butt*, let alone *penis*.

Why It Rocks:
- **Voice:** While Ruby's voice (à la Bridget Jones) is familiar, Lockhart's writing is exceptional in its realism. This particular passage really tickled me: "I always figured a boyfriend would ask me out, then pick me up on Saturday night. . . . We'd have plans. I never thought he'd swing by Saturday morning to see if I wanted to run his errands with him and we'd end up buying fifteen lollipops at the drugstore and opening them all and having blind taste tests."

- **Plot:** Like Nick Hornby's slacker opus to ex-girlfriends, *High Fidelity*, *The Boyfriend List* effectively uses past relationships with the opposite sex as a lens through which Ruby can view herself and learn how to change her behavior. This premise allows readers to dig a little deeper into what appears to be just another chick lit book.
- **Pacing:** The text is peppered with detailed funny footnotes that provide the reader with some of Ruby's inner thoughts and may slow some readers down as they laugh themselves silly before going on to the next page.
- **Characterization:** Ruby's spot-on, self-deprecating, and witty first-person narration and the details of her life that are just different enough to make readers take notice (the houseboat, the performance-artist mom, the notes left in old-fashioned student mailboxes) ensure that readers will relate to Ruby but also find her interesting.

Hook It Up With: *Gingerbread* by Rachel Cohn and *Girl, 15, Charming but Insane* by Sue Limb.

Read More about It:
Booklist: 04/01/05
Horn Book: 10/01/05
Kirkus Reviews: 02/15/05
Publishers Weekly, starred: 02/28/05
School Library Journal: 04/01/05
V.O.Y.A. (Voice of Youth Advocates): 04/01/05

Mackler, Carolyn. 2003. *The Earth, My Butt, and Other Big, Round Things.* Cambridge, MA: Candlewick. 246p.

The Story: Fifteen-year-old overweight Virginia has never felt like a real member of the attractive and accomplished Shreve family. Her mother is a well-known adolescent psychologist, and her father is a successful software executive, while older sister Anais is in the Peace Corp and perfect brother Byron is a sophomore at Columbia. Virginia lives with her parents in a penthouse apartment on Manhattan's Upper West Side; she attends a snobby private school where she couldn't feel more out of place amid an army of skinny, fashion-obsessed girls. Her best friend, Shannon, just moved, forcing Virginia to spend most lunch periods huddled in the girl's bathroom, rather than eating alone in the lunchroom.

The only bright spot in Virginia's life is the Monday make-out sessions she holds in her room with Froggy Welsh IV, a shy, sweet boy who has a crush on her, though she can't imagine why. But those steamy afternoons end when Virginia thinks Froggy (hidden under the bed in haste when her mother unexpectedly comes home) has overheard her mother tell Virginia that she has a doctor's appointment to address her weight issues. Mortified, Virginia promptly begins avoiding Froggy, thinking he couldn't care less, when in reality he is crushed.

Virginia tries visiting her brother at his dorm, hoping to rekindle the easy relationship they used to have when they were younger, but she is disappointed when he blows her off. She likes the doctor her mother takes her to, especially when he tells her mom that the focus shouldn't be on Virginia's body, but on fitness and nutrition. But after her father buys her a full-length mirror to watch herself lose weight, she begins skipping meals and spending lunch in a sympathetic teacher's office. Then, just as Virginia thinks things couldn't possibly get worse, her parents get a terrible phone call from Columbia's dean of students. Byron has been accused of date raping another student, and the student honor board has voted that he be suspended for the rest of the semester. The news is enough to send Virginia on a disastrous days-long binge of junk food and candy.

At home, Virginia's parents seem determined to gloss over the incident and insist that everything is fine. At school, Froggy tries to talk to Virginia, but she continues to avoid him because she can't stand the thought of doing anything sexual in the wake of Byron's accusation. Shannon invites Virginia to Seattle for Thanksgiving, but her mother tells her she can't go because her mother is determined to have a "normal" family holiday for Byron. Virginia is furious. In a silent rage, she purposely burns her finger over a candle as a way to release some of her anger. This isn't the first time she's hurt herself instead of speaking up to her parents, and she begins to wonder what would happen if she just stopped being obedient. She decides to secretly buy a ticket to Seattle with her own savings.

Virginia tells her mother that she's going to Seattle whether her mother agrees or not, and she ends up having a great time reconnecting with Shannon and her family. A week before Christmas, a few of Byron's old friends stop by the apartment but don't stay long. Virginia tells Byron that it's probably because they believe that he is a rapist. Byron becomes completely enraged, shouting expletives at her and forcing her to lock herself in her room. Shaken, she sneaks out later and finds the Columbia dorm room of Annie Mills, the girl Byron raped. Virginia apologizes to Annie for what her brother did, and Annie responds by telling Virginia that Byron hasn't ruined her life because she refuses to let anyone turn her into a victim. Virginia identifies with Annie, and it occurs to her that she doesn't have to be a victim either and can take control of her own life.

Inspired by Annie, Virginia launches a campaign to stick up for herself. She buys a low-cut dress and dyes her hair purple for her parents' holiday party. After Christmas, she takes up kickboxing and begins making friends with people in her class. She confronts Byron about how terribly he's been treating her and tells her dad to please stop commenting on her weight. Finally, she, along with kids from her school, starts a Webzine called *Earthquack* and suddenly has a whole new group of friends to sit with at lunch. But the best thing that happens is when Froggy, who she was always sure was interested only in making out with her in private, kisses her in front of the entire *Earthquack* staff. Slowly but surely, Virginia is realizing that her world, and the people she chooses to have in it, doesn't have to revolve around her "big butt."

The Message: You don't have to be a victim. You can take control of your life by standing up for yourself. Follow your dreams. If you set goals, you can accomplish anything.

Who's it for?: Why, for all the "fat girls," of course! Actually, Mackler's novel is perfect for 7th–12th graders, chubby or not. Virginia's issues span the gamut of female adolescent emotion, and there won't be a 12- to 17-year-old girl alive who can't relate. There are a few rather racy make-out scenes between Virginia and Froggy, where lots of heavy petting goes on but no actual intercourse. Virginia also has frequent daydreams about a certain "green-eyed Yankee's shortstop" (whom readers will recognize as Derek Jeter, though he remains unnamed throughout the book) and enjoys oogling his rear during games. There is also some strong language and bullying issues.

Why It Rocks:
• **Voice:** In a funny, self-deprecating first-person voice, Mackler addresses serious issues of class, body image, emerging sexuality, and self-mutilation in an understated way that never comes off as didactic or excessive.
• **Plot:** Kind of groundbreaking—in the wake of Paris Hilton and Lindsey Lohan-esque Gossip Girls, Mackler dared to write about a girl with a real body who has sexual feelings and deals with them in a realistic manner.
• **Pacing:** Chronological and straightforward, building nicely to the catalytic climax of Virginia meeting Annie.
• **Characterization:** While some reviewers say Mackler assigned Virginia too many issues and didn't deal with them all to the same extent, I completely disagree. By lightly touching on each issue and layering it into Virginia's personality, Mackler created a full picture of a real girl who, despite her family's wealth and prestige, is in quiet crisis. In addition, all of the secondary characterizations of Virginia's family members are excellent, and Mackler is careful to show the impact of each of their individual dysfunctions on Virginia.

Hook It Up With: *Myrtle of Willendorf* by Rebecca O'Connell and *Life in the Fat Lane* by Cherie Bennett.

Read More about It:
Booklist: 09/01/03
Horn Book: 04/01/04
Kirkus Reviews: 06/15/03
Publishers Weekly: 07/21/03
School Library Journal: 09/01/03
V.O.Y.A. (Voice of Youth Advocates): 10/01/03

Marchetta, Melina. 2004. *Saving Francesca*. New York: Random House. 243p.

The Story: Sixteen-year-old Australian teen Francesca "Frankie" Spinelli usually can't stand her outgoing, outspoken mother Mia's morning ritual of waking the household with her 1980s pop songs and peppy demeanor. But when Mia doesn't get out of bed one morning and refuses to leave her room, Frankie is worried. Even though her mother drives her crazy, Francesca loves her family. She is very close to her father, Robert, a strong, quiet building contractor, and her little brother, Luca.

That morning, Francesca gets Luca and herself off to school, only to be confronted by a new set of issues. She has started attending St. Sebastian's, which has only recently begun admitting girls. She is among the first 30 female students and hates it. She misses her friends from her old school, St. Stella's, and the only girls she knows at St. Sebastian's are girls she considers losers. Tara Finke, a self-proclaimed feminist; Siobhan Sullivan, previously known as "the slut of St. Stella's"; and Justine Kalinsky, a studious girl who plays in the school band, have all made friendly overtures to Francesca, but she's not interested. However, when Tara circulates a petition among the girls about the lack of girls' restrooms and sports teams, Francesca reluctantly volunteers to take their demands to Will Trombal, a senior who is one of the school's elected leaders. The meeting does not go well, especially after Will arrogantly looks over her list and coldly informs her that the girls would get along better if they "didn't make waves."

Meanwhile, at home the fridge is bare and the dishes are piling up, as Francesca's dad tries valiantly to maintain his own job as well as manage the household. When Mia has still not left her room after two weeks, Francesca's grandmothers decide Mia needs peace and quiet. They send Luca to an aunt's house, while Francesca is sent to stay with Mia's mother, Nonna Anna. Over the next few weeks, Francesca, out of sheer loneliness, begins to make some connections with a few of the boys at school she had resolutely ignored before. She strikes up sarcastic exchanges with bad boy Jimmy Hailler and class joker Thomas Mackee, and even attends a rugby game that Will is playing in. Nonna Anna has a party, and Will's grandmother comes. When Will comes later to pick her up, he and Francesca chat for a while on the front stoop, and Francesca realizes she has a crush on him.

Shortly afterward, Francesca, Tara, Siobhan, and Justine get invited to an upperclassman party. Everyone is drinking, and Francesca is stunned when a drunken Will walks right up to her and kisses her deeply. But the next day at school, Justine tells her she just found out Will already has a girlfriend. Frankie is crushed. Tara proposes an "Alanis night," for the girls to hang out "listening to Alanis Morissette's music where there's a lot of revenge and anger towards men," and Francesca realizes how much she really likes these girls. She goes home to convince her dad that the family all needs to be together again.

A few days later, Francesca tries to get her father to pinpoint an event that led to Mia's breakdown, but he is frustratingly evasive. Francesca sees Will at her cousin Angelina's wedding, and he tries to kiss her again, but she stops him because of his girlfriend. When she finally hears that Will and his girlfriend have broken up, she waits in vain for him to ask her out. On an all-school camping trip to the coast, she confronts him, and he admits he hasn't wanted to start up a relationship with her because he had planned to go away to school next year and likes her too much to start something he can't finish. On Francesca's 17th birthday, Mia, who has been getting better, has a relapse and spends the day sobbing in her room. In *Sixteen Candles* fashion, no one remembers that it's Frankie's birthday.

Life rapidly goes downhill over the next few days; the girls go to a nightclub to hear a new band, only to be busted for drinking by Siobhan's police officer father, Will tells Francesca he's definitely decided to go abroad, and she gets in a fight with Justine. Frankie leaves school in a daze and goes to a local coffee shop, where she runs into one of Mia's friends, who accidentally reveals the reason for Mia's depression—

she suffered a miscarriage. Francesca goes home and confronts her father, screaming about how he has lied to her. Then she runs to the nearest train station and just rides, until her thoughts have quieted, then gets off and calls her dad to pick her up. When he does, he admits not telling her about Mia's miscarriage was a mistake. At home, her friends are all waiting for her, worried, and she sits down and has a long talk with Mia about the lost baby and everything that has happened. Even though Will is leaving, Francesca is happy with herself and her friends, especially when she leaves school to discover that for the first time in months, Mia has come to pick her and Luca up.

The Message: Believe in yourself and don't be afraid to try on different personalities to figure out who you are. Parents are also just people, with the same feelings and emotions as teens. They don't always know what to do or say in difficult situations. Sometimes you outgrow certain friends, sometimes they outgrow you, and it's not the end of the world. The hardest person to love is often yourself.

Who's It For?: 8th–12th grade. Francesca and her friends engage in underage drinking, converse using strong language, and have frank discussions about sex. Mia is a young, liberal parent, speaking openly to her children about sex and their bodies, often to Robert's chagrin. I read this one aloud to my New York City eighth graders the year it came out, but it's not one I would recommend as a read-aloud everywhere, and I still had to do some on-the-fly editing.

Why It Rocks:
• **Voice:** Rock solid. Frankie's first-person narration is poignant and rich, chock-full of insecurities, bewilderment, and sudden rushes of blind confidence. Some Aussie slang and Catholic school terminology may be confusing to American teens, but all is explained in context.
• **Plot:** What makes this novel more than just another girl-struggling-to-fit-in story is the engrossing subplot of Mia's depression and the gradual development of Francesca's pitch-perfect and scathingly funny platonic friendships with the boys of St. Sebastian's.
• **Pacing:** Occasionally slow. I learned from experience that this isn't the best choice for a read-aloud because of Francesca's many internal musings and memory flashbacks. But don't hesitate to include one of Francesca's sarcastic and witty exchanges with Thomas or Jimmy in a booktalk. They are priceless.
• **Characterization:** While Francesca is fully engaging and rounded, it is her supporting cast that makes her shine so. Besides her crew of Sebastian girlfriends, there are her young, deeply-in-love parents, opinionated Italian relatives, and of course, the tortured, Darcy-like Will Trombal, who generates almost as much reader sympathy as Francesca. Marchetta is a schoolteacher in Sydney, and her wonderful teen characters reflect her keen powers of observation.

Hook It Up With: *Sloppy Firsts* by Megan McCafferty and *Bringing Up the Bones* by Lara M. Zeises.

Read More about It:
Booklist: 10/01/04
Horn Book: 04/01/05

Kirkus Reviews, starred: 09/01/04
Publishers Weekly, starred: 09/06/04
School Library Journal, starred: 09/01/04
V.O.Y.A. (Voice of Youth Advocates): 10/01/04

Moriarty, Jaclyn. 2004. *The Year of Secret Assignments.* **New York: Scholastic. 340 p.**

The Story: Three Australian private school girls engage in a letter exchange with three public school boys, resulting in a dramatic comedy of pranks, mistaken identity, hurt feelings, and true love. High school sophomores Lydia, Emily, and Cassie have been best friends since grade school because they all have lawyer parents who work and socialize with one another. Cynical Lydia is an aspiring writer; hyperbolic Emily, who suffers from malapropism, loves horses and Toblerone chocolate; while quiet, smart Cassie and her attorney mother are trying to survive their first year without Cassie's father, who recently died of cancer. The girls' English teacher, Mr. Botherit, has launched a pen pal project between their institution, Ashbury, and it's public school rival, Brookfield, to help mend the rift between the warring student bodies.

Charlie, an easygoing boy from a working-class family, who admits during the course of their exchange that he's never had a girlfriend, receives Emily's letter. Emily offers Charlie advice about how to talk to girls and proposes they go on a "practice" date where Emily can test his skills. The practice goes well, piquing their interest in each other.

Seb, a boy who is as smart and sarcastic as Lydia, receives her letter. Ever since Cassie's father's death, Lydia has been the mastermind behind a series of "secret assignments": funny missions to distract the girls when they are feeling sad. So when Seb proposes a series of dares to Lydia that involve shutting down his school so that he can avoid taking tests, Lydia is more than up to the challenge. Suddenly, Brookfield is in turmoil daily, with fire alarms and sprinkler systems being set off constantly. Seb is completely charmed by Lydia's daring and keeps pressuring her to meet him in person. When Lydia finally agrees to meet him, she sets a condition that they must recognize each other with no pictures exchanged beforehand. She is completely unnerved when Seb walks right up to her, sure that he has cheated somehow.

Cassie's letter is received by Matthew, a caustic and cruel boy who begins their correspondence by telling her to "eat sh*t and die." Cassie is afraid, but because before his death, her father challenged her to always face her fears, she blithely ignores Matthew's hostility and keeps writing. Matthew finally responds reluctantly that he's been so nasty because a girl from Ashbury got him in trouble at school and he's still angry. He's also a victim of poverty and divorce, so he asks Cassie's forgiveness and requests a meeting at a certain secluded park. Cassie agrees, but Matthew never shows. Both Emily and Lydia question Charlie and Seb about Matthew, but the boys insist there is no one by that name in their school. Emily and Lydia wonder if Matthew is someone that Cassie has made up in her grief over her father.

Matthew writes to Cassie that he was waiting in the agreed upon spot for her, and that he thought *she* stood *him* up. They decide to try again. Emily and Lydia figure out where Cassie is meeting Matthew and go there in case she needs backup. They find Cassie alone, crying under a tree. With great reluctance, she finally tells them that when she met Matthew, he told her that Matthew wasn't even his real name and that he had made up everything in his letters as a cruel joke. Emily and Lydia immediately write to Charlie and Seb and ask their help in uncovering Matthew's real identity so that they can exact revenge on Cassie's behalf. Charlie discovers that Matthew is really Paul Wilson, the most popular guy in the tenth grade and star of the school play.

As the girls plot Paul's downfall, their continued correspondence begins to break down. Charlie discovers that he was an unwitting pawn in one of Lydia's secret assignments and is hurt that Emily didn't tell him. Lydia discovers that Seb actually saw a picture of her before their meeting and feels that he lied to her. Both girls come to an impasse with their Brookfield beaus. When Seb, in his frustration over the stagnation of he and Lydia's relationship, beats up Paul for what he's done to Cassie, Paul threatens to get him expelled for fighting. This infuriates the girls, who put their revenge plan into action. Using Lydia's mom's production studio and staff (she is a retired soap opera star), they convince Paul that he's been tapped as an emergency replacement in a made-for-TV movie. They send him to a distant location to wait for "Heath and Naomi" and are thoroughly satisfied when Paul calls the studio, wondering when the rest of the cast and crew are going to show up. In their triumph, Emily makes up with Charlie, and Lydia with Seb.

But all is still not well! Mr. Botherit suspends the Ashbury/Broookfield pen pal project after someone breaks into Brookfield school and spray paints anti-Brookfield graffiti all over the walls. Soon Ashbury's walls also are defaced, setting off a chain of retaliatory vandalism. Emily, Cassie and Lydia are accused of being the culprits when their headmistress does a surprise locker search and discovers some incriminating letters and notebooks that refer to "secret assignments." In addition, a "very reliable" student from Brookfield has placed the three girls at the scene of one of the acts of vandalism. The lawyer parents immediately mobilize, demanding a school hearing, where the girls' innocence will be defended by Emily, who is thrilled to put her burgeoning lawyer skills to the test. Just as Emily has gotten the teachers acting as judges to agree that the girls' private papers are not admissible evidence, Cassie bursts into the room, with Charlie and Seb. They have acquired Paul's backpack, which contains several half-full spray paint cans. Paul, the "very reliable" witness, actually perpetrated all the vandalism in an attempt to get back at the girls for their prank. He tries to bluster his way out of it but finally rushes out of the room in guilty shame. The girls are acquitted, the pen pal project is reinstated, and the Year of Secret Assignments ends on a hopeful and happy note.

The Message: Friends can be your lifeline in times of trouble. Good friends stick together and stick up for each other. You can't let fear keep you from taking risks. While it is important to grieve, it is equally important not to let grief cripple your life.

Who's It For?: 7th–12th grade. This book will be an easy, breezy read for middle school teens, although older teens are more likely to understand Moriarty's underlying themes about the strength of friendship and the importance of grieving. There is some light sexual banter, some strong language, and an oral sex reference.

Why It Rocks:
• **Voice:** Although Emily, Lydia, and Cassie's voices occasionally feel interchangeable, they are all funny, and Moriarty manages to write realistic, comical dialogue that feels fresh but isn't so full of slang that it dates immediately.
• **Plot:** Almost impossible to summarize in its sheer and impressively wrought complexity. I have listed enough here to remind you of the main plot points; however, there are innumerable other funny asides, serious conversations, and internal musings. This is an excellent example of an epistolary novel, and Moriarty tells her story through letters, e-mails, scripts, Cassie's diary, Lydia's writer's notebook, school flyers, and hilarious deadpan memos to Emily from her lawyer dad. Fans will also notice the several mentions of Elizabeth Clarry, the main character from Moriarty's popular first novel, *Feeling Sorry for Celia.*
• **Pacing:** Media-savvy teens will love the constantly changing forms in which Moriarty has chosen to relate her tale, and the author arranges the correspondence chronologically by school term, with the names of the pair who are writing at the top of the page to help readers keep track of who is speaking.
• **Characterization:** Though the voices of the characters often feel similar, each of these teens learns something about her or himself by book's end, whether it was how to deal with difficult people, come to terms with family, or learn how to effectively channel grief. Despite the glib title and soapy plot, the sincere and realistic characterizations make this a much richer read than it may appear to be at first.

Hook It Up With: *Feeling Sorry for Celia,* also by Jaclyn Moriarty, and *The Sisterhood of the Traveling Pants* by Ann Brashares.

Read More about It:
Booklist, starred: 01/01/04
Horn Book, starred: 03/01/04
Kirkus Reviews: 01/15/04
Publishers Weekly: 02/02/04
School Library Journal: 03/01/04
V.O.Y.A. (Voice of Youth Advocates): 06/01/04

Sones, Sonya. 2004. *One of Those Hideous Books Where the Mother Dies.* New York: Simon & Schuster. 268p.

The Story: Fifteen-year-old Ruby Milliken has suddenly found herself in the same situation as the girls who star in her least favorite teen novels, "those hideous books where the mother dies." Her mother has just lost her battle with cancer, and now Ruby must leave Boston to move in with her biological father in Los Angeles. Ruby's parents divorced before she was born, and her mother refused to talk about or acknowledge her father in any way, so Ruby has never technically met him. But her mother's sister, Aunt Duffy, didn't agree with her mom's decision to hide her father's identity from Ruby, so she has been secretly taking Ruby to see her father, Whip Logan, über-celebrity, whenever one of his movies is playing.

Despite Whip's fame and wealth, Ruby, still grieving for her mother, is desperate to stay in Boston, but Aunt Duffy can't afford to take her in, and there is nowhere else for her to live but with her father. On the plane, Ruby writes the first of many letters to her best friend, Lizzie, and daydreams about her sexy boyfriend, Ray. Whip picks her up at the airport, where they are hounded by paparazzi, a surrealistic moment for Ruby. When they arrive at Whip's home, Whip is incredibly kind, his house is luxurious, and his next-door neighbor is Cameron Diaz, but Ruby can't enjoy any of it because it all feels like it is at the expense of her mother's death. She can't help but wonder why Whip never tried to contact her or send her mom money and thinks that his attempts at making up for all those years of absence are too little, too late. She's also worried about the fact that she can't seem to cry anymore since her mom's death, and in a darkly humorous attempt to cope with the situation, she keeps sending messages to her mother's defunct e-mail account; the messages keep being returned bearing the message "permanent fatal errors," which Ruby finds oddly comforting and amusing.

Her first day of high school in L.A. makes homesick Ruby feel even more out of place. The teachers are addressed by their first names, the electives offered include Dream Interpretation and The Rhythms of Rap, and her assigned guide is Collette, who is "severely tanned" and has a snake tattoo. Ruby is shocked by the some of the information Collette shares with her (where the coke deals are made and who can sell her a term paper for cheap), but they bond over the difficulty of having famous parents, after discovering that Collette's mom once starred in a movie with Ruby's dad.

Ruby soon meets Whip's entourage, including his gay, live-in personal assistant, Max. "Aunt" Max is the sole person in L.A. that Ruby truly gravitates toward, so she spends as much time as possible with him, shunning her father in the process. Ruby gradually begins to get more comfortable with Collette and her other sophisticated classmates. Whip has agreed to allow Ruby to invite Ray to L.A. for Thanksgiving, and Ruby can't wait. On Halloween, Whip throws a huge party, and the number of celebrities who attend floors Ruby. She tries to call Lizzie and Ray to tell them, and also to hear what happened at her old school's Halloween dance, but neither of them returns her calls for several days. While she waits to hear from them, Ruby decides to try out for the school play, *Pygmalion*.

When Lizzie finally contacts Ruby, it is to tell her that she and Ray have fallen for each other; Ruby is devastated. On Thanksgiving, Whip and Max take Ruby to the homeless shelter where Whip cooks and serves dinner to the residents every year. Ruby is touched and wonders if she has been too hard on him. To cheer her up in the wake of Lizzie and Ray's betrayal, Whip takes Ruby to the set of his latest movie to meet his costar and Ruby's favorite celebrity, Eminem. This raises Ruby's spirits for a bit, but when a classmate she doesn't know well is killed in an automobile accident, Ruby is strongly affected and can't stop thinking about her mother.

One night, she awakens from a dream in which she is talking to her mother on the phone and her mother tells her to get out of the house. Ruby decides to take a walk and winds up at the scene of the car accident. Whip finds her there and gives her a hug; suddenly Ruby is crying for the first time since her mom died. As they stand there, there is a mild earthquake, and Whip is quick to protect Ruby. When they arrive home, Max shows them that there was very little damage done to the house—other than the heavy wooden bookcase that fell on Ruby's bed, flattening it. Ruby remembers her dream and nearly faints.

Whip finally tells Ruby the truth about him and her mother: her mom's heart was broken, and she never wanted to see Whip again after Whip came to terms with the fact that he was gay. Ruby is stunned, and even more so when Max admits that he's not just Whip's assistant but also his life partner. Now that she has the whole story, Ruby is finally able to reevaluate her feelings for Whip and her mom and move on. She ends up scoring the lead in the school play, opposite a boy she's been "crushing" on, and makes up with Lizzie. Finally at peace with her mom's death, Ruby can't imagine living anywhere but L.A. with anyone but her dad.

The Message: First impressions aren't always correct. Make sure you have all the facts about a situation before making an assumption. Forgiveness is often easier than it looks. Love is complicated—adults don't even get it right most of time, let alone teenagers.

Who's It For?: 7th–12th grade. Ruby may have a few sexy daydreams about Ray and contemplate going to second base and beyond, but she never does. She gets so angry at Whip she considers "kicking him in the balls," but other than that, there is little strong language. Ruby's family situation and relationship with her father and Max may be a problem for some readers in conservative regions.

Why It Rocks:
- **Voice:** The star of this first-person novel, written in a bright, free-verse poetry/prose style that belies its sad subject, is Ruby's fresh, sincere voice, sometimes shot through with pain but more often crackling with humor.
- **Plot:** Chronological and easy to follow. The titles at the top of each of Ruby's one- to two-page poems provide quick signposts to readers flipping ahead to find out what happens next or going back to reread some of Ruby's wickedly smart observations.
- **Pacing:** Told in multiple formats (poetry, letters, e-mails, lists), Ruby's story moves along quickly, but teens will want to slow down to savor some of Ruby's apt remarks: "That's L.A. down there, / simmering in that murky smog stew. / But from where I'm sitting, / it looks more like / Hell A."
- **Characterization:** While not all of the secondary characterizations are fleshed out (Whip seems one-dimensional and too good to be true, and Aunt Duffy is simply a plot device to explain how Ruby knows anything about Whip), Lizzie and Max shine in their supporting roles. Lizzie's "Marge Simpson-esque" voice comes through loud and clear in her sharply observed letters, while Max's gentle diplomacy is demonstrated as he runs interference between Ruby and Whip.

Hook It Up With: *What My Mother Doesn't Know*, also by Sonya Sones, *Jinx* by Margaret Wild, and *Splintering* by Eireann Corrigan.

Read More about It:
Booklist, starred: 05/01/04
Horn Book: 10/01/04
Kirkus Reviews: 05/01/04
Publishers Weekly: 06/21/04
School Library Journal, starred: 08/01/04
V.O.Y.A (Voice of Youth Advocates): 10/01/04

Stone, Tanya Lee. 2006. *A Bad Boy Can Be Good for a Girl.* New York: Random House. 228p.

The Story: Three different high school girls encounter the same smooth-talking senior cad, each coming away from the experience sadder and wiser for having met him. First there is Josie, a cool, confident freshman who knows who she is and what she wants. That's why she is taken aback by how much she is physically attracted to hot senior T.L. (only identified by his initials throughout the book) after he hits on her at a fall dance. His come-on lines are clichés, yet she finds herself giggling after every comment. He begins pressuring her for sex, and their make-out sessions feel so good that she begins to consider losing her virginity to him. Almost against her will, she finds herself cutting class, ditching friends, and risking her parents' ire to be with him.

When Josie continues to withhold intercourse, T.L. begins to back off, and Josie panics. She agrees to go out with him alone one night on his parents' boat. They come so close to having sex that he has opened the condom wrapper and pulled down her underwear. But something doesn't feel right to Josie, and she tells him to stop. The next day at school, she overhears him tell his buddies that "I've just gotta work a little harder on this one." She is stunned to hear herself so casually objectified. He breaks it off with her soon afterward, and Josie swears to herself that next time she'll be smarter, that she'll remember how good he made her feel, but also how awful after she found out he was really after only one thing.

Josie's emotions remind her of a book she read by Judy Blume, where a girl becomes engulfed by her physical feelings for her boyfriend. The book is titled *Forever,* and Josie is inspired by her experience with T.L. to pen a warning in the back of the school library's copy of the novel in order to warn other girls about his philandering ways. She then makes it her mission to spread the word—every girl in school needs to check out the back of *Forever.*

Next in line is Nicolette, an attractive junior who uses sex as form of power. She hears about Josie's crusade against T.L., and her interest is piqued. She walks right up to him and introduces herself, and they go out that same afternoon after school. He shows her an old art supply closet down a forgotten hall, and they meet there regularly between classes to make out. Yet, he barely acknowledges her when he's with his friends and never calls her to make plans. His idea of a date is to take her to a remote public baseball dugout, where they engage in oral sex.

Nic, overwhelmed by her physical feelings for T.L., is beginning to feel like she is losing the sexual control of which she was so proud. He finally agrees to take her on a real date but won't come in to meet her mom, then only takes her to the local pizza spot, where they end up having sex in his car after dinner. It feels so good to Nic that she's sure she's finally fallen in love. The next day, his friends and their girlfriends smirk at her in the hall, the girls telling her they've heard what she does in the supply closet. Soon after, she hears that he has started dating another girl, a senior named Aviva. Furious, she accuses him of cheating, and he tells her that their relationship was never really serious—they were just messing around, and she wanted it as much as he did. She finds a note from Josie in her locker, telling her that she's sorry T.L. got Nic, too, and that she should check out *Forever*. She does, and is shocked at how many comments have been added since Josie wrote her warning.

The next girl to attract T.L.'s attention is Aviva, an artsy guitar player of hippie parents. She meets T.L. at a beach party but is wary because she has heard he's dating a wild girl named Nicolette. The next day she overhears his friends say that T.L. "has moved on to that Aviva chick," and while it sounds an alarm in her head, she still accepts a last-minute invitation from him to another beach bash. He kisses her at the party, and she's hooked, taken aback by how physically attracted she is to him and how much she enjoys the attention she's getting from his popular crowd of friends. Aviva has never considered herself the type of person who can so easily have her head turned by compliments and attention. After she spends a number of weekends going out (and making out) with him every night, her best friend, Amanda, chastises her for dumping all her other friends. Aviva responds that she can't help it, for she has completely fallen for him.

Soon, Aviva is so overcome by her physical feelings for T.L. that she decides they should have sex. She invites him over to her house one afternoon when she knows her parents won't be home, wearing only her guitar. While she enjoys the connection they share, the actual intercourse is somewhat painful and awkward. Afterward, she tells him she loves him, but he seems to have fallen asleep. He doesn't call her that night, and she is so distraught that she begins to question her decision. When she finally corners him, he admits that her saying she loved him felt too serious and that he thinks they need to slow down. Aviva is livid and calls him a coward because he pressured her for sex but doesn't want to deal with the feelings caused by it. Josie hears about what happened, finds Aviva at school, and tells her to read *Forever*. When she does, she is stunned to see that girls who felt they were taken advantage of by T.L. have written on every square inch of white space. The girls form an initially uneasy but supportive bond over their similar "bad boy" experience, vowing to learn from their mistakes.

The Message: No one is completely immune to feelings of sexual attraction. Even the steadiest person can lose control of his or her emotions in the heat of the moment. There is a distinct difference between love and lust, although sometimes it can be hard to discern. Don't beat yourself up over mistakes; try instead to see them as an opportunity for growth.

Who's It For?: 9th–12th grade, possibly 10th grade and up in some communities. Do you really need me to tell you why?

Why It Rocks:
• **Voice:** Stone's poetry attempts in this first-person verse-novel are merely so-so compared with her intriguing premise of smart girls losing their heads, then sharing their stories in the back of the most revered adolescent sex novel of all time.
• **Plot:** Fantastic. After the plethora of "mean girl" books, it's refreshing to read a story where girls overcome their jealousy and anger over a boy and bond in spite of their differences. And like a DVD with nifty extras, the front and back pages of Stone's novel are full of graffiti to look like the infamous copy of *Forever*.
• **Pacing:** Stone arranges the book chronologically, with each girl telling her story in prose poems that read quickly, if not a bit too simply. Teens will be impatient to learn if the bad boy ever gets his comeuppance.
• **Characterization:** Stone develops a distinct, yet recognizable type for each of the female characters in this book, even as her despicable bad boy sinks into stereotype. She does hint at some family problems in his background (a competitive older brother, parents in an unhappy marriage), so he comes off as only a *nearly* complete jerk.

Hook It Up With: *Forever* by Judy Blume, *Dreamland* by Sarah Dessen, and *Love and Sex: Ten Stories of Truth* edited by Michael Cart.

Read More about It:
Booklist: 01/01/06
Horn Book: 01/01/06
Kirkus Reviews: 01/01/06
School Library Journal, starred: 01/01/06
V.O.Y.A. (Voice of Youth Advocates): 04/01/06

———————

Vance, Susanna. 2003. *Deep.* **New York: Random House. 272p.**

The Story: Birdie Sidwell and Morgan Bera, two completely different girls who have nothing in common except the color of their red hair, are about to be united by fate in a very unexpected way. Thirteen-year-old Birdie is the treasured only child of older, academic parents who indulge her every whim. Her parents have decided to take a break from their hectic schedules as a school superintendent and government scientist to go on a yearlong sabbatical to the Caribbean. Birdie is thrilled to be leaving her hometown of Riverton, Oregon, for the island of St. Petts, where she plans on collecting new experiences to inspire the award-winning novel she intends to write.

In complete contrast, somber 17-year-old Morgan has been raised on the ocean by a pair of unconventional Norwegian sailor parents who have homeschooled her in the way of the sea. Her father sold his insurance practice to sail the world and raise his family on the water. He and his wife made their living helping residents of storm-ravaged islands in the Atlantic collect their insurance money, but as of late they have surrendered to the siren call of alcoholism after the accidental drowning death of Morgan's older sister. Oona was swept from the family boat by a rogue wave on a deceptively clear day, and Morgan, in her grief, is convinced that her dead sister's spirit still guides her.

It is Oona's voice that tells her to leave her parents ashore in Panama for their own good, since they are no longer safe to pilot the boat in their inebriated state. Morgan realizes that she will need forged official papers that place the boat in her name if she is to sail alone. She remembers her parents mentioning a man who specializes in making such documents, so she sails off to the privately owned island of Calista, where this man, named Nicholas, is known to live.

As Birdie and her parents wait for the ferry that will take them on the last leg of their journey to St. Petts, they are invited to board the boat of a handsome stranger named Nicholas. He offers to hold their luggage while they shop at the market, and even though Birdie's father is deeply suspicious, they do just that. Later, when Birdie comes onboard to retrieve her camera, Nicolas guns the engines in full view of her astonished parents and sails away with her.

For the first few days of her capture, Birdie is drugged into submission and only faintly registers Nicholas's ever-changing appearance and the fact that seem to be switching boats often. When she finally comes back to herself, she realizes that Nicholas is a charming but completely merciless modern-day pirate who intends to brainwash her into being his pampered human pet. She learns quickly that if she makes any mention of her former life, he locks her into the cabin of his boat without food or water for days, but if she pretends to be happy, he is very kind, cooking for her and taking her snorkeling.

They are docked on a private island named Calista that Nicholas claims is owned by his millionaire grandfather, Peter Vundermeer. He often leaves the island on mysterious errands, leaving Birdie locked in the boat while he is gone. On one of these excursions, she uses her journal to piece together the fact that she's now been missing for over a month. Birdie realizes that she will have to be very clever if she is to outsmart Nicholas and save herself.

Morgan reaches Calista, somewhat disturbed by the many Coast Guard helicopters that keep flying overhead. She knows the island as the private residence of millionaire recluse Peter Vundermeer and wonders why he would allow someone with as unsavory a reputation as Nicholas to hang around. Nicholas has met Morgan and her parents before, and he greets her warmly. He explains that the Guard are looking for a poor kidnapped girl and have been combing the area for several days. After he puts together her false papers and woos her with wine and a gourmet dinner, he attempts to seduce her. Morgan breaks away and races back to her boat, unaware that Birdie is watching her from her locked cabin. Safe at sea, Morgan slowly registers that the boat she saw docked in Calista's harbor looked familiar. She realizes it was the boat of a retired European couple she had come in contact with before and that Nicholas must have stolen it. Against her better judgment, she turns around and heads back to the island to investigate further.

Nicholas's mood swings are getting more and more frequent, and Birdie begins to fear for her life, after he jokes that the huge wooden crate that has been parked on the dock for the past few days is about to become her new home. He leaves her locked in the ship's cabin again, but this time with a computer that he demands she use to write him a story. Birdie instead works at cracking the password to the Internet so she can send an e-mail. Finally guessing the password (M-O-N-E-Y), she quickly dashes off an e-mail to her parents, giving her location and what she knows of Nicholas's criminal nature.

Nicholas returns and makes good on his threat of putting Birdie in the crate. He has been spooked by the helicopters that keep circling and decides Birdie would be better off hidden. He provides her with canned food and bottled water, but Birdie isn't frightened, as she is sure she will be rescued. In the middle of the night, Birdie awakens as Morgan returns to the island. Before Morgan can free Birdie, however, Nicholas, who has been hiding behind the crate, knocks her out with his flashlight and shoves her in with Birdie. The next morning he returns, furious, after discovering Birdie's e-mail. He picks up the crate with a front loader and dumps it into an abandoned well deep in the island's jungle, where it lodges halfway down.

When Morgan awakes, she and Birdie share their stories and hope for rescue. But after a day of waiting, Morgan tries to kick her way out of the ill-made crate. Instead, the bottom drops out and Birdie plunges into the darkness. Morgan climbs down carefully to retrieve her, and they discover to their horror that they are standing on a mass grave of Nicholas's victims, including poor Peter Vundermeer. They make it back into the crate and fall asleep, exhausted by their efforts. They are awakened by a crazed Nicholas, who plans on hiding in the crate himself until the Coast Guard, who have landed on the island, disperse. Morgan leaps at him, and they wrestle desperately on the jungle floor as Birdie pulls herself out of the crate. As Nicholas tries to strangle Morgan, Birdie beans him with a six-pack of water. Morgan ties his hands with vines just as the Coast Guard arrives. Nicholas is arrested, and the girls are reunited with their parents.

Birdie returns home to Oregon, where she writes her adventures into a novel starring a hero who is a combination of both girls. Morgan's parents enter rehab and get counseling, and the two new friends stay in touch through e-mail.

The Message: Never give up. It's always darkest before the dawn. Don't be afraid to meet new challenges head-on. Learn to trust your instincts—they are often correct. Opposites attract and need each other, not only to maintain balance but also to survive. Morgan's dramatic loss of her sister at sea may also be disturbing and sad for some readers.

Who's It For?: 8th–12th grade. Nicholas is a very disturbing character, but the reader sees him only through Birdie's naive eyes, and Vance keeps the more sordid details of his criminal life to a minimum. His seduction scene with Morgan never gets beyond heavy breathing and some deep kisses, but his palpable anger when she rejects him is frightening. For those teens who collect serial killer DVDs, this story will seem tame, but it may be too much for younger middle school students.

Why It Rocks:
• **Voice:** Vance's wonderfully eccentric brand of storytelling is a cross between writer Dorothy Parker and filmmaker Christopher Guest (*Best in Show, A Mighty*

Wind), with a little Tennesee Williams added in for some Southern Gothic flavor. She maintains alternating, pitch-perfect voices for Birdie and Morgan that remain consistently unique, never melding into each other.

• **Plot:** Vance's offbeat plot won't be for every reader but will be unforgettable for those who choose to take the plunge. Her attention to detail is riveting, from her fascinating exploration of Caribbean cultures and environment to her chronicling of Birdie's bubble bath oil collection and Morgan's vast folkloric knowledge of the sea.

• **Pacing:** The alternating voice chapters help build suspense toward the inevitable climax as the reader wonders how on earth these two disparate personalities will ever meet.

• **Characterization:** Birdie starts out light and shallow, Morgan dark and deep; but, by the end of the story, Birdie has learned to take care of herself and recognize her weaknesses, while Morgan has learned that life need not always be taken so seriously and that it's okay to enjoy the simple pleasures of a good-looking boy's attention. Birdie's sunny, oblivious optimism contrasted with Morgan's solemn reserve is just one of the many ways Vance carries through her theme of opposites attracting and benefiting each other.

Hook It Up With: *See You down the Road* by Kim Ablon Whitney and *How I Live Now* by Meg Rosoff.

Read More about It:
Booklist: 04/15/03
Horn Book: 10/01/03
Kirkus Reviews: 05/01/03
Publishers Weekly: 05/19/03
School Library Journal: 06/01/03

CHAPTER 3

THE CLOSET CLUB: GLBTQ FICTION FOR TEENS AND THEIR FRIENDS

I have to admit, the first time I heard the acronym *GLBTQ* I was confused. *GLBT* I knew and understood as gay, lesbian, bisexual, and transgender. But *Q*? What did *that* mean? (I figured it couldn't mean "Queer," since we had already covered that with *G* and *L*.) When I read that it stood for "Questioning," I was struck by how a simple addition of one more letter to the popular acronym could go a long way toward making more teens feel safe waving a Rainbow Flag or standing next to someone who is. Sexual orientation can be fluid during adolescence (a fact I fear many teens are woefully unaware of), and the teens who aren't completely sure of themselves can feel lost among the labels of gay, straight, and bisexual, wondering which one to choose and probably feeling resentful that they have to choose at all. Now, with the addition of the *Q*, they can be curious, they can be inquiring, they can be *questioning*! And best of all, they don't have to feel pressured to choose a label they may not feel is right for them.

While a few of the books in this chapter deal with teens who know for a fact that they are either gay (*Hard Love, Boy Meets Boy*) or straight, most are about teens who are in the process of discovering and/or questioning whether they may be gay (*Eight Seconds*), lesbian (*Kissing Kate*), or bisexual (*My Heartbeat, Empress of the World*). I would argue that there are probably more teens on the Yellow Brick Road to discovering their sexual orientation than there are those who have reached the Emerald City of Identity, so along with teens seeing positive, confident examples of gay youth in YA fiction, it is equally important for them to see the process of discovery, the process of understanding, of growing, of *questioning*.

Of course, this entire chapter and introduction assumes the fact that you, as an educator or librarian working with teens, believe that GLBTQ youth deserve the same level of professional service and representation in the collection that you would afford any other teen interest group. If for some reason you don't, I leave you with this quote from David Levithan, author of *Boy Meets Boy*, from his article about gay teen lit in the October 2004 issue of *School Library Journal:* "Discrimination is not a legitimate point of view. Silencing books silences the readers who need them most. And silencing these readers can have dire, tragic consequences."

Ferris, Jean. 2000. *Eight Seconds*. New York: Harcourt. 186p.

The Story: Eighteen-year-old John Ritchie has always felt like an outsider and attributes these feelings to the heart surgery he underwent as a child. Ever since the operation, John has felt there was something missing in him that other people seemed to have, but he is too busy to think about it much the summer before senior year. He lives with his parents and four sisters on their working ranch, where there are always chores to be done and siblings to appease. And, he's just broken up with his girlfriend of six months, Kelsey, who had been pressuring him to think about marriage after graduation next year. So when his father suggests sending him to a weeklong "rodeo school," John jumps at the chance to get away from all the women in his life, including Kelsey. He is happy to learn that his best friend, Bobby, is also enrolled but less than thrilled to discover that so is Russ Millard, the biggest bully at school.

As John meets some of the other boys in the program, he is immediately drawn to handsome, friendly Kit Crowe, whom he recognizes as a fellow college classmate of one of his older sisters. After the instructor explains that most cowboys choose one event to specialize in, both John and Kit, along with Russ, choose bull riding, while Bobby elects to join the calf ropers. They spend their first full day working on mechanical bulls and by the third day have worked their way up to riding the real thing. Although no one has yet stayed on the full eight seconds required for rodeo competitions, it is clear that the rider with the most natural talent and style is Kit, which brings out the worst in Russ. But Russ backs off after he tries to dump his dinner tray on Kit and the older boy responds with a quick knee to the groin.

That night, John is too sore from riding to sleep, so when Kit whispers that he's going out for some air, John joins him. Soon they are sitting on a fence rail, sharing details about their lives; but the conversation seems different, more intimate than the talks John has had with Bobby. Over the course of the next three nights, after being slammed in the dirt by bulls all day, the two boys continue their conversations on the fence. John tells the story of his heart surgery, revealing to Kit his feeling that he is missing a sort of inner peace that everyone else seems to have. Kit also confesses to feeling like an outsider, and John wonders how someone as seemingly self-assured as Kit could feel that way. By the end of the week, John knows he's going to miss his nightly talks with Kit and looks forward to seeing him at upcoming rodeos.

When John returns home and tells his sister about meeting Kit, he is stunned when she tells him Kit is known for his active participation in a gay student group on campus. John can't help but see his conversations with Kit in a whole new light, and he worries about what his attraction to the other boy means. At the first rodeo of the season, John discovers that both Bobby and Russ have heard that Kit is gay when Russ starts taunting Kit on the fairway. Officials pull Russ away for using foul language, while John and Bobby assure Kit that they don't agree with Russ. But John still feels conflicted about being friends with Kit, and to avoid thinking about it, immerses himself in farm work until the next fair.

At the next rodeo, Kit tells John beforehand he knows the difference between friendship and romance and hopes that he and John can still be friends. John doesn't ride well this time, but Kit does, and John's father wants to meet him. When Kit invites John over to his house in front of his father, John agrees to come. He spends the day with Kit and his family, feeling better about Kit but worse about himself. What does it mean that he is thinking about Kit so often, far more often than he ever thought about Kelsey?

The third rodeo is rainy. John and Kit both score higher than Russ, who is thrown in four seconds. He storms up to Kit afterward, shouting that it isn't fair that he should lose to a "fairy." Kit keeps his cool, but John punches Russ and gets disqualified for fighting. The storm grows worse, and Kit and John retreat to Kit's RV to wait it out. They strike up another meaningful, interesting conversation, and John ends up staying late. When he returns to his own pickup, Russ is waiting. He's been spying on the RV since the rodeo and threatens to tell everyone that John and Kit are a couple. John is furious, but controls himself and just drives home.

For the next two weeks before the final rodeo of the season, John rarely leaves the ranch. Bobby, who has heard and dismissed the rumors circulating about John and Kit, warns him that this will make it seem like he has something to hide, but John doesn't care. He works to keep from thinking. Finally, John has to go into town to run some errands for his dad, and he coincidentally meets up with both Kit and Russ at the local Diary Queen. No one is more surprised than John when Russ starts taunting Kit and John turns on Kit as well. He is irrationally furious with Kit for being gay and angry that Kit's very existence has made him question his own feelings and fears. He shoves Kit and shakes him, asking him, "Why?" Kit breaks his grip, and John leaves, ashamed at what he has done and more confused than ever.

At the State Fair, John both hopes to and dreads seeing Kit. He watches him ride, and is horrified when Kit takes a terrible spill and doesn't get up. An ambulance takes him away. Numb, John performs his best ride ever, winning the rodeo while completely consumed with thoughts of Kit. As soon as he can, he goes to the hospital, where he learns that Kit has a broken leg and fractured pelvis. He resolves to come back the next day and apologize for what happened at the Dairy Queen. He is stunned when Kit flatly refuses to forgive him, saying that he simply doesn't trust John anymore and that just because he wants a second chance doesn't mean that he may have one.

John is devastated. He finally realizes that what he felt for Kit was love, and because he was too ashamed to admit it to himself, he pushed Kit away and blamed him for being able to express what John couldn't even articulate. He goes back to the DQ and picks a fight with Russ, just to get the beating he feels he deserves for betraying Kit and lying to himself. He calls Kit one last time at the end of the summer, and when Kit gently hangs up, John knows that even though he'll probably never talk to Kit again, he will never forget him.

The Message: Love hurts. Authentic feelings cannot be denied. Second chances are not guaranteed. Before you can stand up for what you believe in, you have to know what those beliefs are.

Who's It For?: 7th–12th grade. Despite the rodeo setting, Ferris stays away from strong language, and while John constantly refers to the intensity of his feelings for Kit, they are no sexier than, "I wanted to touch the hot muscle of his forearm." In terms of violence, there are descriptions of fistfights and parking lot brawls. The gradual unveiling of John's true feelings towards Kit, conveyed by Ferris's nuanced, evenhanded writing, will probably be most appreciated by high school students.

Why It Rocks:
• **Voice:** John's confused first-person narration is painfully convincing and will ring true to teen readers exploring their own vague stirrings of same-sex attraction.
• **Plot:** With the rampant popularity of *Brokeback Mountain*, the time is ripe for teens to rediscover this story of a same-sex cowboy crush published way back at the turn of the millennium. The unusual setting and particularly subtle exploration of adolescent sexual questioning are what make this plot unique.
• **Pacing:** Measured. The book is chronologically arranged over the course of several rodeos, and John's internal thoughts fill the pages between the money shots of bucking bulls and cheering crowds. Ferris maintains John's sense of fear of naming his feelings right up until book's end, providing a mental suspense that parallels that of the physical anticipation and apprehension of riding the bulls.
• **Characterization:** Even though this is John's story, Kit is a fully realized character who dispenses both wisdom and doubt in equal measure. Two other secondary characters shine as brightly as a first-place rodeo belt buckle: John's six-year-old sister, Clemmie, whose rambunctious nature forces John to interact with his family when he would rather withdraw; and Howdy, John's happy poodle pup, who serves no practical purpose on the farm and is a powerful metaphor for John's own sense of displacement.

Hook It Up With: *Brokeback Mountain* (the short story) by Annie Proulx (for older teens) and *Tex* by S. E. Hinton.

Read More about It:
Booklist, starred: 10/01/00
Horn Book: 04/01/01
Publishers Weekly: 11/13/00
School Library Journal: 01/01/01
V.O.Y.A. (Voice of Youth Advocates): 10/01/00

Freymann-Weyr, Garrett. 2002. *My Heartbeat.* **Boston: Houghton Mifflin. 154p.**

The Story: Fourteen-year-old Ellen has always hung out with her elder brother, Link, and his best friend, James. Teachers from junior high commented on her "unwillingness to form any firm social attachments" with kids her own age, but frankly, Ellen has never needed more than Link and James, who tend to invite her along on most of their excursions. Even when they completely ignore her, she loves listening to their heated debates about literature, foreign films, or college programs. She also never misses an opportunity to be with James, on whom she's been nursing a serious crush since seventh grade.

Ellen and Link's parents are left-leaning New York intellectuals whose dinner conversation tends to center on books, family projects, or their children's schoolwork. Link is a certified genius who attends a special math course for gifted students at

Columbia on Saturdays, while Ellen, a self-described good girl, earns high grades but seems to escape the scrutiny her parents level on Link, who is the more vocal and dramatic of the two. Ellen loves her family but notes that everyone goes out of the way to avoid conflict and that sometimes, because their conversations are more academic than personal, her family can feel like strangers to her.

When Ellen starts her freshman year at the private prep school that Link and James both attend, her curiosity is piqued when one of her classmates asks her if seniors Link and James are a "couple." Despite Link and James's closeness, this notion has never occurred to Ellen. When Ellen broaches the subject one night with them after they have finished watching a film at James's house, Link becomes furious, claims he isn't gay, and storms out. James explains to Ellen that Link doesn't know if he's gay, "which makes him afraid he is. Which makes him swear he isn't." James isn't sure about himself either, but the idea doesn't scare him the way it scares Link, and while he finds girls "interesting," he's only slept with men up to this point. Ellen knows her brother fears their father's disapproval, because he has made it clear without saying it directly that he would have a problem with Link's being gay.

When Ellen returns home, Link reiterates that he and James are not a couple, that he doesn't want to talk about it anymore, and that he doesn't want her discussing this matter with their parents. He begins avoiding both Ellen and James and starts dating a girl named Polly. Ellen understands that while Link allowed her and James to spend time with him, he permitted it only on the unwritten condition that they not try to "know" him. By pushing the question of his sexuality, they have gone too far and subsequently been banished from his life. Ellen is confused but not completely sad, since this has opened the door for her and James to define who they are to each other without Link. She finds a way to reconnect with Link by running with him in the mornings, and while she feels forgiven, he still remains very private.

Ellen and James begin spending more time together, and on a rollerblading date near Thanksgiving, they finally kiss. Ellen is thrilled with this romantic development, although she sometimes has the feeling that when she makes out with James, she is giving him the physical affection that Link refused to offer. This feeling is reinforced when James admits that he and Link used to think of her as their "insurance" against anything happening between the two of them, and as a result, James often lavished the attention he wanted to give Link on Ellen. Ellen doesn't care; she is just happy that she and James are a couple, something she always dreamed about.

When Link sabotages his midterm exams by turning them all in blank and reveals that he dropped out of the Columbia program months ago and has instead been taking piano lessons on Saturday mornings, his parents call a family meeting. The school will allow Link to retake his exams if he goes into therapy. Mom responds by saying she thinks Link did this to get their attention to tell them something. Dad just thinks Link has performance issues. Link tells his parents he finds it interesting that Dad raised his allowance because of the "expense" of taking out Polly, which Link views as a bribe to date a girl instead of James. Mom didn't know this and is furious. Ellen notices that no one uses the word *gay*. The conversation ends in a draw, with Link agreeing to therapy but refusing to take his exams over.

After the family meeting, Link asks Ellen to arrange a meeting between the two of them and James, to see if they can be as they were before. Link, Ellen, and James meet at a diner, but when the talk turns to Link's sexuality, Link grows tense when

James states that his parents will always be afraid of Link's possible homosexuality as long as Link is. Link still insists that he is not gay and goes back to avoiding Ellen and James. Meanwhile, Ellen has discovered art as a way to express herself after her father gives her a sketchbook and pencils as a present. She finds some of her social awkwardness going away as she shares her drawings with others and asks for their opinions. Through her new way of "seeing," using pencil and paper, Ellen begins to realize that there are limits to how well you can know people, even your own family. She's been reading books on homosexual history and politics, but James tells her that all the books in the world won't help her understand Link if he is unwilling to share his feelings with her.

Link's therapist suggests music and languages as a way to express his mathematics gift, which Dad is able to live with. Link also gets accepted to Yale, and he agrees to attend, to his father's glee. James gets accepted to a German art school, and when he and Ellen say good-bye, they have sex for the first time. It is a bittersweet experience, since Ellen knows this is the end of something instead of the beginning. But she leaves his house with a light heart, believing that someday they will meet again, after they have both garnered more life experience, and maybe then the time will be right.

The Message: Love comes in all shapes and sizes and cannot always be labeled. Some relationships defy definition and just must be accepted on their own terms. If you don't respect the boundaries people set, you risk alienating them.

Who's It For?: 9th–12th grade. There are no issues of sex, violence, or strong language in this novel, other than the stray curse word. Ellen and James's sex scene at the end of the book is less than a paragraph. But the complexity of the relationships, the subtleness of the conversations, and the sheer weight of the words that go unsaid among these brilliantly wrought characters call for the decoding skills of an older teen reader.

Why It Rocks:
•   **Voice:** Ellen's first-person narration is both naive and sophisticated, as befitting a sheltered, smart girl of privilege living in New York City. But the riveting show-don't-tell dialogue among Ellen, Link, and James is the greatest strength of this intellectual character study.
•   **Plot:** Solidly character driven and very emotive. The complicated interweaving of relationships, the idea of the unwritten laws that govern our interpersonal interactions, and the fascinating examination of love—friendship love, romantic love, sibling love, and parent love—all combine to create a story that is deeply moving, despite its lack of action.
•   **Pacing:** Slow and very thoughtful. Although the novel clocks in at just over 150 pages, readers shouldn't expect to finish quickly. The philosophical tone and weighty conversations will have teens going back and rereading significant passages over again to glean more insight into the characters' inner lives.
•   **Characterization:** *My Heartbeat* is the Woody Allen movie of YA fiction, full of neurotic, complex, intellectual characters who reveal clues to their personalities through their thought-provoking conversations and studied silences.

Hook It Up With: *Hello, I Lied* by M. E. Kerr.

Read More about It:
Booklist, starred: 06/01/02
Horn Book, starred: 05/01/02
Kirkus Reviews: 04/01/02
Publishers Weekly: 03/18/02
School Library Journal, starred: 04/01/02
V.O.Y.A. (Voice of Youth Advocates): 04/01/02

Hartinger, Brent. 2003. *Geography Club.* New York: HarperCollins. 226p.

The Story: High school sophomore Russel Middlebrook is in the closet. He studiously averts his eyes in the boys' locker room after P.E.; carefully avoids the subject of romance when chatting with his two best friends, nervous Gunnar and brainiac Min; and goes out of his way to fly under the radar at school. Although he often feels guilty when he sees how badly Brian Bund, the school outcast, is treated, he never attempts to intervene, terrified that he might draw the bullies' scrutiny onto himself. The result of all this secrecy is that he often feels very alone.

Russel assuages his loneliness by chatting online with other gay teens. One evening he is surprised to meet a teen who claims to go to Russel's high school. Intrigued, Russel agrees to meet the boy at a nearby park and is shocked to discover his new friend is popular jock Kevin Land. They cautiously embark on a secret friendship, and Russel feels so relieved to have found someone else like himself that he confides in Min, whose surprising reaction is to laugh. It seems that Min identifies as bisexual and has been dating Teresa from the soccer team. Russel proposes that the closeted teens all meet at a nearby pizza place to get to know one another. He brings Kevin; Min brings Teresa and Teresa's friend Ike. At first the conversation is stilted, but once they loosen up, they are reluctant to end the evening, and all go home wishing they had a private place to meet where they could talk freely. The next day, Min proposes that they apply to become an after-school club, so they can have access to a classroom. To discourage others from joining, they dub the group the most boring title they can think of—"Geography Club"—hoping no one else will be interested enough to join.

But getting the Geography Club off the ground isn't Russel's only worry. Gunnar, who's desperate for a girlfriend, asks Russel to help him out by going on a double date with Trish, the best friend of the girl Gunnar has asked out. Russel reluctantly agrees, and while the evening is uneventful, he is uncomfortable because he has the distinct sense that Trish likes him much more than he likes her. Gunnar continues to pressure Russel to go out with Trish so he can date her friend, Kimberly, and Russel doesn't know how he can refuse without blowing his cover. Meanwhile, he has joined the baseball team to get closer to Kevin, and their relationship is heating up to the point where they are meeting regularly for secret make-out sessions. Russel is also enjoying a newfound popularity as one of the baseball jocks and is surprised at how much he likes being in the spotlight after so many years of trying to avoid notice.

Just as everyone is becoming comfortable in the Geography Club, a girl named Belinda with a genuine interest in geography shows up and wants to join. They allow her in because they don't know what else to do and fear that they will have to disband. But when Belinda overhears them talking about the club's true purpose, she reveals her own secret (that her mother is an alcoholic) and swears to keep theirs. So, they welcome her as the Geography Club's first straight member.

Russel couldn't be happier with the way things are progressing at school and in his relationship with Kevin, but soon his carefully constructed world begins to fall apart. First, Min witnesses him making fun of Brian Bund while Russel is with a group of baseball payers, and refuses to talk to him. Then, Gunnar asks Russel to take Trish out a third time, and Russel refuses. Gunnar retaliates by insinuating Russel is gay, and in order keep Gunnar from finding out for sure, Russel feels pressured into giving in to Gunnar again. The date ends in disaster, with Russel having to fend off Trish's amorous attentions at her parents' remote beach house and then walk two hours to a pay phone and call Kevin when a drunken Gunnar refuses to drive him home. Finally, there is strife in the Geography Club when Min proposes that they invite Brian to join. The jocks have added "gay" to the list of insults hurled at Brian, and Min feels that even if it isn't true, they should try to help him. Everyone else, however, is worried about being exposed if they include Brian and votes against her, including Russel and Teresa. Min and Teresa break up as a result, and the Geography Club disbands.

But the worst is yet to come. Russel comes to school the Monday after his awful date and discovers that Gunnar, who is furious that Russel left, has spread the rumor that Russel is gay. Russel is instantly shunned by the jocks, including Kevin, and is forced to sit with Brian at lunch, who he discovers is an articulate and funny guy. Russel then makes up with Min and accepts Gunnar's heartfelt apology after finally telling Gunnar the truth about himself. The next day Brian submits a petition for a Gay-Straight Alliance, which takes the heat off Russel, because everyone begins to make fun of Brian again. Russel decides to repay Brian's kindness by continuing to sit with him at lunch, to Kevin's horror. Russel knows that his relationship with Kevin is over if he can't understand why Russel would defend Brian. The Geography Club, now the GSA, reconvenes with Min, Gunnar, Belinda, Brian, and Russel as its proud founding members.

The Message: Be true to yourself. Let your light shine. Stick up for the underdog. Popularity is fleeting and can disappear as quickly as it materializes. Hardship builds character.

Who's It For?: 7th–10th grade. Hartinger keeps the tone light even as he deals with such serious issues as sexual identity, betrayal, and bullying. Sex is insinuated but not described beyond a few steamy kisses, and an occasional f-word appears in the text. In what is probably the most upsetting scene in the book, bullies thrust a lipstick-wearing, bra-clad Brian through the cafeteria doors, to his horror and embarrassment. Despite the age of the characters, this is an excellent introduction to the growing body of GLBTQ literature for older middle school students.

Why It Rocks:
• **Voice:** Russel's first-person voice is realistically self-deprecating and ironic while remaining hopeful and humorous. His confiding, honest tone is the book's greatest strength.
• **Plot:** Contrived, with just a few too many coincidences to come off as completely realistic. For example, Russel's best friend, Min, is gay. Russel's crush object, Kevin, also just happen to be gay, Belinda is instantly sympathetic when she discovers the secret of the Geography Club. Still, it reads like romantic comedy with a relatively happy ending, a familiar and welcoming format to most teens.
• **Pacing:** Swift. Clocking in at just over 220 pages, the book maintains light tone, and the high drama will keep teens turning pages.
• **Characterization:** Realistic but with the exception of Russel, relatively superficial. Parents and teachers are either entirely absent or completely one-dimensional. Hartinger attempts to make some of the secondary characters more complex by giving them some quirks (Gunnar is a bit of a hypochondriac, Kevin is "sensitive" under his jock exterior), but the story is mainly anchored by Russel's well-wrought voice.

Hook It Up With: *Geography Club's* sequel, *The Order of the Poison Oak*, and *Totally Joe* by James Howe.

Read More about It:
Booklist: 04/01/03
Horn Book: 10/01/03
Kirkus Reviews: 12/15/02
Publishers Weekly: 02/03/03
School Library Journal: 02/01/03
V.O.Y.A.(Voice of Youth Advocates): 04/01/03

Hyde, Catherine Ryan. 2006. *Becoming Chloe.* New York: Random House. 215p.

The Story: The first time 17-year-old Jordan meets 18-year-old Chloe, she is being gang-raped in the alley outside the abandoned cellar where he has crashed for the night. He scares away the rapists and tries to comfort the girl, who seems strangely unaffected by what has just occurred. She is tiny and blond, and she looks far younger than she is. All Jordan can get out of her is that she used to be a ward of the state and has been living in a corner of the cellar she has just recently begun calling home.

Jordan himself isn't in great shape. He has an infected wound on his forehead from a fight with his father, who threw him out of his upper-class home in Connecticut when he found out Jordy was gay. He's been living on the streets of New York City ever since, sleeping with older men in order to earn money for food and clothes, bathing in public restrooms, and eating in diners. He is drawn to Chloe's fragile innocence and touched by how quickly she comes to trust him. He even helps her choose a new name after she tells him she hates her name, which is Wanda. Jordan suggests "Chloe," which she immediately adopts as her own.

They set up a home of sorts in the cellar, complete with a padlock on their entry window and a pile of mattresses in the corner. They adopt each other as family; Chloe repays Jordan's kindness by getting him food and antibiotics from the free clinic when he gets a fever from his infected wound, and she also brings him a tamed pigeon to keep him company while he is sick. Jordan is troubled by Chloe's odd, childlike manner, but decides to accept it after a clinic doctor tells him most likely she suffered great trauma at some point in her life and her innocent affect is probably a coping mechanism. But no matter how much he asks, Chloe refuses to talk about her previous life.

Jordan covets a beautiful leather coat in a store window, and when the storeowner offers him the coat in exchange for oral sex, Jordan considers it. Instead, he waits until the man's pants are literally down, then makes a run for it while wearing the coat. The storeowner gives chase, and when Chloe, who was nearby, tries to stop him, the man slaps her and twists her arm. Jordan, furious that someone would try to hurt Chloe, throws a heavy trash can at him. They run away, with Jordan fearing he has killed the man. Jordan decides it isn't safe to continue living in their cellar, so he takes what money they have and buys train tickets to his hometown in Connecticut.

Once there, Jordan goes to his house and confronts his parents. His mother is cold and distant, hastily scribbling him a check for a thousand dollars so he will leave, while his father refuses to even look at him. Jordan uses the money to rent a furnished room from an old man named Otis and his ancient Doberman, Bruno. Jordan gets a job as a waiter, and Otis's sister also pays him to cook and clean for her brother. Chloe loves Bruno and Otis, but they haven't been living there a year when the old dog dies and is soon followed by his master. Before he dies, Otis wills his 1954 Chevy truck to Jordan. Otis's sister puts the house up for sale, and Jordan and Chloe are forced to move out.

Before they leave town, Jordan takes Chloe to a therapist named Dr. Reynoso, who prescribes Zoloft. Chloe can't swallow the pills, however, and finally gives up. She knows the pills are supposed to help her feel happy, so instead she proposes a road trip, suggesting that if Jordan can show her what is so beautiful about the world, maybe she can be happy without pills. Dr. Reynoso agrees that it would do no harm but makes Jordan promise to call her if they run into trouble.

Driving Otis's old truck, Jordan and Chloe set out from Connecticut on their adventure, deciding to drive slowly and see all the sights. Chloe is keeping track in her notebook of any examples of beauty that they see, and Jordan is quick to point them out, especially those instances when people help them. When they visit Niagara Falls, a kind middle-aged couple buys them tickets to a boat ride under the falls. In Pennsylvania, when Otis's truck breaks down, a friendly mechanic brokers a deal for them to sell the antique truck to a car collector, who pays them $2,400 for it. A young married couple with a baby drives them into Kentucky, and when the father admires Jordan's leather coat, Jordan gives it to him, relieved to get rid of it and what it represents.

Next, they meet Randy, a bicycle repairman who uses a wheelchair and loves cats and hiking. He encourages Jordan to continue his journey by bicycle and outfits Jordan and Chloe with bikes, bike trailers, and hiking and mountain gear. In exchange, all he asks is that they climb a certain mountain for him in the Rockies, leave a sign there that states Randy was there in spirit, and take a picture. He shows them an album full of pictures of mountaintops he has traveled to vicariously. Chloe loves the idea, and soon they are on their way again, noticing small things, like cats in trees and kids on swings, that they might have missed were they traveling any other way.

They see the Mississippi, and in Arkansas stay the night with an African American couple named Dodd who feed them and let them sleep in their hayloft. Jordan is mutually attracted to their son, Trent, but realizes that his sexuality is something he must put on hold while he is trying to help Chloe. They make it to Randy's mountain, where they climb to the top and plant the sign, later biking to the Grand Canyon, where Chloe falls and breaks her foot. Because of Chloe's cast, they are forced to give up the bikes and go back to hitching, but they are able to take a helicopter ride out over the canyon, and a friendly campground owner lets them stay for free and drives Chloe to the hospital when it is time for her cast to be removed.

They hitch a ride to the Painted Desert, but outside of Phoenix, Jordan is jumped and beaten by a carful of drunken college boys. Chloe is traumatized by the event and has to be restrained from hurting herself. Jordan, who has suffered a concussion, worries that this incident will undo all of Chloe's good experiences. After they are released from the hospital, they take a bus to California, and hitch a ride to Big Sur with a 90-year-old man named Maximilian, who tells Chloe that despite his age he hasn't even come close to seeing all the beauty the world has to offer. They ride an Appaloosa named Cisco on the beach, swim in the ocean, and see a whale breach. Jordan is relieved to hear Chloe say that despite the attack, she has taken Maximilian's words to heart and wants to see what more beauty she can find. Their story ends with their letters to Dr. Reynoso letting her know that they successfully made it to the end of their journey, in more ways than one.

The Message: Families come in all shapes and sizes and are sometimes composed of good friends. The world is neither all bad nor all good, but a mixture of both. Beauty is in the eye of the beholder. Never give up hope.

Who's It For?: 9th–12th grade. In terms of content, this is solidly a high school novel. The rape on the opening page is not graphically described but disturbing nonetheless. Jordan's parents are cruel; it is implied that his father beat him and his mother let it happen while claiming no responsibility. The beating Jordy suffers near the end is frightening and causes Chloe, in her distress, to smash her head against a hospital mirror. There is also the issue of Jordy's street hustling and occasional thievery. Chloe's past is never fully revealed, but she offhandedly remarks that in the state home she was raped repeatedly.

Why It Rocks:
• **Voice:** While Jordy's first-person narration occasionally sounds wise beyond his years, his voice is compelling and his observations of the people and places he visits with Chloe are perceptive and honest. His dialogue with Chloe, who is prone to

obvious, unintentionally humorous statements, lends the book some much-needed comic relief.

• **Plot:** Despite the grim opener, this story is infused with the hope that the world is mostly beautiful and that when given a choice, people tend to do the right thing. While this rather unsubtle theme of love and redemption may seem hokey to adults, who have seen this premise illustrated ad nauseam in popular media, it will feel moving and fresh to teen readers.

• **Pacing:** Decidedly measured for a book just over 200 pages. This is not a quick read, mostly owing to the philosophical tone and tough content. Some reviewers noted that the first half of the book, set in New York City and Connecticut and more fraught with danger, doesn't jibe with the second half, which takes place on the road and is much more meandering; but I found the pacing matched the circumstances nicely, echoing the characters' states of mind in different settings.

• **Characterization:** Realistic, although Jordan is uncommonly mature and Chloe uncommonly wise and simple, sometimes simultaneously. Both have suffered pasts that make their reactions and decisions believable, and Jordy's homosexuality lends an interesting dimension to his character, while not being the main "issue" of the novel.

Hook It Up With: *St. Iggy* by K. L. Going and *Defining Dulcie* by Paul Acampora.

Read More about It:
Booklist: 01/01/06
Kirkus Reviews, starred: 01/15/06
Publishers Weekly, starred: 04/10/06
School Library Journal: 06/01/06
V.O.Y.A. (Voice of Youth Advocates): 08/01/06

Johnson, Maureen. 2004. *The Bermudez Triangle.* New York: Penguin Group. 370p.

The Story: A jealous classmate at Nina's eighth birthday party christened best friends Nina Bermudez, Avery Dekker, and Melanie Forrest the "Bermudez Triangle." Now it's the summer before senior year, and the über-close Triangle is splitting up. Smart, hyperorganized, natural-born leader Nina is attending a precollegiate program at Stanford, while sarcastic hipster Avery and quiet, girly redheaded Mel stay behind in upstate New York and take waitressing jobs at a local Irish-themed chain restaurant, P. J. Mortimer's.

Nina quickly acclimates to her new surroundings and soon falls for a fellow student, Steve Carson, a cute blond "eco-warrior" from Oregon whom she ends up kissing after a grueling all-night study session. Meanwhile, to their combined great surprise, Avery and Melanie discover they have a mutual physical attraction when they jokingly kiss one morning after a sleepover, and it turns into the first of many make-out sessions. Mel has always sensed she was gay but never had the courage to tell anyone. Avery knows she likes Mel but isn't sure that she wants to be labeled a lesbian just yet, and she insists that their relationship stay secret. Both of them are concerned about Nina's reaction when she returns but can't decide how to tell her. In the end, they simply keep quiet and begin avoiding Nina, who senses something is wrong when she tries to invite Avery and Mel out for a girls' night out not long after she returns, and instead they ask along good-natured fellow P.J.'s waiter Parker, who has no idea what is going on but is happy to be included because he is nursing a slight crush on Mel.

The truth comes out when the Triangle goes school shopping and Nina accidentally walks in on Avery and Mel kissing in a fitting room. The resulting conversation is awkward and leaves Nina feeling like a third wheel. Nina, who has enough to keep her busy and distracted as student council president, decides to focus on getting early acceptance to Stanford, where she will see Steve again next fall. Meanwhile, Mel is making Avery feel claustrophobic because she constantly wants to be with her, even during Avery's piano-practicing time, which Avery considers sacrosanct. Avery and Mel get in a huge fight after a classmate witnesses and comments on seeing them in the gay/lesbian section of a bookstore. Neither of them tells Nina about it, but one of the students Nina is on council with asks, "How long have your friends been gay?" which causes her to worry.

Rumors begin to spread about Avery and Mel, so Avery decides to take matters into her own hands by joining a garage band with some guys she knows to get out of hanging out with Mel. She also begins a casual romantic relationship with bandmate Gaz, whom Nina sees her kissing in a car after the student council fall hayride. Nina confronts Avery, who begs her not to tell Mel. Parker, who's heard the rumors at school, asks Mel if she's gay, and when she confirms it, he becomes her new confidante, since Avery is avoiding Mel and Nina is too busy to listen to her problems.

When Avery cancels their Thanksgiving weekend plans, then doesn't call her for two weeks, Mel finally turns to Nina for help. Nina sees a chance for them to all be friends again, so she confronts Avery and tells her that they all need to talk, but Avery gets angry at Nina's interference and tells her to butt out. The same day she finds out she is accepted to Stanford, Nina has to tell Mel that Avery doesn't want to go out with her anymore. Mel is inconsolable and becomes completely withdrawn, which doesn't help Nina when she needs someone to talk to after Steve dumps her over the phone. Avery sees how sad Nina is after the breakup and tries to talk to her, but Nina doesn't trust her any longer and blows her off. Avery worries that she's pushed Nina too far and their lifelong friendship may be over.

Everyone coincidentally meets up at the school Valentine's Day dance. Nina is staffing the ticket booth when Mel shows up with Parker and Avery comes with Gaz. Avery and Mel meet in the bathroom, and Avery, tired of trying to figure out her sexuality, suggests getting back together. Mel wisely turns her down and leaves. Meanwhile, Parker, who has transferred his crush from Mel to Nina, gives Nina a ride home and asks if he can kiss her. Nina agrees on one condition: that Parker is not her "boyfriend," because she is loath to get into another serious relationship after Steve. Parker consents, sure that he can eventually change Nina's mind.

On Nina's birthday in March, Steve e-mails, saying he's sorry about the breakup. The same day, Mel tells Nina she's finally going to come out to her dad (Mel's parents are divorced, and she lives with her father). Parker takes Nina out for her birthday but gets angry when she tells him about Steve's e-mail and he learns that she's thinking about getting back together with him. Then, to make matters worse, when Nina gets home, she gets a call from Mel's dad, who wants to congratulate her about getting into Stanford. Nina misunderstands and thinks "the news" he is referring to is Mel's coming out and then accidentally outs Mel, who hasn't told her father yet. This has clearly been Nina's worst birthday ever.

Mel weathers the storm of her mom's disapproval about her sexuality with her father and Avery's support. She slowly begins to gain confidence in herself as she carries on a flirtation with a girl she met at a dance in a neighboring high school. So she is ready to support Avery when she has to audition for acceptance to a New York City music college. Mel convinces Nina and Parker to drive with her to Avery's audition to surprise her, but everything goes wrong: a freak snowstorm makes driving impossible, Mel accidentally locks the keys in the car at a rest stop, and Parker can barely bring himself to talk to Nina. Despite all odds, however, they make it in time to wish a touched Avery well. Avery passes her audition, everyone makes up with everyone else, and the Triangle even manages to rustle up another girl at the audition for Parker to flirt with. They end the day by celebrating with coffee and hot chocolate.

The Message: Life is change; learn to embrace it. Nothing stays the same forever. A strong friendship can weather any storm. Good friends bring out the best in one another.

Who's It For?: 8th–12th grade. The breezy text could make this work for younger readers, but the exploration of coming-of-age issues such as sexual identity and romantic relationship navigations, along with the sheer number of underage drinking scenes, makes this better suited to older teen readers.

Why It Rocks:
• **Voice:** Johnson tells her story in third person, from multiple perspectives, allowing the reader to understand and experience each of the Triangle's unique points of view.
• **Plot:** Despite the lighthearted tone, this is a surprisingly in-depth examination of the amorphous nature of adolescent relationships and how the shifting landscape of those relationships helps shape the character of the future grown-up inside. And by focusing on the three-way friendship and love in all its wonderful, terrible forms, Johnson neatly dodges the "Gay Problem Novel" label.
• **Pacing:** Chronologically arranged by seasonal holidays and school events, dialogue-heavy chapters and changing formats (e-mail, letters, locker notes) make this thick book read fast.
• **Characterization:** The three girls are sympathetically portrayed and nicely rounded. Nina learns to take change in stride, Avery learns not to be too hard on herself, while Mel discovers both her voice and her inner "butch." Minor characterizations also add zing to the story, including Nina's klepto Stanford roommate, Ashley, and the endearing Parker, whose off-the-wall remarks provide welcome comic relief amid all the female angst.

Hook It Up With: *The Sisterhood of the Traveling Pants* series (*The Second Summer of the Sisterhood, Girls in Pants, Forever in Blue*) by Ann Brashares and *The Girls* series (*Girls in Love, Girls Out Late, Girls under Pressure, Girls in Tears*) by Jacqueline Wilson.

Read More about It:
Booklist: 11/01/04
Horn Book: 04/01/05
Kirkus Reviews: 10/01/04
Publishers Weekly: 12/06/04
School Library Journal: 11/01/04
V.O.Y.A. (Voice of Youth Advocates): 10/01/04

LaRochelle, David. 2005. *Absolutely, Positively, Not . . .* New York: Scholastic. 219p.

The Story: When 16-year-old Steven DeNarski begins noticing how good-looking his health education teacher, Mr. Bowman, is, he worries about what this observation says about him. Steven, who is meticulously neat, attends square dancing with his mother, and has been collecting images of Superman, a muscular hero in tights, since he was a little boy, has always assumed that a physical attraction to girls would kick in sooner or later. But this new feeling is so troublesome that Steven not only tears up the male underwear catalogs he's been hiding under his bed for the past two years, but also decides to embark on a plan of heterosexual immersion. Steven DeNarski is absolutely, positively not gay! And he's going to prove it!

At the library, Steven finds an ancient book about parenting teenage boys written by a Dr. Trent Beachum, and he is relieved to discover that the doctor has several suggestions for how to curtail "deviant sexual behavior." Steven starts with Beachum's first directive: surround oneself with masculine role models. Even though he dislikes sports, Steven begins sitting with the school hockey team during lunch. He observes the importance of male-bonding practices, like swearing and belching, and joins in as much as he can, along with wearing a backward baseball cap. But he is soon exiled from the table after he witnesses one of the jocks chug a milk carton full of leftovers and is so grossed out that he pukes on the table. Shortly afterward, a cute, female Norwegian foreign exchange student fills his seat, and he is rejected.

Next, Steven attempts aversion therapy. Beachum suggests wearing a rubber band around his wrist and snapping it every time he has an "impure thought." He breaks the first band less than three blocks from home, and by the end of the day his wrist is painfully red. All he manages to do is inadvertently start a rubber band-wearing fad, which is quickly outlawed by the principal after it turns into a rubber band-shooting fad. More troubling is that Steven has a dream in which he is naked and being shot at with rubber bands when Mr. Bowman, as Superman, saves him. His attraction to Mr. Bowman is getting out of hand, and Steven knows he needs to step up his game.

Steven decides that next he should enter the dating scene, so he becomes a serial dater; he gets such a good reputation among the girls at his school for his consideration and kindness that soon *they* are calling *him.* He is even approached by the sexy Norwegian exchange student, Solveig, who asks him out, but when she drives right past the movie theater and down a deserted dead-end road, Steven knows he's in trouble. When she starts kissing him, he tries to respond but finally admits to himself that he is simply not interested. He tells Solveig he feels ill, but he can tell she feels rejected, which makes him feel terrible. After she drops him off, he goes straight to his room and calls his best friend, Rachel, to see if she has time for a serious talk.

When Steven admits to Rachel that he thinks he might be gay, Rachel is unsurprised and informs him she's been waiting for him to come out for years. Then, to his great chagrin, she announces to her entire household that Steven has finally come out, after which he is heartily congratulated by her parents and even her little sister. While he's relieved to have told Rachel and her family, he decides to wait to tell his own parents.

When one of his mother's friends tries to set him up with her granddaughter, Steven panics and makes up a girlfriend, modeled after the first thing he thinks of, Rachel's golden retriever, Kelly ("long blond hair and chestnut brown eyes"). He also tells his mother that he's taking Kelly to an upcoming school dance. Rachel doesn't help matters by thinking that taking the dog to the dance makes a great nonconformist statement about what it means to be a couple. Steven's deception concerning Kelly gets so out of control that he does end up taking the dog to the dance, creating a scene he never intended, although he unexpectedly attracts the attention and approval of Mr. Bowman. The next day, when his mom wants to know all about the dance, Steven decides to tell her the truth. She is initially in denial but eventually accepts what Steven is telling her. He also tells his father, whose reaction is to tell Steven about the two "great big queers" in his army unit who were the "bravest, most decent guys" he ever knew.

Steven is relieved to have come out to his parents, but he still feels the need for a gay mentor. He looks online but is put off by the explicit sex talk in the gay chat rooms. He almost tells Mr. Bowman his secret when the teacher drives him home and he notices a familiar men's underwear catalog in the backseat, but reconsiders after he overhears Mr. Bowman, who is also an assistant hockey coach, laugh when the other coach calls the opposing team a bunch of "faggots." When he, full of hope, attends a gay teen support group that meets in the next town, it turns out to be made up of mostly girls. Finally, Steven discovers through the friend of a friend that one of the hockey players he used to sit with at lunch is gay. In an act of desperation, he calls the boy up and asks him out. Mike agrees to meet him, and Steven is thrilled to be able to admit to himself and the world that he is absolutely, positively gay.

The Message: Be true to yourself. Honesty is the best policy. Situations are often not as dire as you anticipate. If at first you don't succeed, try, try again.

Who's It For?: 7th–10th grade. This hilarious send-up of a serious topic is genuinely sweet and good natured, and LaRochelle mostly steers clear of sexual content and strong language. There is a little heavy breathing, groping, and kissing (mostly on the part of Solveig the exchange student) and some use of the word *faggot* in bullying situations. Probably the book's most disheartening scene is when Steven witnesses the teacher he has almost trusted with his secret laugh along with another adult who has used the hateful word. Like *Geography Club, Absolutely, Positively Not...* is a great introduction to GLBT literature for older middle school students.

Why It Rocks:
- **Voice:** Steven's first-person narration is humorous while still paying tribute to the significance of the coming-out experience. There's no doubt that Steven's realistically worried yet determinedly optimistic voice will help ease the fears of the closeted teens who meet him in these pages.
- **Plot:** Although the story occasionally slips into farcical sitcom circumstances, Steven's utter sincerity makes the reader care, even as he escorts his best friend's dog to a school dance.
- **Pacing:** Brisk. LaRochelle dispenses generous helpings of laughter that effortlessly propel readers through each of Steven's excruciating, exhilarating experiences.
- **Characterization:** While Steven is the undeniable star of this coming-out show, his caring but clueless parents and his well-meaning, overly enthusiastic friend Rachel also are nicely rounded out. Of course, there are the stereotypical bullying jocks, but LaRochelle provides a foil in the form of Matt the hockey player, who isn't afraid to exclaim, "Damn right I'm gay. Who the hell wants to know?" when Steven cautiously feels him out on the phone.

Hook It Up With: *A Really Nice Prom Mess* by Brian Sloan (for older YAs) and *The Hookup Artist* by Tucker Shaw.

Read More about It:
Booklist, starred: 07/01/05
Horn Book: 04/01/06
Kirkus Reviews: 06/01/05
School Library Journal: 09/01/05
V.O.Y.A. (Voice of Youth Advocates): 10/01/05

Levithan, David. 2003. *Boy Meets Boy.* New York: Random House. 185p.

The Story: High school sophomore Paul lives in a progressive Anytown, U.S.A., where "there isn't really a gay scene or a straight scene ... they all got mixed up a while back." Personal sexuality and gender roles are nonissues in Paul's hometown, in which the Joy Scouts outnumber the Boy Scouts, the cheerleaders perform their routines on motorcycles, and the star quarterback, Paul's good friend Infinite Darlene, is both a triumphant Homecoming *and* drag queen. As a result of his open-minded environment, Paul has always been very comfortable with himself. He came out to his best friend, Joni, in second grade when she tried to kiss him, was the first openly gay president of the third grade, and formed his school's first Gay-Straight Alliance in the sixth grade. But after a rocky freshman romance with Kyle (who claimed to be straight and told everyone Paul "tricked" him into kissing him), Paul is having a harder time reentering the high school dating and social scene. He is hopeful, however, that the beginning of the new school year will bring a fresh romance into his life.

Paul meets new boy Noah in the self-help section of the local bookstore right after school starts, and it's love at first sight. Noah is a sensitive artist and photographer, and he invites Paul over to his house after school to "paint some music," which Paul discovers is Noah's process of letting music guide the direction of the paintbrush. He is utterly enchanted by both the experience and the boy. Soon they are exchanging soulful notes between classes, sharing details about their lives and past relationships, and going on a romantic first date aboard a paddleboat at the local park.

But other complications arise in Paul's life that distract him from his new romance. First, his best female friend, Joni, has dumped her regular steady, Ted, and started dating Chuck, a dim-witted football player who was scorned by Infinite Darlene the year before. Paul finds Chuck brutish and offensive, and he doesn't know how to break it to Joni that he can't stand her new squeeze. Next, Paul's old flame, Kyle, apologizes to him and asks if they can be friends again; it seems that Kyle needs someone to talk with about his confusion over his sexuality. Paul knows it's not a good idea to get close to Kyle again while he is pursuing Noah, but he is drawn to Kyle's vulnerability and sincere regret over the way their relationship ended. Finally, Paul's best friend, Tony, who lives in a neighboring town that is not nearly as open as Paul's, is chafing under the restrictions that his religiously conservative parents have placed on him after he came out to them, and Paul is trying to be there for him. To top it off, Paul has also been named the "architect" of the annual "Dowager Dance," an event held each year in memory of a local spinster who left behind a large sum of money to be spent for that purpose. His emotional and social plates are both more than full.

And things get worse before they get better. As a gesture of goodwill, Paul agrees to go out with Joni and Chuck, along with Tony. But they run into Ted and his date at a local diner, where Ted and Chuck get into a fight that Tony good-naturedly breaks up by breaking into "If I Had a Hammer." Paul tells Joni about his conversation with Kyle, and soon the news is all over the school, courtesy of Chuck. Kyle corners Paul in a janitor's closet at school, tells him that he thinks they had a good thing and should get back together, and kisses him. Paul worries that Noah will hear the gossip and believe he is interested in Kyle again. Then, one of Tony's mother's friends witnesses Paul and Tony hugging and sounds the alarm to Tony's parents, who ground him indefinitely.

Noah tells Paul he's been thinking things over and wants to take a little break because of the intensity of their courtship. Paul is upset but has no one to talk to, since Joni is spending all her time with Chuck and since Tony is grounded. Also he discovers that Noah heard he had kissed someone, and when Paul unwittingly reveals that it was Kyle, Noah refuses to talk to him anymore. Paul tries to repair his relationship with Joni, but she sees it as a negative judgment of her relationship with Chuck, and they have a huge blowup in the girls' locker room. He momentarily distracts himself from all his relationship woes by focusing on the upcoming Dowager Dance. His committee decides on the uplifting theme of Death, emphasizing the aspects of rebirth and renewal. They tour the local graveyard for tombstone images and decide that everyone should wear some token from a deceased ancestor or relative. Kyle approaches Paul in the graveyard, and Paul uses the opportunity to tell him that he will have to accept the fact that they will be nothing more than friends because he is in love with Noah.

Paul goes to Tony for advice on how to win back Noah, and Tony tells him his best bet is to show Noah how much he cares. So, Paul embarks on a weeklong campaign of love, during which he surprises Noah with a romantic gesture every day. First he showers him with hundreds of handmade origami flowers, then a long list of interesting words and definitions. He gets his musician friend, Zeke, to write a song for Noah and sing it under his window. He sends Noah rolls of film, delivered in creative ways by all of his friends, and, finally, he writes him several long letters about how sorry he is. It all pays off when Noah forgives him and asks him to the Dowager Dance.

Tony is still under house arrest, but he wants to go to the dance and is tired of trying to sneak out, so he enlists Paul, Joni, and all of their friends to come and pick him up, hoping his parents will cave in front of such a big group. Paul has his doubts that Joni will show, but she does, proudly proclaiming to Tony's parents, "We're all his date." In the end, they reluctantly allow him to leave, but before they go to the dance, Tony asks if they could all go to his special spot, a clearing in the woods where he camped for a few nights when his parents threw him out. There, they stage an impromptu pre-dance party with candles, flashlights, and a boom box, and Paul's heart is contented and full as he looks around at all his friends laughing and mingling in the dark.

The Message: There is strength in numbers. If enough people decide to accept a certain idea or notion as the "norm," that is how it will be perceived. Friendships are important lifelines during times of trouble. Adversity builds character.

Who's It For?: 7th–12th grade. With no strong language and nothing naughtier than a few deep kisses, this revolutionary "gaytopian" romance is as clean and shiny as a bright new penny. However, Levithan's lyrical writing and angst-ridden romantic complications will probably be most understood and enjoyed by older teens.

Why It Rocks:
- **Voice:** Paul's first-person narration is sweetly self-deprecating and often wise beyond his years, but his idealistic voice perfectly matches Levithan's romanticized world.
- **Plot:** Levithan's big-hearted debut novel is quite simply the "John Hughes movie" of gay teen literature—a tender teen romantic comedy that leaves one reaching for tissues in the final scene every time. By creating a better-than-real-life setting, Levithan's gay characters get to experience a giddy first romance the likes of which was previously available only to straight teens.
- **Pacing:** Measured. This is a character-driven novel hallmarked by long, expository dialogue between characters and Paul's angsty internal thoughts.
- **Characterization:** Paul's supporting cast is lovingly depicted with loads of little details that bring them to whimsical life, such as Infinite Darlene's love of leather, Noah's predilection for gluing Matchbox cars to his wall, and Paul's mother's

habit of making pancakes in the shapes of countries. Conservative readers won't even be able to find fault with Levithan's portrayal of Tony's parents, which he goes to great lengths to humanize and whom Tony forgives every step of the way.

Hook It Up With: *Rainbow Boys* by Alex Sanchez and *Baby Be-Bop* by Francesca Lia Block.

Read More about It:
Booklist, starred: 09/15/03
Horn Book: 04/01/04
Kirkus Reviews: 08/15/03
Publishers Weekly: 10/06/03
School Library Journal, starred: 09/01/03
V.O.Y.A. (Voice of Youth Advocates): 10/01/03

Myracle, Lauren. 2003. *Kissing Kate.* New York: Penguin Group. 198p.

The Story: High school juniors Lissa and Kate have been friends since seventh grade, when beautiful, blonde Kate offered to be shy, dark Lissa's headstand partner in gym class. But ever since that night two weeks ago, when Kate got a little tipsy at Rob's and kissed Lissa in the gazebo in the backyard, things have been strained between them. Kate doesn't want to talk about it, but Lissa can't stop thinking about it and how it has awakened feelings in her that are both exotic and strangely familiar.

Lissa's parents died in a plane crash when she was eight. She lives in Atlanta with her little sister, Beth, who is now in fifth grade, and her Uncle Jerry, who manages a plant nursery. After school and most weekends, she spends her time taking care of Beth, or in her old Nissan truck, picking up food orders for her flamboyant boss, Darlin Dupriest, who owns "Entrees on Trays," a restaurant delivery service. Her life is full but was never lonely as long as Kate was around, but now Kate is avoiding her and spending all her time with Ben, the boy she conveniently started dating right after the incident in the gazebo.

To add to Lissa's misery, Darlin has hired a new driver to help out on Saturday nights, a weird girl named Ariel who was in Lissa's English class last year. Ariel dyes her hair different colors, has a nose ring, and talks way too much, in Lissa's opinion. But no matter how many times Lissa blows her off, Ariel keeps trying to be friends, enlisting her help in getting Darlin to join a singles' club and asking questions about the book on lucid dreaming that Lissa has in her car. The book, which Lissa bought after she and Kate stopped speaking, provides different techniques on how to "stay awake" during dreams in order to gain some control over them, and Lissa hopes to use her dreams to figure out what to do about her relationship with Kate. She keeps having a reccurring dream about walking through a parking lot as a little girl, away from the safety of a shopping mall, where her mom waits for her inside. The dream is partially based on a memory of an incident in which Lissa was almost kidnapped as a little girl while her mother was shopping. But Lissa is sure that the dream contains a greater message, if she could just decode it.

Kate eventually approaches Lissa at school and tells her they should talk soon, but Lissa can't bring herself to call Kate, and she's tired of being alone. Even her usually reticent uncle has started dating a woman from work, and Darlin is the hit of the middle-aged singles' group. So she finally gives in to Ariel's enthusiasm and begins hanging out with her and her friend Finn, another outsider teen, who has a withered hand. They begin eating together at lunch and frequenting the local IHOP.

When Kate finally calls, Lissa brings up the kiss, and Kate abruptly hangs up. The next day, Kate approaches Lissa at school, apologizes for hanging up, and pleads with Lissa to put what happened behind them because it's "not normal." Lissa reluctantly agrees, even though her feelings of attraction to Kate haven't changed. In the meantime, she accepts a date with Finn, who, according to Ariel, has a crush on her. But when she brings up the topic of the date with Kate, she acts strangely possessive and makes unkind remarks about Finn's hand. Lissa becomes further confused—she senses Kate feels the same way she does, but simply won't discuss it. This makes Lissa more appreciative of her friendship with Ariel, who doesn't seem to be afraid to admit who she is or speak her mind.

Lissa's date with Finn is awkward and stiff. When he tries to kiss her at the end of the night, she backs away, and he goes home, disappointed. It's still early, so out of habit, she heads over to Kate's house. Their conversation quickly turns to the night of the gazebo kiss, and Kate finally admits that she has physical feelings for Lissa as well, but she is too frightened to explore them and would prefer to pretend that nothing ever happened between them. Lissa kisses Kate again, hoping to persuade her, but Kate pushes her away, exclaiming that she's not "a fucking dyke," and Lissa knows their friendship is over.

Lissa leaves Kate's house and calls Ariel. They meet at a local coffeehouse, where Lissa tells her about Kate and admits that she might be gay. Ariel is kind and sympathetic, confiding that she's glad Lissa doesn't like Finn because she kind of likes him herself! The next weekend, she takes Lissa to meet her gay cousin, Jessica, who works in a bookstore in a neighboring town. Jessica's girlfriend joins them, and they spend a pleasant afternoon talking about books, movies, and music. When it is time for Lissa and Ariel to leave, Jessica tells Lissa she's available anytime she needs to talk, and Lissa is grateful.

The next weekend, Ariel helps Lissa figure out the meaning of her latest lucid dream about the parking lot. When Lissa reveals that in this dream she turned around and saw her five-year-old self safely on the sidewalk, Ariel tells her that the parking lot must have represented all the people in her life, including Kate, who were asking her to be someone she wasn't, but now that she has admitted who she is, she is finally able to face herself and call herself back to safety. At last Lissa feels as though she may be able to move past kissing Kate and start a new chapter in her life.

The Message: Be yourself. Trust your intuition. You can't change others; you can change only yourself. If you can't solve a problem the usual way, be open to alternative methods (like lucid dreaming).

Who's It For?: 7th–12th grade. There is some strong language in the text but no sexual content beyond kissing. The concept of lucid dreaming is clearly explained, but the New Age idea may be confusing to some younger readers.

Why It Rocks:

• **Voice:** Lissa's first-person voice is realistically poignant and uncertain, but it might have made a richer novel had Myracle provided the reader with Kate's conflicted point of view as well.

• **Plot:** Myracle manages to incorporate three other subplots into this less-than-200-page novel that all serve as effective mirrors reflecting Lissa's painful search for companionship: Uncle Jerry's budding relationship with Sophie, the cashier at the nursery; Darlin's recovery after ending a long romance; and Beth's realization that the school friend she idolizes is really petty and mean.

• **Pacing:** Throughout the novel, Lissa flashes back to scenes of her and Kate's close friendship before the kiss. These flashbacks, combined with the descriptions of Lissa's lucid dreams, tend to slow the action, but the suspense of seeing whether or not Lissa and Kate will get together at the end will keep teens reading.

• **Characterization:** Lissa is a rich, rounded character, as is her little sister, Beth, whose middle school machinations to secure the popular girl's favor provide the book with much of its comic relief. But Uncle Jerry remains stubbornly offscreen, Darlin seems to be quirky just for quirky's sake, and Kate's motives are disappointingly unclear.

Hook It Up With: *Keeping You a Secret* by Julie Ann Peters and *Name Me Nobody* by Lois-Ann Yamanaka.

Read More about It:
Booklist: 09/15/03
Horn Book: 10/01/03
Publishers Weekly: 03/17/03
School Library Journal: 04/01/03
V.O.Y.A. (Voice of Youth Advocates): 04/01/03

Ryan, Sara. 2001. *Empress of the World.* New York: Penguin Group. 213p.

The Story: Sixteen-year-old Nicola "Nic" Lancaster, theater-tech girl and aspiring archaeologist, is spending her summer at the Siegel Institute Program for Gifted Youth. After the first assembly, she quickly stakes out the group of teens who seem the most likely to become her new friends and records all her thoughts and observations about them in her "field journal." There is manic Katrina, who has curly red hair, dresses in kaleidoscope colors, and loves computers; Isaac from San Francisco, who has a crush on Katrina and is suffering through his parents' divorce; mellow Kevin, who composes music and talks really slowly; and finally, Battle, the blonde minister's daughter from North Carolina, whose beautiful long hair and cool demeanor intrigue Nic the most.

Nic has never had a serious romantic relationship or friendship outside of her theater crew and is troubled by the intense feelings she is suddenly having for Battle. When she twists her ankle on a group hike, Isaac splints her leg and helps her back to the nurses' station. He is so kind that Nic feels she ought to have crush on him, but Battle is the one she can't get off her mind. When she has a difficult time understanding her latest anthropology assignment, she uses it as an excuse to ask Battle, who took the class the year before. Nic is pleased when the talk shifts from classwork to their personal backgrounds and Battle shares her deepest secret: that she hasn't heard from her elder brother, Nick, since he ran away from home when he was 17, and her parents act like he never existed. She keeps a beautiful handmade puppet that represents Nick in a special box, which she shows to Nic, who is touched by Battle's vulnerability.

Everyone is on edge after Parents' Weekend. Isaac's parents are strained, Battle's mother claims Battle is an only child, which infuriates her, while Nic's dad keeps trying to lighten the mood with bad jokes. After all of their families leave, Battle tells Nic and Katrina that her parents boarded her beloved corgis in her absence, so she has decided to punish them by cutting off all her hair and shaving her head. Nic spirits away the shorn braid, hiding it in her dresser drawer, and returns to help Katrina shave Battle's head. Nic makes such a dramatic production of cutting Battle's hair that Katrina asks if something is going on between the two. Nic responds that there isn't but she wishes there was, and feels as though her feelings for Battle must be completely obvious to everyone. After a group volleyball game the next day, she takes Isaac into her confidence and is relieved when he doesn't make a fuss over her same-sex crush.

A few days later, when Nic is suffering from a PMS headache and Battle brings her a cold washcloth, they share a sweet first kiss. Nic writes in her journal that she might be gay, but she questions her feelings because Battle refuses to discuss exactly what they are to each other. One night, Battle suggests taking a hike after curfew and brings along a bottle of wine to share. Nic notes that their sexual awkwardness with each other is eased by the alcohol, but when she tries to talk about what is happening between them, Battle tells her to "Shut up and feel." Nic is also uncomfortable with how much Kevin flirts with Battle in public, but she feels helpless to say anything. She decides to give her feelings an outlet by creating a sister to the "Nick" puppet, made from a pair of Katrina's old velvet leggings and Battle's shorn braid. But when she presents the toy, which she has christened "Empress of the World," to Battle, Battle is upset instead of pleased and orders Nic to leave her room. Nic is devastated when Battle stops speaking to her and begins hanging out and holding hands with Kevin.

Nic decides to throw herself into her studies to distract herself from her broken heart. But she keeps seeing Battle and Kevin everywhere, and after accidentally witnessing them kissing in an elevator, she finds herself confiding in her anthropology teacher, Ms. Fraser, and Isaac. Ms. Fraser warns her that using her studies to avoid her feelings won't work, and Isaac advises confronting Battle directly and to quit analyzing so much. Nic feels so lonely that she kisses Isaac, who wisely notes that it probably happened because neither of them can have the person they really want. She is further confused when she goes on a field dig with her class and is strongly attracted to one of the good-looking male graduate students working at the site. On that same trip, she is teased for being gay by a couple of her male classmates and is proud of herself for standing up to them and not allowing them to label her.

Nic and Battle finally talk when Katrina engineers a meeting between them, then removes herself by falling asleep, exhausted from working on a complicated computer program for 48 hours straight. Battle admits that it is hard for her to get close to anyone and that she became frightened by how vulnerable she had allowed herself to become with Nic. She also felt like Nic was overanalyzing everything she did and said, which Nic claims she's trying to stop. The conversation makes Nic feel much better, and she goes to bed with a lighter heart.

By summer's end, Nic still doesn't know exactly what she and Battle are to each other, but she tries to be content with Battle's statement that "words don't always work." She is pleased to note that Battle has quietly taken back the Empress of the World puppet. After a dance celebrating the end of the seminar, at which Katrina and Isaac finally debut as a couple, Nic and Battle meet once more in the woods by the river to seal their promise to keep in touch with a make-up, make-out session.

The Message: Not all relationships can be defined. Trust your intuition. It is important to learn how to be comfortable with being uncomfortable.

Who's It For?: 8th–12th grade. Even though more is sometimes *implied* in sexual situations between characters, nothing more is *described* beyond a few swoon-y kisses. Katrina contemplates a romance with her computer teacher but never follows through. Nic endures some realistic mean-spirited taunting that includes the word *dyke,* and there are a few f-bombs scattered throughout the text.

Why It Rocks:
• **Voice:** Nic & Co.'s conversations are painfully realistic. Ryan completely captures the voices of brainy, insecure teens trying to impress one another with their big vocabularies and throwaway curses that are supposed to prove, despite their high GPAs, that they are still rule-breaking rebels.
• **Plot:** Groundbreaking for its time. Ryan was one of the first authors to write and publish a book that explored the sexual ambiguity of adolescence, refusing to label her characters as being either fully gay or straight.
• **Pacing:** Meandering, punctuated by tangential subplots, like Isaac's parents' divorce and Katrina's computer teacher crush, that aren't nearly as interesting as the drama unfolding between Nic and Battle.
• **Characterization:** While Nic's questioning, analytical character is laid bare through her first-person narration and journal entries, Battle remains maddeningly mysterious and aloof. Like Nic, readers get that tantalizing glimpse into Battle's life only when she lets down her guard to talk about her brother, and they will be left wanting more. And Katrina, Issac, and Kevin, despite the quirky attributes assigned them, are little more than amusing background noise.

Hook It Up With: *The Rules for Hearts,* the sequel to *Empress;* and *Dare Truth or Promise* by Paula Boock.

Read More about It:
Booklist: 07/01/01
Horn Book: 09/01/01
Kirkus Reviews, starred: 06/15/01
Publishers Weekly: 07/23/01
School Library Journal: 07/01/01
V.O.Y.A. (Voice of Youth Advocates): 08/01/01

Wittlinger, Ellen. 1999. *Hard Love.* New York: Simon & Schuster. 240p.

The Story: Angry and alienated since his parents' divorce five years ago, 16-year-old loner John Galardi spends most of his time crafting his 'zine, *Bananafish*, and listening to the romantic woes of his best (actually only) friend, Brian. John splits his time between his mom's suburban house during the week and his dad's place in Boston on the weekends, though neither place feels like home. His mom is still mourning the end of her marriage and spends hours in a dark room "thinking" at the end of the day, while his father leaves John alone most weekends after their cursory Friday night dinner to pursue his own interests.

But John's life takes a sharp turn after he meets Marisol Guzman, "Puerto Rican Cuban Yankee Cambridge Massachusetts, rich spoiled lesbian private-school gifted-and-talented writer virgin" author of John's favorite 'zine, *Escape Velocity*. John has always admired Marisol's writing, so he invites her to have coffee with him after he introduces himself to her at Tower Records while she is dropping off copies of her latest issue. Marisol is witty, brutally honest, and completely unlike anyone John has ever met before. He is initially so dazzled by her that he comes up with an alias, "Giovanni" (which Marisol shortens to Gio), to make himself appear more interesting. They spend that first meeting discussing the technical aspects of putting together a 'zine, and soon they are spending part of each Saturday hanging out together and sharing their stories. John tells Marisol about his self-imposed isolation and anger toward his parents, while she tells him about her first failed lesbian romance and how difficult it is to deal with her overprotective adoptive parents. Soon John is living for his Saturday morning dates with Marisol.

Back at school, his friend Brian has scored a freshman girlfriend and is pressuring John to get a date for the junior prom so that they can double. Tired of Brian's nagging, John lies and tells Brian that Marisol is his new girlfriend. The next time John is in Boston, Marisol surprises him with Ani DiFranco concert tickets. They have such a great time at the concert that John dares to bring up the question of the prom. But Marisol makes a joke out of it, and John quickly drops it. Then, Marisol is forced to stay the night at John's dad's when she misses the last train home, and while they lie talking in the dark, she reveals through a piece of her writing how insecure she is about her and John's relationship. John is secretly thrilled to see this chink in the armor of cool and collected Marisol. The next morning, after he corrects his father's assumption that he and Marisol are a romantic couple, she abruptly changes her mind and agrees to go to the prom with him.

John has been corresponding with another 'zine writer, Diana Tree, who invites him and Marisol to an informal 'zine convention in Provincetown that's taking place the weekend after the prom. Marisol tells John she'll think about it but that they've already been spending a lot of time together. John panics at this suggestion that Marisol needs space and comes to attach even more importance to their upcoming prom date.

The night of the dance, John reveals his deepest secret to Marisol: since his parents' divorce, his mother has subconsciously refused to touch him, and this is a big part of the reason he has walled himself off emotionally. Marisol is sympathetic, but after they go through the prom rituals of pictures, limo riding, and eating a rubbery chicken dinner with Brian and his date, Marisol is sighing and rolling her eyes. She finally agrees to slow dance with John, and he is so moved by her innocent touch after being denied physical affection for so long, that he refuses to let go. She gets angry and storms out of the prom. John follows her, and they get in a terrible fight, during which Marisol takes him to task for lying about everything, from what he told Brian about her to his own name. She also accuses him of trying to turn their friendship into a romance, when he knows she is a lesbian. John responds by telling her he loves her, and Marisol makes him take her home without another word.

The next morning, John gets in a fight with his mother, during which he finally realizes the reason why his mother refuses to touch him—because he looks like his father, whom she despises. He grabs her hand on purpose just to see what she will do, and she is so startled that she ends up dropping and shattering a jar of honey. Afterward, John is momentarily cheered when Marisol calls and tells him that she would still like to go to the conference, even though she emphasizes that the reason she's going is that Provincetown has a large gay community and she thinks that it's important for John to see her among other lesbians.

When John and Marisol arrive in Provincetown, they are greeted by Bill, the conference leader; and the kind, shy Diana Tree. Marisol quickly makes friends with three lesbian women and, to John's dismay, ends up sharing a cabin with them. He senses that Diana likes him, but he bitterly refuses to acknowledge it, feeling that if he can't have Marisol, he doesn't want anyone. He reads aloud a revealing poem about Marisol at the 'zine share and continues to shadow her movements at the conference. Finally, Marisol tells him that she will not be coming home with him, but is instead going to New York City with some of the girls she has met. At a sing-along that evening, Diana sings a song called "Hard Love," that John feels was written just for him and his situation.

At last, John painfully comes to terms with the inevitable. He resolves to try to have a better relationship with his parents. Diana asks him to write her, and he promises her he will. Finally, when John says good-bye to Marisol, she admits that she was actually very flattered he had asked her to the prom and that she loves him "as much as I can."

The Message: Learn to accept the things you cannot change. "There is no great loss without some small gain." "'Tis better to have loved and lost than never to have loved at all."

Who's It For?: 7th–12th grade. Despite an occasional f-bomb, this is a clean, highly readable text. The mix of formats within the story (letters, fuzzy photocopied 'zine excerpts) adds another dimension to the character-driven plot that will engage teens visually as well. Conservative readers may take issue with John's utter contempt and disrespect of his parents, even though it is amply justified by their self-centered behavior.

Why It Rocks:
• **Voice:** John's first-person narration is so permeated with the need to connect with another human being that it's almost too painful to read, and his funny, frank, and irreverent dialogue with Marisol serves as a welcome contrast to his dark internal thoughts.
• **Plot:** While Wittlinger's premise of unrequited love between a straight and gay may be a familiar story to some readers, the well-integrated infusion of 'zine culture and the painfully honest examination of John's distant, bitter relationship with his parents are what catapult this Printz Honor–winning novel into the contemporary classics category.
• **Pacing:** Measured. This is a character-driven story and as such, Wittlinger takes her time developing and revealing the layers of John and Marisol, through extended internal dialogue and conversation.
• **Characterization:** Both John's and Marisol's characterizations are compelling and rounded. The two teens change and grow by story's end, with Marisol's willingness to wear her emotions on her sleeve through her honest 'zine entries helping John to understand that putting his feelings out there for everyone to examine and comment on is much braver than trying to pretend he doesn't care. John's parents are provided with motives for their distant behavior, and while they are not necessarily sympathetic, they are realistic.

Hook It Up With: *Whistle Me Home* by Barbara Wersba and *From the Notebooks of Melanin Sun* by Jacqueline Woodson.

Read More about It:
Booklist, starred: 10/01/99
Horn Book: 07/01/99
School Library Journal, starred: 07/01/99
V.O.Y.A. (Voice of Youth Advocates): 08/01/99

CHAPTER 4

THE TERRIBLE TWEENS: 10–13 GOING ON 30

INTRODUCTION

C'mon, you know exactly who I'm talking about—that middle school sister of the cool Goth tenth grader on your T.A.B. (Teen Advisory Board). She's 11, looks 14, and is reading *Gossip Girls*. Or the bespectacled, freckled boy who is dragged up to the reference desk by his mother, who tells you in no uncertain terms that he has read "all the Harry Potters" and everything else recommended for his grade level and now needs something "more." Neither you nor she is quite certain what that means, but she's sure she'll know it when she sees it. What about the bubbly ten-year-old fifth grader who announces she's done with horse stories and now wants something more "romantic?" Or the super-serious sixth-grade boy who has been reading historical nonfiction above his grade level for years and now needs your help to find a work of historical fiction that will be acceptable to his teacher, who refuses to believe that he read the John Adams biography on his own?

If you've spent any time at all working behind a reference desk, you're familiar with the type of patron of whom I write—the sophisticated, born-too-short-but-on-his-or-her way up, twenty-first-century "Tween!" Not quite a teenager, but far removed from the ankle biters who reside in the J section of the library, this is the child aged 10–13 who can't wait to graduate into adolescence, and whom you better not call a "kid." The sad fact is that our hyperconnected, moving-at-the-speed-of-light society is requiring that kids grow up faster and faster. They long to be taken seriously by the adults in their lives—at least as seriously as their older high school–aged brothers and sisters—and they know that one way to prove their knowledge and experience is to expand their reading base. They want to skip ahead to reads that are "heavier," either physically (*Eragon*) or in content (*Gossip Girls*) to show the world that they aren't little kids. Their parents take them to the bookstore or library, stare at the bewildering array of covers, and end up letting them take home something like *Girls in Pants* ("well, the movie was pretty tame") or *Bucking the Sarge* ("didn't he win the Newbery Medal?") without ever once peeking inside to make sure that the content matches the young-looking cover.

Here's where you come in—what? You thought your job was strictly 7th–12th grade? Guess again. Tweens are your future teen advisory board members. They're going to be the ones coming to your Knit & Read after-school club or your D&D

Saturday tournaments. Don't underestimate the power of tween word of mouth. The marketing executives who scoop up their allowances don't, and you shouldn't either. Tweens will always remember that you were the cool teen services librarian who treated them like a grown-ups and gave them books that they found engaging but that were still just the right size, shape, and comprehension level for their SpongeBob backpacks. And they will tell all their friends! Serve them now, and you will have them for life. Ah, the terrible tween—not so terrible if you have the right attitude and, more important, the right books on hand to recommend.

Boyce, Frank Cottrell. 2004. *Millions.* New York: HarperCollins. 247p.

The Story: British fourth grader Damian Cunningham and his fifth-grade brother, Anthony, have just lost their mother and moved to a new neighborhood. Since his mother's death, Damian has been obsessed with the lives of saints and believes they appear and speak to him. He builds a hermitage out of cardboard boxes near the railway that runs behind his house, where he goes to meditate. One morning near the end of November, Damian is nearly flattened by an enormous bag of money that comes tumbling out of a speeding train. Convinced he has witnessed a miracle, he quickly gets Anthony. The two boys haul the bag back to the house, where they discover they are in possession of a cool 22 million pounds. But their excitement is tempered with the knowledge that England is on the brink of adopting the euro and the stacks of paper money will become worthless in just a few short weeks.

The boys quickly begin spending the cash at school on chauffeured bike rides, watches, Game Boys, and footballs. Damian longs to do something more altruistic with the cash. He sets free several pet shop birds and stuffs handfuls of bills into the letter slot of the next-door neighbors, a group of frugal Mormon missionaries. Anthony is more ambitious, attempting to buy a house through a real estate agent, who leaves in a huff when she realizes an adult does not accompany them. The boys' father notices some of their new possessions, but Anthony's convincing lies keep him in the dark.

After Damian offers some money to a mysterious, poor-looking man with a glass eye who is lurking around the hermitage, Anthony warns him that he can't just offer money to anyone he thinks needs it. Damian then drops thousands of pounds into a charity bin at school during an assembly on water aid for developing countries. Anthony is furious and only then reveals to Damian that the cash was not a miracle, but stolen, and shows him the Internet article he found about the robbery. The clever crooks planned to drop the bags from freight trains all over the country, then collect them later and innocently join the crowds of British citizens changing over their money at the local banks.

The principal calls the boys into his office the next day about the large donation, along with their father and Dorothy, the woman who led the school assembly. Anthony lies and claims to have stolen the money from the Mormons next door, who meekly accept the money that was never theirs, believing that it came from the same miraculous source that stuffed their letter slot. Meanwhile, the boy's father begins a flirtation with Dorothy, who invites herself to the school nativity play.

Damian and Anthony have taken to carrying the money with them everywhere, even filling the saddlebags of the fake donkey (ridden by Damian, who plays Joseph) the night of the play. When the man with the glass eye (who Damian now knows must be one of the robbers) shows up backstage, Damian escapes with the saddlebags, taking the money to the one place he knows is safe—his old house. When his dad and Anthony find him there, the boys finally tell their father the whole story, except that Damian omits Glass Eye.

They return to their new home that night to find it ransacked and all their Christmas decorations ruined. Their dad decides to get the money changed and spend it to make up for the ruined holiday presents. After everyone is in bed, Glass Eye sneaks out of the attic where he has been hiding since wrecking the house and tells Damian he will contact him by cell phone tomorrow after the money's been changed. The next day, Damian, Anthony, their dad, and Dorothy go together to change the money at different banks around town. They are having so much fun that Damian almost forgets the phone call.

When the crook calls later that night, Damian goes to let him in and instead finds hundreds of begging people filling the street outside his house, most of them parents and friends of the kids at school who told about the money. Damian takes the cash and runs down to the train tracks. Glass Eye gets in through the back door, but once in the house, he is questioned and arrested by the police, who have come to investigate the crowd outside. Meanwhile, Damian has set fire to the remaining money on the tracks, and through the smoke sees his mother, who dispenses some last-minute advice and tells him she loves him. Damian's dad tells him he deserves to spend the held-back changed money any way he wishes, so he uses it to pay for 14 wells to be dug for water in Nigeria.

The Message: Money can't buy happiness. The best things in life are free. Wealth complicates relationships.

Who's It For?: 5th–8th grade. Boyce's writing is so clever that eighth grade and above can appreciate it, while the universal themes can also be easily understood by a fifth grader. Some reviewers mentioned that American audiences may be confused by Boyce's fictional conversion of English money from the pound to the euro, but that minor detail shouldn't stand in the way of the enjoyment of the story.

Why It Rocks:
• **Voice:** Damian's sweet first-person narration is innocent and questioning, without being cloying.
• **Plot:** Could author/screenwriter Boyce add anything significant to what has already been written on the theme of the poor longing for fortune, then discovering that being wealthy also has its problems (*The Prince and the Pauper, The Little Princess*)? Absolutely. Boyce's premise may be a sprawling cliché, but the specific details he shares about these brothers make the story feel fresh, intimate, and utterly sincere.

- **Pacing:** Measured and thoughtful. Damian's gradual realization that poverty is ubiquitous and that even a billion dollars wouldn't be enough to address it worldwide is a concept that many tweens will struggle with long into adolescence, and that many adults still have difficulty explaining.
- **Characterization:** The funny, articulate conversations Damian holds with imaginary martyrs, Anthony's encyclopedic knowledge of real estate and interest rates, and the priceless moment when the brothers stand in the middle of an aisle in the toy store and realize there is absolutely nothing they want to buy are the sorts of character-rounding details that make this book so much more than its surface premise.

Hook It Up With: *Lunch Money* by Andrew Clements and *Double Fudge* by Judy Blume.

Read More about It:
Booklist: 08/01/04
Horn Book: 04/01/05
Kirkus Reviews: 07/01/04
Publishers Weekly, starred: 08/23/04
School Library Journal: 10/01/04
V.O.Y.A. (Voice of Youth Advocates): 10/01/04

Broach, Elise. 2005. *Shakespeare's Secret.* New York: Henry Holt. 250p.

The Story: Sixth grader Hero Netherfield is the new girl ... again. Her family has just moved from New York to Washington, D.C., so that her Shakespeare-scholar father can accept a job in an Elizabethan-era archives. Now Hero must start over at a new school, where other kids are inevitably going to make fun of her name, a name Hero has always hated along with anything else that smacks of Shakespeare. The day before school starts, Hero meets her next-door neighbor, elderly Mrs. Roth, who lets slip that Hero's family has moved into the infamous "Murphy diamond house." Hero waits impatiently for the end of school the next day to find out the rest of the story.

Arthur and Eleanor Murphy were Mrs. Roth's next-door neighbors. Eleanor Murphy owned an heirloom necklace that had been passed down from her English ancestors, the Veres. The Murphys insured the diamond at the center for a million dollars because they could not afford to insure the entire necklace. Last year, a thief who took nothing else stole the diamond from the necklace. The insurance company was certain the Murphys committed the robbery in order to receive the insurance money. Mrs. Roth also believes that Arthur Murphy committed the robbery, because Eleanor was dying of cancer, and he needed money for her expensive treatment. The insurance company finally released the money but only after a long investigation, during which Eleanor died. Arthur moved away, and Mrs. Roth believes he hid the diamond somewhere in Hero's house.

Over the course of the next several weeks, Hero visits Mrs. Roth often, gathering more clues about the missing diamond. Her father tells her he understands Mrs. Murphy's relatives to be descendents of Edward de Vere, the 17th Earl of Oxford, who some scholars believe was the real author of Shakespeare's plays. When Hero shares this with Mrs. Roth, the elderly woman shows her the necklace, given to her by Mr. Murphy when he moved. Included with the necklace is a note saying that Mr. Murphy believed his wife would have wanted Mrs. Roth to have the antique, along with a quote from a poem by Dylan Thomas, ending with "Rage, rage against the dying of the light." Hero believes it is a clue to the diamond's whereabouts. Hero's father also sees her working on reproducing a symbol she saw on the back of the necklace and remarks that it looks just like the family crest of Anne Boleyn, one of Henry the Eighth's wives and the mother of Queen Elizabeth.

Meanwhile, Hero's problems at school have eased somewhat owing to an unexpected friendship that has sprung up between her and Danny Cordova, the most popular eighth-grade boy at school and the son of the local police chief. Danny also befriends Mrs. Roth and quickly becomes involved in solving the mystery. From a conversation with Danny's father, Hero learns that Danny's mother left his dad and now lives in California trying to make it as an actress, and that Mrs. Roth used to be married to Mr. Murphy before he was married to Eleanor. Hero confronts Mrs. Roth and accuses her of lying. Later, she apologizes, and Mrs. Roth tells her she and Mr. Murphy divorced after 19 years because their adopted teenaged daughter ran away, and they haven't heard from her since. Mr. Murphy later married Eleanor, and they all became good friends.

Hero shows Mrs. Roth the Boleyn crest, and the two speculate on how de Vere would have come to own Anne Boleyn's necklace—perhaps he was Queen Elizabeth's lover, or maybe even a nonmarital son she had to keep quiet about. When Hero shows Danny the Dylan quote, he thinks the clue means the diamond is hidden in a light fixture. The next evening that Hero's parents are out, she and Danny search for the diamond and find it in the back porch light, which has never worked. They go the next day to tell Mrs. Roth they found the diamond, but Danny shamefacedly admits he mailed it that morning to his mother in California because she needs money. Mrs. Roth invites them in nevertheless, and Danny notices a picture of Mrs. Roth's runaway daughter, saying it looks exactly like his mother.

Putting together the dates of when Danny's mother left and when Mrs. Roth's daughter ran away, Hero is the one who finally realizes that Danny's mother and Mrs. Roth's daughter, Anna, are one and the same. Mrs. Roth writes to her daughter that she has met Danny, and Anna sends back the diamond because she doesn't want Danny to get in trouble. Hero suggests telling her dad about the necklace, so his archives can pay off the insurance company and then purchase the heirloom for their own collection, a suggestion Mrs. Roth and Danny happily agree to.

The Message: Appearances can be deceiving. Putting your trust in someone new is often a risk worth taking. Never give up—sometimes the answer is right in front of you. To solve a problem, at times you need to step back and look at it a different way.

Who's It For?: 5th–8th grade. In terms of content, there are some bullying issues concerning Hero. Also, Danny mentions being suspended from school for pushing a teacher and for vandalizing school property. There is also the matter of Danny's mother leaving the family. All of these issues are dealt with in an age-appropriate manner and necessary to the telling of the story. Interested readers will find that, despite Hero's bias, they pick up quite a few facts about the lives of Shakespeare, Edward de Vere, Anne Boleyn, and Queen Elizabeth. The author's note and historical timeline at the back will provide curious young historians with even more background. Both readers new to the Bard and those who consider him an old friend will enjoy this literary mystery.

Why It Rocks:
- **Voice:** Broach's crisp, third-person prose allows readers the necessary distance to try to solve the mystery themselves.
- **Plot:** Broach underlines the history mystery with a strong family story that rounds out the characters, making them more than just stereotypical, chin-rubbing sleuths.
- **Pacing:** Purposeful. The action moves at a realistic, measured pace while still maintaining a suspense that will keep young readers flipping pages.
- **Characterization:** It is endearingly realistic how Hero moves from despising all things Shakespeare to begrudgingly admitting to her dad how she can understand why he finds all this history stuff so interesting. This is also a wonderful study of intergenerational relationships, with the friendship between Hero, Danny, and Mrs. Roth resulting in the solving of a mystery that no one of them could have accomplished alone.

Hook It Up With: *Chasing Vermeer* by Blue Balliett and *The Shakespeare Stealer* (and sequels) by Gary Blackwood.

Read More about It:
Booklist: 05/01/05
Horn Book: 04/01/06
Kirkus Reviews, starred: 04/15/05
School Library Journal: 06/15/05
V.O.Y.A. (Voice of Youth Advocates): 08/01/05

Choldenko, Gennifer. 2004. *Al Capone Does My Shirts.* New York: Penguin Group. 225p.

The Story: It is January 1935, and 12-year-old Matthew Flanagan, (a.k.a Moose) is none too pleased when his father, an electrician, beats out 247 other applicants for a job at the infamous Alcatraz Island prison off the coast of San Francisco. Moose is far too nervous living next door to criminals to appreciate the fact that the prison provides housing for employees' families during a time when many Depression-era families have lost their livelihoods. His mother is thrilled, because the new job puts the family in close proximity to the Esther P. Marinoff School, a place for children who are "different." Moose's 15-year-old sister Natalie barely speaks, rocks back and forth, and counts her button collection over and over again. Unfortunately, the school sends her home after one day, insisting that she is unable to be helped. Now Moose must come right home after school each day to watch Nat while his mother teaches piano lessons on the mainland.

Meanwhile, Moose meets the rest of the Alcatraz kids, including the warden's beautiful and manipulative daughter, Piper. She tries to get him to agree to help her with a moneymaking scheme to sell prison laundry service to the kids at school. For five cents a shirt, their classmates can have their clothes laundered by famous criminals such as Al Capone and Machine Gun Kelly. Moose reluctantly agrees after Piper promises to be kind to Natalie.

The one bright spot in Moose's life are the pick-up baseball games that are organized by his new friend Scout after school on Mondays, but now that Moose must come home right after school, he can no longer play. The warden finds out about, and puts an end to, the shirt-laundering scheme after he receives a letter from an angry parent, but clever Piper is able to divert most of the blame onto Moose and the other Alcatraz kids. Moose's father is very disappointed in him and takes away his baseball equipment.

Moose discovers that the convicts play baseball in the prison recreational yard, and that occasionally their baseballs come over the fence. He hopes to find one to give to Scout, who has been sore at him since he has no longer been able to play after school. Every day during the spring, Moose parks Natalie in the fields with her button box while he goes hunting for baseballs. One day he returns to find Natalie in the company of prisoner #105, a low-risk convict who has been given grounds privileges. #105 hands Moose one of the coveted baseballs, but Moose is too distraught to enjoy it as he drags Natalie away, sure that she has been compromised in some way by the man. Moose wants to tell his parents about #105 so they will take the responsibility of Natalie's care away from him, but he can't face disappointing his father again or dashing his mother's hopes. She has arranged another interview with the Marinoff School, and is working daily to prepare Natalie.

Moose is too frightened to take Natalie outside anymore, but she throws a huge tantrum when she realizes she can no longer see #105. The day before her second interview is Nat's birthday, and Moose takes her back to the hill where she first met the convict. He realizes that their relationship is innocent and that #105 actually isn't much older than his sister. At Nat's birthday party, Moose confronts his mother about putting ten candles on the cake, something she has been doing for the past five years. His mother tearfully responds that if they admit Natalie is 16 and no longer a child, then it is too late for her to get help.

The day after Nat's interview, the school calls to say that Nat still isn't ready. Frustrated, Moose turns to Piper and asks her to help him get a letter to Al Capone, asking the gangster to use his influence on the outside to get Natalie accepted. A week later, the school suddenly agrees to take Natalie. Later, when Moose puts on one of his shirts from the prison laundry, a slip of folded paper with the word *DONE* written on it falls from one of the sleeves.

The Message: While rules aren't made to be broken, they can be bent for a good reason. Sometimes the only person you can depend on is yourself. Responsibility builds character. Question authority. Never give up hope.

Who's It For?: 6th–8th grade. The most disturbing issue raised is the possibility that Natalie has been molested or hurt by #105, but the author implies that while this is Moose's greatest fear, nothing inappropriate happened between Natalie and the convict. Natalie displays some upsetting behaviors (for example, large-scale tantrums or taking off all her clothes for no reason) that are symptomatic of her mental disability. Choldenko reveals in an endnote that Nat's condition is most likely autism, since the disease had not yet been named in 1935. There is no strong language, and though many of the criminals of Alcatraz are famous mobsters, not too much is made of their violent crimes.

Why It Rocks:
• **Voice:** Moose's first-person narration is authentic, and his worries about parents, school, and friends are as true for tweens now as they were in 1935. In an interesting and informative author's note, Choldenko discusses which parts of the book were fact and which were fiction, gives more background about Alcatraz, and explains that Natalie's character was based on her experiences with her own autistic sibling, Gina.
• **Plot:** It's not difficult to understand how Gennifer Choldenko's unusual Depression-era historical fiction scored a Newbery honor. Choldenko's use of Alcatraz as a metaphor for Moose's feelings of imprisonment is nothing short of inspired, as is her seamless blending of historical fact with fiction.
• **Pacing:** Measured. Besides the well-drawn characterizations, the suspense of whether or not Natalie will be accepted to her school will keep readers going.
• **Characterization:** Despite the prominence given to Natalie's condition in the story, this is not a "disease" book. Instead, Choldenko emphasizes how family bonds are strained when one member requires more time and attention than the rest. Tween readers will empathize with Moose's battling feelings of both tenderness and resentment toward his sister and her neediness. The scheming Piper adds some light-hearted comic relief with her many plans to capitalize on the celebrity of Alcatraz's famous criminals.

Hook It Up With: *The Teacher's Funeral* by Richard Peck and *The Cloud Chamber* by Joyce Maynard.

Read More about It:
Booklist: 02/01/04
Horn Book: 10/01/04
Kirkus Reviews, starred: 03/01/04
Publishers Weekly, starred: 01/02/04
School Library Journal, starred: 03/01/04

Clements, Andrew. 2002. *Things Not Seen*. New York: Penguin Group. 176p.

The Story: One morning in February, 15-year-old Bobby Phillips awakens to discover he has inexplicably turned invisible. He immediately tells his mom and dad (a literature professor at the University of Chicago and a physicist, respectively), whose reactions range from disbelief to amazement. After his parents leave for work, Bobby heads off to the university library, where he spends the morning wandering around naked, marveling at and getting used to his new condition. On his way out, he crashes into a girl, who he notices is blind.

Later, Bobby falls asleep on the couch with the television on, waiting for his parents to come home. He awakens to a local news report about a car accident, recognizes his dad's car, and hears that his parents have been taken to the hospital. Bobby realizes how serious his condition is in light of this new twist, and, after receiving a reassuring phone call from the doctor in charge of his parents, quickly goes to the hospital. His mother gives him money and instructs him to tell authorities that his Aunt Ethel from Florida is staying with him.

Bobby spends the next few days behind closed curtains, avoiding the neighbors and checking in with his parents by phone. He visits the library again and sees the blind girl, whose name is Alicia, in one of the study rooms. Over the next two days, they meet in a study room and begin sharing the details of their lives. Alicia reveals that she has been blind for only two years, after falling out of bed and hitting her head, and Bobby is forced to confess his condition when Alicia accidentally jostles against him and discovers he is naked. Her father comes to the library to pick Alicia up and is worried when he sees her speaking to no one, so Bobby also tells Alicia's parents about himself, which is helpful because Alicia's dad is a famous astronomer who lends his expertise to the problem.

Meanwhile, Bobby's school wants to know when he will be returning to class. Social Services tells Bobby's parents, who are now home from the hospital, that they have five days to produce him or his disappearance becomes a police matter. The two scientist dads theorize that Bobby's electric blanket may be to blame because it puts out too much energy and is creating a type of electromagnetic disturbance. Bobby begins to do research on the blanket and decides that he and Alicia need to travel to the Sears headquarters and somehow, using his invisibility, get the names of all the customers who have complained about it. The plan goes smoothly, with Alicia charming the Human Resources staff while Bobby hacks a computer in customer services and finds the names.

Bobby begins calling the list of names and finally speaks to a Mr. Borden, whose daughter Sheila disappeared three years ago. Bobby uses the Web to track down Sheila and calls her. After an initial shock, she admits the same thing happened to her and she ran away, setting up a life for herself in which she does everything electronically. She makes him swear not to tell anyone about her. Bobby tells the dads what he has learned without revealing Sheila's name—just the date and place where she first became invisible.

The dads use a computer program to match the dates and locations and discover a solar wind passed over both places at the time of invisibility. They theorize that this atmospheric occurrence, coupled with the faulty blanket, caused the invisibility—but they still don't know how to reverse it. Bobby goes online to discover that the same solar wind that caused his problem almost four weeks ago is still blowing. Alicia suggests that two negatives might make a positive: if Bobby uses the blanket again, he might become visible. Bobby decides to try it and awakens to police crashing into his room during a surprise search. They turn on the lights and reveal Bobby, visible again. He mails the blanket with all the data to Sheila in case she ever changes her mind about staying invisible, and then embarks on a new stage of his relationship with Alicia, with whom he realizes he has fallen in love.

The Message: Life isn't fair. Sometimes the only person you can trust is yourself. Adults don't have all the answers and can't always protect you. Invisibility takes many forms.

Who's It For?: 6th–8th grade. Bobby may be 15, but this story isn't as much about what it's like to be 15 as it is about what it's like to be invisible. The sweetly chaste romance will intrigue your typical sixth-grade girl, yet is kept in the background enough to keep from discouraging her opposite-sex-oblivious male classmate, who's just digging the science stuff. The science in *Things Not Seen* is also surprisingly convincing and fun to ponder. The explanations of solar winds and faulty electric blankets seem plausible, but not so technical that your typical tween won't be able to grasp the principles being discussed. A perfectly safe booktalk choice for large, mixed tween groups.

Why It Rocks:
• **Voice:** Because Bobby's first-person narration is loaded with astute observations about the physical sensations of being invisible—the disorientation of trying to walk when you can't see your feet, the constant chill of being out, about, and nude in the middle of an early Chicago spring—readers will quickly be able to put themselves into his shoes (or bare feet!).
• **Plot:** This is the tween novel with everything: adventure, technology, suspense, romance, and even some (necessary) nudity! The author's winning formula of science, fiction, and humor works so well because Clements never lets readers lose sight of the fact that this extraordinary situation is happening to an ordinary boy.
• **Pacing:** Increasingly stressful. Clements knows how to ratchet up the suspense by introducing numerous plot complications, like having Bobby's parents end up in the hospital the same day that he turns invisible.
• **Characterization:** Just like any other kid, Bobby fights with his parents, is scared of the dark, and falls for a pretty girl. Tweens can't help but relate to this sincere, fallible boy.

Hook It Up With: *The Radioactive Boy Scout: The True Story of a Boy and His Backyard Nuclear Reactor* by Ken Silverstein and *The Schwa Was Here* by Neal Schusterman (also featured in this chapter).

Read More about It:
Booklist, starred: 04/15/02
Horn Book: 03/01/02
School Library Journal: 03/01/02
Kirkus Reviews, starred: 02/01/02
Voice of Youth Advocates (V.O.Y.A.): 02/01/02

Jocelyn, Marthe. 2004. *Mable Riley: A Reliable Record of Humdrum, Peril, and Romance.* **Cambridge, MA: Candlewick. 279p.**

The Story: In turn-of-the-century rural Ambler's Corner, Ontario, 14-year-old Mable Riley longs for adventure and to become a writer. To that end, she records everything in her private diary. She is thrilled when her elder sister, Viola, who has accepted a teaching position the next county over, allows Mable to accompany her as her teaching assistant. They board with the stoic Mr. and Mrs. Goodhand and their 20-year-old son, Alfred.

After quickly settling into a routine of schoolwork and chores, Mable is disappointed to realize that living with the Goodhands is not all that different from living in Ambler's Corner. She amuses herself by writing an adventurous romance story in cliff-hanging chapters to post to her best friend, Hattie, back home, and by "spelling down" her new school rival, Elizabeth Campbell, who was the spelling bee champion until Mable arrived. She also enjoys a mild flirtation with Tommy Thomas, a boy at school.

One Sunday afternoon, Mrs. Goodhand asks Mable to take a loaf of bread to the town oddball, the Widow Rattle. Mable is shocked and intrigued by the woman, who lives happily by herself, wears trousers, and rides a bicycle. She continues to bring the "Christian bread" to the widow every Sunday afternoon and learns that Mrs. Rattle came from a wealthy family and was until very recently a newspaper journalist. Fired because of her desire to write serious stories about women's issues, Mrs. Rattle has decided to take a job at the local cheese factory, run by the Goodhands' neighbors, Mr. and Mrs. Forrest.

The Goodhands, like many of the local dairy farmers, sell their milk to the Forrests. Mable dislikes Mrs. Forrest, a judgmental, self-important busybody, because she called Viola a "hussy" for daring to sing out loud while walking home with Alfred after church choir practice. When Mable mentions Mrs. Rattle one time too many, Viola forbids her to visit the controversial woman, worried that Mable's actions will reflect on her as the teacher. In spite of this, Mable is able to convince Viola to let her attend a "Ladies' Reading Circle" meeting that is to be held at Mrs. Rattle's house. Mable is shocked to discover, when Mrs. Rattle declares that the working conditions for women at the cheese factory are appalling and that she wants to organize a strike, that the reading circle is a cover for a secret suffragist group.

Later, an anonymous editorial appears in the town newspaper, revealing the hardships suffered by the workers at the factory. Soon after, Mable and Viola attend the local Harvest Social with the Goodhands. Mrs. Rattle also shows up and is confronted by the Forrests, who accuse her of writing the editorial and fire her on the spot. Mrs. Forrest comes to the Goodhands' house to suggest the town replace Viola as teacher. Then she brags that if the workers strike at the factory, she and Mr. Forrest will alert the police, who will not hesitate to break up the strike. Mable overhears the conversation and sneaks out of the house after everyone is asleep to warn Mrs. Rattle, who refuses to cancel the protest.

Mable feigns illness the next day, takes the Goodhands' horse and wagon to the factory as soon as Viola leaves, and joins the protest. The police do break up the strike, and Mable and Mrs. Rattle end up at the courthouse with the rest of the protestors. When the Goodhands arrive to take Mable home, there is another confrontation between the Goodhands and the Forrests, who point out that because of the strike, all of Mr. Goodhand's milk will go to waste. Mable suggests later to Alfred and Mr. Goodhand that the farmers should threaten to sell their milk to other dairy factories further away unless Mr. Forrest agrees to changing the working conditions. Mr. Goodhand and the other farmers approach Mr. Forrest with this threat and add that they don't want to lose their milk again if there is another strike. Mr. Forrest reluctantly agrees.

Mable is jubilant and now wants only one more thing—her sister and Alfred to admit their love for each other. She is soon satisfied when they announce their engagement, and Mable gets a taste of romance herself when Tommy kisses her on the way home from school. Mrs. Rattle recovers from the strike, finds a new job, and prepares to move away. Mable and Viola move into Mrs. Rattle's old house until the end of the school year, when Viola will get married.

The Message: Be careful what you wish for. There is no great risk without some small gain. Don't be afraid to be wrong, or to apologize when you are. Conversely, don't be afraid to speak up for what you know is right or for those who aren't always heard. Dream big.

Who's It For?: 5th–8th grade. Most of the violence and romance to be found between the pages of Mable's diary take place in the melodramatic story she writes to her friend Hattie, and even that will be tame stuff to 21st-century tweens. This book is about as clean as the country church services Mable suffers through every Sunday. Recommend widely and with no reservations, especially to prairie-struck fans of those March and Ingalls girls.

Why It Rocks:
• **Voice:** Mable's cozy first-person narration in diary format will cause her to become even more real in the minds of readers.
• **Plot:** While the story and format may seem familiar, Jocelyn adds several distinctive details that take this snappy historical fiction up a notch from those tired Dear America diaries. Yes, it's a pioneer story between sisters, but a pioneer story set in Ontario, an altogether different frontier. Jocelyn notes both President McKinley's assassination *and* Queen Victoria's death in the pages of Mable's diary. And while there has lately been a renewed interest in the suffrage movement in juvenile literature, Jocelyn also references the roots of the labor movement by highlighting the poor working conditions at the cheese factory.
• **Pacing:** Mable's purple-prosed romance story, replete with train robberies, shallow rogues, and fainting spells, may slow some readers down from the main plotline, but the laughs are well worth the side trip.
• **Characterization:** Irrepressible and utterly charming, Mable can't help but secure a place in the hearts of booky, misunderstood girls everywhere, right next to Anne Shirley, Jo March, and Elizabeth Bennet.

Hook It Up With: *With Courage and Cloth* by Ann Bausum and *A Year Down Yonder* by Richard Peck.

Read More about It:
Booklist: 03/01/04
Horn Book: 10/01/04
Kirkus Reviews: 02/15/04
Publishers Weekly: 02/23/04
School Library Journal: 03/01/04

Nelson, Blake. 2006. *Gender Blender.* **New York: Random House. 224p.**

The Story: When Tom Witherspoon and Emma Baker were younger, they were best friends, but now that they're in sixth grade they just don't seem to have anything in common anymore. Emma is cautious, conservative, and driven. Tom is competitive and rash, and he doesn't believe in homework. In Mrs. Andre's health class, they are paired for an assignment about gender roles. For the next week, Mrs. Andre wants each boy-girl pair to observe every aspect of each other's life and focus on how gender affects society's expectations of each person.

Tom nearly misses the explanation of the assignment because he is busy showing one of his friends the arrowhead he found in the woods behind his house. Later that afternoon, he is fooling around on the school's trampoline when Emma, who's at gymnastics practice, orders him off. They end up jumping, arguing, and colliding in midair. They hit their heads and pass out. When they awaken, they have somehow switched bodies. They are surprised by the eighth-grade boys' track team and have to hide in a janitor's closet, but they are discovered, and Tom—as Emma—pretends they have been making out so they can escape.

Over the next few days, Tom and Emma suffer through each other's daily life. Tom attends one of Emma's piano lessons, which is a disaster, since he has no idea how to play. Emma's formal family dinners also flummox him, and he can't believe how much of the conversation revolves around Emma's activities and grades. Emma meanwhile has to contend with Tom's rambunctious friends, who push her in a shopping cart headlong down a hill in the name of fun, and his bratty little brother, who is constantly stealing Tom's possessions and either hiding them or blowing them up. Emma does some research and discovers an ancient Eskimo myth involving a squabbling married couple and a cursed arrowhead, which forces them to switch bodies in order to learn to get along with the opposite sex. In the story, the couple had four days to make things right. Emma remembers Tom's arrowhead and believes that the two of them are now in the same predicament.

Emma shares what she has learned with Tom, and the two agree to try and get along as best they can, despite their continual dismay at being trapped in one another's body. Tom is thrilled that he can finally look at a naked girl as long as he wants (in Emma's bathroom mirror) but has no idea how to negotiate the seemingly endless bottles of hair-and-body products in the shower. He is dismayed to learn that teachers expect Emma to come up with the right answers in class but delighted to realize he'll get to see Kelly Angstrom naked after PE class. He also learns how mean girls can be to one another when classmates who claim to be Emma's friends tease him about being caught in the janitor's closet while making out with a boy. Tom runs to the bathroom to escape, where he makes an even worse discovery: while trapped in Emma's body, he's just had her first period.

Meanwhile, Emma is finding out that teachers basically ignore Tom, but coaches admire his pitching arm. Using Tom's strength, Emma easily wins him a place on the first-string Little League team after pitching tryouts. She discovers how callous boys can be when she overhears her crush, class hottie Jeff Matthews, giving crude pointers to the other boys about how to score with girls. She is horrified to wake up with an erection, made even worse by the fact that Tom's mother walks in while she is trying to make it go away.

The final day of the curse, Tom and Emma are both invited to Kelly's birthday party, which everyone knows is going to feature a kissing game. Tom almost doesn't make it because he bungled his way through Emma's gymnastics meet and sprained his ankle. After a few arguments about who likes whom and who's going into the closet for "Seven Minutes in Heaven," Emma and Tom end up together again in the dark. After they pledge to stay with one another forever should it turn out that the curse can't be reversed, one of Tom's friends kicks the door too hard in jest, knocking both of them in the head. They pass out, and when they come to, they are each back in their own body. They both receive an A on their health report on gender differences, which they deliver together the following week, good friends once more.

The Message: The best way to understand someone else is to put yourself in his or her shoes. Both girls and boys have gender strengths and weaknesses. True compromise is hard.

Who's It For?: 6th–8th grade. The age of the characters is a good way to gauge the age group this particular book is best suited to. Sixth grade is a cusp year during which some tweens have already tipped over into adolescence, trying on bras and eyeing the opposite sex, while others are completely clueless when it comes to puberty and are still pulling out their old Barbie dolls or superhero action figures. The scenes dealing with Tom's first period and Emma's surprise erection are sympathetic and humorous, and they will go a long way toward easing tween fears about these uncontrollable body changes. Seventh and eighth graders will be able to read this book with a sense of having been there and done that while still appreciating Nelson's all-too-accurate portrayal of middle school politics.

Why It Rocks:
- **Voice:** Nelson's decision to write in intimate third-person from alternating points of view between the two main characters allows readers an interesting dip into both Emma and Tom's heads.
- **Plot:** The body switcheroo bit is old news, but Nelson worked it over and made it new again. He not only gets the grade-level humor right (innocent Emma initially thinks her "morning wood" is a wayward chipmunk; Tom uses exfoliator on his hair because he is confused by the sheer number of bottles in Emma's shower) but also

successfully uses the body-switch basis to nail the absurdity and awkwardness of puberty.

*   **Pacing:** The alternating perspectives keep the readers on edge as they wonder if Emma and Tom will ever be free of each other's strange body.
*   **Characterization:** What makes the book work is Blake's skillfull balance between slamming-locker, eavesdropping, slapstick episodes and realistic, empathetic moments that tweens will instantly relate to. Emma's focus wins Tom a prized spot on the baseball team, while Tom, who believes that gymnastics isn't a "real sport," comes away from Emma's meet with a sprained ankle and a new respect for all the training it takes to be a gymnast. Likewise, no reader will come away from this very funny book without some idea of how hard the other side has it.

Hook It Up With: *The Day Joanie Frankenhauser Became a Boy* by Frances Lin Lantz and *Are You There God? It's Me, Margaret* by Judy Blume.

Read More about It:
Booklist: 03/01/06
Horn Book: 10/01/06
Kirkus Reviews: 02/15/06
Publishers Weekly, starred: 02/06/06
School Library Journal: 04/01/06
V.O.Y.A. (Voice of Youth Advocates): 06/01/06

Nickerson, Sara. Illustrations by Sally Wern Comport. 2002. *How to Disappear Completely and Never Be Found.* New York: HarperCollins. 288p.

The Story: Margaret is a lonely sixth grader who, ever since her father's mysterious drowning death four years ago, is obsessed with natural disasters, especially those of animal varieties, like killer bees. Her mother has coped with her grief by completely shutting down. The only cheerful presence in the house is Margaret's seven-year-old sister, Sophie, who entertains herself with The Hardest Jigsaw Ever Made. Both girls are surprised when their mother suddenly takes them to a broken-down mansion that they have never seen before, on an island near their Pacific Northwest home. Their mother posts a "For Sale by Owner" sign on the front lawn and refuses to answer any questions.

Boyd, the 12-year-old boy who lives in the house next door, secretly watches and wonders about the new neighbors. Boyd is an outsider at school, mainly because he spends his lunch hours at the town's unique library, which is presided over by a man named Mr. Librarian, who collects only unpublished manuscripts. There, Boyd pours over a set of hand-drawn comic books about a man named Ratt, who is half human, half rodent, lives in an old mansion (identical to the house next to Boyd's), and turns other people's trash into works of art.

At the mansion, Margaret finds a mysterious package on the back porch that is addressed to her mother. She brings it home with her, opening it to find a homemade comic book starring a character named Ratt, an old rusty key, and a tarnished swimming medal with her father's name on it. The medal troubles Margaret. If her father was a championship swimmer, how could he have drowned? Margaret knows little about the circumstances of her father's death and decides she must know if it was an accident or a suicide. Telling Sophie to cover for her, she pretends to head off to school and then rides the ferry to the island where she first saw the mansion and found the package.

It takes Margaret a long time to walk to the mansion, and it is twilight before she arrives. Once inside, she discovers a junk room, a tool room, and an artist's studio, before a hulking shape in the hall frightens her. As she runs out, she leaves her backpack on the stairs in fright. Boyd sees Margaret run out, stops her, and introduces himself. He tells her that because of the comic books he believes Ratt lives in the mansion, but Boyd's never seen him.

That night, Boyd hides Margaret in his room under the bed, and they share what they know about Ratt and the house. She tells Boyd about her father's death, and he tells her the story of Ratt and his rival, the Drowning Ghost from the comic books. Before they were Ratt and the Drowning Ghost, they were just two regular boys who enjoyed collecting garbage and turning it into treasure. But as they grew older, one boy began to turn into a rat and the other became a popular swim jock. Something happened that made them enemies, but Boyd doesn't know what because the story is in the first volume, resting in Margaret's backpack on the mansion stairs.

The next morning after Boyd leaves for school, Margaret goes to the library, where she plans to hide overnight so she can go through the old newspapers without Mr. Librarian looking over her shoulder. Back home, Sophie has decided to come looking for Margaret. After school, Boyd is ambushed by a pack of bullies, who tie him up and leave him in his parents' boathouse. That night in the library, Margaret finds a clipping of her father as a teen wearing the medal with his younger brother in the background, looking decidedly rodent-like. She is startled by someone coming into the library and hides under the reference desk. It is Ratt, and he takes the clipping and leaves a new comic strip, which shows Boyd trapped in the boathouse.

Margaret rescues Boyd, then goes back into the mansion to look for the missing first volume of the comic book. She finds it and reads a story about two men who used to be friends as children. They went canoeing one night, and only one came back. Margaret is sure now that Ratt is her uncle and the Drowning Ghost her father. There is another comic on the desk showing Sophie meeting Ratt and going with him to his canoe. Margaret and Boyd race back to the boathouse, where they take Boyd's parents' motorboat and go looking for Ratt and Sophie.

Meanwhile, Margaret's mother has discovered the girls are gone and is on her way to the island. While Ratt and Sophie are in the canoe, he tells her about growing up with her father, about turning into a rat, and about how her father tried to force him back into civilization four years ago. But before he can tell her how her father died, Margaret and Boyd arrive. When Sophie tries to jump into Boyd's boat and falls into the water, Margaret goes in after her, though neither can swim. Ratt rescues both of them, but he slips under the water before Margaret can question him.

Search-and-rescue squads look for Ratt while Margaret and Sophie are reunited with their mother, who finally tells them the truth. Four years ago, when her father tried to bring Ratt back to live with them, Ratt staged his own drowning death to convince his brother that he was dead so that he would leave him alone. Instead, Margaret's father jumped in to save him and accidentally drowned in the cold water.

By the next morning, the police still can't find Ratt's body. Margaret is sure that he is dead. As the family goes home on the ferry, Boyd and Ratt suddenly pull up alongside the ferry on Boyd's motorboat, and the girls and their mother wave a fond farewell to Ratt who isn't dead afterall. Margaret's mother decides to keep the house and let Ratt live there. Boyd begins showing the Ratt stories at school, and soon kids begin leaving small gifts at the door of the mansion to encourage Ratt to make multiple copies of the now popular comic books.

The Message: There are two sides to every story. Stories change depending on who is telling them. Each person has a story, and every person's story impacts everyone else's. In order to move on in our own stories, we have to find the answers to our important questions.

Who's It For?: 6th–8th grade. The content is fine for as young as fifth grade, but the complexity of the storytelling and multiple points of view may confuse a younger reader. The mysterious dark house, the Drowning Ghost, and the half-rodent man are mildly spooky but unlikely to faze middle schoolers who have placidly sat through all six *Star Wars* movies and the *Lord of the Rings* trilogy. The very real issues of parental death and bullying are dealt with sensitively and age-appropriately, and Sophie and Mr. Librarian's characters leaven some of the scary and sad scenes with humor. Owing to its happy ending, it's a pretty safe recommendation for those tweens who want "a scary book, but not *too* scary."

Why It Rocks:
•   **Voice:** Nickerson tells her story using four points of view that come together seamlessly and compliment one another beautifully: Margaret's first-person, Boyd's third-person, Ratt's comic panels (gorgeously inked by illustrator Sally Wern Comport and a quirky stand-alone story in their own right), and several italicized "Editor's Notes," which the reader discovers at the end have been written by Mr. Librarian, that curmudgeonly keeper of the world's slush pile.
•   **Plot:** Woven into this complex, offbeat mystery are timeless themes about the importance of stories—and our need to tell them—and how every person's story impacts and influences every other life story it touches. Although there were a few subplots that Nickerson didn't carry through as successfully as others (including one featuring an odd friend of Margaret's named Tina Louise who is knocked out by a baseball), overall this is an ambitious, thought-provoking first novel that shows a great deal of promise and deserves much more notice and praise than it initially received.
•   **Pacing:** This is a very plotty, deliberately paced novel. By adding a comic book component to her story, Nickerson tapped into a trend that was just beginning to go mainstream in popular culture, and it gives her book an added dimension. The format change, however, may slow some readers.
•   **Characterization:** Nickerson's characters are eccentric and unforgettable, especially anxious Margaret, with her fears of attacking Chihuahuas and killer bees;

lonesome Boyd, with his Peeping Tom tendencies; and the forlorn Ratt, who could have been saved from a life of isolation had he only learned how to reach out.

Hook It Up With: *Coraline* by Neil Gaiman and *The Curse of the Blue Figurine* by John Bellairs.

Read More about It:
Booklist: 04/01/02
Horn Book: July/August 2002
Kirkus Reviews: 03/15/02
Publishers Weekly: 04/15/02
School Library Journal: 04/01/02
Voice of Youth Advocates (V.O.Y.A.): 06/01/02

Shusterman, Neal. 2004. *The Schwa Was Here.* New York: Penguin Group. 228p.

The Story: Anthony "Antsy" Bonano is an eighth-grade Brooklynite, the wisecracking but average middle child in his boisterous Italian family. His classmate Calvin Schwa is functionally invisible. No matter what he says or does, this permanently nondescript kid always gets passed over. When the two meet, Antsy realizes he has gone to school with Calvin for years but never really noticed him. So Antsy suggests putting Calvin through a series of experiments to test his level of forgettableness, or as Antsy calls it, "The Schwa Effect."

After making him sing the national anthem in the boy's restroom while wearing an orange sombrero, and putting him through security at the airport with very little hubbub, Antsy is convinced that the Schwa really is invisible to most people. He quickly grasps the Schwa's moneymaking potential and sets up a series of jobs for the Schwa to undertake for cash, like slipping late homework into a teacher's briefcase or eavesdropping on cheerleaders to find out whom they like on the football team. But Antsy gets a little overconfident when he accepts a dare for the Schwa that involves sneaking into the apartment of Old Man Crawley, the meanest and richest man in Brooklyn, and stealing a dog dish from one of his twelve Afghan hounds.

Antsy and the Schwa make it into Crawley's apartment, only to discover that all of the dog dishes are nailed down. Crawley catches both of them and demands that they work as his dog walkers for the next 12 weeks or he will use his influence to get their fathers fired from their jobs. But it isn't long before Crawley informs Antsy that he wants him to perform a new job: entertaining his granddaughter Lexie, who is coming to stay. Antsy is apprehensive until he meets Lexie, who is smart and funny and also happens to be blind. Calvin also is smitten because Lexie seems to be able to sense his presence like no one else can. The two boys jockey for Lexie's attention, but she ends up falling for Antsy.

Things get complicated when Lexie accidentally kisses Antsy in front of Calvin, who storms off. Antsy goes to apologize, and the Schwa tells him the story of his missing mother: how she disappeared one day in the supermarket when he was five, leaving him in a shopping cart. How he cried and cried and no one seemed to notice or care. Calvin believes he is so forgettable that one day no one will remember him and he too will disappear. His own father, a housepainter brain-damaged from a fall, can hardly remember who he is. Later, he unveils to Antsy his big plan to get noticed: he has used his college fund to rent a giant billboard of his face. Unfortunately, the highway over which he rented the space has been closed for construction.

With a little detective work, Antsy discovers there was a very real explanation for Calvin's mother's disappearance, and he tells Calvin the truth: his mother didn't just disappear into thin air; she ran off with a supermarket employee. The Schwa questions his father about his mother's whereabouts, and his father reluctantly shows him a box of letters she sent to Calvin over the years. Antsy calls a few days later to find that Calvin's number has been disconnected and his house empty, like he was never there. Antsy is moved to draw an upside down "e," the symbol of a schwa ("the faint vowel sound in many unstressed syllables in the English language"), on every available surface in Brooklyn to prove Calvin's existence. He suspects Calvin has left in search of his mom, and his hunch is proven correct when he receives a letter six months later containing a picture of Calvin and his mom together.

In addition, there are a number of subplots, including Antsy's ongoing defini-tion of his role within his family, his parents' resolution to end their bickering by making real their dream of opening a restaurant, and Crawley's change from a crabby eccentric to a generous grandfather who is happy to help fund the Bonanos new restaurant and enjoys being "kidnapped," or taken out of his house to exciting new places once a month by Antsy and Lexie.

The Message: Invisibility is a state of mind. There are many different ways of being invisible in our society, including being of a certain age, race, or gender in any given situation. You don't have to let society decide to label you; you get to decide who you are and who you want to be. You are in charge of your destiny.

Who's It For?: 6th–8th grade. Despite the sophisticated themes, this is an easy read, mostly because of Antsy's wisecracking first-person narration and his down-to-earth philosophies, like, "Life is like a bad haircut. At first it looks awful, then you kind of get used to it." Tweens can definitely read between the lines to the substantial embedded themes, or they can just enjoy the rollicking plot. And lest you think I'm just loving this book from an adult perspective, I have to tell you it is one of my most popular booktalk titles. My middle school students are nuts about it. I own three copies, and they're never in.

There is no strong language, and the only violence occurs during a subplot involving Anthony's father's job as the product developer at a plastic factory. He brings home an allegedly unbreakable mannequin, dubbed "Manny Bullpucky," and asks Antsy and his friends to test it. They do everything from tossing it off a bridge to throwing it into the path of an oncoming subway train (which any New Yorker will tell you is extremely dangerous and could cause an accident or derailment). Parents who don't want to give their serious pranksters any more ideas may want to steer clear; everyone else: enjoy!

Why It Rocks:
- **Voice:** Antsy's wisecracking first-person narration will have middle school students chuckling in sympathy and recognition.
- **Plot:** There are many subtle, well-executed examples of societal invisibility woven throughout Shusterman's text: Antsy's invisibility as an average middle child in a big family, Lexie's invisibility as a person with a disability, and Crawley's invisibility as a senior citizen.
- **Pacing:** Decidedly measured. Readers really can't tell until more than halfway through the book if the Schwa is really invisible or if they're being treated to a little magical realism.
- **Characterization:** It's the small details that make Shusterman's wonderfully realized characters jump off the page, like the Schwa's famous paperclip collection, which symbolizes the importance of seemingly inconsequential objects. Instead of important documents, Calvin collects the instruments that hold them together. At one point, Antsy realizes he is like a paperclip, since his biggest talent is keeping peace between his parents, a talent that is completely taken for granted and never recognized like his siblings' academic smarts. Or the fact that forgettable Calvin's last name is also the name of the "most common vowel sound in the English language."

Hook It Up With: *Things Not Seen* by Andrew Clements (also in this chapter) and *Holes* by Louis Sachar.

Read More about It:
Booklist: 12/01/04
Horn Book: 04/01/05
Kirkus Reviews: 10/01/04
School Library Journal, starred: 10/01/04
V.O.Y.A. (Voice of Youth Advocates): 10/01/04

Weeks, Sarah. 2004. *So B. It.* New York: HarperCollins. 245p.

The Story: Ever since she can remember, 12-year-old Heidi has lived with Mama and Bernadette, the kind neighbor who lives on the other side of their adjoined apartment wall in Reno, Nevada. Mama is mentally disabled. She can't understand numbers, tell time, use money, or read. She also suffers from debilitating migraines. There are only 23 words in her limited vocabulary, among them *Heidi, 'Dette,* and *So B. It,* her name for herself. Bernadette found Mama standing outside the apartment building one day when Heidi was an infant, confused and alone. Mama walked into the apartment like she lived there, Bernadette discovered the door that connected their two apartments, and she has been caring for Mama and Heidi ever since.

Bernie, a prolific reader, suffers from agoraphobia, so she schools Heidi at home. Whenever they run low on cash, Heidi disguises herself in Bernie's clothes and plays the slot machine at the local Laundromat. Owing to her uncanny luck, she always wins, but Bernie warns her not to abuse her talent, so she never takes more than they need. Bernie pays her own utility bills once a month, but she has never seen a bill delivered to Mama's apartment. She simply accepts this as another aspect of Heidi's luck.

As Heidi grows older, she can't help but wonder where she and Mama came from and who her father is. She believes that one of the clues to her background is Mama's nonsense word *soof,* which neither she nor Bernie knows the meaning of. Heidi finds an old camera hidden in the back of a kitchen drawer, gets the film developed, and discovers the film contains images of her mother, younger and pregnant, attending a Christmas party at a place called Hilltop Home in Liberty, New York. Bernie looks up the phone number for Hilltop, but the operator there won't answer her questions. After three weeks of unsuccessful calls, Heidi decides to take matters into her own hands and travel to Liberty on her own. Bernie vehemently disagrees, but Heidi insists and uses the slots to get money for her bus ticket.

On her three-day journey, Heidi sits with two different women who have strong family ties and connections, making Heidi long even more to know her own roots. She checks in with Bernie by phone at each stop. When she finally arrives in Liberty, she is tired and has lost all her money to a pickpocket in New York City. She uses her lucky streak to guess the number of jelly beans in a jar at the local cab company and wins a ride to Hilltop Home, an assisted-living center for mentally disabled adults.

At Hilltop Home, Heidi meets Ruby, one of the home's nursing aides; Mr. Hill, the owner; and his disabled adult son, Elliot, who seems oddly familiar to her. She shows Mr. Hill her pictures, and he grows angry, accuses her of extorting money from him, and orders her to leave. Heidi is sad and confused but agrees to leave and spend the night with Ruby and her kind husband, Roy, the local sheriff. The next day, Roy takes her back to Hilltop to meet with Mr. Hill and his lawyer. Right before she leaves, Bernie calls and tells Heidi she needs her to come home right away, but Heidi is so excited to finally hear the truth about herself that she impatiently gets off the phone and runs to Roy's car.

At Hilltop, Mr. Hill finally tells her the truth: a local woman named Diane DeMuth had a brain-damaged child named Sophia, who is Heidi's Mama. Diane talked Mr. Hill into accepting Sophia into Hilltop for free when she was a young woman. Sophia lived there for a year and became best friends with Mr. Hill's son, Elliot. Diane came to Mr. Hill and claimed that Sophia was pregnant and Elliot was the father. In order to save the reputation of Hilltop and keep his son from Sophia and her mother, Mr. Hill agreed to pay all of Diane's living expenses if she took Sophia far away and never contacted Mr. Hill again. When Bernie called asking for information, Mr. Hill thought it was Diane asking for more money. Mr. Hill's lawyer tells Heidi that Diane was killed in a bus accident that took place near her house in Reno, right around the same time Bernie found Mama and Heidi. Their bills continued to be paid by the account Mr. Hill set up for Diane and Sophia. "Soof" was how Elliot pronounced Sofia, and "So B. It" was how Sofia pronounced her own name.

Ecstatic to know the truth, Heidi calls Bernie only to hear the sad news that Mama had died in her sleep after a particularly bad headache. Heidi is devastated and stays with Roy and Ruby until Mama's body can be flown to Liberty for burial. Roy and Ruby ask her if she would like to live with them, but Heidi wants to go back to Bernie. After she comes home from Liberty, Heidi seems to have lost her lucky streak.

But Roy and Ruby claim she must have passed it on to them: Ruby gives birth to a baby girl after years of trying to have children.

The Message: Not knowing all the facts of a situation leaves room to imagine. Everyone has the need to know where they come from. Whether you know your family background or not, you still have worth and value as a person in your own right. Sometimes you have to make your own luck.

Who's It For?: 6th–8th grade. Similar in tone to books like *Harry Sue* by Sue Stauffacher and *Bud, Not Buddy* by Christopher Paul Curtis, Weeks tackles tough topics in an age-appropriate manner. There are discussions of mental illness, under-age gambling, and nonmarital birth, but Weeks breaks these subjects down into kid-sized bites that students can understand and empathize with. Although Weeks focuses far more on the mystery of Heidi's origins than on her mother's mental illness, this is a comforting and sympathetic read for kids who may have mentally ill adults or relatives in their lives.

A fun approach to booktalking this title that lightens the somewhat somber aspects of the story is to come to class with the list of So B. It's 23 words. Ask students that if they had only a handful of words, what would they be? How few could they get by on and still get across what they needed and wanted?

Why It Rocks:
• **Voice:** While readers may have to suspend disbelief about Heidi's incredible luck and atypical circumstances, her simultaneously wise and naive first-person narration makes it all feel true.
• **Plot:** Weeks takes the archetypal quest-for-identity story and does it up differently in this bittersweet novel that is an unusual mix of mystery, magical realism, and old-fashioned tearjerker.
• **Pacing:** Deliberate and revealing. Weeks carefully plants clues but does a nice job of keeping So B. It's history a secret until Heidi is strong enough to hear the truth.
• **Characterization:** The secondary characters are well rounded, especially tender, open-space-challenged Bernie and brokenhearted Ruby, who still keeps drawers full of clothes for the babies she has lost.

Hook It Up With: *My Louisiana Sky* by Kimberly Willis Holt and *Becoming Naomi Leon* by Pam Munoz Ryan.

Read More about It:
Booklist, starred: 06/01/04
Horn Book, starred: 07/01/04
Kirkus Reviews: 05/15/04
Publishers Weekly: 05/31/04
School Library Journal: 07/01/04

Winerip, Michael. 2005. *Adam Canfield of the Slash*. Cambridge, MA: Candlewick. 336p.

The Story: Eighth grader Adam Canfield and his best friend, Jennifer, are the current coeditors of the *Slash*, the student newspaper of Harris Elementary/Middle School. Phoebe, an overenthusiastic third grader, is one of their new cub reporters. As the school year starts, two stories come to their attention that will put everything they've learned as ethical and responsible reporters to the test. First, Jennifer notices a short article in the local paper mentioning that the zoning board has decided to enforce an old law that states, "accessory structures in the front half of a housing lot" must be removed. Jennifer has a hunch that *accessory* includes freestanding basketball hoops but leaves the investigation to Adam. Next, the coeditors become suspicious when their tyrannical principal, Mrs. Marris, orders them to write an article about a local woman named Minnie Bloch, who died recently and left the Harris school district a large amount of money to be used for "general improvements." But she refuses to tell Adam and Jennifer what those improvements are or how much money was gifted to the school.

Adam does some digging and finds out that Minnie Bloch lived in one of poorest neighborhoods in town. When he goes to see her house, he runs into her neighbor, Mrs. Willard, who tells him that Miss Bloch was extremely frugal and had saved almost half a million dollars. She also tells him that as executor of Miss Bloch's will, she knows that $75,000 of that money was left to the school, with the understanding it would be spent on the students themselves. Meanwhile, Phoebe has written a story about the school's kind, long suffering janitor, Eddie, who mentions in his interview that he is currently working on installing a posh new bathroom adjoining Mrs. Marris's office.

Adam is also trying to get the definition of the meaning of *accessory structure* from zoning board enforcement officers Herb Black and Herb Green, but he can't seem to get past their obfuscating secretary. Jennifer suggests visiting them in person during a teacher in-service day and, with some fancy verbal footwork, getting the Herbs to admit that Mrs. Boland, the zoning board chair and wife of Sumner Boland, local media mogul, is determined to rid the town of "unsightly" driveway hoops. Adam and Jennifer decide to push back the Bloch article until they have more information, and the October issue of the *Slash* contains the basketball hoop story and Phoebe's story on Eddie the janitor. Mrs. Marris looks over the proofs and tells them to remove the mention of her new bathroom. Suddenly, the editors realize where Miss Bloch's money is going.

Mrs. Boland sees the student paper and warns Mrs. Marris that she should better control her reporters or find a new job. Meanwhile, Adam and Jennifer receive plenty of positive feedback about the issue from both kids and parents, since many of the members of the community are fed up with the subjective pap being produced by Sumner Boland, who owns all the local papers and television stations. A lawyer who's been hired by one of the families to protest the hoop law contacts Jennifer to let her know that the judge on the case has granted a temporary restraining order against the removal of the hoops that's likely to become permanent because of the huge outpouring of criticism against the law, generated by the *Slash* article.

Jennifer, Adam, and Phoebe focus on collecting more proof that Mrs. Marris is using the Bloch money for herself. They discover that Eddie has work-order slips for all the jobs he has completed for the school, including Mrs. Marris's gold-plated bathroom. Using the slips and a copy of Miss Bloch's will, Adam and Jennifer write up their exposé. Knowing that Mrs. Marris will never approve the piece, they put together a plan with the help of the *Slash* staff to e-mail everyone they know an electronic version of the article. Then they deliver the proofs to Mrs. Marris, who threatens them with expulsion, an indelible stain on their permanent record.

As planned, Adam still orders the e-mail to go out. Phones start ringing, and heads begin to roll. Mrs. Marris disappears, and all that the school board will say is that she has taken a leave of absence to care for a sick relative. With their permanent records and basketball hoops intact, Adam and Jennifer, with Phoebe's help, begin planning the next issue of the *Slash*.

The Message: The truth depends on who's doing the telling. Media should strive to be objective but can be biased. It's important to understand the difference between fact and opinion. Kids are often much smarter than adults give them credit for.

Who's It For?: 6th–8th grade. The squeaky-clean content is fine for as young as fourth grade, but younger readers probably won't get all the sly embedded jokes about media bias and personal ethics. This is a wickedly funny and outrageously smart tween read, where kids rule and adults are forced to give them their due. Recommend this one to every soccer mom and her kids who come past your reference desk.

Why It Rocks:
- **Voice:** Pulitzer Prize-winning *New York Times* reporter Winerip provides third-person narration for Adam (and occasionally Phoebe), whose point of view is smart and funny and blithely assumes that his intended middle school audience is sophisticated enough to get his jokes. They are, and they do.
- **Plot:** Winerip's brilliant and hilarious satirizations of everything from biased media to standardized testing are often humorous and always thought provoking. Students see through "Multicultural Month," where they tried recipes from other countries but "never talked about the real stuff that went on between different kids at school." Adam is on the verge of being "enriched to death" because of his monstrous schedule: jazz band, Math Olympiad, Geography Challenge, soccer, swimming, and, of course, the "Say No to Drugs Community Players." Adam's parents' friends and neighbors start asking for subscriptions to the relatively objective *Slash*, because Sumner Boland (clearly a send-up of Rupert Murdoch) has bought all the local papers and merged them into one bland, biased publication entitled "The Tremble County Citizen-Gazette-Herald-Advertiser." Take your pick: the opportunities for classroom discussion are endless.
- **Pacing:** Crisp and well maintained. Readers will have to work at keeping the two strands of Adam's exposés straight, but Winerip makes the ride so much fun that they will enjoy every minute of it.
- **Characterization:** Although Adam, Jennifer, and Phoebe are like the super-smart, well-spoken versions of the real middle school students we know and love,

tweens will easily relate to them, since they believe themselves to be just as clever and precocious as they see themselves portrayed in the media.

Hook It Up With: *Hoot* by Carl Hiassen and *The School Story* by Andrew Clements.

Read More about It:
Booklist: 05/01/05
Horn Book: 10/01/05
Kirkus Reviews: 04/01/05
Publishers Weekly, starred: 04/01/05
School Library Journal: 03/01/05

CHAPTER 5

TRUE GRIT: THE MOST CHALLENGING (AND POSSIBLY CHALLENGED) TITLES

INTRODUCTION

Oh, dear. You knew we were going to have to deal with the hard stuff sooner or later, so here are my favorite parental button–pushing titles that deal with touchy topics like sex, drugs, violence, strong language, child abuse, murder, questioning of adult authority, and challenging of religious beliefs. "Why are these scary books being published for innocent adolescents?" parents moan, and "Why, oh why, is the public or school librarian promoting this trash to my precious teen angel?" Why indeed. At some point in your career, you will have to defend all that "trash" in your collection. Will you be ready? Besides having stacks of challenge forms next to my computer, here is how I have come to respond to parents and other members of the adult tribe who wonder why gritty reality fiction is so appealing to teens (and so appalling to grown-ups).

Adolescence is a time of awakening. The innocence and security of childhood are being replaced by serious disillusionment and endless questions. Teens see mixed messages about their bodies, sexuality, and politics on television, in movies and video games, and even in advertisements as they walk down the street. They are looking for reading that reflects what they see around them but that will also help them decode what they see. Inevitably, topics such as sex, drugs, and body image are going to come up in conversations among their peers, and they naturally want to decide how these topics fit into their burgeoning belief systems. As librarians, we know that when teens get the lowdown from a skillful and compassionate young adult author, it is preferable to their receiving misinformation from a friend or experimenting with dangerous behavior themselves. It's also far better for teens to get this content from a book as opposed to video games, movies, and other popular media, where graphic imagery meant to entertain adults is provided to adolescents, who can't always look at these stereotyped and otherwise distorted images with the sense of irony or detachment that their parents will.

Teens are going to seek out information on these topics whether or not their parents want them to. They want to read about sex, drugs, and rock and roll because they are developmentally curious. It is our duty to make sure that books on these subjects, both fiction and nonfiction, are available when they come looking. Anything less, and we are not fulfilling our commitment to teen services. And let's be brutally honest—the juiciest sex scene or most violent street fight depicted in a morally complex and multilayered YA novel doesn't even come close to being as graphic as what teens have seen depicted on *Sex and the City* or in a Quentin Tarantino movie or while playing *Grand Theft Auto*. Instead of hiding the darker side of life from teens, we need to help parents understand that it is okay to let teens discover those truths, when they feel ready, at the hands of an articulate and understanding young adult author.

Now, considering the potential for challenges, will you want to booktalk these titles to classroom groups? Maybe not across the board, but they are certainly excellent choices for one-on-one recommendations when a teen comes to you asking for a book on any of these gritty topics. Use your own good judgment.

You may also notice that these summaries are quite a bit shorter than some of the other selections. That's because, even more so than for any of the other titles in this book, you must READ these titles before recommending them. Too much detail, and you might be tempted to just go on my words—and that would be a mistake. This content is heavy. Take the time to read these titles and give them the serious consideration they deserve while thinking about your own community and teen audience.

Burgess, Melvin. 2003. *Doing It*. New York: Henry Holt. 336p.

The Story: Dino, Ben, and Jonathan are three British teenage boys attempting to navigate messy sexual relationships with a limited understanding of the opposite sex. Dino is the informal leader of the trio, mostly because of his phenomenal good looks and confidence with the ladies. He is on the brink of scoring with Jackie, the best-looking girl in school, when his family life begins to unravel. Dino discovers that his mother is having an affair, and in a fit of anger, he reveals that fact to his father.

As his parents begin to negotiate a divorce, Dino struggles with his new and not entirely welcome knowledge of adult relationships while trying to date Jackie and a new girl named Zoe at the same time. Bookish Ben finds himself fulfilling every schoolboy's dream when his sexy drama teacher, Miss Young, makes a pass at him and they embark on a secret sexual relationship. But when he begins to realize how out of his depth he is, he attempts to end things with the unstable and emotionally immature teacher. She cuts her wrists in response. Fearing he will never be free of her, Ben enlists the dubious help of Miss Young's domineering mother, who sweeps in and neatly dispatches her out of school, but not before scolding the astonished Ben about his taking advantage of Miss Young's "vulnerability."

In perhaps the most humorous story line, worrywart Jonathan is torn between what his friends' opinions are and how he really feels about dating Deborah, an overweight classmate. As he tries to decide if he is strong enough to go public with his romance, he is horrified to discover a mysterious bump on his penis and has to go through an agonizing visit with a female doctor, where he finds out that it's just a large vein. At book's end, each boy has muddled through his problems more or less successfully, but it is Dino who has the last word when he characteristically ends up seducing the one girl Ben has had his eye on since ditching Miss Young.

The Message: Be true to yourself. Young men and women are equally mystified by sexual relationships. Question authority. Parents and other adults don't always make the right choices or have the best interest in mind of the teenagers in their lives.

Who's It For?: 10th–12th grade. The title and titillating cover art offer ample warning about what lies between the covers. So, hopefully, older teens won't be too surprised by the long, descriptive, almost gleefully constructed paragraphs about shagging, snogging, wanking off, licking, groping, bum grabbing, boob feeling, and "knobby knobster"(Jonathan's name for his penis) handling. While younger readers are certainly going to be curious about the contents, it's unlikely they will be developmentally interested past the first page, and the Britishisms for making out are apt to add even more confusion.

There is no doubt that reading *Doing It* has generated a great many teenaged sighs of relief, from both male readers, who believed themselves to be the only ones suffering from sex on the brain, and female readers, who may be shocked to realize that boys are just as anxiety ridden about sex as they are. For that reason alone, you need this book in your YA collection.

Why It Rocks:
- **Voice:** Burgess messily switches back and forth from first- to third-person narration within the same chapter with little or no warning, making it hard to determine whose point of view the reader is supposed to be following.
- **Plot:** Burgess deserves props for being brutally honest when it comes to telling the truth about how much time adolescent boys spend thinking about, well, *doing it.*
- **Pacing:** Tangential. Burgess indulges in several subplots, including drawn-out reactions from the females in Dino's life, when he would have been better off getting on with the, er, action.
- **Characterization:** In terms of writing, Burgess has done better, and this is not the best example of his wordsmith skills. There is little character development, and the boys' voices are static and interchangeable.

Hook It Up With: *Girls for Breakfast* by David Yoo and *Funny Little Monkey* by Andrew Auseon.

Read More about It:
Booklist: 06/01/04
Horn Book: 07/01/04
Kirkus Reviews: 05/01/04
Publishers Weekly: 04/26/04
School Library Journal: 06/01/04
V.O.Y.A. (Voice of Youth Advocates): 06/01/04

Crutcher, Chris. 2001. *Whale Talk.* **New York: HarperCollins. 220p.**

The Story: Tao Jones (T.J.) is an adopted multiracial teen who lives with his loving, retro-hippie parents in a rural Northwestern town. His rocky beginnings with a crack-addicted biological mother have left him with a big chip on his shoulder. Luckily, between his New Age parents, an understanding therapist named Georgia, and his girlfriend Carly, T.J. usually manages to keep his anger under control.

Although T.J. is athletically gifted, he stays away from organized sports at Cutter High, because he is philosophically opposed to the cultlike status commanded by the school athletes. When his teacher and mentor, Mr. Simit, asks him to help start a brand-new school swim team, T.J. sees it as an opportunity to rally Cutter's so-called "losers" to a common cause and stick it to the jocks at the same time. T.J. is bound and determined that every single guy on the swim team will earn his own letter jacket, an act that will annoy the jocks to no end.

There are a number of subplots, including T.J.'s connection with a bi-racial toddler named Heidi, whose racist stepfather, a former Cutter High football hero named Rich Marshall, is teaching her to hate her brown skin; and T.J.'s attempt to help a developmentally disabled student face down his bullying tormentors. There is also his struggle to understand why his easygoing father can't seem to forgive himself for a tragic accident he was involved in that caused the death of a toddler over 30 years ago.

As tensions build at both school and home, T.J. works hard to control his anger over Heidi's hopeless situation and the jocks' relentless bullying of the swim team. In a bittersweet finish, the team earns their letter jackets, but T.J.'s father is killed when he takes a bullet from Rich Marshall's gun that was intended for Heidi. T.J.'s father dies in his arms, finally feeling at peace that although he was responsible for the death of one child, he had saved another.

The Message: Parents are people, too—even the best make mistakes. Learn to take personal responsibility for your actions. Love yourself even when outside forces are giving you reasons not to. It's okay to be angry, but understand why and try to direct anger into a positive outcome. Racism and bullying are wrong but apathy toward these responses is no better.

Who's It For?: 8th–12th grade. This has been a frequently challenged book, owing to Crutcher's forthright attitude about, well, everything. Teens and adults curse freely and realistically, Heidi's therapy includes acting out her anger by beating on her black dolls and calling them the "N" word, and Rich Marshall is portrayed as a drunken, proud racist who hits his wife and children. There is a violent hunting scene near the beginning and a terribly sad scene at the end where T.J.'s father is killed.

It is widely known that Chris Crutcher is a child and family therapist. Even when he frankly discusses topics like child abuse and violent bullying, he does so in a way that is emotional yet also slightly clinical—a writing style that gives Crutcher's many fans breathing space away from the tough topics he tends to address in his work.

Why It Rocks:
- **Voice:** Crutcher employs his signature raw and immediate first-person narration, and if T.J. occassionally sounds more mature than your average high school student, well, the guy was raised by hippies and provided with extensive anger management therapy.
- **Plot:** Is it over the top? Yes. Melodramatic and emotionally messy? Absolutely. But teens love Crutcher's black-and-white universe, where adults are either angels or demons and teen characters are left to navigate the gray area in between.
- **Pacing:** Wandering, but potent. Each subplot Crutcher indulges in packs an emotional wallop.
- **Characterization:** "Crutcher never fails to come up with unique character details that stay with the reader long after the book's finished, like the quote that inspired the novel's title. T.J.'s dad tells him that whale calls can be heard for thousands of miles and once voiced, can't be edited or changed. "Whale talk is truth."

Hook It Up With: *Staying Fat for Sarah Byrnes*, also by Chris Crutcher, and *Tangerine* by Edward Bloor.

Read More about It:
Booklist: 04/01/01
Horn Book: 05/01/01
Kirkus Reviews: 03/01/ 01
Publishers Weekly, starred: 03/12/01
School Library Journal: 05/01/01

Frank, E. R. 2002. America: A Novel. New York: Simon & Schuster. 242p.

The Story: America, so named by his drug-addicted teenage mother because his father could be just about anyone in America, is a lost child. He is lost to his foster family, lost to the social welfare system, and lost to himself.

America's problems begin when he is taken from his loving foster mother, Mrs. Harper, when he is five years old and sent to stay with his biological mother for a short visit. She leaves America and his two half-brothers alone in the apartment to go buy drugs and never returns. The three little boys more or less fend for themselves for weeks until they are discovered by a police officer. America then becomes just another neglected child of the welfare system, drowned by a sea of paperwork and red tape.

By the time America is returned to Mrs. Harper, he has lost all innocence and trust. He is sexually molested by her adult son, Browning, and to escape the situation, runs away after setting fire to Browning's blanket as he sleeps. America finds himself alone in the world of the homeless and halfway houses. After attempting suicide, he comes under the care of Dr. B., a compassionate therapist who refuses to give up on him, even when America physically assaults him. It is as a series of complex and layered first-person flashbacks during his therapy sessions with Dr. B that America's story is told. And it is with Dr. B's help that America is finally able to put his past to rest and look hopefully toward his future.

The Message: Families can be found in the most unlikely of places, and help can come from unexpected sources.

Who's It For?: 9th–12th grade. The dialogue is authentic and real, which means plenty of strong language. Author Emily Frank is a social worker and therapist, and she pulls no punches when realistically describing disturbing scenes of child neglect, sexual abuse, drug use, street violence and suicide. This is powerful, heavy material that is best suited to readers aged 14 and older.

Why It Rocks:
• **Voice:** Frank's channeling of America's voice is chillingly, achingly real. Teen readers will be astonished to discover that the author of this incredible and haunting creation is a petite, white social worker from New Jersey.
• **Plot:** While many of America's situations are bleak and horrific, Frank's treatment of the material is subtle, sympathetic, and never sensationalistic.
• **Pacing:** Frank's polished use of flashbacks allows the reader to draw breath between some of the more brutal episodes of America's life,
• **Characterization:** The irony of Frank's title blends perfectly with her seamless characterization of America. He is just one lost child, but he could be any lost child. He belongs to and is the responsibility of us all. The soothing background character of Dr. B. provides a strong counterpoint to many of the other disreputable adults America encounters on his journey.

Hook It Up With: *The Buffalo Tree* by Adam Rapp and *Speak* by Laurie Halse Anderson.

Read More about It:
Booklist, starred: 02/15/02
Horn Book, starred: 9/2002
Kirkus Reviews, starred: 10/15/01
Publishers Weekly, starred: 01/07/02
School Library Journal, starred: 03/01/02

Hopkins, Ellen. 2004. *Crank.* New York: Simon & Schuster. 537p.

The Story: Seventeen-year-old self-described "good girl" Kristina Snow cajoles her mother into allowing her to visit her ne'er-do-well divorced father over summer vacation. Adam, a hunky neighbor boy in her father's apartment complex, introduces her to the drug crystal meth, or "crank." While under the influence of the drug, Kristina morphs into her alter ego, Bree, a fearless bad girl. She and Adam are caught snorting crank by her dad, a user himself, who, in the novel's most surrealistic scene, joins them in taking the drug.

When Kristina returns home to Reno, she hopes that things will go back to normal, but the voice of Bree is too strong. At her stepfather's company picnic, she meets two different boys, Chase and Brendan. Chase is the good guy, Brendan the bad boy, but they are both able to supply Bree with crank. She manages for a time to balance dating both boys with her escalating drug habit, but her parents are noticing her distant behavior at home, and her grades are plummeting at school.

Everything comes crashing down when Brendan date-rapes Kristina while they are both high. She drops him and confesses what happened to Chase, who is concerned and wants her to stop using. Now she is forced to find another source of crank and partners up with Robyn, a cheerleader who shows Kristina how to smoke crank instead of snort it, which leads to a more intense high. Soon she is trying other drugs like Ecstasy. She sneaks out while grounded and is picked up by a police officer for being out past curfew. She spends the night in jail, and subsequently, finds a new drug connection that allows her to become a dealer. Kristina finds herself using more and more crank, until she discovers she's pregnant—and the baby is Brendan's. She agonizes over what to do, finally opting to have the baby even though she's terrified of the possibility of drug-induced birth defects. Chase offers to marry her, but Kristina isn't in love with him and refuses to ruin his future. She delivers a baby boy and is raising him with her parents' help, but she still hears the siren call of the intoxicating drug and is occasionally using by book's end.

The Message: Don't do drugs (or hang out with people who do)!

Who's It For? 8th–12th grade. Kristina's rape is emotionally devastating to read, but the act itself is not graphically depicted. There is some strong language and descriptions of how to use drugs.

Why It Rocks:
• **Voice:** Told in poetic first-person free verse, *Crank* is basically a better-written and sorely needed modernized version of *Go Ask Alice*.
• **Plot:** Hopkins tells readers honestly from page one who she is (the mother of a former crank addict) and which parts of the autobiographical novel are based in truth. Unlike some of the situations in *Go Ask Alice*, nothing that happens to Kristina throughout the course of the story seems melodramatic or gratuitous. It is all too frighteningly realistic and, therefore, much more effective.
• **Pacing:** A bit long-winded. This book could have been cut in half and still been a forceful, persuasive read. The length may turn off some reluctant readers who are drawn to the topic.
• **Characterization:** Kristina is a well-drawn character, but many of the secondary characters seem a bit outrageous, especially her crank-addicted father.

Hook It Up With: *Go Ask Alice* by Beatrice Sparks and *Smack* by Melvin Burgess

Read More about It:
Booklist: 11/15/04
Kirkus Reviews: 10/01/04
Publishers Weekly: 11/01/04
School Library Journal: 11/01/04
V.O.Y.A (Voice of Youth Advocates): 02/01/05

Jacobson, Jennifer Richard. 2005. *Stained*. New York: Simon & Schuster. 200p.

The Story: It is 1975 in the small, primarily Catholic town of Weaver Falls, New Hampshire, where 17-year-old Jocelyn finds her identity and spirituality being called into question by three very different men. First, there is Gabe, the next-door neighbor whom she has secretly been in love with since they were children. Despite the fact that Gabe has bullied and abandoned her on many occasions, she is more than just a little concerned when he doesn't show up one day at their shared summer job and is subsequently declared missing.

Second, there is Benny, a new boy at her school whom she has been dating for the past few months. Lately, Benny has been pushing her away, claiming to be experiencing massive guilt over their lusty make-out sessions. His mother is terminally ill, and Benny has decided that forgoing sexual pleasure with Joss will somehow balance the spiritual scales in his mother's favor.

Finally, there is Father Warren, the parish priest who has seemingly gained the admiration and trust of the town's young people since he moved to Weaver Falls about a year and a half ago. Benny has told Joss that Father Warren believes she is a sexual temptation to him and that he should stay away from her. Even though Joss is a lapsed Catholic, she is devastated by Benny's admission, mostly due to guilt she still feels over an incident that took place the summer before seventh grade. Gabe and his cousin Jay pulled Joss's clothes off against her will, groped her, and then told everyone she let them. Because of this malicious gossip, Joss's only friends since seventh grade have been bookworm Theresa and Benny.

When Joss goes to confront Father Warren concerning his comments about her to Benny, she spies an old picture of Gabe on his desk. Putting together what she knows about Father Warren's pointed and borderline inappropriate conversations with Benny and his closeness with Gabe's crowd, she suddenly knows where Gabe is and why he has run away. Returning to the clubhouse in the woods where they played as children, Joss discovers Gabe, and he admits that he and Father Warren were having a sexual relationship. During the course of the conversation, Joss finds the strength to talk about her molestation and tell Gabe that it was his fault, not hers.

Even though Joss promises not to tell his parents where he is, Gabe runs again the next day, this time to another state. Joss tells everything she suspects to her mother and Gabe's parents. Gabe stays away, sending only a torn lottery ticket to Joss later in an envelope with no return address to let her know he is okay. Later that summer, at Benny's mother's funeral, with a new priest officiating, Joss finally feels free of the guilt and fear that has "stained" her soul for so long.

Message: Spirituality is personal and experienced individually. Spirituality and religion are not necessarily mutually exclusive. No one has the right to label or judge you based on religion. Some secrets should not be kept, especially if someone is being hurt.

Who's It For? 9th–12th grade. The content is not graphic, but the molestation incident is emotionally upsetting. Older readers will better understand and identify with the challenging underlying themes of spirituality and manipulation that are embedded in the text.

Why It Rocks:
• **Voice:** Joss's first-person voice is the wounded, contemplative voice of an outsider looking in. Some critics were not happy with Jacobson's choice to not explain the priest's motivations, but this is Joss's version of story, not Father Warren's. Ask any teen and they will tell you that they are often completely baffled by the reasons behind the decisions adults in their lives make in real life, let alone in fiction. Joss may never have found out why Father Warren did what he did, but that, unfortunately, is life, and teens understand that.
• **Plot:** Even though the main story line of *Stained* deals with the uncomfortable topic of church sex offenders, it would be a mistake to dismiss this subtly written book as just another issue-driven novel. Jacobson uses the topic of religion as a jumping-off point to explore broader ideas of self-worth and identity and the definition of truth.
• **Pacing:** Thoughtful. Jacobson gives teens time to think about her deep themes as Joss guides them quietly through her reflective, introspective story.
• **Characterization:** Although the story is told from Joss's point of view, Jacobson also writes quietly moving portrayals of Benny and Gabe that make them far more sympathetic than villainous. Each of these teens becomes a fully rounded character by book's end.

Hook It Up With: *The Last Safe Place on Earth* by Richard Peck and *Send Me Down a Miracle* by Han Nolan.

Read More about It:
Booklist: 04/01/05
Horn Book: March/April 05
Kirkus Reviews, starred: 03/01/05
Publishers Weekly: 02/21/05
School Library Journal: 03/01/05
V.O.Y.A. (Voice of Youth Advocates): 04/01/05

Johnson, Kathleen Jeffrie. 2003. *Target*. New York: Roaring Brook Press. 175p.

The Story: Sixteen-year-old Grady West is walking home one night when he is brutally beaten and raped in the back of a van by two anonymous male strangers. Now, Grady defines his life in terms of "Before" and "After" the horrific event. He is silent, unable to eat, and can't bear to be touched. After Grady refuses any type of therapy, his parents decide that their only course of action is to transfer him to a new school and hope that he can manage to put the past behind him.

The rape is never far from Grady's mind, and he finds himself constantly wondering if he didn't fight back hard enough and if being the target of such an attack means he is gay. His silence attracts the attention of Jess, a dramatic male African American student whose endless clowning and outrageous speech beg an audience like Grady, who won't talk back. Grady also begins to make a connection with Pearl, a quiet, overweight girl in his art class.

Grady's anxiety level rises, however, when Gwendolyn, a student reporter who smells a story, starts asking too many questions. Then one of his friends from his old school, Tracy, sees him at the local library with Jess and demands to know why he left town so abruptly. Jess knows something is wrong after meeting Tracy, and arranges for he and Grady to meet back at the library with Tracy and Ted, Grady's old best friend. Grady has no idea what Jess has done until Tracy and Ted sit down next to him. With both of them anxiously questioning Grady, he becomes withdrawn and is unable to speak.

While Grady is still in shock, Gwendolyn shows up with a copy of the article on rape that she plans to publish in the school paper. Jess chases her off but not before everyone sees a copy of the article and finally puts the pieces together about Grady's past. Now that everyone knows, Grady can't believe that instead of disgust they all show acceptance and sympathy as they wait for him to feel well enough to discuss "the Night of" with them. The book ends with Grady on the shaky road to recovery with the support of all of his friends, both new and old.

The Message: Boys are just as vulnerable as girls when it comes sexual abuse. Healing from great trauma takes time and patience. Friends can be valuable resources in times of trouble, if allowed to be. Becoming a victim isn't always a choice, but staying one is.

Who's It For?: 9th–12th grade. Johnson made the choice to graphically describe the rape in detail, which, to my middle school-oriented mind, automatically makes *Target* a book for 14 and up. In addition, Grady has sexually explicit thoughts about both Pearl and Fred, an out gay student, as he tries to understand if the attack affected his sexuality. Jess's language is politically incorrect, to say the least, and may offend some readers; however, his racial, gender, and sexual-orientation sentiments are certainly nothing that most high school students haven't either heard or voiced themselves. While Jess's frankness may shock some adult readers, older teens have most likely seen and heard all this before.

Why It Rocks:
• **Voice:** Johnson's third-person prose feels fresh and original, and other than a rather heavy-handed bird metaphor, she carefully stays away from cliché and instead

peppers her writing with evocative phrases such as, "unhappiness peeling off his skin like a scent."

• **Plot:** *Target* is one of the first books to deal with the sexual abuse of a young man instead of a young woman. Johnson painstakingly details the long, awful minutes of Grady's days, where he endlessly goes over the incident in his mind, trying to understand what made him a target.

• **Pacing:** Almost excruciatingly slow. The reader is forced to travel each awful postrape day with Grady, with the only motivation to finish being the hope that Grady finds his way out of his lonely mental prison.

• **Characterization:** Grady's journey is a dark and painful one, and not a very easy or enjoyable to read. Still, it will serve as an invaluable resource to any teen who has ever been sexually abused. Some comparisons to Laurie Halse Anderson's *Speak*, a Printz Honor novel, are bound to come to mind, but *Target* stands on its own as a powerful and raw character study.

Hook It Up With: *When Jeff Comes Home* by Catherine Atkins, *When She Hollers* by Cynthia Voigt, and *I Hadn't Meant to Tell You This* by Jacqueline Woodson.

Read More about It:
Booklist: 11/15/03
Kirkus Reviews, starred: 08/01/03
Publishers Weekly: 11/03/03
School Library Journal: 12/01/03
V.O.Y.A. (Voice of Youth Advocates): 02/01/04

Nolan, Han. 2001. *Born Blue.* New York: Harcourt. 277p.

The Story: Janie's mother is a heroin addict who almost allowed her to drown when she was four years old. Since then, Janie has lived in a foster home with Harmon, an African American boy whose prized possession is a shoebox full of cassette tapes. Harmon's tapes are all recordings by "the ladies," Aretha Franklin, Billie Holiday, and Janie's favorite, Etta James. The two children dream of futures with real families as they listen endlessly to the tapes in the basement of their foster home. It is there that Janie's lifelong dream to become a singer is born.

Even though Janie has blond hair and blue eyes, she wishes her skin were dark like Harmon's or Doris's (Doris is their cheerful social worker). When the Jameses, an affluent African American family, adopt Harmon, Janie is bereft. Her biological mother, Linda, kidnaps her from her foster parents and trades her to a mixed-race, drug-dealing couple named Mitch and Shelly in exchange for heroin. While living with them, Janie discovers the power of her voice and renames herself Leshaya, after her beloved Doris's daughter. She speaks ebonically, tells her classmates she is really black, and claims Mitch, who is African American, is her real father.

When Mitch and Shelly are arrested, 12-year-old Leshaya runs to Harmon, the only person she can trust. She lives with the Jameses for a short while, going to school and singing in the church choir. But when they attempt to get her to admit to lying and stealing some of Mrs. James's jewelry, she runs again, this time to a small Southern town where she had heard Etta James had once recorded. From here, Leshaya's life tumbles downward. Essentially homeless, she fronts a few different bands, going home with whomever will let her crash on their couch. She becomes pregnant and leaves the baby with the Jameses before racing off again after her singing dream. Her talent is strong enough to get her a recording deal and a single on the radio, but her self-destructive behavior always sabotages any small success she is able to win.

Finally, after losing everything, including Linda, who she watched die of AIDS, Leshaya returns to the Jameses' to try and reclaim Etta, her baby. But when she peeps in the James' window and sees how happy the toddler is with Harmon, she knows it would be a greater wrong to take her back. Leshaya is left with only the burning hunger that has haunted her since childhood, to become the famous singer she knows she was born to be.

The Message: Unchecked passion for any one thing can be destructive. True talent can cover deep flaws, at least at first. Realizing a dream takes work and determination. Don't make life-changing decisions based on emotion. Be proud of who you are and where you come from. Don't be afraid to allow yourself to be reflective and change your mind.

Who's It For?: 9th–12th grade. Leshaya has sex for the first time when she is 12, though this is not graphically depicted. There are numerous references to drug use and underage drinking.

Why It Rocks:
- **Voice:** Leshaya's unique first-person voice, infused with her unfettered passion for music, will allow the iPod generation to root for her, even as they wince at her cringe-worthy choices.
- **Plot:** In this character-driven novel, Nolan challenges traditional ideas of class and race by chronicling the unconventional life of a poor, white foster child who longs to look and sound like the only people who have ever shown her love and acceptance: a stable, affluent African American family.
- **Pacing:** Riveting, since Leshaya is always on the brink of some personal disaster. But teens will keep reading to see if she will manage to turn her love of music into a real career.
- **Characterization:** The James family serves as a strong moral compass in the midst of Leshaya's chaotic existence, even though, crippled by her mother's abuse and neglect, she lacks the social and psychological skills to accept their love. Although the majority of teens will not be able to personally identify with many of Leshaya's horrific circumstances, most will be able to empathize with her habit of making bad choices, then being too proud to admit to wrongdoing, even in the face of over-whelming evidence.

Hook It Up With: *The Facts Speak for Themselves* by Brock Cole and *The Orpheus Obsession* by Dakota Lane.

Paulsen, Gary. 2000. *The Beet Fields: Memories of a Sixteenth Summer.* New York: Random House. 160p.

The Story: "The boy," as he is referred to in third person throughout the text, must leave home when he is 16 years old because of his mother's inappropriate drunken sexual advances. He finds employment in the beet fields of North Dakota, working alongside Mexican migrant workers, who share their food and humor with him. He contributes to the communal pot by climbing the rafters of the farmer's barn and wringing the necks of pigeons. When they travel from farm to farm, he goes with them, until he catches sight of Lynette, daughter of farmer Bill Flaherty.

This time, when the migrant workers move on, the boy stays and works for the Flahertys, in hopes of getting close to the mysterious Lynette. However, during the course of his stay at the Flahertys, the very nature of his grueling, sun-up-to-sun-down tractor plowing never allows him to catch even a glimpse of her. The boy is forced to leave when a crooked local deputy arrests him as a runaway and steals all the cash he's earned from working the fields. Now a fugitive from the law, he hitch-hikes out of town, penniless.

The boy's first ride is a Hungarian immigrant, who is shockingly killed when a wayward pheasant crashes through the driver's side windshield at 80 miles an hour. The boy amazingly escapes the crash unscathed and searches for another ride, knowing there is nothing he can do to help the poor dead man now. His next ride is a lonely old farm woman named Hazel, who takes him home and dresses him in her dead solider son's clothes. He lives with Hazel and works as her farmhand for about two weeks, until he is offered a better job as a traveling carnival worker when the fair comes to town.

Now under the dubious tutelage of carny brothers Taylor and Bobby, the boy learns how to set up, take down, and shill the "rubes." He finally feels somewhat secure, with a real job and money in his pocket. The only thing missing is a warm body to share it with. Enter Ruby, Taylor's wife and the sole dancer in the fair's girlie show. Ruby responds to the longing on the boy's face and invites him to her trailer one night after he's watched her strip naked in front of a group of gape-mouthed farmers. Once he loses his virginity to Ruby, the boy decides he has become a man. A short epilogue describes his first act as such: enlistment in the army.

The Message: What does it mean to be a man? How do you know when you've arrived at adulthood?

Who's It For?: 9th–12th grade. While the sex scenes are not explicit, the implied incest and the boy's underage sexual encounter with Ruby demand a high school audience. Some language and the violent car crash may disturb younger readers.

Why It Rocks:
• **Voice:** In an author's note, Paulsen writes, "... here it is now, as real as I can write it, and as real as I can remember it happening." Of all his autobiographical fiction, *The Beet Fields* is arguably his best-written and most deeply felt novel.
• **Plot:** Paulsen's greatest works are the ones that skillfully meld elements of his real life into an adventurous (*Hatchet*) or heartfelt (*The Cookcamp*) novel. Less than 200 pages, *The Beet Fields* is still loaded with lush descriptions so vibrant you can see, hear, and taste them: the hot summer sun; the delicious smell of beans and tortillas emanating from the migrant workers' camp; and the bright, cheap lights of the fair's midway.
• **Pacing:** Fairly brisk, though Paulsen often pauses to take time to smell the roses (or beet fields, as it were).
• **Characterization:** As he meets people of different classes, races, and levels of morality (the honest migrant workers, the crooked lawmen, the shyster carnies), the boy takes something from each encounter that helps him continue to survive on his own in post–WWII America. Honest and utterly sincere, *The Beet Fields* is a poetically written chronicle of one boy's short and occasionally sweet journey to adulthood.

Hook It Up With: *Rule of the Bone* by Russell Banks and *Tex* by S. E. Hinton.

Read More about It:
Booklist, starred: 07/01/00
Publishers Weekly: 09/04/00
School Library Journal: 09/01/00
V.O.Y.A. (Voice of Youth Advocates): 12/01/00

Rapp, Adam. 2003. 33 *Snowfish.* **Cambridge, MA: Candlewick Press. 179p.**

The Story: Boobie has killed his parents and stolen his baby brother with the intention of selling him to the highest bidder. Custis is an orphan who, for most of his wretched life, has been the sexual slave of a middle-aged pedophile. Curl is a teen prostitute who has a dangerous crush on Boobie. These three misfits, relegated to the far, far edges of midwestern society, have managed to find one another and are now on the run because of the murders Boobie has committed.

After a short reprieve in a run-down motel, where Boobie kidnaps a child from a parking lot and Custis frees him, the three find a temporary home in an abandoned school bus in the woods. But as the fall fades into winter, Curl gets pneumonia from the falling temperatures and exposure and dies. Boobie nearly goes over the edge, almost killing Custis and then himself; however, at the last minute he drops his stolen gun and stalks into the woods, never to be seen again. Custis is left alone with the baby, and it is snowing.

As Custis trudges through the woods, he finds a small house belonging to an elderly black man named Seldom. When he tries to steal Seldom's pet chicken in hopes of eating it, Seldom captures him and tries to tame this now wild boy with love and understanding. Custis leads Seldom back to the bus, where Seldom helps him bury Curl. After a few misunderstandings about how to properly show love (Custis thinks that to please Seldom he must offer up his body for sex), Seldom, Custis, and Boobie's stolen baby brother begin to form a most unusual and strong family unit.

The Message: Family is where you find it. Love can heal the greatest of hurts and humiliations.

Who's It For?: 9th–12th grade. This is probably not a reasonable choice for anyone under 14 unless you know the reader personally. Both Custis and Curl have been used and abused since they were very small children. Neither knows any other kind of life, so they very graphically and offhandedly refer to the horrific events, like being subjects of homemade porn films, as normal and commonplace. Descriptions of rape, murder, and beatings are best handled by readers aged 14 and older.

Why It Rocks:
• **Voice:** Rapp's mesmerizing tale is told in alternating chapters between Custis and Curl. The only input the reader has from Boobie is his disturbing drawings, often reflecting his pyromaniacal urgings.
• **Plot:** This book is a tour de force. Despite the subject matter, it is not a book about rape, murder, or sexual abuse. It is about the calm and clear-eyed resilience of children, about how families are formed and found in the most unlikely of places, and, above all, about how real love can go a long way toward healing the most terrible of crimes.
• **Pacing:** Custis and Curl's rough, uneducated voices, full of profanity and words that are common to them but may need to be puzzled out by some readers, slow the action considerably.
• **Characterization:** *Snowfish* is brutally and unashamedly honest, terribly violent and sad, yet the characterizations are so complete that it never seems heavy-handed or exploitive. These characters became so real to me that when one of Boobie's drawings depicted Custis and Curl slumped in the corner of the motel room, I had to put the book down because it seemed to foreshadow the death of one of these kids and I loved them both so much that I couldn't bear to lose either.

Hook It Up With: *Life Is Funny* by E. R. Frank and *Push* by Sapphire.

Read More about It:
Horn Book: 04/01/04
Kirkus Reviews: 02/01/03
Publishers Weekly: 01/13/03
School Library Journal: 04/01/03
V.O.Y.A. (Voice of Youth Advocates): 04/01/03

Williams-Garcia, Rita. 2004. *No Laughter Here*. New York: HarperCollins. 133p.

The Story: Ten-year-old Akilah is sassy, smart, and thrilled to be starting fifth grade with her best friend, Victoria. Victoria has been away all summer, visiting family in her native Nigeria. Akilah is surprised and dismayed when bright, funny Victoria comes back to their Queens neighborhood all but mute. Akilah expects that returning to school will break Victoria's new reticence, but Victoria sits silent each day, never raising her hand or asking a question.

The situation comes to a head when Akilah forges Victoria's mother's name on a permission slip that will allow students to see a film about adolescent sexual development and puberty. Victoria leaves the classroom during the film and finally confides to an uncomprehending Akilah what had happened to her over the summer. Victoria was taken to Nigeria to undergo an operation where her clitoris was removed, a time-honored tradition among her parents' people.

Victoria makes Akilah promise not to tell, but Akilah's mother, a child welfare worker, surprises Akilah in her room while she is looking up *female genital mutilation* (FGM) on the Internet. Akilah is mortified when her mother marches her up the street to Victoria's house and loudly confronts Victoria's mother about what she has had done to her daughter. Victoria's parents take her out of school after this incident, while Akilah continues to struggle on her own to understand why such a brutal custom is still allowed to take place. Her teacher, Ms. Saunders, explains to her the cultural context of FGM while not condoning it, and Akilah and Victoria are finally able to discuss the issue with each other via e-mail.

Victoria finally returns to school after Akilah's mother uses her professional contacts to put pressure on Victoria's family to get her counseling. Victoria forgives Akilah for revealing her secret, and the two friends agree to try and create a Web site that will tell Victoria's story and the truth about FGM.

The Message: What does it mean to be a friend? How does culture shape our personal belief systems and what we interpret to be right or wrong?

Who's It For?: 5th–8th grade. It is no mistake that Akilah and Victoria are ten years old. In an author's note, Rita Williams-Garcia observes that eight is the age where many African girls are subjected to FGM. Although the subject matter is grim and potentially frightening to younger readers, Williams-Garcia writes about FGM in an age-appropriate manner that is neither too clinical nor too informal while attempting to be objective about the cultural aspect of the practice. For example, Victoria refers to her missing clitoris as a "raisin," while Akilah's mother, Victoria's mother, and Ms. Saunders provide differing viewpoints on both the brutality and cultural significance of FGM.

In addition to the issue of FGM, there is a great deal of informative discussion between Akilah and her mother about her first period, which she has during the course of the book. All in all, this is an excellent book to use in classrooms for introductory discussions about topics ranging from puberty and adolescence to human rights, multiculturalism, and global communities.

Why it Rocks:
- **Voice:** In fewer than 150 pages, Williams-Garcia succinctly discusses puberty, culture clashes, and middle-grade friendships, all in a perfectly pitched ten-year-old's voice.
- **Plot:** This is one brave, incredibly well written book. A less accomplished author would never have been able to cover this complex topic and render these realistic relationships in such a short space, but Williams-Garcia does it with a grace and fearlessness that is a joy to read.
- **Pacing:** Brisk, moving at the speed of Akilah's rapidly growing realization that something is very wrong with her best friend.
- **Characterization:** Despite the book's short length, Williams-Garcia manages to make her secondary characters shine, providing fully realized pictures of Akilah's supportive, boisterous family with a surprising economy of words. The opening scene between Akilah and her mom as they sip iced tea in the backyard and address each other ("Now, girl . . . ") is a masterful example of show, don't tell.

Hook It Up With: *The Fattening Hut* by Pat Lowry Collins and *No Condition Is Permanent* by Christina Kessler.

Read More about It:
Booklist, starred: 12/01/03
Horn Book: 10/01/04
Kirkus Reviews, starred: 11/15/03
Publishers Weekly: 12/22/03
School Library Journal: 02/01/04
V.O.Y.A. (Voice of Youth Advocates): 04/01/04

CHAPTER 6

GRAPHIC FANTASTIC: GRAPHIC NOVELS WITH TEEN APPEAL

The young Adult Library Services Association of the American Library Association (ALA) has just introduced a new selection list into its booklist hall of fame: Great Graphic Novels for Teens, to make its debut at the next Midwinter conference. For some comic book and graphic novel aficionados, it will seem long overdue. But for me, a relatively new comic and graphic novel fangirl, it arrived right on time. I was lucky enough to be on the Best Books for Young Adults (BBYA) committee as graphic novels (GN) were gathering mainstream speed with young adult librarians. The format, popular with teens for like, EVER, was finally beginning to be seen as "necessary" as opposed to "accessory" in most YA collections, and the BBYA committee began nominating more GN titles. Up to that point, I had been reading some graphic novels (mostly the haunting and cerebral *Sandman* by Neil Gaiman) and had even developed a beginning GN collection for the YA room of the large, urban public library I was working in at the time. I read Kat Kan's "Graphically Speaking" column in *VOYA*, and noticed that *School Library Journal* (*SLJ*) and *Booklist* were beginning to sprinkle a few GN titles in and around their regular reviews. I had my own small list of titles on Reading Rants, which mostly contained a handful of already widely recognized YA titles, such as *The Tale of One Bad Rat* by Bryan Talbot and *Pedro and Me* by Judd Winick. I began enjoying, as have many others, reading and watching Robin Brenner's impressive and prolific graphic novel review site (No Flying, No Tights) spread its wings and soar. But the moment it all gelled for me was the first time (during my second year on the BBYA) that I creased the cover of Craig Thompson's *Blankets*, a sprawling, nearly 600-page autobiographical adolescent epic of the author's experience of growing up in a midwestern Christian fundamentalist home. Like I said, I had casually perused GN titles up to that point, but that was the moment I really saw the storytelling potential behind the format and just fell head over heels in love with this raw, intensely personal and beautifully wrought masterpiece. Thompson showed me the length and breadth that comics could be stretched to tell a story and that the format wasn't just for Bat-fans and X-Men wanna-bes; it was also for me. *Blankets* literally changed my reading life, and I wasn't the only one, apparently, since it was one of our BBYA Top Ten committee choices in 2004.

There are lots of teens out there who are waiting to have just such an epiphany, and you can be the YA librarian who helps them experience it. This exciting format has something for everyone; you should explore it in all its many permutations: superheroes, manga, indie, fantasy, spy/espionage, horror, and so forth, in order to be able to recommend widely to your adolescent audience. Choosing just ten for this chapter was incredibly difficult, and in the end I just did my best to highlight recent titles that have been popular with my teens and that I am nuts about personally. So don't expect an exhaustive list and understand that to really get a handle on this medium, you should go back at some point and get grounded in the classics: Art Spiegelman (*Maus*), Jeff Smith (*Bone*), Will Eisner (*Contract with God*), Alan Moore (*Watchmen*), and Frank Miller (*Sin City, The Dark Knight Returns*). And if you're wondering where all the female classic authors are, that's your first clue that comics and graphic novels have traditionally been a boy's club. But as you look over my selections, you'll notice an overabundance of "she-roes," and that's not entirely unintentional. As graphic novels continue to become more and more mainstream, there will be pressure to expand the audience beyond fan boys and Dungeon Masters. Graphic novels written by female authors and for a female audience are widely sought and highly prized by GN publishers right now, and this will no doubt continue to be a trend in the coming decade.

Finally, while there is a manga-style title here and there on this list, *manga* (literally the Japanese word for "comic book") is a global force unto itself that is so far reaching, and encompasses so many subgenres, it demands its own chapter just to cover it adequately. I personally am not a fan, but there are beginning to be many guides for librarians on the subject of animae and manga, so go and grab yourself one if you're interested. And, just to make sure we're all on the same page, I should say that when I use the term *graphic novel,* I mean either a stand-alone story that is published as such or a collection of comics that was originally published serially, and is now available in a bound paperback or hardcover volume. Also note that in this chapter, under the "Why it Rocks" section I state whether the book is serialized or a standalone story. I replace the "Voice" category with commentary about the artwork.

Cooke, Darwyn. 2002. *Catwoman: Selina's Big Score.* New York: DC Comics. 96p.

The Story: Selina Kyle, a.k.a Catwoman, is desperate for cash. After faking her own death and disappearing from the streets of Gotham City, she has ended up in Morocco, where a botched burglary leaves her penniless and out of ideas. She returns to Gotham in search of a new heist. She finds one through her old friend Swifty, a pawnshop broker and petty crook who puts her in touch with Chantel, a gorgeous black call girl whose "regular meal" is mafia crime boss Frank Falcone. Chantel had overheard Falcone and his cronies discuss the rail transport of an ill-gotten $24 million through Canada in order to launder it. She's willing to get all the details for Selina in exchange for a cut of the cash.

Selina knows she will have to assemble a team in order to properly pull off the job and contacts her old crime partner and former lover, the leather-faced and white-crew-cut-topped Stark. This is a dangerous idea because the last time Stark and Selina saw each other was when Selina double-crossed him on a diamond heist and disappeared with the goods. But she knows that Stark is the only one smart enough and experienced enough to help her. He reluctantly agrees, but he makes it known he doesn't really trust her and will kill her if she crosses him again.

Selina and Stark travel to Las Vegas to further engage one of Stark's connections, Jeff, a young Latino Lothario with loads of charm and technological know-how. He designs a type of motorcycle/rocket vehicle that runs on one track and can easily catch up with the money train. Using the train's route, e-mailed to Selina by Chantel, the three hatch a plan to board the train over the St. Lawrence River, overpower the Mafia muscle, drop the money bags attached to inflatable rafts down to the water, parachute off the train themselves, then gather the money into a waiting boat, captained by Swifty.

But before they can congratulate themselves on their brilliant plan, things begin to go wrong. First, Falcone discovers that Chantel accessed the train routes from his computer; he tortures the names of Selina and Stark out of her, then murders her. Then Falcone quickly calls his Canadian contact, Henri LaPerier, to warn him that the train may be attacked. But then he himself is caught and killed by Gotham detective Slam Bradley, who has been hired by the mayor to find out if Selina Kyle is really dead. Before Chantel and Falcone die, they both reveal enough details to lead Slam to the site of the proposed train heist, so he is able to engage a small plane to fly him there.

Meanwhile, the three robbers have pulled off their heist as planned, except LaPerier, who has intercepted their boat, unpleasantly surprises them. He shoots Swifty and Jeff. Stark immediately suspects that Selina may have double-crossed him again and is in cahoots with LaPerier. Slam arrives on the scene, but LaPerier's man shoots down his plane. Selina and Stark leap overboard to avoid LaPerier's gun. He thinks they have drowned, but they hold onto a towrope and quietly reboard. While Selina distracts LaPerier, Stark sneaks up behind him with a gun and asks him if he was in league with Selina. He says no; then the two engage in gunplay that leaves LaPerier dead and Stark mortally wounded. He dies in Selina's arms. Selina checks the shore and the crashed plane to make sure there are "no loose ends." She discovers Slam, who survived the plane crash. He tells her he must take her in, and she responds by shooting him in the leg so he can't follow her. In the final panels, as she makes her $24 million getaway on the boat, Selina gently lets Stark's body slide from her arms and into a watery grave.

The Message: No crime goes unpunished. There can be honor among thieves. A family is where you find it. Regret is a useless emotion. Women can be just as tough, brutal, and ruthless as men.

Who's It For?: 9th–12th grade. The violence is realistically but not graphically depicted. Chantel's torture is not shown, and blood appears only sparingly throughout the story. Selina and Stark are shown in bed, but there is no nudity. Depictions and discussion of guns, murder, organized crime, and prostitution make this most suitable for older teen fans of adult mystery novels and popular crime television shows like *CSI, Law & Order,* and *The Sopranos.*

Why It Rocks:
• **Art:** Cooke's Selina is a classy criminal, reminiscent of a slinky 1940s era Joan Crawford, complete with thick, perfect eyebrows; pencil waist; and a notably normal-sized bosom. Cooke uses color lavishly, often filling in backgrounds with muted reds and blues to evoke pain, passion, or regret. Several panels that depict Slam outside in a storm as he confronts Falcone are full of movement and misery as the thickly falling rain slants across his hard-bitten face.
• **Plot:** This high-stakes tale of love, money, and betrayal combines old school noir with cutting-edge toys and technology, resulting in a dazzling drama that is equal parts Bogart, Bacall, and Bond.
• **Pacing:** Flashbacks and several different points of view are employed well, and the action is nonstop.
• **Characterization:** Classic noir-girl Selina fits right in with the recent reincarnation of pulp fiction and detective stories, such as *The Hard Case Crime* imprint of both old and new pulp stories and the repackaged Dashiell Hammett paperbacks by *Vintage*.

Stand-alone or Serial?: Stand-alone.

Hook It Up With: *Catwoman, Vol. 1: The Dark End of the Street* by Ed Brubaker and Darwyn Cooke; *Birds of Prey: Batgirl/ Catwoman #1* by John Francis Moore, Darick Robertson, and Jimmy Palmiotti; and *Catwoman: When in Rome* by Jeph Loeb.

Read More about It:
Library Journal: 11/01/02
Publishers Weekly: 03/10/03
School Library Journal: 04/01/03

Clugston-Major, Chynna. 2005. *Queen Bee.* New York: Scholastic. 112p.

The Story: Seventh-grader Haley Madison is determined to be popular no matter what the cost. Having always been the target of bullies at her school, she is thrilled to learn that her mother has accepted a new job and they are moving. Haley decides she is going to change her whole personality in order to fit in with the popular crowd at JFK Intermediate School. The only thing she can't change is her secret power of psychokinesis, or the ability to move objects using her mind, which occasionally acts out when she least expects it.

On Haley's first day, she is shown around school by Trini, a perfectly nice but not exactly popular girl. She introduces Haley to the "Hive," the most popular group of girls in school, which is headed up by Anjelica, a raven-haired ice queen. The Hive takes notice of Haley as word gets around how about how kind she is. It seems whenever someone is in trouble, Haley shows up and saves the day, usually using a subtle form of her psychokinesis to do it. Soon, Haley and Anjie are going head to head as they compete for the title as Queen of the Hive. Eventually, Anjie gives in to the inevitable, and Haley becomes the new Queen Bee. But Haley is quickly bored with her new role and dismayed to discover that being popular seems to consist of making fun of people and reading nothing heavier than the latest fashion magazine.

One day, another new girl shows up at school. Her name is Alexa Harmon, and the moment she and Haley make eye contact, they recognize the power of psychokinesis in each other. Haley senses this girl is trouble, and she is proven right when Alexa proceeds to try and unseat Haley from the Queen Bee throne using her powers. Alexa gets Haley in trouble for cheating when she plants a cheat sheet in her bag; in retaliation, Haley makes Alexa's cell phone ring in class, then sends an unflattering text message to the teacher who had confiscated it. The pranks continue to escalate and culminate when both girls enter a schoolwide talent contest, each determined to win first place.

Haley is helped by her new crush, Jasper, a cute drummer who suggests she go the retro-route and sing "We Got the Beat" by the Go-Go's. Alexa decides to cover the Gwen Stefani single "If I Was a Rich Girl." As Jasper and Haley grow closer, Haley confides in him about her psychokinesis and the fact that she was adopted as a baby and knows nothing about her birth other than she thinks she has a sister, as evidenced by the picture locket that was around her neck when she was found abandoned on the steps of a church.

The night of the show, Haley and Jasper try desperately to keep Alexa from using her power to make the other contestants mess up, but one by one, she causes other students to trip, fall, or lose their place. Alexa sings her piece unharmed because Jasper refuses to let Haley stoop to using her power on Alexa, but when it is Haley's turn, she does use her power to deflect Alexa's attempts to ruin her set. Backstage, just as the two are about to claw each other's eyes out, the judges announce that Haley is the runner-up. Alexa begins to gloat, but before she can really get started, the judges announce that they made a mistake and that Alexa is the runner-up while Haley is the winner. Alexa is furious, Haley, triumphant.

The following week at school, mostly because of Jasper's influence, Haley decides she's done with the Hive and would rather hang out with Trini and her gang. Alexa flounces up to Haley at lunch and announces that while she may have lost the contest, she scored a deal with a talent agent who was in the audience. The agent helped her get a contract to be the new teen model for a famous make-up company. Haley responds by using her powers to cause Alexa to trip and fall in front of everyone in the cafeteria. In a sneak peek at the next book in the series, Jasper and Haley see the new poster featuring Alexa advertising the teen makeup line. Haley is quick to give the poster Alexa a beard and horns, but not before Jasper comments on how much the two of them actually look alike. . . . Could Alexa be Haley's long lost sister?

The Message: Two wrongs don't make a right. Popularity isn't everything. Just because someone else is cruel doesn't mean you should sink to his or her level.

Who's It For?: 5th–9th grade. This is a solidly middle school offering. There is no strong language, sex, or violence (unless you count various trips and spills as the girls battle each other with their mental powers). This proposed new series from Chynna

Clugston is groundbreaking in that it is the debut of an indie comic queen on a mainstream label. Scholastic was wise enough to woo Clugston, most well known for her 1980s mod, manga-style indie teen dramedy series *Blue Monday* and *Scooter Girl*, over to its Graphix label and bring her college-bound 20s' tone down to a tween timbre.

Why It Rocks:
•   **Art:** While the content is fine for as young as fifth grade, the densely crowded black-and-white panels and small dialogue bubbles may pose a problem for younger readers.
•   **Plot:** Obvious? Yes, but we have to remember that while we've read hundreds of variations on the same chick-lit theme, teens have not and very well may welcome this über-cute version that is sweeter than *Mean Girls,* more innocent than *Gossip Girls*, and contains a supernatural element that lends some lift to this well-worn story line.
•   **Pacing:** Like a lighter-than-air sitcom, this one can be finished in under 45 minutes.
•   **Characterization:** Clugston successfully channels Betty, Veronica, Josie's Pussycats, and Sabrina's twinkle in this bouncy middle school romp that is sure to induce giggles and squeals.

Stand-alone or Serial?: First in a proposed series.

Hook It Up With: *Mary Jane, Vol. 1: Circle of Friends* by Sean McKeever and Takeshi Miyazawa, *The Clique* series by Lisi Harrison, and *The Girls* by Amy Goldman Koss.

Read More about It:
Booklist: 09/15/05
Publisher's Weekly: 08/08/05
V.O.Y.A. (Voice of Youth Advocates): 12/01/05

Loeb, Jeph, and Tim Sale. (2004). *Spider-Man: Blue.* **New York: Marvel Comics. unpaged.**

The Story: An older and wiser Peter Parker, still saving the world as Spiderman and married to Mary Jane Watson, decides to tape record the tragic story of his lost love, Gwen Stacy. Peter is a web-slinging college student the first time he meets beautiful blond Gwen. He has just faced down the Green Goblin for what he hopes will be the last time. Business mogul Norman Osborn, father of Peter's college pal Harry, has no idea that he becomes the flying criminal bomber when he blacks out. Spiderman battled the Goblin in a burning building and saved Osborn's life after he was knocked unconscious during the fight. Later, when Peter comes to the hospital to visit Harry and Norman, he sees Gwen accompanied by some of Harry's other friends, and it is love at first sight.

But the road to true love never did run smooth, especially for Peter. Before he can begin to pursue this new love interest, he must answer the call of duty as Spiderman. A shadowy hulking figure is enabling some of the city's worst criminals to slip their bonds in order to challenge Spiderman. The first of these is the Rhino, a muscle-bound giant in a purple suit with horns. But Spiderman dispatches the Rhino in enough time for Peter to get ready for a night out with Gwen and the rest of the gang. Before he can leave, Aunt May introduces him to the daughter of a friend whom she has been wanting Peter to meet for a long time: fiery redhead Mary Jane Watson.

Aunt May persuades Peter to take Mary Jane (MJ) along to the club, and she quickly wins over Harry and the rest of the guys with her flirtatious wit and bodacious bod. Gwen is less than impressed, and the two begin to vie for Peter's attention. Suddenly, Peter sees a news report on the club's television set about a man-sized lizard that is wreaking havoc in the city's subway system. He is relieved to rush off and leave the uncomfortable situation behind.

After dealing with the Lizard, Peter returns to Aunt May's house to find Harry waiting for him. Harry wants to talk about the possibility of Peter's sharing an apartment with him. Peter takes Harry up on the offer, and the new roomies decide to throw a housewarming party. Peter is slinging his way toward the new place as Spiderman, when the Vulture, a flying villain with razor-sharp wings that can slice through webbing, sideswipes him. Peter is momentarily confused because he had sent the Vulture to prison in the past, but it turns out this is a new young upstart who has stolen the old Vulture's wings and legacy. The Vulture knocks out Spiderman, and he lies unconscious and exposed on a rooftop for awhile before slowly coming to and making his way to Harry's, having completely missed the party and Gwen.

Peter gets sick from his cold night out and is in bed when MJ and Gwen arrive simultaneously to nurse him back to health. Out his bedroom window, Peter sees the Vulture fly by and has to dismiss both the girls so he can dispatch the villain, but he quickly discovers that he has both the new and old birds on his hands as the two criminals battle each other for the Vulture title. Spiderman clips both of their wings, and then hurries home to bed to recover. Meanwhile, the shadowy scoundrel who has been releasing these monsters on Spiderman and watching the results has decided that it's his turn to act.

The night of a Valentine's Day bash that Peter and Harry are throwing at their apartment, the mastermind literally crashes the party and reveals himself to be Kraven the Hunter. Because Harry has borrowed Peter's aftershave, Kraven's sensitive nose mistakes Harry for Peter. But before Kraven can throw Harry over the side of the building, Spiderman shows up, saves Harry, and beats down Kraven. Before the Hunter slips into unconsciousness, he reveals to Spiderman that the Green Goblin had hired him to study and then murder the web slinger. Peter knows that for all practical purposes the Green Goblin is dead, since Norman Osborn still hasn't recovered his memory from the night Spiderman "killed" the Goblin and saved his life. But now Peter is wondering if he made a mistake in allowing Osborn to live.

Peter returns home to find he has missed the party again, but Gwen has stayed to ask him to be her Valentine, and the two finally physically consummate their love.

Flash forward to the present as Peter is finishing his recorded message to a long-dead Gwen. He records that he married MJ and that he is happy, but every year around this time of year he still feels blue because he misses Gwen.

The Message: With great power comes great responsibility. (C'mon, I couldn't resist!) Duty is stronger than love. Regret is a powerful, useless emotion. Keep your friends close and your enemies closer.

Who's It For?: 7th–12th grade. There are plenty of "Pow," "Wham!" and "Thunk!" punches being thrown, but no blood is depicted and no actual deaths occur. While it is implied that Peter and Gwen have sex, it all takes place offstage, and the only nudity is Peter's bare (albeit, hunky) chest.

Why It Rocks:
• **Art:** The art is idealized; the author and illustrator evoke classic superhero genre archetypes: beautiful, witty women; righteous, strong young men; dastardly villains; hard-nosed bosses; and so on.
• **Plot:** Although this is a 2004 title, *Blue* is a nostalgic homage to the good old comic book days of bloodless, virtuous violence; innocent flirtation; and heartbreaking romance. Peter and crew are just the right age for our target teen audience, and the plotline, which balances action, romance, and good vs. evil, will appeal to both sexes.
• **Pacing:** Peter bounces back and forth between romantic and criminal crisis in this fast-paced romantic adventure.
• **Characterization:** This is a great introductory volume for Spiderman initiates, because it includes many classic Spiderman foes and explains the initial relationships among such recurring characters as Mary Jane, Harry Osborn, and, of course, Gwen Stacy. *Blue* is actually a retelling of stories done by Stan Lee and John Romita back in the 1960s. It turns out that Peter was right in regretting that he had allowed Norman Osborn to live, since it is the Green Goblin who ends up killing Gwen. Gwen attained cult status among Spidey fans when she was taken hostage and hurled off a bridge by the Goblin. Spiderman attempted to save her, but her neck snapped when he tried to break her fall with his webbing. While the reason for Gwen's death is not revealed in *Blue,* the uninitiated will still be able to enjoy this action-packed romance.

Stand-alone or Serial?: Serial, collecting issues 1–6 of *Spiderman: Blue.*

Hook It Up With: *Daredevil: Yellow, Hulk: Gray,* and *Spiderman for All Seasons,* all by Jeph Loeb and Tim Sale; and *Ultimate Spiderman, Vol. 1* by Brian Michael Bendis and Mark Bagley.

Read More about It: Regrettably, *Spider-Man: Blue* was not reviewed by mainstream library media. For more information and opinions on this title, check out the very entertaining customer reviews on Amazon.com.

Niles, Steve, and Ben Templesmith. 2003. *30 Days of Night.* **San Diego: IDW Publishing. 104p.**

The Story: In the small arctic community of Barrow, Alaska, the sun doesn't rise between November 18 and December 17. It is the final evening before the monthlong period of darkness, and married cops Stella and Eben Olemaun are following up on a series of petty crimes that have broken out. It seems that all the cell phones in town have disappeared simultaneously, there are problems with the town's generator and satellite communications, and, finally, a weird stranger is making trouble over at the local diner. After finding all the phones destroyed in a smoking hole in the snow, the two chalk it up to a teenage prank and stop for a moment to enjoy the last sunset they will see in a while.

They then drive over to the diner, where the stranger has been demanding raw hamburger meat for dinner and threatening the owner. Stella and Eben handcuff the man and take him over to the cell in their office to calm down. After muttering darkly about how they can't stop what's coming, the man suddenly bends the iron bars and bursts out of the cell. Eben shoots him in the head and Stella plugs him a few more times for good measure. Now thoroughly terrified, the two head out to the satellite communications center to find out why the computers and phones aren't working. They discover a grisly sight: the head of their friend Gus the engineer mounted on a pole and the building utterly destroyed. As they speed over to the diner again to round up the rest of the citizens, they spot a light far out on the frozen waste. Eben uses his high-powered binoculars and sees a crowd of darkly clad, black-eyed figures shambling toward town.

Meanwhile, in New Orleans, a series of e-mails have been hacked by a voodoo priestess and her son, Taylor. The priestess, or Momma, explains to her son that the e-mails are exchanges between two vampires, Marlow and Vincente. They indicate that there will be a huge gathering of their kind in Barrow. Momma knows this is her chance to finally document the existence of vampires. She sends Taylor on a mission to film the vampires, ordering him not to be a hero and to simply fly in, get the pictures, then get out.

Back in Barrow, the massacre has begun. The vampires, led by a pierced, bald bloodsucker named Marlow, are enjoying a feeding frenzy as they revel in the fact that there is no need to hide from the sun. The corpses are piling up as they hunt down every man, woman, and child, drain their blood, and cut off their heads, in order to keep them from "turning." A small group of survivors, led by Stella and Eben, are hiding in the base of an old industrial furnace, scavenging food, and waiting for an opportunity to escape.

As they share what little food they have left, they hear a commotion outside. Peering out of the basement furnace slot, they see the arrival of Vincente, clearly known to all of the vampires as a powerful leader. Instead of congratulating Marlow on his discovery of Barrow, Vincente chastises him for creating such a disaster site. Now humans will have definite proof of their existence. Vincente then decapitates Marlow and orders the other vampires to incinerate the town and wipe out all traces of vampire presence.

Suddenly, a helicopter appears over the horizon. It is Taylor with his camera. He hovers low to capture the carnage. Unfortunately, he has underestimated the vampires' power. Vincente leaps straight into the air, breaks the windshield, and causes the copter to crash—but not before a doomed Taylor is able to send the live-feed film back to Momma. Vincente is pleased because now the helicopter crash will be blamed for the burning of Barrow.

Eben sees only one solution. He has obtained a sample of vampire blood and intends to inject it into himself, knowing the only way these powerful beings can be destroyed is by one another. He is able to retain enough of his own personality to issue a challenge to Vincente as the other vampires watch. The two engage in a bloody battle, which Eben, full of righteous anger, wins. He then orders the rest of the vampires to leave. A few days later, when the sun finally returns, Eben kisses Stella. He then disintegrates at her side as the rays touch him, and she begins to weep.

The Message: Never give up hope. Sometimes a great sacrifice must be made to right a great wrong. It's always darkest before the dawn. Love conquers all.

Who's It For?: 9th–12th grade. This is an extremely violent graphic novel that is appropriate only for the high school audience. There are multiple decapitations, eviscerations, and explosions. Having said that, Templesmith's gorgeous, gory, blood-and-tear-stained artwork is singularly stunning, and you could justify having this title in your collection for that reason alone. Templesmith does a good job of making the actual decapitations and throat ripping smeary and vague, so while a great deal of blood is being spilled, the carnage is fairly indistinct.

Why It Rocks:
• **Art:** Templesmith's flinty-skinned, merciless killing machines sport rabid, red pupils; slick, black-lipped mouths crowded with sharklike layers of fangs; and numerous piercings and tattoos. When they take a bite out of a victim, it's not a delicate sip but a mighty CRUNCH! Ruby-red blood, the only color to relieve the unrelentingly gray panels, scatters across each page like sprays from Jackson Pollock's paintbrush, and the result is both sickening and mesmerizing.
• **Plot:** This horror comic stands out from the rest of the undead pack because of Steve Niles's singularly brilliant, yet simple premise of vampire bloodlust unleashed during an endless arctic night.
• **Pacing:** The panels flow quickly into one another, paced like a fast-moving horror movie. In fact, *30 Days* has already been optioned for film by Sam Raimi, director of the *Spider-Man* movies, and an added extra are the first few pages of the screenplay for those teens hungering for more.
• **Characterization:** While the vampires play to type, Eben and Stella are their stalwart opposites, and when Eben makes the ultimate sacrifice, teens will cheer even as they weep for Stella alone.

Stand-alone or Serial?: Stand-alone, with sequels that were initially published serially and are now available in bound format.

Hook It Up With: Niles and Templesmith's sequels: *Dark Days* and *30 Days of Night: Back to Barrow; The Walking Dead, Vol. 1: Days Gone By* by Robert Kirkman and Tony Moore; and *Richard Matheson's I Am Legend,* adapted into a graphic novel by Steve Niles and Elman Brown.

Read More about It:
Library Journal: 03/01/04
Publishers Weekly: 01/26/04

Parker, Jeff. 2003. *The Interman.* Hermosa Beach, CA: Octopus. 128p.

The Story: The Interman Project, developed in the 1960s by five of the most powerful countries in the world and directed by the Pentagon, was charged with the creation of a race of super spies—operatives who could perfectly adapt to their surroundings no matter what the circumstances. With DNA manipulation, these super humans would have the ability to breathe underwater, automatically moderate body temperature, absorb poison with no ill effects, and have the strength of ten in one body. Unfortunately, after the project's first successful prototype was born, the project was curtailed as the Vietnam War began and the Pentagon came under more public scrutiny. Afraid that their genetic tinkering would come to light, the governments abandoned the Interman Project, adopting out their baby spy to a scientist's family named Meach.

Now 30 years later, thanks to the work of an industrious accountant who has been hired to purge military expenses from the Pentagon files, the heads of state have uncovered Van Meach's paper trail and decided that their genetic mistake must be erased once and for all. William Marcy, the current director of the CIA, has ordered each country involved in the project to send an assassin after Van to ensure he is "disposed of." Van, now in his thirties, knows very little about his origins and has been working as a privately hired benign mercenary, carrying out difficult and dangerous tasks normal men can't perform.

On his way to the Galápagos Islands to visit an old family friend, Dr. Keele, who is an expert on animal adaptation and was a consultant on the Interman Project, Van is attacked by the first of the trained assassins the government agencies have hired. He eludes the man, and Dr. Keele is able to give him enough information to begin putting together the pieces of his past. Angry and confused, Van begins a global search for the story of his birth. He travels from the Galápagos to Greece, London, Calcutta, and Bhutan, and at each stop, he meets and deals with another assassin determined to kill him.

In Greece, an MI-6 agent tries to kill him with a blow dart and a gorgeous, blond French agent seduces him over poisoned prosciutto. In London, he battles and kills in self-defense an assassin in a sword fight in the Tower of London. He also visits the widow of the scientist, Vance Sirraman, who was the head of the Interman Project. Sirraman's widow gives him her husband's journals so that Van can learn more about himself. In Calcutta, "The Compass," a gang of four unstoppable assassins who have never missed a target, attacks Van, yet he quickly and inventively dispatches each one. Along the way, he is aided by Outcault, a shadowy professional assassin who has chosen, for reasons known only to himself, to help instead of hinder Van.

From Sirraman's journals, Van learns of a scientist named Turgis, who also worked on the Interman Project and now runs a free clinic in Bhutan. Van travels there to find more answers. It turns out Turgis took the last remaining Interman sample when the project was closed and sold it to the Soviets to create their own spy. The result was May, a female superspy and deadly assassin who could have been Van's twin. Turgis had tutored her, until the KGB sent him away and took over May's training themselves. Turgis, who regrets helping the Soviets, offers to help Van get the assassins off his back by placing a call to William Marcy and confessing his role in the Interman debacle.

Marcy agrees to meet Turgis and Van at the ruins of the old Interman lab in Wyoming and hear them out. But before the two can go very far, Turgis is attacked and murdered by May, under the orders of her Soviet masters. Van is literally buried alive when May wrestles him out of the small plane he's flying out of Bhutan, then sets off a bomb to trigger an avalanche. He survives, owing to his ability to go for long periods without oxygen, and continues on the rendezvous point. May, believing that Van is dead, goes on to Wyoming to eliminate Marcy, whom she blames for creating her and making her the murderous monster she believes herself to be.

Once she reaches the ruined lab, May effortlessly destroys all of Marcy's defenses and is about to kill him when Van parachutes in and draws her off. The two are equally matched, but during the course of their fight across the rocky landscape, May slips and tumbles over the edge of a cliff. Van saves her, despite her claim that if he pulls her up, she will kill him. May kicks Van's legs out from under him and is about to smash his skull with a rock when Outcault shoots her from behind.

Van realizes, as he cradles May's dying form, that she had never had the Interman powers he possesses. Sirraman's journals revealed that the rest of the fertilized egg samples for the project remained normal; Van was the only true Interman. May had been such a successful assassin because she believed she had the power, and belief was enough to make her almost as strong and as resourceful as Van. Outcault reveals that he was working for Marcy all along but couldn't resist watching Van dispatch all the world's greatest assassins with ease. Now that May is dead and Marcy realizes that Van has no intention of using his powers for evil, he calls off the manhunt, and Van begins his life anew as a regular taxpaying American.

The Message: Nothing is just black or white, good or evil; there are many shades of gray in between. Nature vs. nurture: are people born talented or can talent be developed through discipline and training? There is a universal need to discover our identity: who we are and where we came from. Adaptation is the key to survival.

Who's It For?: 6th–10th grade. The Cold War references and dense, text-heavy panels may challenge some younger readers. The violence is mostly of the explosive, bloodless type, and there is no nudity or sex.

Why It Rocks:
- **Art:** The energetic art has a look and feel that is reminiscent of the old Hanna-Barbera 1960s-era *Jonny Quest* cartoons, with rich colors, realistically depicted figures, and nonstop action.

- **Plot:** This is author Jeff Parker's first independent project (though he has contributed drawings to Dark Horse, Marvel, and DC Comics), and it is obviously a labor of love. *Entertainment Weekly* called *The Interman* "The best genetically engineered spy-on-the-run flick you've never seen," and I quite agree. Buy multiple copies and help an indie talent out, would ya?
- **Pacing:** The densely drawn panels are colorful and eye catching, but the loads of text and slightly irregular aesthetic will slow down some readers.
- **Characterization:** Van's search for identity and constant worry that he is "adapting" to the use of violence with each new attempt on his life add real depth to what would appear to be just another derivation of James Bond meets X-Men. Van is depicted as a character of color, most likely meant to be Indian like his creator, Dr. Sirraman, but whose dark eyes, hair, and olive skin could be seen as Latino or Middle Eastern. So, *The Interman* may be the perfect choice to booktalk to teens of these populations whose experiences with superheroes may begin and end with square-jawed, Caucasian strongmen.

Stand-alone or Serial?: Stand-alone.

Hook It Up With: *Abarat* by Clive Barker, *Wolverine: Origin* by Bill Jemas, et al., and *Superman: Birthright* by Mark Waid and Leinil Francis Yu.

Read More about It:
Publishers Weekly: 06/30/03
V.O.Y.A. (Voice of Youth Advocates): 02/01/04

Smith, Jeff, and Charles Vess. 2002. *Rose.* Columbus, OH: Cartoon Books. unpaged.

The Story: In the medieval kingdom of Atheia, two royal sisters meditate under supervision of the Disciples of Venu. They are trying to train their "dreaming eyes" to open. The sister whose mental eye opens first will become the successor to the throne, since leaders of this world rule with the intuition that comes from dreams. The younger sister, Rose, shows more promise than her sibling, but she is brash and impetuous. Briar, the elder sister, is cold and pragmatic, lacking imagination. Her dreaming eye is said to be blind by the girls' teachers, and even though she is techni-cally next in line to the throne, all signs point to Rose as becoming the next ruler. Under the protection of Lucius, the hunky captain of the palace guard, the teenage sisters are traveling to the Disciples' cave, where they will be tested to see which one of them will be queen. Rose brings her two clumsy, sweet Great Danes, Euclid and Cleo, whose telepathic canine speech she can understand.

Once at the cave, the girls begin their lessons to open their dreaming eyes. The folklore of their people tells of a dragon queen whose name was Mim. It was Mim's job to keep the world safe and peaceful by holding the balance of dreaming in check, but she became possessed and driven mad by the evil Lord of the Locusts. The other dragons were forced to turn their queen into stone to trap the evil Lord within her so he could do no more harm. She became the mountain range that frames the valley in which the girls live. But now, warns their teacher, the Lord of the Locusts has found an emancipator who is strong enough to free him from his prison, and fate is leading this person closer and closer. Briar becomes frustrated with the meditation and the story and claims not to believe in dreams and destiny, which appalls both Rose and their teacher.

Meanwhile, a river dragon named Balsaad has gone rogue and turned against the humans, burning and pillaging villages around the valley. Rose, who had a dream that she freed a small dragon from a stream, believes it is her fault that the dragon is loose. She goes on a hunt with her dogs and encounters Balsaad, who confirms that she freed him in her dream. In a rage, she slices off his hand with her sword, but he has become so strong he can reattach his own limbs. The fight comes to a draw, and Balsaad leaves in search of easier prey.

Rose returns to the cave to tell her sister about the dream. Briar warns her not to tell their teachers or the good Red Dragon, who works with the Disciples, because then the others might believe Rose is the emancipator they fear. Rose is called before the Red Dragon and the Headmaster of the Disciples and asked if her dreaming eye has given her any clue about the Lord of the Locusts. As her sister suggested, Rose tells them about her initial battle with Balsaad but not about the dream. She knows that the Red Dragon realizes she has held something back. She swears to her sister that she will go to the Headmaster and tell him the whole truth first thing the next morning.

But Briar manipulates Rose into believing that Rose's strong dreaming eye must mean that she truly is the emancipator. Rose becomes determined to prove she is not the person who will free the Locusts by rushing off in the middle of the night to slay Balsaad. Briar also goes out into the night but for entirely different reasons. She is counting on Balsaad to get rid of Rose, but now she has to rally the Hairy Men, great ratlike creatures who hate humans, to attack Lucius and his guard, who also have gone out hunting for Rose. Of course, Briar, jealous of her sister's talent and determined to be queen, has been the emancipator all along.

On her way to find Balsaad, Rose encounters the Red Dragon. She confesses her dream to him, and he tells her that if she kills Balsaad, there will be an imbalance in the cycle of dreaming. She must promise to kill the first living creature she sees after defeating Balsaad so that balance can be maintained, or all will be lost. Rose promises with a heavy heart, then goes off with her dogs to find the dragon. Lucius and his guard are attacked by the Hairy Men as they search for Rose but manage to drive them back. Euclid, ordered by Rose, has come to lead them to where she has cornered Balsaad to provide reinforcements and help the people who have been under his attack.

Following the Red Dragon's instructions, Rose leads Balsaad toward the river where she freed him. She begins to slice him into pieces with her sword, even managing to chop off his head. But as the dragon blindly searches for his head, Rose slips into a trance where the "Lord of the Locusts" reveals himself to her, admits he needs her strong dreaming eye to free himself, and offers her great power in exchange. Briar also appears in the dream, revealing her part in the deception and confessing her hatred of Rose. Finally, Rose is awakened by Cleo's barking. Balsaad has found his severed head, reattached it, and is after her again. Rose plunges into the river and turns to face him. As she hacks away at him, his limbs are washed away in the current and the evil magic that allowed him to reattach them in the past is useless. Soon, Balsaad is no more.

As Rose struggles back to shore, she hears a scuffling step and remembers the Red Dragon's warning. She turns to kill the living being behind her, only to discover it is Briar, shriveled up into an old lady as punishment for failing the "Lord of the Locusts." Briar pleads for her life and for forgiveness, asking that Rose kill Cleo in her stead. So Rose, who longs for her sister's love in spite of all Briar has done to her, kills her beloved dog to spare Briar's life. Rose returns home with Lucius and his crew to become the new crown princess, and all the people think she is a hero for defeating Balsaad. She is left wondering, however, if she did the right thing in sacrificing Cleo to save a sister who tried to destroy her, as the shadow of the "Lord of the Locusts" continues to hang over the land.

The Message: Be careful who you trust; blood isn't always thicker than water. Question others' motivations and loyalties; don't expect that everyone will always have your best interest at heart. Not everyone is your friend. Growing up means making grown-up decisions and dealing with the consequences.

Who's It For?: 6th–10th grade. There are some sword fights and scary monsters, but the novel's only real bloody scene is when Rose kills Balsaad. Using a flood of pink blood, Vess spares no detail as Balsaad is hacked to pieces by Rose, with muscle and sinew writhing across the panels. Balsaad is a baddie who gets what he deserves, however, and few readers will mourn him. Prepare for some of your tenderhearted readers to shed tears at the novel's most emotionally wrenching scene, when Rose must tell Euclid she had to kill Cleo (which thankfully takes place off the page). Sniff!

Why It Rocks:
•   **Art:** Vess's art evokes old-school fairy lore, with sinister red-eyed dragons, snow-covered hills that reflect glowing sunsets, and hood-covered mystics whose faces hold the secrets of the universe. His subdued palette is soft and dreamy, with a hand-lettered font that looks like it sprang from a medieval illuminated manuscript and speech bubbles that are colored green for dragon speech, blue for dogs, and pink for the evil "Lord of the Locusts."
•   **Plot:** The brutality of Briar's betrayal and Balsaad's gory end will remind readers of original, Grimm-like tales, where endings weren't always happy, witches ate children who were too inquisitive for their own good, and the devil could trick you out of your soul.
•   **Pacing:** The softly drawn panels and extended dream sequences will cause readers to linger over Vess's romantically drawn scenes.
•   **Characterization:** Rose's journey from wide-eyed innocent girl to heavy-hearted, remorseful woman is inevitable, yet each time I read this story, I hope the ending will be different. It never is, and that is the terrible beauty of Smith and Vess's sad, gorgeous epic. Rose's regret and uncertainty about the choices she made will resound with teen readers, who will quickly identify with this all-too-human hero.

Stand-alone or Serial?: Stand-alone, originally published as a three-issue miniseries.

Hook It Up With: *Seven Wild Sisters* by Charles de Lint and *Stardust* by Neil Gaiman.

Read More about It:
Locus: July 2003

Vaughan, Brian K., and Adrian Alphona. 2003. *Runaways: Pride and Joy.* New York: Marvel Comics. unpaged.

The Story: It's just another quiet evening at computer geek Alex Wilder's house in Malibu, where his millionaire parents are hosting their annual fundraising party. Every year, they invite the same six wealthy couples to sit down and write checks for charity. And each year, Alex is expected to entertain the couples' children: Karolina Dean, gorgeous, blond vegetarian; Chase Stein, surfer dude; Molly Hayes, cutesy tween, and the youngest at 11; Nico Minoru, black nail polish–wearing alterna-girl; and Gertrude Yorke, purple-haired, brilliant bookworm.

Except this year is a little different. Instead of hanging out in the video game room like usual, Alex convinces everyone that it might be fun to spy on their parents in the library, using his father's extensive security tunnels. They are horrified when they witness their usually boring parents, dressed in what look like elaborate Halloween costumes, utter strange incantations, then murder a frightened teenage girl as part of what looks like ritual sacrifice. As they piece together what they've seen and heard, they realize their parents are part of a secret society of supervillains called the Pride.

Shocked and confused, Alex calls a meeting of all the teens the next night (except Molly because she's too young to sneak out) to discuss what their plan of action will be. They decide to report what they know to the police, but the officer they get on the phone hangs up in disgust when Alex mentions superpowers. They then decide to drive to Gertrude's house to look for evidence of their parents' crimes. There they discover a hidden room with a genetically modified pet dinosaur, which obeys only Gert, that her parents (who turn out to be future- and alternative-past-time travelers) were saving to give her on her 18th birthday. They also discover a sort of handbook that contains information about the Pride, but it's entirely in code. Next, they travel to Karolina's house, where she discovers that she is the daughter of powerful aliens from another world, and that she has the ability to fly and send out concentrated streams of light and heat.

Meanwhile, the police, who work for the Pride, alert Alex's parents to his phone call. At Chase's house, the teens look through his parents' secret lab, where Chase discovers all sorts of interesting gadgets including X-ray glasses and giant mechanical hands that shoot fire. But it is here that Chase's and Nico's parents, who were called by Alex's dad, finally confront them. There is a brief battle between the young Runaways and their evil parents, where Nico is attacked by her own mother and strangely absorbs into her own body the staff her mother accosts her with, and where Gert's dinosaur shows up and saves the teens at the last minute. As they make their escape, Gertrude's parents call her on her cell phone and tell her that unless all of the teens come home, they will be forced to execute Molly, who is still home asleep in her bed.

The teens, realizing that there is no going back now, plan an attack and head for Molly's house to rescue her. Nico, Alex, and Gert storm the house with Gert's dinosaur. Gert's and Molly's parents drive them back, but when Nico is cut, the staff her body absorbed reemerges, and she is able to use it to freeze the bad guys. Meanwhile, Chase and Karolina are behind the house waiting for Alex's signal. They are attacked by Karolina's mother but quickly subdue her. Nico goes to Molly's room and knocks out Molly's mother, who is watching over her. Molly wakes up, and not understanding what is going on, almost attacks Nico. Molly's parents are powerful mutants who have apparently passed on their powers to Molly, who suddenly has enough superstrength to throw Karolina's mom through the wall when she shows up again.

Once more, the Runaways make their escape, this time with Molly in tow, and are about to try and contact the police again when Alex's father calls his cell. He tells Alex the Pride basically owns the police department and that there is a giant manhunt for the six of them because Alex's parents have framed Alex for the murder of the girl sacrificed by the Pride. Chase suggests a hideaway, an old hotel he knows of that is in ruins of an old earthquake. The teens go there and try to decide what to do next. Back at Molly's house, the parents have recovered, regrouped, and discovered an unsigned note from one of the teens that was left at the scene. The note indicates that whoever wrote it is still "loyal" to his or her parents, no matter what. The Pride is somewhat heartened by the fact that there is a mole in their group of rogue children. But who?

The Message: Never trust anyone over 30. Occasionally, your parents really ARE as evil as you believe them to be.

Who's It For?: 6th–9th grade. No sex, only explosive violence, and the only death is that of the young girl sacrificed in the beginning, and even that is shown without blood or gore. There is an extended gag where young Molly keeps wanting to talk about her changing body with the other girls in the gang, which the reader is led to believe is about getting her first menstrual period but is really about her coming into her mutant powers.

Why It Rocks:
• **Art:** Relatively standard issue; it's really Vaughan's sparky writing that sets these panels on fire.
• **Plot:** Besides having a smashing good premise that turns *The Incredibles* on its ear, this GN is also just incredibly well written. Vaughan, a relatively new but lauded talent, has outdone himself here. The many puns, wordplays, and pop culture references included in his dead-on, realistic teen dialogue are bound to date this GN quickly, but even so, I was lovin' every minute of it.

- **Pacing:** Faster than a speeding bullet. The fledgling crime fighters tumble from one crisis into another, always a hairbreadth from being caught by their diabolical parents.
- **Characterization:** This group of adolescent heros contains characters of color, with realistic body types. No teen can come away from reading this series without being able to identify with one of these classic teen archetypes, reminiscent of John Hughes's landmark adolescent angstfest, *The Breakfast Club.* Which one are you? The Brain, the Basket Case, the Princess? They're all here, reinterpreted by Vaughan for the 21st-century teen.

Stand-alone or Serial?: Serial; collects Runaways #1–6, with subsequent sequel collections.

Hook It Up With: *The Shadow Club* by Neal Shusterman and *Alt Ed* by Catherine Atkins.

Read More about It:
Library Journal: 09/01/04
Publishers Weekly: 06/28/04

Vaughan, Brian K., and Pia Guerra. 2002. *Y: The Last Man—Unmanned.* New York: DC Comics. 126p.

The Story: Amateur magician and unemployed new college grad Yorick Brown is the last man on earth—literally. The year is 2002, and a bizarre plague has killed every living being with a Y chromosome, except Yorick and his male pet monkey, Ampersand. In a surprisingly hostile landscape, where packs of militant biker women who believe themselves to be the new Amazons hunt along the highways, Yorick makes his way in disguise from Brooklyn to Washington, D.C., to try to find his mom, a Democratic congresswoman, using a few of his trusty magic tricks to evade capture by suspicious girls.

While Yorick's mom is thrilled to discover that he is still alive, she is, along with some of her elected friends, pretty busy trying to hold down the White House as the wives of deceased Republicans lay siege to it. Once Yorick's mother reveals his existence to the secretary of agriculture (who is now the president, because everyone else in the chain of command is dead), the new leader of the free world sends Yorick on a quest with special agent 355, a kick-ass, dreadlocked martial arts expert, to find Dr. Allison Mann, a top scientist who specializes in cloning. The hope is that Dr. Mann will somehow be able to isolate whatever it is that kept Yorick and his monkey alive, when all other males dropped dead, and replicate it. Yorick, still in shock, refuses to take his situation very seriously and keeps trying to sidetrack 355 in order to make an escape to Australia, where his blond bombshell anthropologist girlfriend Beth is working somewhere in the Outback.

Meanwhile, Yorick's sister, Hero, has been brainwashed by Victoria, the brainy militant feminist who heads the Amazon movement. These women believe that the plague was a divine justice; as a sign of their loyalty to the new matriarchy, they have one of their breasts removed to resemble the Amazon warriors of myth, who cut off a breast in order to shoot arrows more accurately. One of Victoria's minions spots Yorick and 355 and reports the former's existence to Victoria, who asks for volunteers to hunt down and kill this last man. Hero, who has no idea that the offending male is her brother, is the first to raise her hand. There is also a pack of female Israeli soldiers who have traveled to America after being tipped off about Yorick's existence; they want him for their own reasons.

Agent 355 and Yorick make it to Dr. Mann's lab in Boston, but when they leave briefly to go chasing after Ampersand, they return to find the entire building engulfed in flames, including Dr. Mann's lab and all her samples. The Israeli soldiers set the fire to prevent the doctor from cloning any men in the future. Dr. Mann has a contingency lab that contains some duplicate records and materials, but it is in California. Yorick, 355, and Dr. Mann are left somberly contemplating their next course of action.

The Message: Thirst for power knows no gender. In their own way, women can be just as brutal as men. Not everyone is your friend. No one has all the answers. Cooperation is the key to survival.

Who's It For?: 10th–12th grade. There is a great deal of graphic gun violence and blood depicted in this postapocalyptic world, along with partial female nudity and strong language. The men die all at once, with blood streaming from every orifice. There are corpses piled in the streets, and some of the Amazons' mutilated chests are shown. As previously mentioned, this is tame stuff compared with other media aimed at teens, but this title is one you might want to examine personally to determine whether or not it meets the selection criteria for your collection. Subsequent volumes in this ongoing series are equally as violent and even more sexual in nature. I would give this to a high school student who dug *30 Days of Night* but not to a middle school fan of *Queen Bee*.

Why It Rocks:
- **Art:** Serviceable; again it is Vaughan's words that make the package work. Guerra's art is very straightforward; she doesn't linger on the violence, but she doesn't shy away from it either.
- **Plot:** Although I hesitated to include another title by Vaughan, I decided to go ahead because while the two stories share the same brand of snappy, clever writing, they are for two very different audiences. The back cover of *Y* states that it is "suggested for mature readers," and while that is certainly true, maturity is relative: Yorick's headstrong, lovesick, impetuous, wisecracking character is still an adolescent in every sense of the word.
- **Pacing:** Occasionally uneven, juxtaposing philosophical sections that ponder the reality of a female-ruled world with sometimes shockingly violent action sequences.
- **Characterization:** Vaughan's vision of a female-ruled world is a balanced, sobering, and occasionally hilarious view of the fairer sex's strengths and shortfalls. Despite the widely accepted generalization that female leaders are more cooperative

than male ones, Vaughan's female politicians don't seem to get along any better now that their male counterparts are gone. The women in D.C. who are grieving the men who have passed set up a makeshift memorial at where else? The Washington Monument. (Insert giggle here!) The Amazons may be brutal man haters, but the author shows just as many devastated wives, sisters, daughters, and girlfriends mourning their lost loved ones. Teens are going to love how brutally honest Vaughan is about the realties of both genders and how his postapocalyptic plotline challenges and questions the ultra–politically correct atmosphere in which they have grown up.

Stand-alone or Serial?: Serial; collects *Y: The Last Man,* #1–5, with subsequent sequel collections.

Hook It Up With: *Tomorrow, When the War Began* by John Marsden and *Z for Zachariah* by Robert C. O'Brien.

Read More about It:
Booklist: 02/01/03
Library Journal: 05/01/03
Publishers Weekly: 10/06/03

Whedon, Joss; Karl Moline; and Andy Owens. 2003. *Fray.* Portland, OR: Dark Horse Comics. unpaged.

The Story: In the gritty, grimy futuristic city of Haddyn, where cars fly and just breathing in some parts of town is a biohazard, lives professional thief Melaka Fray. With blue-black hair that tumbles down into magenta curls, a trusty stun gun, and astonishing reflexes, Mel is one the best "grabbers" in the business, a fact that is not lost on her most frequent employer, a fish-mutant black market art dealer named Gunther. Mel enjoys her work as a thief, mainly because it riles her elder sister Erin, a police officer, and helps shut out the pain of the death of her twin brother, Harth, who was killed four years ago while on a grab with Mel. She keeps her distance from most people but allows herself to love Loo, the motor-mouthed, pigtailed five-year-old daughter of the local bar owner who doesn't let the fact that she is missing half her right arm and is blind in one eye stop her from following Mel everywhere.

One particularly harrowing day, when Mel has already fallen off a building and had a nasty fight with her sister, she returns to her apartment to discover a giant, red, horned and hoofed demon named Urkonn, who informs her that he has been assigned to prepare and train her for her upcoming battle against the legions of vampires currently planning to take over the human world. Mel, who has never even heard of vampires, is confused. From Urkonn she comes to understand that vampires are what her society calls "lurks," shadowy addicts who crave blood and live in the city's sewers.

As long as there have been lurks, there have been Slayers, powerful self-healing female warriors who were created by the very first shamans and magicians at the dawn of civilization to thin the vampire ranks. Melaka is the current incarnation of the Slayer. The last active Slayer, from the 21st century, was able to banish all demons from the earthly realms but was lost in the process. Since then, there have been other Slayers, but they haven't been called on to defend the earth, since much of the evil threat had been removed. But now, the ranks of undead have swelled, and they have a new leader who has the power to open the portals of hell and release the demons back into the earthly dimension.

Mel has always wondered about her body's fast-healing properties and incredible physical flexibility. But she has no desire to assume the Slayer's mantle; because it was a lurk who murdered her twin on the ill-fated grab four years, and as a result they are the only beings Mel is truly afraid of. Urkonn also tells her she should have had some inkling about her destiny through dreams of being a Slayer that should have come to her in her sleep, but Mel has never dreamed and doesn't believe Urkonn at first. But then Icarus, the very vampire that killed her twin, accosts her. He brings her to meet his powerful leader, whom Mel is shocked to discover is her lost brother, Harth. Instead of dying, Harth was turned into a vampire by Icarus, and subsequently became very evil. As the twin of the Slayer, Harth inherited all of Mel's dreams of being the Chosen One. Only now that he has gone to the other side, he is using his part of the Slayer's powers to raise an army of vampires and work the dark magic that will release demons back into the world.

Harth physically beats Mel and tosses her down into the sewers. She painfully makes her way to Erin's apartment, where she tells her sister everything she has learned, then goes back to her own place, where Urkonn is waiting. She is devastated to discover that someone has trashed her apartment and murdered little Loo. Enraged, she rallies the petty criminals and shady citizens of her rundown neighborhood by showing them Loo's body and telling them about the true nature of the lurks. Erin shows up with a flying fleet of cops she has persuaded to join the fight. As the human vigilantes assemble, Harth is readying his minions for battle. He has also managed to raise a huge demon that is part centipede, part rattlesnake, and whose womb is the portal into hell. Harth plans to ride it out into the city streets, where its hideous eggs will hatch and release hordes of monsters.

As the two armies come together, Mel is snapped up by Harth's demon. Never one to give up, she begins to hack her way through the monster's head and comes out through its eye, killing it just as Harth and Erin are fighting each other to the death on the demon's back. All three are thrown clear as the monster crashes into the side of a building. The vampires scatter, and Harth escapes unscathed in the ensuing chaos. Although the city has been saved and the demon portal closed, Mel is still troubled about Loo's death. It appeared that vampires killed Loo, but she accuses Urkonn of the murder, and he admits that he felt he was forced to kill Loo to push Melaka into accepting her role as Slayer. In a violent fight that takes place mostly underwater in the unfortunate Gunther's fish tank, Mel finishes Urkonn as well.

A frame story concerning two powerful head demons who had originally sent Urkonn to "deal with" Melaka suggests that Urkonn wasn't the ally he pretended to be, and her decision to off him was probably wise. Having finally accepted her calling, Melaka rebuilds her relationship with her sister as she continues to slay vampires and watch over the city she loves.

The Message: Fate may decide our destiny, but we decide how we fulfill it. Learn to depend on yourself, but don't be afraid to ask for help when you need it. Good will always triumph over evil.

Who's It For?: 7th–12th grade. Lots of gore, stabbing, and hand-to-hand violence, but the candy-apple-red blobs of seemingly impenetrable blood that dot the faces and clothes of vampire victims look cartoonish and not especially frightening. What are sad and somewhat scary scenes are those where Harth is viciously and violently bitten by Icarus while Mel stands by helplessly and where Mel finds Loo's poor little broken body and carries it back to her parents. There is one obligatory shower scene, but Mel's body stays firmly in shadow; so, while nudity is implied, it's not shown.

Why It Rocks:
• **Art:** Using white space to highlight his splashy Technicolor palate, and panels tipped at surprising angles, Karl Moline's layout feels very cinematic. Burning trash cans, bombed-out buildings, and fiery explosions provide the perfect postapocolyptic playground for Mel to gambol in. From her tricolor hair and biohazard tattoo to her belly-baring tank tops, (thankfully) small chest, and clunky Doc Martens, Mel is a stylish street kid who manages to kick vampire butt while never smudging her toxic-purple lipstick.
• **Plot:** Former *Buffy* fans, who still may be feeding their vampire-hunter habit with the glossy DVD sets, will love reading this new chapter in Slayer mythology, (if they don't already know about it), but even teens who've never watched a single episode will still be able to enjoy this stand-alone Slayer story.
• **Pacing:** The action rocks and rolls, but Whedon does take the time to lay down the background of the Buffy legend.
• **Characterization:** Buffy creator Joss Whedon continues the tradition of the flawed hero with the heart of gold— complex, fraught with anger and regret, and full of contradictions. With a background worthy of a Dickens character and some serious emotional baggage, Mel may not always come out on top, but she always looks good trying and goes down fighting. Whether they love her for her power punches or her streetwise fashion sense, your teens are going to fall hard for Fray.

Stand-alone or Serial?: Stand-alone, originally published as an eight-issue miniseries.

Hook It Up With: *Twilight* by Stephanie Meyer and *Sunshine* by Robin McKinley

Read More about It:
Publishers Weekly: 03/08/04
School Library Journal: 05/01/04

Willingham, Bill, et al. (2002). *Fables: Legends in Exile.* **New York: DC Comics. 128p.**

The Story: Several hundred years ago, an evil force, known only as "The Adversary," assembled a massive army and conquered all of fairy-tale lands and kingdoms. Those mythical beings of story who were able to escape fled to the only land The Adversary was completely uninterested in: the boring land of the humans, or "mundanes." Now they live immortally in, around, and under New York City, trying to escape notice of the "mundys" while they scheme about how to get their homelands back. This underground community is known as Fabletown and is run by the mayor, Old King Cole (of the merry old soul), and his hardworking deputy, Snow White, from a luxury apartment building called The Woodlands.

One day, Jack, formerly known as the Giant Killer, races into the office of Fabletown's head of police, Bigby Wolf, where he gasps out some terrible news: he has just come from the Greenwich Village apartment of his girlfriend, Rose Red, and found it trashed and covered in blood, with Rose nowhere to be found. Bigby informs Snow White of this matter, since she is Rose Red's sister, and the two of them go back to the apartment with Jack. After finding the apartment as Jack claimed and nosing around a bit, Bigby arrests Jack as a possible suspect. However, he's not ruling out Snow White as a suspect, as she has had a public feud with her wild-child, party-loving sister ever since she caught Rose in bed with Snow's now ex-husband, Prince Charming. He also has his eye on Bluebeard, who has dated Rose in the past and has a reputation for murdering the women he loves.

When Bigby questions Bluebeard, the rich pirate informs him that Rose Red and he had a secret contract that stated she would marry him in a year's time if he provided her a considerable "dowry" in advance. The year is almost up, and Bluebeard insists he can't be the murderer because he intends to claim Rose as his bride at the next Remembrance Day (a holiday celebrated by the Fables to remind them of their lost homelands), which is just a few days away. Bigby and Snow are worried that Rose is not just missing, but dead, since Bigby has determined that the blood splattered around the apartment not only is Rose's, but also has been spilled in such a high volume that the person who lost it can't still be alive.

Bigby continues his investigation, questioning the Black Forest Witch (known for her fondness for eating flesh) and Prince Charming, while Old King Cole urges Snow White to wrap up the disturbing investigation by Remembrance Day, so as not to ruin everyone's good time. Meanwhile, Bluebeard sneaks into Jack's cell and threatens his life if he doesn't tell the truth, and Bigby is forced to arrest him as well. By the time the Remembrance Day gala ball rolls around, tensions are high because Rose is still missing and Bigby doesn't seem any closer to solving the case. But looks can be deceiving. In a dramatic move, Bigby unmasks Rose Red's killer in front of everyone at the ball, then proceeds to tell them how and why the killer committed the crime but wasn't quite able to pull it off.

No one is more surprised than Snow White when Rose's killer is revealed to be: Rose herself. According to Bigby, Rose needed a large amount of money to bail Jack out of a get-rich-quick Internet scheme he'd gotten himself involved in, so she conned Bluebeard into agreeing to marry her and giving her an advancement on the dowry. Jack was supposed to earn the money back in enough time for Rose to buy herself out of Bluebeard's contract, but the year was almost up and Jack was still losing money on his dot com business. Rose began collecting and saving her own blood so that she could stage her death and disappearance in order to buy herself and Jack more time to decide what to do.

Rose and Jack sheepishly admit their wrongdoing and apologize. Snow steps in and uses some creative accounting to get money out of her ex, Prince Charming. She uses that money to pay Bluebeard what he's owed, and everyone lives happily every after, more or less. Except Bigby, who over the course of the investigation has developed a serious crush on Snow White. Could there be a romance in the works for the hard-bitten detective and the beautiful civil servant? Only subsequent sequels will tell . . .

The Message: It's easier to tell the truth than to stage an elaborate deception. The more lies you tell, the more entangled in deception you become. Liars never prosper.

Who's It For?: 9th–12th grade. There is strong language, a great deal of blood, and lots of sexual innuendo, which while screamingly funny is not necessarily appropriate for students under 14. Prince Charming is shown having (covered) intercourse with one of his many conquests, and Pinocchio bitterly states that he hates the Blue Fairy because she "interpreted my wish too literally." Now he's "over three centuries old" and still waiting to go through puberty so he can "get laid." Subsequent sequels are increasingly dicey, with one suggesting a sexual relationship between Goldilocks and Baby Bear. This title will, however, work as a wonderful bridge for older reluctant readers who are into dark, fractured fairy-tale prose like *Breath* by Donna Jo Napoli or Melvin Burgess's gruesome soap opera *Bloodtide*, based on ancient Norse mythology.

Why It Rocks:
• **Art:** Lan Medina's artistic style isn't particularly distinctive, but it's serviceable and at least doesn't distract from Willingham's overall vision.
• **Plot:** Twisting the fairy-tale archetype until it screams, Bill Willingham gives us a wonderfully inventive, grown-up version of classical childhood favorites. He also parodies the hard-boiled detective novel with the gradual unraveling of Rose Red's complicated scheme and Bigby's insistence on announcing her guilt during his "parlor room scene," where traditionally "the clever detective reveals all."
• **Pacing:** Although the story may appear to meander, every clue that's dropped throughout ties into the clever ending.
• **Characterization:** Older teens are going to cheer Willingham's sheer nerve in daring to question the folklore canon by transforming their beloved characters into cursing, cigarette-smoking, martini-drinking disgruntled strangers in a strange land. I'm sorry, but there's nothing more delightfully subversive than watching a prim Snow White utter the f-word!

Stand-alone or Serial?: Serial, collecting *Fables* #1–5, with subsequent sequel collections.

Hook It Up With: *Sirena* by Donna Jo Napoli and *Poison* by Chris Wooding.

Read More about It:
Booklist: 02/01/03
Library Journal: 05/01/03
Publishers Weekly: 05/05/03
V.O.Y.A. (Voice of Youth Advocates): 06/01/03

CHAPTER 7

HISTORICAL FICTION FOR HIPSTERS

Whenever I ask a student if he or she wants to try historical fiction, the reaction is always the same: "Do I hafta? [insert groan here] It'll probably be *boring.*" Granted, I'm sure there are many little history heads out there who just eat up your historical fiction suggestions, but by and large very few of them seem to have run into me. What is it about historical fiction? Is it because of the "history" part? Maybe it has to do with the way we phrase it. Maybe instead of saying, "Would you like to try a work of historical fiction?" we should say, "Would you like to try this incredibly exciting and tremendously deep story that will provide you with insight about the world around you and that just happens to take place in the past?" (See how I did that?) How is it that some teens have gotten the idea that historical fiction is boring? It might be because they are assigned to read some historical fiction in their classes, and as we all know, once a book is assigned, that's the death of it and all its kind. It also might be because they're not reading the *right* kinds of historical fiction. You know the kind I mean—the kind that's full of pirates, prostitutes, witches, jewel thieves, wise men, fools, kings, queens, patriots, and survivors. The kind that makes you realize even though this character lived and loved in the past, he or she is just like you. The kind that stays with you long after you've taken the book back to the library. You know, *the good kind.* Teens definitely want to read historical fiction; they just don't always know it yet. So here are some exciting, deep stories that happen to take place in the past and are guaranteed NOT to be boring. Because, they're the, you know, *good kind.*

Carbone, Elisa. 2005. *Last Dance on Holladay Street*. New York: Alfred A. Knopf 196p.

The Time and Place: 1878, Denver, Colorado.

The Story: Thirteen-year-old Eva Wilkins was adopted by her parents, Daddy Walter and Mama Kate, when she was just an infant. A white woman approached the middle-aged African American couple on the streets of Denver on a visit from their farm and asked them if they would take the light-skinned, African American baby and give her a home. Past child-bearing age, they eagerly agreed. Now, Daddy Walter has been dead a year from tetanus and Mama Kate is near death from consumption. Eva doesn't know what she will do or where she will go when Mama Kate passes on. Their only kind neighbor, Mrs. Santini, an Italian immigrant, is leaving the farming community with her husband as he looks for work in Georgetown, one of Colorado's mining towns.

Just before her death, Mama Kate gives Eva a silver dollar and the name and address in Denver of her biological mother, who has been sending money to Mama Kate to take care of Eva. After Mama Kate's funeral, Eva boards a train for Denver. Once there, the sheer number of people and the many different ethnicities they represent overwhelm her. She is lucky enough to run into a kindly African American janitor at the train station named Mr. Stonewall, but he has a dismayed and startled reaction when she shows him the address she's looking for: 518 Holladay Street. When she explains that it is the only contact information she has, he reluctantly agrees to take her there. Eva is surprised to see that the house he leaves her in front of is so rich and fine. She wonders how, if her mother lives in such a house, could she have given her away?

Eva knocks on the door and asks for Sadie Lewis, the name Mama Kate gave her. The woman who answers, Miss B, doesn't seem pleased by her query. When Eva is finally introduced to Sadie and her teenage daughter, Pearl, she is stunned to discover that they are both white. As Sadie faints at the sight of Eva, Eva suddenly understands where she is and what her mother's job is. Sadie is a prostitute; this house, run by Miss B, is what Mama Kate would call, "a house of sin," and Miss B is so furious because Sadie hid the fact that she had given birth to a "colored" child.

While her mother recovers from the shock, a woman named Lucille gets Eva settled and tells her she can share a bed with Pearl, who seems none too happy with the arrangement. Eva spends her first night in the brothel heartened by Lucille's kindness and a good meal. But the next morning, Miss B informs her that she is putting Eva to work in the "dance hall" with Pearl. This is a back room with a bar where men pay 25 cents to dance with Pearl or Eva or a dollar for a watery "cocktail" and the privilege of talking to the girls for a few minutes at the bar while they wait to go "upstairs." Eva knows Mama Kate wouldn't approve, but she needs the money, so she reluctantly agrees. Pearl, who hasn't been too friendly, takes Eva to be fitted for a short silk dress and dancing shoes.

Afterward, Lucille takes Eva aside and tells her the story of her birth—how Sadie met a "colored" miner when Miss B took the girls to a mining town one summer to entertain the men and he fell in love with her. Miss B had a rule about the girls fraternizing with African American men, but the miner persisted until Sadie agreed to have sex with him. She hid the subsequent pregnancy from Miss B, even though she nearly died from blood loss. Later, before her first night in the dance hall, Eva hears all of the women's hard luck stories: tales of orphanages, husbands who left, and uncles who were too friendly. Whenever a girl had no other choice, she ended up at Miss B's.

Eva's dance hall debut is a disaster. She withstands two sweaty, grabby dances before trying to quit, but Pearl asks her how she expects to pay for the room, board, and clothing she's gotten this week without dancing? Eva is shocked to discover that nothing she's been given is free. Afterward, Miss B shows Eva her debt account. According to Miss B's numbers, no matter how hard Eva works, she will always be in Miss B's debt. Pearl tells her it's the same for her and Sadie. Pearl and Eva overhear Miss B threatening Sadie that she'll send Eva and Pearl to work "upstairs" to pay off some of Sadie's debt.

Eva decides to run away and use her silver dollar to buy a train ticket to go to Georgetown and look for Mrs. Santini, but when she gets back to her room after what she had hoped was her last night in the dance hall, she discovers that Miss B has stolen all her clothes to prevent her from leaving. Undeterred, Eva flees in only her camisole and a curtain over her shoulders. She runs barefoot all the way to Mr. Stonewall's rented room. He helps her to get some clothes and food and puts her on the next train out of town.

Eva finds that it's easier to pass as an Italian immigrant than a African American, so she pretends not to speak or understand English. She gets to Georgetown and asks after Mrs. Santini at the post office, but the postmaster, Mr. Flanagan, tells her she has moved on to the next town. After a disastrous attempt to find the Santinis on her own, which results in Eva's withstanding a mountain lion attack and a short recuperation with the postmaster and his family, Eva returns to Denver, worse off than she was before, with no choice but turn herself in to the orphanage.

But at the last moment, Eva evades the orphanage matron at the station and runs back to Mr. Stonewall instead. She discovers that in her absence, Miss B has refused to bail Sadie and Pearl out of jail after a raid until Sadie agrees to let Pearl work upstairs. Eva stays with Mr. Stonewall while trying to convince Miss B to give her the bail money. She sees long lines outside the restaurants run by women and suddenly sees a way out of her situation. She tells Miss B that if she will bail Sadie and Pearl out of jail, they will pay back their debt by starting a "cook house" out of a rented room. Eva uses her silver dollar from Mama Kate to buy their initial supplies, and soon, their little restaurant is doing a brisk business with Eva cooking, Sadie baking, and Pearl serving. Although they still have to sleep on the floor of their room on bedrolls, they are paying off their debt to Miss B a little at a time and Eva finally feels at peace, knowing she is leading the kind of life that Mama Kate and Daddy Walter would be proud of.

The Message: Sometimes, the solution to a problem is right in front of your face. Listen to your conscience; it's usually right. Never give up trying to do the right thing.

Who's It For?: 7th–12th grade. While the length and tone of this novel suggest a young audience, the topic is more fitting to an older teen. That quality, however, makes it perfect for a hi-lo reader. Carbone chooses her words carefully, and the text is never graphic or sensationalistic, despite the subject matter. There are some scenes of violence, such as Eva's witnessing the choking of a prostitute (who survives) at the hands of a drunken customer, and the mountain lion attack. There is also mention of drug use, and Sadie survives a laudanum overdose after discovering Eva is her long-lost child.

Why It Rocks:
- **Voice:** By telling this story in third person, Carbone succeeds in keeping what could easily have become a sensationalistic story from feeling too raw and immediate; however, her third-person telling sometimes has the unintentional effect of feeling too distant and antiseptic. Hearing Eva's own voice may have made for a richer narrative, but young readers will still find her quest for a home compelling.
- **Plot:** Unusual and well wrought. It's certainly not easy to spin for a YA audience an age-appropriate treatment of such a difficult topic that also effectively addresses issues of race, gender, and class. In her author's note, Carbone shares that her story was inspired by the photo of a 15-year-old girl in a book about "fallen women" from the Old West.
- **Pacing:** Plot-driven and quick. Eva's short journey to look for Mrs. Santini may seem too tangential for some readers, but it serves to add excitement to the plotline with the mountain lion attack and to provide more examples of Eva's growing self-reliance.
- **Characterization:** Eva's character is sweet and earnest, realistically naive, but also a fast learner in the ways of the world. Secondary characters are less well developed, and some, like Mama Kate and Miss B, are almost cartoonish in their extremes, but overall this is still a solid story that only occasionally misses its mark.

Hook It Up With: *Witness* by Karen Hesse and *Daughter of Venice* by Donna Jo Napoli.

Read More about It:
Booklist: 02/01/05
Horn Book: 10/01/05
Kirkus Reviews: 02/01/05
School Library Journal: 04/01/05
V.O.Y.A. (Voice of Youth Advocates): 04/01/05

Donnelly, Jennifer. 2003. *A Northern Light*. New York: Harcourt. 389p.

The Time and Place: 1906, a small Adirondack Mountains community, upstate New York.

The Story: Sixteen-year-old Mattie Gokey dreams of going to college and becoming a writer, but a terrible promise and her own insecurities stand in her way. Mattie promised her mother on her deathbed that she would take care of her three younger sisters no matter what; but she is finding that keeping that promise is harder than it seems as she tries to run the entire household on her own and still attend school. Mattie's elder brother, Lawton, who blames their father for their mother's death, left the farm after she died, so Pa often keeps Mattie home from school to help in the house and fields. The Gokey farm is one of many that supply the upscale hotels and resorts in the area with fresh milk and produce, but times are hard in the off-season. Her two best friends are Minnie, who is already married and pregnant, and Weaver, a prideful African American boy whose college dreams match Mattie's. Weaver has received a scholarship to Columbia University, where he plans to go in the fall, while Mattie is still waiting to hear from Barnard. Their teacher, Miss Wilcox, encourages and inspires them with her passionate lectures and shelves full of books.

When Mattie finally gets an acceptance letter from Barnard that includes a full scholarship, she is thrilled but despairing, knowing that her father would never let her go, and even if he did, she could never break the promise she had made to her mother. She tries to stay hopeful about her situation by focusing on the romantic attention she has been garnering lately from Royal Loomis, an attractive neighbor whose family owns the farm adjoining her father's. Mattie can't believe he's interested in her, and she wonders if she could still be happy if she gave up her college dream and married Royal. She witnesses how her friend Minnie always seems tired and careworn after getting married and giving birth to twins, and she remembers how her mother, who loved to read and look up words in her beloved dictionary, rarely had time for books after working on the farm all day.

In spite of her promise, Mattie begins to save a dollar here and there from selling wild berries or helping to organize Miss Wilcox's library, but it isn't until the family mule dies that she gets her chance to earn some real money. Pa needs money for a new animal, so he allows Mattie to work in the restaurant of the Glenmore Hotel with Weaver. Mattie will send some of her earnings to pay for the mule, but the rest she can keep for herself. Miss Wilcox is so happy for her that Mattie can't bear to tell her that she's already written to Barnard to tell them she won't be accepting the scholarship. She has decided she will marry Royal if he asks her, even though he never talks of anything but farming and finds her attachment to books strange. When he finally offers her a ring and suggests a wedding date in the fall, Mattie accepts, even though he has never once said he loves her.

The hotel is a bewildering new world, and Mattie is amazed at everything—from the sheer amount of food she helps serve every day to the decadent lifestyles of the vacationing rich. After Mattie has been working there a short while, she meets a young woman named Grace Brown. One night as Grace is about to go out on a boat ride with her fiancée, she thrusts a packet of letters into Mattie's hands and tells her to burn them in the stove. Startled, Mattie agrees, but becomes busy in the kitchen and forgets all about the letters until the next day, when Grace's dead body is brought up from the lake, her fiancée nowhere to be found.

Mattie struggles with her conscience before reading the letters, which are a correspondence between Grace and her fiancée, Chester Gillette. From the letters, Mattie learns that Grace was pregnant and Chester was responsible, though he refused to marry Grace. When Grace reveals in one of her letters that she can't swim, Mattie realizes that her death was no accident. Chester had lured Grace to the hotel with the promise of marriage, when all the while he was planning to murder her. As Mattie dithers over what to do and whom to tell, the hotel is preparing for their annual Fourth of July extravaganza, which the whole countryside turns out for.

While Mattie is visiting with her friends, she is confronted by Royal's ex-girlfriend, Martha, who spitefully informs her that the only reason Royal is pursuing her is because he has his eye on getting a piece of Mattie's father's farm. When she asks him about it, he all but confesses and Mattie realizes that it is over between them. The day after the celebration, she packs her bag and leaves Grace's letters, with a note explaining what they are and how she got them, on the hotel manager's desk. She also leaves a note for Royal, folded around the ring she is returning and a note for her father with the rest of the money due on the mule. From her savings, she has just enough to buy a train ticket to New York City. Thinking of Grace's lost love and life, and of her own future, she makes peace with herself about her decision: "I know it is a bad thing to break a promise, but I think now that it is a worse thing to let a promise break you."

There are also numerous well-developed subplots that contribute to the richness of the story and Mattie's character development, including Weaver's refusal to become subservient when called "nigger" by some backwoods trappers, who subsequently burn down his family's house and steal his college savings. Mattie is emboldened by Weaver's courage, and his example helps her to make her decision. Also, Miss Wilcox, Mattie's teacher and mentor, turns out to be a renegade poet whose unconventional writings have incensed her husband and caused her to live a life on the run. Mattie admires Miss Wilcox's ability to live alone rather than in an unhappy marriage, which also aids in her efforts to come to terms with her decision not to marry Royal.

The Message: "There is no great loss without some small gain." Education is often the most valuable thing any of us owns. Never underestimate yourself or what you can accomplish if you set yourself a goal and work toward it. Some promises are unfairly asked and meant to be broken. As long as you are alive, you have choices, even when it seems like you don't.

Who's It For?: 8th–12th grade. There are some semi-graphic scenes of childbirth and breast-feeding. A hotel guest exposes his genitals to the female waitresses, and Mattie accidently witnesses Royal's father engaging in sex with a poor neighbor woman who is his longtime mistress. There is also an incident of abuse when Pa hits Mattie for spending money on writing paper when they need it for food.

Why It Rocks:
• **Voice:** Woven throughout Mattie's brave and poignant first-person narration is an insatiable love of books and reading. Through Miss Wilcox, Mattie comes to know Louisa May Alcott, Emily Dickinson, Walt Whitman, and William Blake. This is an unabashed love song to literature, and any booky teenage girl who picks up this novel will fall deeply in love with Mattie and her beloved writers.
• **Plot:** Donnelly's sumptuously detailed, Printz Honor–winning plot is based on a true story. In her author's note, Donnelly explains that Mattie's character was

imagined but Grace Brown and Chester Gillette were real. Grace's body was pulled from a lake in upstate New York on July 12, 1906, and Chester Gillette was later convicted of her murder and executed in 1908.

- **Pacing:** Told in flashbacks between Mattie's present, as she reads through Grace's letters, and the past spring and early summer before she came to work at the hotel, this almost-400-page novel flies along, with numerous intriguing subplots to fuel the action. Donnelly delineates between Mattie's present and past by having the past chapters each start with a word that Mattie has chosen for that day from her mother's precious dictionary.
- **Characterization:** Mattie is a round, fully realized character who changes and grows right before the reader's eyes. In addition, each of the secondary characters is incredibly well drawn, from stubborn Pa and prideful Weaver to selfish Royal and independent Miss Wilcox.

Hook It Up With: *Ashes of Roses* by Mary Jane Auch and *The Awakening* by Kate Chopin.

Read More about It:
Booklist, starred: 05/15/03
Horn Book: 05/01/03
Kirkus Reviews: 03/15/03
Publishers Weekly, starred: 03/03/03
School Library Journal, starred: 05/01/03
V.O.Y.A. (Voice of Youth Advocates): 04/01/03

Hearn, Julie. 2005. *The Minister's Daughter.* **New York: Simon & Schuster. 263p.**

The Time and Place: 1645, a small rural village during the English Civil War, and 1692, Salem, Massachusetts.

The Story: In a small English village, two young women are drawn together by jealousy and circumstance as one tries to fulfill her destiny while the other tries to escape it. Nell is the granddaughter of the village "cunning woman," and she is a "merrybegot," a child conceived on the first of May who is sacred to nature. All Nell knows of her mother is that she came from "across the border" to practice her pagan rituals in secret with the members of Nell's village. She was married to an unforgiving man who sent her away after another impregnated her during a spring fertility ritual. She died giving birth to Nell, and Granny's son, who was Nell's father, left Nell to be raised by Granny. Nell and her Granny are both pagans, who know for a fact that fairies and "piskies" exist, but they keep quiet about it and attend church with the rest of the villagers.

Grace is the rebellious eldest daughter of the new minister, a strict Puritan who has no tolerance for Catholics or pagan worshippers of the "Old Religion." She has a plain, younger sister, Patience, who is prone to wild flights of imagination. Grace has been slipping out at night for secret trysts with Sam, the blacksmith's son, and subsequently finds herself pregnant. The minister believes that it is Nell who is "frolicking" with Sam, and he accuses her in front of everyone at church of indulging in "wanton pleasures." Nell is furious that Sam doesn't deny it, when they both know it is Grace who he has been with.

Meanwhile, the fairies have informed Granny that a new fairy is about to be born and they will need a human midwife. Granny decides that Nell should go, so she is whisked away in the middle of the night by a fairy horseman who takes her to the expectant mother. She is given the birth caul as payment for her service, which, when used properly, can save a human life. Grace tells Sam that she is pregnant, but he is unsympathetic and leaves shortly afterward to become a solider. Grace goes to Granny in hope of securing a potion to end the pregnancy, but Nell is the only one home and refuses to help her on the grounds that the baby is a merrybegot, therefore sacred and not to be harmed.

Grace decides to accuse Nell of witchcraft to distract her father from her growing belly. She takes to her bed and begins to feign illness, claiming Nell has cursed her. She also forces Patience to take part in the fraud, and soon the town is buzzing with gossip about the minister's daughter's bizarre affliction. Additionally, Grace orders Patience to take a jeweled frog charm, which belonged to their dead mother, and hide it somewhere near Nell's cottage, so that she can later claim Nell stole it. Nell feels responsible for the safety of Grace's baby, so she goes to the minister's house to see if Grace will accept a protection potion. But Grace and Patience go wild in her presence, alerting the minister, who comes running. Nell escapes his grasp but screams out Grace's secret as she flees down the stairs, hoping that the minister will hear and know the truth.

The minister realizes Grace is pregnant but has managed to convince himself that the swelling is a product of a curse put on her by Nell. The minister invites Matthew Hopkins, a famous witch hunter, to the village, to rout out any evil. With the encouragement of the minister and Hopkins, the villagers begin to suspect Granny of witchcraft, and one Sunday they form an angry mob and go to the cunning woman's cottage. Nell is not home when they tie her feeble old grandmother to a rope and dunk her in the pond to see if she will float. The villagers come to their senses and feel badly for what they have done, but it is too late: Granny is in shock and near death. Nell wants to use the caul to save her life, but Granny won't let her. Before Granny dies, she gives Nell her secret box of pagan ritual objects and a small jeweled frog she found in the garden, which used to belong to Nell's mother. Although Nell and her grandmother don't realize it, Nell's and Grace's mothers are one and the same.

After her grandmother's death, Nell keeps the fairy caul with her for protection. One day in the forest, she comes across a dying young soldier. Against her better judgment, she uses the caul to save his life. Meanwhile, Hopkins has been planning her arrest and decides to formerly accuse her on All Hallow's Eve. Hopkins and the minister find Nell half-dressed, wearing the frog pendant, and lying on the floor of the cottage, high on the ritual "flying" ointment pagans use to feel free of their bodies. It is all the evidence they need, and she is interrogated and imprisoned. The minister orders a gallows built to hang the accused witch, but after Nell's death, he plans on taking his family to the New World, where no one will know them and they can start over.

Nell is taken to the gallows, but just as the rope is put around her neck, she is reprieved by the boy she saved, who was not just any soldier, but Prince Charles, the king's son. He was alerted to Nell's plight by a rare cooperation between the piskies and fairies, who worked together to send him a message about Nell's impending death. The prince moves Nell to a coastal town, where she lives happily under his protection until her death. Grace's son is born, and the minister orders him left in the woods to die, where he is found by a kindly village woman, who raises him as her own. Patience, now an old woman living in Salem, Massachusetts, during the infamous witch-hunts, ironically finds herself accused of witchcraft. Still angry and jealous of her pretty, elder sister, she tells the tale of her sister's teenage pregnancy and sets the elders on Grace, who she still believes (or does she?) bore the "devil's spawn."

The Message: Liars never prosper. "What goes around comes around." No good deed goes unpunished. Be true to yourself in all situations, and you can't go wrong.

Who's It For?: 8th–12th grade. This novel is a twofer: an original blend of historical fiction and fantasy that will interest fans of both genres. The discussions of unwed pregnancy, abortion, and sexual rituals associated with pagan religious practice are not explicit, but devout religious teens may be offended by some of the content.

Why It Rocks:
- **Voice:** This richly woven story is told in two voices: an omniscient third person, where the reader is allowed into the minds of several of the characters (including Nell, Granny, and Grace), and the first-person voice of Patience, now an old woman, who is telling her accusers in 1692 Salem the events of her childhood that led her to believe that her sister, Grace, is a witch. Both points of view are equally well wrought and complement each other well, as the plot twists, turns, then twists again!
- **Plot:** Inventive and wildly entertaining. Hearn tells her story with the authoritative assumption that not only did piskies and fairies exist, but also their actions helped shape the course of human history. This enlivens the actual historical events considerably, and while the lines between fact and fantasy are somewhat blurred, readers will easily be able to tell the difference.
- **Pacing:** Quick, and full of foreshadowing. The reader is dropped right into the rising conflict between Nell and the minister, the old ways and the new. Arranged chronologically from April to the following January, the suspense builds as Grace's belly swells and the minister's wrath grows.
- **Characterization:** Each character in Hearn's tale is wonderfully, tragically human. Even the minister himself, who would have been easy to portray one-dimensionally, has a moment of uncertainty as Nell is about to hang when he recognizes his unfaithful wife in Nell's features. Patience is a complicated, unreliable narrator who seems simple but may actually be the most clever one in the bunch. And many readers will be surprised to learn in the author's note that witch-hunter Matthew Hopkins was actually a real person!

Hook It Up With: *Juniper, Wise Child,* and *Colman,* all by Monica Furlong; and *A Break with Charity* by Ann Rinaldi.

Read More about It:
Booklist: 05/15/05
Horn Book: 10/01/05
Kirkus Reviews, starred: 05/15/05
Publishers Weekly, starred: 06/27/05
School Library Journal: 06/15/05
V.O.Y.A. (Voice of Youth Advocates):

McCaughrean, Geraldine. 2002. *The Kite Rider.* **New York: HarperCollins. 272p.**

The Time and Place: 13th-century China, near the beginning of Kublai Khan's reign, around 1281.

The Story: Twelve-year-old Haoyou is in a terrible bind. His sailor father, Pei, has died of a heart attack after being sent aloft on a homemade kite to "test the wind," a common tradition among Chinese sailors before a journey. Now, the man responsible for sending his father, Di Chou, the ship's brutish first mate, has petitioned Haoyou's greedy uncle, Bo, for Haoyou's beautiful widowed mother's hand in marriage. If Haoyou doesn't stop the marriage, then he; his mother, Qing'an; and his little sister, WaWa, will be forced to answer to the murderous Di Chou.

Luckily, Haoyou has a wise ally in his second cousin, Mipeng, a local medium. There is no love lost between her and Di Chou because he beat her and cut off all her hair after she stated during a family séance that it would be bad luck for Qing'an to marry again. The two cousins happen to see Di Chou duck into an unsavory bar the night before the wedding and spy on him as he drinks himself into a stupor. Thinking fast, they haul the unconscious criminal down to the wharf, where they sign him into service on the next departing ship. The nervous captain wants to wait until morning to do a wind test, but Haoyou offers to go up on the spot, willing to do anything to get rid of Di Chou. Haoyou's flight is straight and successful, and he is surprised at how much he enjoys it.

The next day, when Uncle Bo is livid over Di Chou's failure to show up for his own wedding, a tall, handsome, well-dressed stranger comes to the door. His name is The Great Miao, and he is the head of the traveling Jade Circus. He happened to witness Haoyou's impromptu flight at the wharf and wants to offer him an apprenticeship in the circus as a kite rider. Uncle Bo eagerly agrees, seeing a way to get back some of the money that Qing'an's widowhood has cost him as head of the family. Haoyou insists that he must bring Mipeng, whom he needs to summon the spirits that allow him to "fly."

When Haoyou gets to the circus grounds, he is not pleased to see that Miao's company is made up of both Chinese and Mongol members. The barbarian ruler

Kublai Khan has recently conquered China, and there is still a great deal of tension between the native Chinese and their Mongol conquerors. Mipeng and Haoyou build a huge, red kite for him to fly on, complete with painted golden characters of good luck, bamboo whistles, and a long horsehair tail. Haoyou's first flight in his hometown is successful, so he leaves with The Great Miao, promising to send his mother money. The circus is on its way to Kublai's court to perform for the new ruler.

Soon, Haoyou and Mipeng have created an act that is half spectacle, half fortune-telling. Haoyou rides the kite into the wind, and Mipeng "translates" the squeaks and squeals that comes from the bamboo whistles, which she claims are the voices of the ancestor spirits. Haoyou feels guilty about lying to people, but when he sees how much money he is making to send home to his mother, he feels a little better. But after he suffers a bad fall while aloft and looking for a lost circus worker's child, sustaining a concussion that leaves a small blind spot in one eye, he is nervous about flying; Miao kindly doesn't push him.

Unexpectedly, Uncle Bo and Aunt Mo show up at the circus, demanding hospitality and all of Haoyou's earnings. Mipeng warns Haoyou not to give Bo anything because he will just gamble it away, but Haoyou wants to be seen as an obedient nephew, so he turns over the money. Miao is disappointed in him and furious that Bo has attached himself to the circus retinue with no intention of leaving.

On their way to the khan's summer place in Xanadu, the circus runs into the ruler's traveling court. As they prepare to perform for Kublai, Miao shares a dark secret with Haoyou, Miao is actually a member of the royal Sung family, the dynasty Kublai Khan destroyed. Before Miao's father died, he made Miao pledge to assassinate Kublai. Miao has decided not to do it, because he believes it is wiser to try to understand why God chose Kublai Khan to rule, but Haoyou's unwavering sense of obedience has made him think again. Haoyou is troubled and confused by this news but still performs successfully for the ruler.

Later, Uncle Bo makes a dangerous wager with some of the khan's brutal knights: that they can't keep one of their own on a kite in the sky longer than Haoyou. This ends in disaster, with one of Kublai's knights dead and Haoyou in disgrace and in danger of being beheaded. Haoyou is saved when one of the Mongols points out to the khan that the boy could serve as a spy in the sky for the his armies. In the ensuing chaos as Miao tries to smuggle Haoyou away from Kublai Khan's army, with the disgraced Uncle Bo and Aunt Mo, Haoyou accidentally spills Miao's secret. Uncle Bo confronts Miao and tells him that if he doesn't sign over the circus to Bo, he will tell the khan who Miao really is. Instead, Miao proudly tells the khan himself and waits to be executed. But when all the circus people, Chinese and Mongol alike, line up with him, the khan decides it is too much trouble. He leaves with his army but still insists on taking Haoyou and his kite.

On his first assignment for Kublai Khan, Haoyou is sent up in terrible weather, and in the subsequent storm and battle, he crashes into a river and is swept away. Kublai and his army, also ravaged by the weather, reassemble and leave, believing the kite boy lost or dead. Haoyou is battered but alive, having finally completely lost his vision in one eye. He works his way home, where he discovers that his mother was sold by Uncle Bo to work as a serving maid in a filthy bar. Miao and Mipeng, who have fallen in love and married and are now traveling with the rest of the company in a lavish dragon-shaped circus boat, come looking for Haoyou and his family. Haoyou,

Qing'an, and Aunt Mo join them after Uncle Bo is left alone to gamble away his last penny, and Haoyou cleverly tricks a returned Di Chou into being responsible for all his mother's debts. Free at last, the happy family sails away to its next adventure.

The Message: Blind obedience isn't a good guiding principle. Question authority, especially if it seems you are being taken advantage of. "What goes around comes around." Crime doesn't pay. When in doubt, be honest and tell the truth. Don't be afraid to dream big or fly high (literally or figuratively).

Who's It For?: 6th–12th grade. While Haoyou is chronologically young, his adventures and this richly detailed narrative will appeal to older teens and middle schoolers alike. There is no sexual content here, but obviously lots of historically accurate violence. The brutality of Kublai Khan's armies is noted, Miao is nearly executed by being rolled up in a rug and trampled to death by a horse, and Uncle Bo almost strangles Mipeng to death when he hears of her marriage to Miao, for which he didn't give permission. Everything McCaughrean writes is historically accurate and necessary to the story, and I personally have used this title in sixth-grade medieval literature circles.

Why It Rocks:
•   **Voice:** McCaughrean employs a limited third-person point of view, mostly from Haoyou's viewpoint, and occasionally from Di Chou's or Uncle Bo's position, that emphasizes how integral each character is in this carefully constructed ensemble piece.
•   **Plot:** Exhilarating and absorbing. The attention to historical detail is meticulous and complete, and the sight, sounds, and smells of the 13th-century circus and Kublai Khan's traveling court are brought to such vivid life that it will be difficult for readers to extricate themselves from the pages and return to their 21st-century world.
•   **Pacing:** The action rises and falls steadily, and just when the reader is breathing a sigh of relief, Haoyou begins to ride the crest of yet another hair-raising adventure. This page-turning pace is a real accomplishment in such a densely plotted piece of historical fiction.
•   **Characterization:** Arguably the best character is Mipeng, Haoyou's stubborn, wise cousin, who was the catalyst for his character development, but this is truly a cast of equals, where each character, from the mighty Kublai Khan to the circus worker's lost toddler, is given room to shine.

Hook It Up With: *I Rode a Horse of Milk White Jade* by Diane Lee Wilson, *A Single Shard* by Linda Sue Park, and *Dragon Keeper* by Carole Wilkinson.

Read More about It:
Booklist, starred: 05/15/02
Horn Book, starred: July/August 2002
Kirkus Reviews, starred: 05/15/02
Publishers Weekly: 07/08/02
School Library Journal, starred: 06/01/02
V.O.Y.A. (Voice of Youth Advocates):

Meyer, L. A. 2002. *Bloody Jack: Being an Account of the Curious Adventures of Mary "Jacky" Faber, Ship's Boy.* New York: Harcourt. 278p.

The Time and Place: 1797, London, England, and the high seas aboard the H.M.S. *Dolphin.*

The Story: Mary Faber is only eight years old when her family is killed by a deadly fever. Thrown out of her middle-class home, Mary is adopted by a gang of homeless orphans, who beg and steal to survive. When Mary is 12 years old, the beloved leader of her gang is killed, and she decides that it's time to make a clean break from the London slums. She cuts off all her hair, trades her skirts for trousers, and heads down the Thames to the sea, hoping to find a job on the docks.

Mary quickly discovers that moving about without suspicion is much easier as a boy than a girl. So she rechristens herself "Jacky" and names her charade "the Great Deception." Because of her ability to read, she wins a treasured spot as a ship's boy aboard a British naval ship named the H.M.S. *Dolphin.* She is quickly apprenticed to Mr. Tilden, the ship's schoolteacher, and meets the other ship's boys: Davy, Benjy, Willy, Tink, and Jaimy. Of all of the boys, Jaimy is the only one who's not an orphan or from a desperately poor family, and after standing a few midnight watches with him, Jacky decides she likes him best.

After an initial bout of seasickness, the ship's boys all settle in to life on the boat. There are lessons to learn, riggings to climb, and decks to scrub. Jacky likes most of the adult sailors, except the sneaky Bill Stoat, who looks at her with predatory eyes. Her "sea dad," Liam, an Irish sailor who is teaching her the ways of the ship, warns her to keep clear of Stoat and his troublemaking friends. The ship's boys form a close-knit group, creating "The Brotherhood of the Ship's Boys of His Majesty's Ship the *Dolphin*," complete with a secret handshake and a blood oath. The *Dolphin's* course is set toward North Africa in search of pirates that threaten England's merchant ships. The sailors drill daily with cannons to prepare for battle, and Jacky's role is to drum while the captain gives commands.

After several months at sea, Jacky is becoming more and more aware of her attraction to Jaimy and wonders if he would find her desirable if he knew she were a girl. When Jacky gets her first period onboard, she becomes so convinced she's dying that she writes a last will and testament. When the bleeding stops, Jacky is relieved to still be alive and resolves to do more study on the mysterious matter. Finally, after much drilling and preparation, the *Dolphin's* crew comes upon a pirate ship. In the confusion and fear of her first battle, Jacky's only fear is for Jaimy, and she ends up killing a pirate who is about to attack him, saving his life. She hates what she has done, but earns the respect of the crew, who begin calling her "Bloody Jack." One of the Brotherhood, Benjy, is killed in the battle, but despite their sadness, the ship's boys' morale is high, since the *Dolphin* captured the pirate ship and secured its treasure.

The *Dolphin* docks in the tropical port of Palma, and the Brotherhood get matching anchor tattoos with their first pay. Jacky goes first, so she has time to stop at a brothel she saw on the way and ask the women there about the mysterious bleeding. She is relieved to find out that she is not dying but worries that as her puberty progresses, she will be found out. She is already strapping down her growing chest with a tight-fitting vest under her shirt, and she makes excuses not to join the boys in the ship's "head" (toilets).

The *Dolphin* heads next to the Caribbean on the trail of the dread pirate LaFieve, who is known for his brutality. As they continue their search, Jacky is fighting her own battle onboard. Sloat is stalking her, and when he finally corners her in the middle of a dark night with the intention of sexually assaulting her, Jacky panics and runs him through with her hidden knife. Sloat stumbles overboard and drowns. Jacky hides, hoping everyone will think Sloat's death is an accident; but blood is found on the rail, and Liam is blamed for his death. Jacky is horrified that her "sea dad" has been accused, and she quickly confesses to the Captain herself, claiming self-defense. Luckily, the Captain believes her, but she decides that the deception has become too difficult to maintain and resolves to tell the truth soon and ask to be left off in Jamaica.

Meanwhile, Jaimy has become distant and cold, and finally confesses to Jacky that this is because he is afraid he is turning "sodomite," since he finds himself sexually attracted to her. So she tells him her secret and seals his stunned silence with a kiss. They get a chance to act like a real couple when they dock in Jamaica, when Jacky brushes out her hair and buys a bright tropical dress and the two of them lunch together in public. Jaimy swears he'll marry her, but Jacky knows it is impossible, owing to their unusual circumstances.

Not long after they leave Jamaica, the *Dolphin* happens upon LaFieve and his pirate fleet. After a long, violent battle the pirates blow a huge hole in the side of the *Dolphin* and make their getaway. The crew manages to find shelter in the cove of a deserted island, where they make repairs on their ship. Mr. Tilden creates an enormous kite capable of carrying a person, with the intention of sending someone up to signal a passing ship. Jacky is elected to be the kite's passenger because she is the smallest and lightest of the crew. The Captain promises her midshipman status when she lands, the first step in becoming a ship's officer. Unfortunately, the breeze is so strong that it tugs up the shallowly rooted palm tree the kite is tethered to and flies away.

Jacky is sure she's about to die, but after a day of floating, she comes down safely on yet another deserted island. Relived to be able to drop the Deception, Jacky lives the happy life of a castaway for almost 20 days. Then she spots both her ship and LaFieve's coming to her island from different directions. She runs to warn the *Dolphin's* crew but is captured by LaFieve's band. They almost hang her in an attempt to get the Captain to surrender the *Dolphin*, but Jaimy and Liam rush in to save her just as LaFieve kicks the barrel out from under her feet. The Captain, finally learning of Jacky's secret, locks her in the brig until she can be dropped off in Boston, where her share of the pirate money will be used to pay for her to attend a finishing school for young ladies. Jaimy swears his undying love, and that he will come for her as soon as he is able. Jacky resolves to wait for him while wondering what waits for her behind the doors of the Lawson Peabody School for Young Girls, which suddenly seems more frightening than an ocean full of ruthless pirates.

The Message: There are both advantages and disadvantages of being either male or female in any given society. You make your own luck, you are the master of your own fate. Honesty is (usually) the best policy. Loyalty and shared values are essential values in any good friendship.

Who's It For?: 7th–12th grade. The descriptions of the horrors the orphan gangs must endure on the streets of London may upset some younger readers. Jacky's near rape by Sloat is short but somewhat graphically depicted. Jacky also comments frequently on the many physical changes she is undergoing and on her passionate make-out sessions with Jaimy once she tells him her secret. The battle scenes are realistically violent, complete with bloodshed and death. Teen fans of C. S. Forester's *Horatio Hornblower* series, or Patrick O'Brian's Jack Aubrey novels (*Master and Commander*) will also find much to like here.

Why It Rocks:
- **Voice:** Meyer does a wonderful job of approximating the street slang and dialect of the time period. In this first-person narrative, Jacky starts out sounding and acting like a grubby little boy, but slowly, as she matures and gains experience, her voice begins to age subtly, though she remains as foul-mouthed as ever!
- **Plot:** Like many of you reading this, I am *so tired* of the girl-dressed-as-a boy premise, however, *Bloody Jack* transcends this stock formula because of the meticulous attention Meyer pays to historical detail. Every aspect is perfect, from the description of the ship's boys' duties down to the buttons on the Captain's uniform.
- **Pacing:** Warn teens that they may end up reading this one in a single sitting. It's a thrill a minute, and a breathless suspense is maintained by whether Jacky's "Deception" will be discovered.
- **Characterization:** Other than the sassy, vulnerable Jacky herself, the rest of Meyer's characters remain stubbornly stock, from the stalwart Captain to the snarling pirate LaFieve. That's no great loss, however, because the rocketing plot is so exciting that most readers won't notice or care.

Hook It Up With: the rest of the titles in the *Bloody Jack Adventures* series (*Curse of the Blue Tattoo, Under the Jolly Roger, In the Belly of the Bloodhound*) by L. A. Meyer, *Pirates!* by Celia Rees, and *Stowaway* by Karen Hesse.

Read More about It:
Booklist, starred: 11/15/02
Horn Book: January/February 2003
Kirkus Reviews: 08/01/02
Publishers Weekly, starred: 10/07/02
School Library Journal: 09/01/02
Voice of Youth Advocates (V.O.Y.A.): 12/01/02

Morpungo, Michael. 2004. *Private Peaceful.* New York: Scholastic. 202p.

The Time and Place: Turn of the century to the beginning of WWI, 1914, rural Devon County, England, and the battlefields of France.

The Story: It is close to midnight, and Private Thomas Peaceful is using his brother Charlie's watch to count down the hours until morning. At dawn something terrible is going to happen that Thomas can't bear to think about, so instead, he begins to review memories of happier times and the significant moments that have brought him to this place. He begins by recalling his first day of school, how his beloved elder brother, Charlie, took him to his class and he made his first friend, Molly, who showed him how to tie his shoe.

Thomas's family is made up of Mother, Charlie, Thomas, and Big Joe, Thomas's eldest brother, who, as result of childhood meningitis, is developmentally disabled but much adored by his siblings. Molly, a neighbor girl who is distant from her own strict parents and spends as much time as possible visiting the Peaceful home, is like their sister. Thomas's family lives on the Colonel's estate, where his father was the forester, but when his father is accidentally killed by a falling tree, the Colonel comes to their cottage and tells Mother they will have to move, since their housing was contingent upon her husband's job.

The Colonel offers Mother a job as a lady's maid to his ailing wife, and she accepts, although that will mean leaving her boys on their own. "Grandmother Wolf," the name the boys have bestowed on their mother's controlling aunt, comes to stay and watch them, but she is mean to Big Joe, and the children hate her. Then the Colonel's wife dies and Mother comes home. Once again, the family is worried that they will be put out, but the Colonel's wife made him promise before she died that he would let the family stay in their house.

The close siblings' childhood is mostly idyllic as they hike, fish, and roam the Devon countryside. Molly, Charlie, and Thomas are the best of friends, but as they grow older, Thomas feels the other two begin to pull away from him and closer to each other. The gap grows wider when they finish school and take jobs on the estate: Molly as a maid in the house and Charlie as dog keeper in the kennels. This brings Charlie in close contact with the Colonel and provides greater opportunities for conflict. Ever since he and Thomas were caught poaching on the Colonel's land when they were younger, the Colonel has been suspicious of Charlie. He fires him for daring to rescue an old hunting dog that he intended to shoot and later kills the dog anyway, causing Big Joe to run away in grief and go missing for two days. He also tells Molly's parents that Charlie is a bad influence, and they forbid her to see him anymore.

Thomas begins carrying letters back and forth between Charlie and Molly, happy to get to spend any time at all with Molly, whom he misses. Meanwhile, talk of war with Germany has begun to spread through the countryside, and Thomas has left school and joined Charlie working at a local dairy farm. One day when the two return home from work, they find Molly sobbing into Mother's lap. She is pregnant, Charlie is the father, and her parents have disowned her. Molly and Charlie marry quietly, and Molly comes to live with them.

As the war escalates, the Colonel makes the announcement that he wants every able-bodied man living or working on his estate to volunteer for the service. He tells Mother that if Charlie doesn't go, he's putting the family out of their house. Thomas, although he is only 16, resolves to go with his brother. They go through their basic training, and to Thomas, the trench digging and rifle drills are like "playing" at being a soldier. Then he boards a ship to France with the rest of his company and as he disembarks, sees the lines of walking wounded soldiers on their way home—suddenly it's all too real.

Thomas and Charlie are assigned to Sergeant Hanley, who forms an immediate dislike for the brothers. When the sergeant makes Thomas run laps until he passes out for some minor infraction, Charlie breaks rank and charges at him. For that, Hanley has Charlie tied spread eagle on a gun wheel in the pouring rain and marches the rest of the company past as a warning against insubordination. After that the brothers and their company begin their move closer and closer to the front, under different commanders. They are happy to leave Hanley behind and move on to serve under the kind Captain Wilkie in Belgium. Although life in the trenches is endlessly wet and full of rats and lice, Captain Wilkie is encouraging and Charlie is like everyone's big brother. During a raid on enemy lines, Captain Wilkie is seriously injured, but Charlie carries him back to safety. When he is sent home to recuperate, he leaves Charlie his fine wristwatch in appreciation.

The brothers' new commander is Lieutenant Buckland, and though he is kind, he is young and inexperienced. They undergo the heaviest shelling yet, and the noise keeps them from being able to sleep or talk. Thomas does his first hand-to-hand fighting at Charlie's side, relieved to discover that he is not a coward. When the Germans retreat, the brothers' company follows and Buckland is killed right next to Thomas. Thomas loses Charlie in the chaos, but he turns up a day later, shot in the foot but otherwise fine. He is sent home on leave, while Thomas is left alone under the new commander, Sergent Hanley.

Hanley hasn't changed one bit and soon crushes the company's spirit with his verbal abuse and obsessive drilling. Thomas survives his first gas attack and receives word that Molly had a baby boy and that Charlie was there to greet him. Charlie comes back in time to take part in the next big push toward enemy lines, but while they are charging forward, Thomas is wounded. Charlie refuses Hanley's order to leave the relative safety of a dugout in No Man's Land, because Thomas cannot move. Hanley warns Charlie that if he doesn't follow orders, he will be brought up on charges. Charlie holds fast, and Hanley leaves the hole with the rest of the company, most of whom are immediately killed. Hanley makes it back to the hole, enraged, and the minute they make it back to their own lines under cover of darkness, Charlie is arrested and taken away.

Thomas isn't allowed to see Charlie for six weeks, and by then the court martial is over and he has been sentenced to death by firing squad for refusing to obey the order of a commanding officer. The brothers don't cry; Charlie solemnly asks Thomas to take care of Molly and gives him Wilkie's watch. Having come full circle, Thomas has been awake the entire night before Charlie's death, committing to memory every moment of his life with his brother, knowing that it will soon be over. Although he is not present at his brother's execution, he hears that Charlie refused the hood and died singing. He stands watch over his brother's grave for 24 hours before he is dispatched to a new location. He is not afraid, because he knows he must live to honor Charlie's memory and go home to Mother, Molly, and Big Joe. Because he promised Charlie he would.

The Message: Life isn't fair, and even when you're right, you may still be punished. Sometimes it's hard to see the big picture when you're in the center of the storm. War isn't romantic or chivalrous. It is brutal, bloody, and harsh, and no one comes away unscathed. There is enough horror in war without men from the same side killing one another.

Who's It For?: 7th–12th grade, but I consider it an excellent adult crossover as well. Younger readers may be disturbed by the second half of the book, which contains frightening (but not graphically depicted) battle scenes and descriptions of poison gas attacks. There is also the issue of Molly's nonmarital pregnancy, which may offend some conservative readers.

Why It Rocks:
• **Voice:** Thomas's first-person narration is occasionally wise beyond his years, but that is fitting for a boy who has lost his innocence on the front lines of war. It is moving but never melodramatic or pitying.
• **Plot:** In his author's note, Morpurgo tells readers that the title of his award-winning novel comes from a name on an actual WWI gravestone in Belgium and that Charlie's story is meant to represent the over 300 British soldiers who were executed by their own comrades for cowardice, desertion, or disobedience. Morpurgo calls these executions "shameful," and after becoming so close to Thomas and Charlie's fictional life and family, every reader, probably awash in tears, will agree.
• **Pacing:** Morpurgo moves the action along by framing each chapter with the present hourly countdown that Thomas is keeping on the watch Wilkie gave to Charlie. As the past rushes toward the present, suspense is beautifully sustained as readers wonder why Thomas never wants the night to end.
• **Characterization:** Achingly real. From childhood through adolescence and into young adulthood, each of these characters is painted with a subtle brush but none so beautifully as Big Joe. I didn't have room here to list all of his scene-stealing subplots, but he is as memorable and captivating as Lenny from *Of Mice and Men* or Boo Radley from *To Kill a Mockingbird*.

Hook It Up With: *Lord of the Nutcracker Men* by Iain Lawrence and *All Quiet on the Western Front* by Erich Maria Remarque.

Read More about It:
Booklist, starred: 10/01/04
Horn Book: November/December 2004
Kirkus Reviews: 09/15/04
Publishers Weekly, starred: 12/06/04
School Library Journal, starred: 11/01/04
V.O.Y.A.(Voice of Youth Advocates): 12/01/04

Napoli, Donna Jo. 2003. *Breath.* New York: Simon & Schuster. 260p.

The Time and Place: Around 1280, the village of Hamelin, medieval Germany.

The Story: Twelve-year-old Salz has coughed and suffered terrible stomach pains for as long as he can remember. Although he has no name for this chronic illness, modern doctors would know it as cystic fibrosis, a disease that causes mucus to fill the lungs and intestines, resulting in coughing fits and sharp stomach cramps. Grossmutter Salz's grandmother, is constantly testing out new potions and poultices on him, but little else works for Salz except standing on his head, which helps loosen the mucus in his lungs. His three elder brothers resent the fact that he can't do heavy farm work because of his cough and instead is sent once a month to a neighboring town, where he is learning history and philosophy at a monastery.

This spring has been very rainy, and one morning when Salz is collecting herbs for Grossmutter between cloudbursts, he comes across a stranger in the woods. The man is a traveling piper who brags that his music is so enticing, he can summon any being he chooses with it, be it man or beast. The piper soon bids Salz farewell, but he has made a deep impression on the boy, who commits the man's music and his unusual claims to memory.

Back at home, the unrelenting rain is threatening to rot the crops in the field and is driving large numbers of rats insides, while the cows are giving less milk. Salz is in charge of taking the cows to the fields to graze, and he notices a new pink-and-purple grass growing there and wonders if it is a fungus brought on by all the rain. Grossmutter, who, along with Salz, is part of a secret pagan coven that also incorporates Christian practices, holds a ritual that includes burying one of the sick cows alive as a sacrifice. Pater Michael, the village priest, attends the ritual and gives it his blessing, to Salz's surprise. This makes the boy wonder about the difference between miracles and magic, one condoned by the church, the other condemned. Salz is sickened by the cow's sacrifice, but thrilled when he is deemed old enough to take part in the "flying" ritual that happens after the priest leaves, which includes spreading a hallucinogenic ointment on the skin that causes the coven to fall into a state of delirium and lust.

But the ritual doesn't help. Soon all of the town's grazing animals are sick or dying. The situation continues to worsen throughout the summer as the disease progresses to people. It is now past harvest, and townsfolk are coming to Grossmutter's door, asking for potions to help cure the hallucinations, convulsions, paralysis, and swelling of the hands and feet that rapidly turns into gangrene. Many have heard of the plague caused by rats in other parts of Europe and wonder if that is what this sickness is. Grossmutter brings home a little girl named Ava whose mother died in her arms while she was trying to help her. Father is none too pleased, but Grossmutter insists, and Salz offers to be her caretaker. He quickly grows fond of the little girl, who doesn't speak.

Soon it is time for Salz's family to take their homemade beer to market. Their beer is renowned throughout the countryside, and the selling of it is a welcome distraction from all the talk of illness. Salz himself never drinks the beer because Grossmutter thinks it may worsen his condition. After the sale the family members sit down to drink the first round of the new beer themselves, which is as delicious as always, but after dinner, they begin to behave strangely: muttering to themselves, crashing into the furniture, and putting their hands in the fire until they burn. The only ones unaffected are Salz and Ava, and they lock themselves in the loft until the fits pass. Salz thinks that an angry ghost has possessed them and moved on, but the same behavior happens the next night and the next.

The odd behavior finally comes to a violent climax when Bertram, Salz's oldest brother, tries to attack Salz with a scythe. Grossmutter steps in front of Bertram to stop him, and Bertram slashes her with the scythe, killing her. Bertram is tried in the village court, but he claims that St. Michael told him to kill Salz because he alone has remained unaffected and so must be causing the sickness. The hysterical townspeople release Bertram and imprison Salz, but Pater Michael convinces the crowd that Salz is not to blame but the rats are. Salz remembers the piper and his claim and tells the town council that if they can find him, he can rid the town of rats.

The piper is summoned and brought before the mayor, who promises him 1,000 guilders if he completes the task. He agrees, and warns all the townspeople to block their ears and the ears of their livestock with wool until dusk. The rats are soon gone, and the townsfolk celebrate by holding their annual fall beer festival. Salz and Ava eat their first fresh bread of the new harvest while sitting at a place of honor next to the piper. After they eat, the mayor pays the piper in front of the village, but it is much less than promised. Before the piper can react, people begin howling, laughing, and taking off their clothes. Some fall into convulsions, while others vomit. It is the sickness again, and Salz, who is suddenly feeling ill himself, understands that it is not the rats, that is causing the townspeople's illness, but the grain that the beer and the fresh bread were made from.

The piper, enraged that he has not been paid his due, begins to play, and all the people get up and follow. But because so many of them can't walk or run because of their various afflictions, they fall down, leaving only the healthy children to follow, even Ava to Salz's dismay. He is stopped by his cough as she marches away. All he can do, after he recovers, is to pack a small bag and follow the piper's path in search of her. In an author's note, Napoli reveals that Salz's neighbors were not suffering from the Black Plague, as some had believed, but ergot poisoning, a type of fungus that prospers in field grasses during long stretches of wet weather and looks like tiny purple-and-pink flowers. The fungus was present in the grain used to make the town's bread and beer.

The Message: Reason and logic always triumph over superstition. There is a logical answer to every problem if you just have the patience to puzzle it out. Respect tradition; it is usually the basis for all things new.

Who's It For?: 7th–12th grade. This is an especially gruesome fractured fairy tale that contains dark passages detailing sexual rituals, bodily functions, and gory symptoms of illness. There are also extended sections that explain the religious and class hierarchy of medieval Europe, fairly big ideas that are easier for older readers to grapple with.

Why It Rocks:
•   **Voice:** Salz's first-person narration is often wise beyond his years, and his logical reasoning seems beyond that of a 12-year-old peasant boy. But, as Napoli explains, he has been more educated than his family members and his illness has made him more careful and observant.
•   **Plot:** Using the story of the "Pied Piper of Hamelin," as her basis, Napoli has spun a rich historical mystery that is chock-full of teachable moments. Her impeccable research is evident in the meticulous descriptions of medieval European life, in the food characters ate, and in the religions they espoused. Of special interest is

Napoli's discussion of the Arab contribution to European culture after the Crusades, which will be fascinating to young scholars.

- **Pacing:** Slow, and occasionally sidetracked into discussions of philosophy or history that add to the understanding of the time period but do nothing to further the story. While the first half of this novel wouldn't fall under the category of page turner, once poor Grossmutter is killed, the action takes off and suspense builds as the reader wonders if Salz will solve the mystery of the poisoned grain in time to save the townspeople from themselves.

- **Characterization:** Napoli is more interested in filling in the details of her time period and setting than in penning rounded secondary characters. Salz grows and develops over the course of the novel, while his family members, priests, and neighbors remain somewhat flat. The exception is Grossmutter, who is sympathetically rendered and plays an important role in Salz's development.

Hook It Up With: *Crispin: The Cross of Lead* by Avi and *The Dark Light* by Mette Newth.

Read More about It:
Booklist: 09/15/03
Horn Book: 04/01/04
Kirkus Reviews, starred: 10/15/03
School Library Journal: 11/01/03
V.O.Y.A. (Voice of Youth Advocates): 12/01/03

Salisbury, Graham. 2005. *Eyes of the Emperor.* New York: Random House. 229p.

The Time and Place: 1941, Honolulu, Hawaii, and Cat Island, Mississippi.

The Story: Sixteen-year-old "nisei" (American-born person of Japanese descent) Eddy Okubo faces fear and racial prejudice when he joins the army shortly before the Japanese attack on Pearl Harbor. Eddy's parents moved from Japan to Honolulu in 1921. His father, Koji, makes his living crafting Japanese fishing boats with Eddy's help and that of and his younger brother Herbie. Tension is growing in the Hawaiian Japanese American community owing to the growing threat from their homeland, which has recently joined the Axis powers of Germany and Italy.

Eddy's two best friends, Nick Matsumara ("Chick") and Takeo Uehara ("Cobra"), have recently been drafted into the army, and Eddy wants to sign up too, even though he is too young and his father wouldn't approve. But Eddy is resolved to join after his father's latest boat is torched in the middle of the night, which he believes is the result of anti-Japanese feelings. Six weeks later, Eddy lies about his age and enlists. After he tells his parents, his father stops speaking to him. Eddy leaves home in October to begin basic training at Schofield Barracks. After seven weeks of basic, he receives a weekend pass and is dismayed to discover that his father still refuses to speak to him.

Eddy goes to bed, defeated, only to awaken the morning of December 7 to a horrifying air raid. Two hundred Japanese fighter planes appear over Oahu, dropping bombs. Their target is the American military base of Pearl Harbor. Once Eddy's father realizes what is happening, he speaks for the first time in weeks and urges Eddy to return to the base as soon as possible and fight for his country with honor. Eddy miraculously finds Chick and Cobra in the midst of all the chaos, and they try to make their way back together. They flag down a passing car, and the "haole" (white) driver views them with suspicion until they flash their military IDs. As the man drives them back to the base, they witness firsthand the utter destruction of Pearl Harbor.

When they finally arrive at their camp, they fall under the command of Lieutenant Sweet, a racist officer who believes that no "Jap" is to be trusted. He sets all the Japanese American soldiers to digging endless ditches and threatens them with the stockade if they don't cooperate. He separates them from everyone else and puts them under machine-gun guard. The guns stay only one day, but the Japanese American soldiers are no longer allowed to train in combat. Instead, they are forced to perform endless rounds of cleanup duties. A new officer named Captain Parrish comes to the barracks. He used to be Eddy's old high school teacher, and he is far kinder than Lieutenant Sweet. Parrish apologizes for the machine-gun guard and orders the Japanese American soldiers to resume their ammunition training. There are other racially charged incidents in which Sweet tries to target Eddy and his friends, but Parrish is quick to head them off.

After being assigned to guard an empty Hawaiian beach for a month, Eddy's company is deployed to the mainland. They travel by ship to California, then on to Wisconsin by train, where they end up at Camp McCoy. They aren't there long before Eddy and several other Japanese American soldiers are awakened by Sweet in the middle of the night and told to pack their bags. They are flown to Mississippi and taken to a fishing boat, captained by a friendly, smelly local named Leroy. Leroy takes them to an old, empty barracks on Ship Island in the Mississippi Sound, their final destination. Sweet tells them to get settled and Leroy will come back for them in a few days to take them to their new top-secret assignment. Eddy, Chick, and Cobra wonder what is in store for them.

They soon find out when Leroy takes them to nearby Cat Island, where they are met by Captain Parrish. The boys are initially happy to see a friendly face, but as Parrish begins to describe their new assignment, their spirits sink. Parrish explains that they are taking part in an experimental secret trial that will test the theory of whether or not dogs can be trained to specifically trail and attack Japanese enemy soldiers. The proponents of this theory believe that Japanese people have a different scent than that of Caucasians, and Eddy and his friends are here to act as "bait" for the pet dogs, which have been donated by their owners to take part in the war effort. Eddy is devastated by Parrish's words but swears to himself he will do his best, as he had promised his father.

Eddy is assigned to work with dog handler Smith and Kooch, a German shepherd. For the next several days, Eddy and Smith train Kooch with a series of exercises that become increasingly more difficult and frightening for Eddy. At first, he just trails a string of horsemeat through the swamp for Kooch to track him with, but soon he and the rest of the Japanese soldiers are forced to hit the dogs with burlap sacks and slingshots, then whip them from the relative safety of a padded suit in order to establish themselves as the enemy.

One day going back to Ship Island after training, Leroy's boat breaks down and he signals for help. The coast guard arrives but with guns drawn and aimed at Eddy and his friends. They don't know about the secret mission and believe the Japanese American soldiers to be enemy saboteurs. Only after Leroy screams out that these are American soldiers do they put away their weapons. Each day the men become more grim and demoralized. They all feel ashamed but are duty bound to do what is being asked of them.

For Kooch's final test, Eddy has to hide wearing only padded sleeves to protect him, while Kooch hunts for him off the leash. When the dog finds Eddy, Smith hesitates for a terrifying moment before calling him off, and the dog goes for Eddy's throat. Eddy is so furious that as soon as Kooch backs down, he launches himself at Smith. The confused dog attacks both of them, and Smith feels what it is like to be at the business end of Kooch's teeth. Both soldiers return to camp sober and silent.

Four days later, top military personnel arrive at Cat Island to see a demonstration of the dogs' ability to track only Japanese soldiers. Kooch is chosen to go first, and Eddy hides along with several other non-Japanese soldiers in the swamp. But Kooch flushes out a Caucasian soldier first. The secret mission is plainly a failure. Eddy doesn't know whether to be relieved or disappointed that something he put so much effort into has failed. Captain Parrish tells them that although the experiment has been terminated, they are to be commended on their hard work and dedication and should prepare themselves for active combat. Eddy finally feels that the army recognizes him as a loyal and trustworthy American soldier, instead of a security risk with the "eyes of the Emperor."

The Message: Character is defined through trial and hardship. Sometimes it is very difficult to do the right thing. Stay true to yourself and your beliefs.

Who's It For?: 7th–12th grade. There is no sex, strong language, or active warfare (other than a short eyewitness account of the attack on Pearl Harbor). This is a powerful all-ages story that works just as well with middle school students as it does with high schoolers.

Why It Rocks:
•   **Voice:** Eddy's first-person narration, peppered with Hawaiian pidgin English phrases and Japanese vocabulary, is boyish and spare. His matter-of-fact, and occasionally naive, tone concerning his circumstances offsets the offensive conditions he is asked to endure without minimizing them.
•   **Plot:** Fascinating and thought provoking. Salisbury has used a little-known historic episode to make a powerful statement about courage, loyalty, and patriotism. This title is a perfect tie-in to present-day events, ironically mirroring some of the same issues the United States has been facing since the 9/11 attack.
•   **Pacing:** Quick and action packed. Salisbury plunges us into the horror of the Pearl Harbor bombing by page 37, and it isn't long after that Eddy and his friends are shipped off to their secret assignment. Salisbury isn't afraid to compress some of the

time periods in order to get on with Eddy's story, a fact that many teen readers are sure to appreciate.

- **Characterization:** Rich and authentic. Eddy feels real because in many respects he is. In Salisbury's author's note, he recounts how he was able to meet and interview 8 of the 26 men who served on Cat Island. Salisbury also draws sympathetic and humorous portraits of cynical Cobra, loverboy Chick, and Eddy's strong, silent pop, Koji Okubo.

Hook It Up With: *Under the Blood-Red Sun* by Graham Salisbury and *B for Buster* by Iain Lawrence.

Read More about It:
Booklist, starred: 05/15/05
Horn Book: July/August 2005
Kirkus Reviews, starred: 07/01/05
Publishers Weekly, starred: 07/01/05
School Library Journal: 09/01/05
V.O.Y.A. (Voice of Youth Advocates): 08/01/05

Spinelli, Jerry. 2003. *Milkweed.* New York: Random House. 208p.

The Time and Place: 1939–1942, Warsaw, Poland.

The Story: The unnamed narrator doesn't know where he came from or who his family is. He is small and fast and has stolen to live for as long as he can remember on the streets of Warsaw. A redheaded boy named Uri, the informal leader of a gang of orphan Jewish boys, rescues him. Uri christens him "Misha Pilsudski" and, based on his dusky skin and dark eyes, invents a personal history for him that includes a lost family of Russian Gypsies who died in German bombings.

The Germans are bombing Warsaw in their attempt to take over Poland, and Uri's gang grows fat from the goods they steal from bombed-out buildings. Misha is thrilled the first time he sees Hitler's army march by, calling them "Jackboots." He even dreams of becoming one until Uri tells him they hate him—and all Jews. Misha thinks he is safe because he is a Gypsy, not a Jew. He meets a little girl named Janina on his daily travels. She invites him to her birthday party, where he misunderstands the use of candles, having never had a birthday cake himself. He thinks they mean to burn up the cake, so he grabs it and runs away. Later he feels guilty, steals a cake from a bakery, and leaves it on Janina's doorstep. This begins a ritual enjoyed by both of them, of Misha's stealing food and leaving half of whatever he takes at Janina's door. Later, Uri introduces him to Dr. Korczak, the head of a Jewish orphans' home. Uri tells Misha it is also good to give to the orphans, so Misha leaves food and coal that he scavenges at the orphanage as well as at Janina's house.

Soon, Misha notices that it is getting harder and harder to steal bread, since few people seem to be carrying it on the street anymore. He also notices more and more destroyed storefronts and more businesses labeled with a yellow star. Misha can't stay away from a merry-go-round in a town park that is forbidden to Jewish children. Uri always warns him not to draw attention to himself, but one day Misha can't stand it anymore and jumps astride one of the horses without a ticket. He gets a taste of things to come when the guard throws him off and the other children take turns kicking him and calling him a "dirty Jew." Misha is frightened by the event, but when shortly after his favorite horse goes missing from the ride and a passing Jewish man is blamed and doused with a fire hose by German soldiers as punishment, Misha finds himself going along with the crowd as they bay for the man's blood.

More time passes, which doesn't hold much significance for Misha in his small world and limited understanding, and one day he sees all the Jews marching in a big parade. He knows they are Jews because of the armbands they wear, and when he asks Uri where they are going, Uri tells him they are headed for the ghetto. Misha follows them and finds Janina and her family and Dr. K and his orphans in the crowd. It is almost like a game as he helps Janina and her parents secure an apartment and set up housekeeping in the ghetto. Soon a wall is erected to keep the Jewish people inside, but Misha finds a drainage hole too small for anyone else and uses it to come and go as he pleases. The boys in Uri's gang get rounded up by Jackboots and sent to the ghetto, but Uri is not among them. Misha splits his time between staying with Janina's family, who have adopted him as one of their own, and sleeping in a rubbish heap with the rest of the gang.

As more Jews are forced into the ghetto, food becomes scarcer and scarcer. Enos, one of Uri's friends, tells Misha that the Jackboots are starving them in order to save bullets. They are also often subjected to brutal lineups, where they have to stand at attention for hours as the Jackboots beat and abuse them. Misha treats this like a game, trying to stand as still as he can in order to win. But life in the ghetto is gray, full of rumors of available food, and lice. Dead bodies, covered in newspaper, appear on the streets every day, and Misha notices that before they are picked up, their clothes and shoes often disappear.

Misha continues to pass back and forth between the ghetto and the city outside, which he has taken to calling Heaven. He always shares at least half of his smuggled food with Janina's family and Dr. K and the orphans. Janina's mother is getting sicker and sicker, and Janina is reacting badly, playing cruel jokes on Misha and hysterically begging her mother for food. But once she starts sneaking out with Misha on his nightly food-smuggling missions, she comes out of her depression.

The Jackboots have become aware that people are sneaking in and out and have begun hanging those they suspect and shooting flamethrowers down the sewers to discourage those who sneak out that way. On Sundays, the Jackboots come with their girlfriends and take pictures of the starving children and throw bread to them like they are birds, which astonishes and angers Misha. The ghetto is so colorless and bare that the day Misha and Janina find a stray milkweed growing in the rubbish is cause for celebration.

On one of his nightly food runs, Misha sees Uri in Heaven. Uri is passing as a Pole and working in a laundry. He warns Misha away from him. Janina's mother dies, their friend Olek is hung from a light pole for smuggling, and still no one comes to their rescue. They can see and hear Russian bombs in the distance, and Misha is finding that it is even beginning to be hard to scavenge food in Heaven. As a joke, some Jackboots set a live cow on fire and send it into the ghetto, where it falls off the edge of a building and is immediately mobbed and eaten.

One day, Uri seeks out Misha and tells him that the Jackboots are going to begin deportations and that whatever happens, Misha should not get on a train. Rumors fly as whole ghetto blocks are emptied at a time and people begin to disappear. An old man appears who claims to have escaped the work camps that the Jackboots are sending them to; he tells of gas, ovens, and electric fences, but no one believes him. Janina's father tells them to leave the ghetto on one of their nightly smuggling missions and not return, but Janina refuses.

One night, the drainage hole is blocked up, and Misha and Janina can't get back in. They slip through the gates the next morning as crowds of Jews are coming out, being led to the trains. Janina searches for her father but can't find him. Misha loses her in the crowd, only to see her at a distance being thrown into a train car by a Jackboot. He is grabbed by a solider, has his ear shot off, and when he wakes, discovers he has been left for dead and all the trains are gone. He begins walking along the tracks, hoping to follow them to Janina.

On his journey, he does farmwork and steals to survive, eventually stealing enough to buy a ticket to America. He holds many jobs and is married and divorced because he can't stop crying, stealing, and compulsively talking about the ghetto. He ends his life living with his daughter and granddaughter, who love and take care of him. He never speaks of Janina again.

The Message: Incredibly difficult circumstances can be overcome with perseverance, wit, and luck. Brutality can't always be explained, but it can be lived through. Life does go on, despite all the evidence to the contrary. Sometimes it is enough just to have survived a horrifying event. "What doesn't kill us makes us stronger."

Who's It For?: 7th–12th grade. While Misha's first-person narrative is simplistic at times, the conditions he is describing are not. It will take a sophisticated reader to understand Misha's unique point of view. The horrors of the Warsaw ghetto were many, and while Misha doesn't always understand what he is seeing, he reports what he has seen in honest, sometimes brutal detail that is best suited to older readers or readers well versed in Holocaust literature.

Why It Rocks:
•   **Voice:** Original and pure. Misha's limited first-person point of view gives the reader the feeling that he or she has been dropped into an alien landscape with no understanding of the environment or atmosphere. To readers new to Holocaust literature, Misha's voice will cause them to seek out other titles, and to those veterans of Anne Frank, Elie Wiesel, and Corrie Ten Boom, it will provide a disturbing fresh perspective.
•   **Plot:** To add yet another title to the already massive and intimidating body of Holocaust literature that says something new seems virtually impossible. But Spinelli not only pulled it off, but also did so with great grace and aplomb by viewing the Warsaw ghetto through the eyes of a complete innocent, thereby making the horrors seem even more alien and inhumane.

- **Pacing:** Misha's narrative is largely chronological, but because time has little meaning for him (other than cold in the winter, lice in the summer), his observations and musings sometimes feel disorganized and scattered. Spinelli helps by roughly organizing Misha's experiences into seasons.
- **Characterization:** Secondary characters are brought to life using evocative little details that ring with truth. Janina rages against the injustice of the ghetto existence by taunting the ghetto police and screaming at her bedridden mother to get up, because, unlike Misha, she has known better. Uri's shame at "passing" comes out in his rough speeches to Misha, and Janina's Uncle Shepsel copes with his new life by claiming he has renounced Judaism and is becoming a Lutheran. Like Misha, all of these characters are wonderfully, painfully real.

Hook It Up With: *Yellow Star* by Jennifer Roy and *Soldier Boys* by Dean Hughes.

Read More about It:
Booklist, starred: 10/15/03
Horn Book: 04/01/04
Kirkus Reviews, starred: 08/01/03
Publishers Weekly: 09/01/03
School Library Journal: 11/01/03
V.O.Y.A. (Voice of Youth Advocates): 02/01/04

Updale, Eleanor. 2004. *Montmorency: Thief, Liar, Gentleman?* **New York: Scholastic. 232p.**

The Time and Place: 1875, London, England.
The Story: An anonymous thief crashes through a skylight while fleeing police and is badly wounded but still alive when apprehended. A young local doctor named Robert Farcett agrees to take on his case, excited by the prospect of being able to test some of the latest medical technologies on a human patient. He names prisoner 493 "Montmorency," after the brand name on the expensive tool bag he was captured with.

Dr. Farcett belongs to a professional group of scientists, philosophers, and historians known as the Scientific Society, and they hold both public and private lectures to enlighten one another on the latest discoveries and theories in their respective fields. Dr. Farcett often takes Montmorency out of prison to show the results of his medical handiwork to the rest of the Society. As a result, Montmorency is also exposed to several scholarly lectures while he waits his turn onstage, and commits everything he hears to memory.

Montmorency is especially interested in a presentation on London's improved sewer system, and it is after this lecture that he has a brainstorm as to how he will make his criminal living after prison. He will use the sewers as his gateway to upper-class neighborhoods, where he will commit burglaries, then literally disappear underground. He will use the money from his loot to set himself up like a proper gentleman, like Dr. Farcett and his colleagues. There is only one problem. How will he fence his stolen goods looking (and smelling) like a sewer rat? He decides he will cultivate a dual personality: Scarper, the sewer thief, and Montmorency, the gentleman. He will lead people to believe that rough Scarper is Montmorency's servant.

Back in the regular prison population, Montmorency is put in a cell with "Freakshow" Frank, a pickpocket and talented mimic who can twist his face into all sorts of configurations. Montmorency gets Freakshow to teach him everything he knows about mimicry and imitation, with the intent of copying Dr. Farcett's gentlemanly mannerisms.

After three long years, Montmorency is released from prison, ready to begin his dual life of crime. As Scarper, he rents a room near the marketplace from raggedy landlady Mrs. Evans and her daughter, Vi. The first time he enters the sewers, he is overwhelmed by the dark and the smell, but soon, he is navigating the tunnels like a pro, with the use of stolen lanterns, chalk, and fishing waders. He commits a series of small but lucrative jewelry robberies, and begins amassing the fortune that will enable him to transform into a gentleman. He enjoys reading about himself in the papers and the thrill of evading the "flushers," the men whose job it is to maintain the sewers.

Once he has gathered enough loot, he commits one more "common" burglary. He goes to Dr. Farcett's house, steals a suit of fine clothes and shoes, and uses a sheet of his stationary to write a letter of introduction to the manager of one of London's finest hotels, The Marimion, asking for a suite of rooms to be set aside for Mr. Montmorency, a gentleman who will be arriving shortly. He delivers the letter as Scarper the servant, who is let into his master's rooms with his luggage. He comes out scrubbed, shaved, and stunningly dressed as Montmorency, gentleman.

Soon Montmorency has slipped into a pattern of using the sewers to continue his life of crime as Scarper at night, and perfecting his Montmorency personality by day. He purchases clothes, studies etiquette, and reads all the local newspapers every day. He acquires a taste for luxury, attending the opera and traveling extensively, in order to auction his goods far from where they were stolen. He has a close call when a nosy hatmaker notices that he is wearing Dr. Farcett's stolen top hat, but by forging a note and implying that the hats had been accidentally mixed up at a brothel, he is able to gain the hatmaker's assurance that he will not say anything to Dr. Farcett.

Montmorency hears about another robber who is working in the same neighborhoods, and while he is relieved to hear that the man has been captured and that all of his own crimes have been pinned on this man, he is troubled to learn the robber's identity: Freakshow, his old prison mentor. He attends the trial and sentencing, ashamed when Freakshow is sentenced to hang but relieved that his secret is still safe. After a bad fright when he gets trapped in the sewers during a storm and nearly swept out to sea, he slowly recovers, but it is a long while before he can convince himself to go back underground.

Meanwhile, he has made a new friend named George Fox-Selwyn. They meet by chance when Montmorency calms a horse that is pulling Fox-Selwyn's cab, and F-S invites Montmorency to his gentleman's club, Bargles. The two soon become fast drinking and gambling buddies. F-S never asks Montmorency about his past, but he has noticed his many scars. They look similar to some diagrams that his physician, Dr.

Farcett, keeps in his home office of a badly wounded criminal that he studied.

After spending several weeks together, F-S decides to take Montmorency into his confidence. It seems that F-S is not only a distinguished gentleman but also an undercover spy for the British government, and he needs Montmorency's advice about his latest assignment. He needs to gain entrance into the heavily guarded British embassy of a small Balkan country named Mauramania. It seems that the Mauramanian ambassador is planning a coup of his own country that could affect British financial interests, but the government needs proof before they can stop him. Montmorency can't resist the challenge, especially when F-S bets him 2,000 pounds that he can't do it. He doesn't tell F-S how he plans to gain entry (through the sewers, of course), and F-S discreetly doesn't ask.

Montmorency becomes Scarper once more, sneaks into the embassy through the sewers, hides under a dining room table, and overhears all the information he needs to implicate the ambassador. He takes a dropped fork as proof that he was there and sneaks out the same way he came in. Together, he and F-S report their findings to the foreign secretary, who is so pleased with Montmorency's work that he offers him a job on the spot as F-S's partner. Montmorency decides to retire Scarper for good. He gives up Scarper's rented room and his own suite at the Marimion and moves into one of the bedrooms at Bargles, ready to start his new life as an international spy. But he keeps a pair of fishing waders under his bed—just in case.

The Message: It is possible to reinvent yourself. There is always a solution to any problem; sometimes the answer is right in front of you. You don't have to be born wealthy to be a success in life. There are many ways of being intelligent, and not all of them come from being formally educated.

Who's It For?: 6th–10th grade. Although there is nary a teen character to be seen, the themes of reinvention, equality vs. class structure, and self-worth will appeal to readers of all ages but especially teens. This is a clean mystery with no strong language or graphic violence, since Freakshow's hanging happens offstage. Some of Montmorency's wounds and operations are grisly, but Updale refrains from describing them in great detail. Young fans of Agatha Christie will love this book, but be aware that subsequent sequels are more explicit about Montmorency's grown-up activities.

Why It Rocks:
*   **Voice:** Updale writes Montmorency's story in a stylish third-person voice that contains enough Victorian vocabulary to be interesting but does not have so formal a tone as to discourage reluctant readers.
*   **Plot:** Action-packed. Updale carries Montmorency from one breathless danger right into another as his dual lifestyle is constantly threatened with discovery.
*   **Pacing:** Measured but certainly not slow. The action moves the story along at a brisk pace while not sacrificing important period detail.
*   **Characterization:** While Updale's text is mostly peopled with familiar stock Victorian characters (ruddy gentlemen, bawdy pub girls, earnest scholars), one standout is the obnoxious daughter of the Marimion's manager, Cissie. Described as having an unflattering poodle-like hairdo, replete with hanging ribbons that trail into

her food, and a babyish lisp that she uses to flirt with Montmorency, Cissie provides some welcome comic relief to readers who are on the edge of their seats worrying about the possibility of Montmorency's secrets being uncovered. Montmorency himself is delightfully layered, and readers will enjoy watching him grow a (small) conscience.

Hook It Up With: All the other titles in the *Montmorency* series (*Montmorency on the Rocks, Montmorency and the Assassins, Montmorency's Revenge*) and *A Drowned Maiden's Hair: A Melodrama* by Laura Amy Schlitz.

Read More about It:
Booklist: 05/01/04
Horn Book: 10/01/04
Kirkus Reviews: 03/15/04
Publishers Weekly: 04/05/04
School Library Journal, starred: 04/01/04
V.O.Y.A. (Voice of Youth Advocates): 06/01/04

CHAPTER 8

NAIL-BITERS: TEEN TALES OF MYSTERY AND SUSPENSE

Introduction

No one likes their thrills, chills, and spills more than teen readers; yet there seems to be a dearth of genuine Nancy Drew/Hardy Boys/Scooby-Doo-like mysteries, where teens act like mini-Columbos and save the day through either their bumbling cluelessness (they just happen to stumble onto the solution) or their youthful ingenuity (their fresh eyes see the clues that their cynical elders missed). The kind of mystery that seems to flourish in YA fiction is the suspense/psychological thriller, which tends to be more *Silence of Lambs* than *Secret of the Old Clock*—mysteries where the villain is either a serial killer (*Acceleration*), an abusive or unmerciful grown-up (*The Rag and Bone Shop, Nothing to Lose, The Rules of Survival, You Don't Know Me*), or even a ruthless or conscience-less peer (*Shattering Glass, Inexcusable, Inside Out*) that the teen protagonist must outsmart and overcome. Those kinds of mysteries are fine, and they certainly have their audience, but personally, I'd love to see more honest-to-goodness, clue-laden mysteries that feature a slightly older and/or wiser Frank or Velma who, through either bumbling cluelessness or youthful ingenuity, tracks down the villain and saves the day. Some of those qualities can be found in Kate Morgenroth's excellent police procedural *Jude* and Nancy Springer's perfectly executed Victorian mystery *The Case of the Missing Marquess*, also included in this chapter. So dim the lights, pull your sweetie or your cat a little closer, and begin your investigation of these ten nail-biting, suspenseful teen mysteries!

Cormier, Robert. 2001. *The Rag and Bone Shop*. New York: Random House. 154p.

The Story: Jason Dorrant is a shy 12-year-old who has just graduated from the seventh grade and is looking forward to the freedom of summer, so when his 7-year-old neighbor's body is discovered in the woods near her house, he is understandably shaken and upset. Jason, who has always been more comfortable around younger children than his own peers, had gone over to Alicia's house to help her work one of her eternal jigsaw puzzles the afternoon she went missing, and he was the last person to see Alicia alive. The police have no leads, no clues, and no evidence. The local senator, whose grandson was in the same class as Alicia, begins to put pressure on the department to solve the case as quickly as possible in this election year. So it is not difficult for the detective in charge to convince the district attorney (DA) to bring in Trent, an ambitious police officer with a growing reputation for his success in securing confessions, to wring a statement out of Jason, their only suspect.

Even though Trent is mentally exhausted after scoring two major murder confessions in just the last week, he accepts the job because of the positive impact it could have on his career owing to the senator's connections. When he arrives at the station, he discovers that the "scenario" has been set for him: Jason and his mother believe that Jason, along with several other boys from his school, is "helping" with the investigation. Although the police have called in other boys, they are quickly questioned for appearance's sake and sent home. It is only Jason who is isolated in a small, hot room, awaiting Trent's attentions. A young woman named Sarah Downes from DA's office, who reminds Trent of his late wife, briefs him on the case. He is drawn to her and wants to impress her, even though her presence brings back disturbing memories of his wife's accusing him of loving the interrogation process, whether or not the confessions he obtained were true.

Trent introduces himself to Jason and begins by asking him questions about himself that establish his personality. He gets Jason's permission to record the conversation and offhandedly suggests having counsel or his mother present, knowing full well that the adolescent boy will manfully refuse. Trent watches Jason's body language as he talks about the day he last saw Alicia alive and doesn't see any guilt, but he does lead Jason into admitting he likes fantasy and horror books with elements of violence; Trent mentally notes that information to exploit later.

Jason is uncomfortable with how Trent keeps emphasizing his personal thoughts and feelings. The room becomes hot and uncomfortable. Trent suggests a break, and leaves the room. Jason is confused, he wants to help, but he doesn't know if he's giving the correct answers or not. Trent makes him feel odd, acting both approachable and forbidding at the same time. Jason doesn't know if the man is his friend or enemy, but something about the questioning feels wrong, and he decides to leave before Trent returns. Trent catches Jason in the parking lot and knows that he should let him go, since the fact that he wants to leave indicates guilt. But Trent feels as if he must secure this confession, to prove to the senator, to Sarah Downes, to his dead wife that he is a master of his skill. He implies to Jason that his leaving makes him seem "suspicious," which worries Jason, and he comes back in easily.

Trent asks about Jason and Alicia's relationship and insinuates that it was odd because of their age difference. He gets Jason a Coke but makes Jason feel like his thirst somehow makes him guilty. After he drinks his soda, Jason decides to reveal a piece of information he had held back: that Alicia's elder brother, Brad, was teasing her on that day, and it seemed particularly mean. He hadn't mentioned it before in case it was just typical sibling quarreling. Trent purposely steers him away from that thought by telling him that Brad has an airtight alibi. Even if the brother did something, Trent is not interested, because his suspect is Jason.

Trent becomes impatient to wrap things up and goes in for the kill. Just to see Jason's response, Trent suggests that Jason was physically attracted to Alicia, but the boy's repulsed body language signifies his innocence. Trent switches to describing the scene of the crime, asking Jason questions about the weapon and motive as if he were the murderer, which confuses and frightens the now terrified boy. Trent then begins to speak rapidly, using everything Jason has artlessly mentioned to implicate him—the horror novels, his knowledge of the woods where Alicia was killed, the fact that they sometimes argued over Alicia's puzzles. All of Trent's instincts tell him that Jason is innocent, but what if Jason is the "perfect deceiver," his innocent voice hiding a foul deed? Trent knows that Jason didn't commit the murder, but his ego and the promise of a reward from the senator won't let him quit.

Trent tells Jason that he is Jason's only friend. He tells him that if he confesses to Alicia's murder, he will be treated with understanding, and that his belief that he didn't kill Alicia is just a coping mechanism of self-denial. Jason finally becomes so tired and hot and badgered that he eventually tells Trent what he wants to hear.

But when Trent exits the room triumphantly with the taped confession, Sarah Downes greets him with the news that Brad's friends have implicated Alicia's brother in the girl's murder. Trent's career is ruined. Jason becomes sick with nightmares, terrified by the notion that if someone could make him *say* he did something so horrific, then maybe he is capable of committing murder. He would never hurt a little child like Alicia, but what about school bully Bobo Kelton? One afternoon while his parents are out, Jason gets a butcher knife from his kitchen and goes in search of Bobo.

The Message: Question authority. Tell the truth no matter what. Adults can be cruel enough to use children as an end to their own selfish means. Power corrupts.

Who's It For?: 8th–10th grade. Besides the obvious ethical issue of adult manipulation of children, some of Trent's past murder cases are described in the kind of detail that may disturb certain readers. But all the violence described in the story is integral to the plot, and if a student is attracted to the story, he or she is unlikely to be surprised by the mentions of murder.

Why It Rocks:
• **Voice:** Cormier's use of third person allows him to switch back and forth between Trent's and Jason's points of view, providing the reader with a mesmerizing look at the interrogation process.
• **Plot:** This is Cormier's last novel, and while his signature dark examination of the depths of the human soul is present, the abrupt, extreme ending had some fans speculating whether Cormier's editor had finished the job. But teen readers will relish the fascinating details of Trent's interrogation techniques, such as the use of two sizes of chair to make the interrogator appear bigger; the purposely small, crowded room

intended to induce claustrophobia; and the deliberate "forgetting" of a cold drink for the suspect as the questions grow more and more uncomfortable.

• **Pacing:** Measured. Each of Trent's questions is calculated and precise, and the slow delivery of them heightens the tension as readers wonder which question will be the one that breaks Jason's inner resolve.

• **Characterization:** Both Jason and Trent are fully rounded characters, and each has been irrevocably changed by novel's end. But readers will also be left wondering about the ending—which doesn't seem wholly plausible—and about what prompted Brad, whose motivations are never explained, to kill Alicia in the first place.

Hook It Up With: *Shadow People* by Joyce McDonald.

Read More about It:
Booklist: 07/01/01
Horn Book: 11/01/01
Kirkus Reviews, starred: 10/01/01
Publishers Weekly: 10/15/01
School Library Journal: 09/01/01
V.O.Y.A. (Voice of Youth Advocates): 10/01/01

———

Flinn, Alex. 2004. *Nothing to Lose*. New York: HarperCollins. 277p.

The Story: Michael Daye is a 16-year-old boy whose life has narrowed to one focus: protecting his mother, Lisa, from the abusive attentions of his stepfather, successful attorney Walker Monroe. Michael begs his mother to leave Walker, but she makes excuses for his behavior and claims that the marriage has bettered their situation because they no longer have to live hand-to-mouth on her tiny paralegal salary. But Michael would give up the big house by the beach in Miami in a second if it meant he could stop worrying about his mother's safety. He tried telling a teacher at school once about Walker, but the lawyer was able to convince the social worker sent to the house that Michael was lying; then he beat Lisa severely. Since then, Michael has become a helpless witness of his mother's abuse, unable to act partially because Lisa won't acknowledge that anything is wrong, but also out of fear that no one will believe him.

A talented football player, Michael is forced to quit the team so he can come right home after school to watch over his mother, who isn't allowed to leave the house without Walker's permission. As his rage against Walker builds, Michael begins alienating all his jock friends by picking fights with them to keep them from asking questions about why he left the team. His grades begin to plummet, and he is reduced to hanging out with an old friend from grade school, nerdy outsider Julian, who respects Michael's space. He reluctantly agrees to go with Julian to the fair when it comes to town, and it is at the "Whack-a-Mole" game that he meets beautiful carny worker Kirstie; it is love at first sight.

After a brief but intense courtship, which includes midnight Ferris wheel rides and long walks around the deserted big top, Kirstie invites Michael to come away with her when the fair leaves. They have revealed their histories to each other, and Kirstie understands Michael's need to escape. She ran away from her family after her bipolar mother committed suicide, and Kirstie, believing it was her fault for not watching over her mother closely enough, tried to commit suicide by cutting her wrists. After getting out of the hospital, she joined the carnival to leave her painful past behind. And now she offers Michael the same choice. Michael is torn, but he finally decides to leave after his mother is rushed to the hospital late one night with internal bleeding from Walker's punches and she still refuses to speak against him.

Michael has packed his bag and is ready to leave with the carnival when Lisa reveals that she is pregnant. He knows now that he can never escape; his conscience won't allow him. So he goes back to the fairgrounds and tells Kirstie good-bye instead. Less than a week later, however, Michael awakens to the sounds of his mother's screaming. He races down to the living room, where he witnesses Walker beating Lisa again. But this time, fueled by the fear that Walker will kill both his mother and her unborn baby, he grabs a fire poker and hits Walker from behind, crushing his skull and killing him. His mother panics and then calmly tells him to run. She tells him there never was a baby, that she made it up only to keep Michael from leaving her. So that Michael's life isn't ruined, she will tell the police she killed Walker. So he runs and catches up with the carnival a week later, where he is given a job, but Kirstie has left, and no one knows where she went.

After a year, the fair has completed its circuit, and Michael is back in Miami when he sees the headlines for his mother's murder trial. As a carny, he has been traveling under an assumed name, and he worries that his picture, printed in all the papers, will cause someone to recognize him. He still hasn't been able to locate Kirstie, although he has been searching for her via the Internet using public library computers. He is finally recognized by Julian, who offers to introduce him to his stepmother, Angela, who is a lawyer and may be able to help him.

Angela agrees to help Michael, but she isn't sure if his testimony about how brutal Walker was will help his mother, who has been painted as a gold-digging "trophy wife" by the press. (Michael hasn't told Angela that he was the one who killed Walker.) Lisa's plea of self-defense is questionable, since it is clear from the evidence that the killing blow came from behind, and the newspapers are speculating she will be sentenced to prison. Angela arranges for him to visit his mother in jail, where Lisa tells him to leave, that she deserves all of this for being such a bad mother. Meanwhile, Michael's fellow carny Cricket has packed Michael's bag and ordered him to leave. The other carnies have discovered his true identity, and his presence at the fair endangers all of them, many of whom are on the run from the law themselves. Michael agrees and goes to stay with Angela. As a good-bye present, Cricket gives him $50 and a piece of paper with Kirstie's phone number on it.

Michael finally admits to Angela that he was the one who had killed Walker, and she is able to help him craft a defense, claiming Walker's death was a "justifiable homicide." His mother is released, and they begin to put their lives back together. Michael calls Kirstie and discovers that she is working in a rehab center as a receptionist, trying to help others, including her estranged sister, who is a recovering addict. She is finally happy, having made peace with her past, and they part as friends.

Michael returns to school, where he is a year behind everyone else but happy to be back on the football team and back home where he belongs.

The Message: Don't be afraid to ask for help. Not all adults can be trusted, but some can be. Loyalty has its limits. There is no excuse for physical abuse. Sometimes you have to set aside others' needs and do what is best for yourself. Never give up.

Who's It For?: 8th–12th grade. The tough content, which includes domestic violence, details of gritty carny life, a mention of sexual intercourse between Michael and Kirstie, portrayals of underage drinking, and the bloody description of the final showdown between Michael and Walker, makes this title more appropriate for older teen readers.

Why It Rocks:
• **Voice:** Michael's first-person voice is heavy with the kind of guilt and regret that no 16-year-old should have to bear. The sharp dialogues between he and Walker are fraught with tension, which helps add to the suspense.
• **Plot:** The *Carnival* meets *Law & Order* story line will immediately grab teens' attention, while the police procedural details, coupled with the dark psychological impact of domestic abuse, and the surprisingly tender romance between Michael and Kirstie will keep it.
• **Pacing:** Flinn utilizes tight, clean flashbacks to tell her compelling murder mystery. Short, briskly written chapters, which alternate between "This Year" and "Last Year," lead readers through a tautly woven timeline that builds suspense and explains how Michael went from celebrated student athlete to drop-out carny worker.
• **Characterization:** Despite the brisk pacing, Flinn takes the time to really develop Michael's character, as he seesaws back and forth between caring too much about his situation and trying to convince himself that he doesn't care at all. Kirstie is also nicely rounded, as is Michael's mother, whose estrangement from her family after her first marriage helps to explain why she clings to Walker. Even Walker is kept from being portrayed as a total monster when he reveals to Michael that he grew up in an abusive home.

Hook It Up With: *The Body of Christopher Creed* by Carol Plum-Ucci

Read More about It:
Booklist: 03/15/04
Horn Book: 10/01/04
Kirkus Reviews, starred: 02/15/04
Publishers Weekly: 03/29/04
School Library Journal: 03/01/04
V.O.Y.A. (Voice of Youth Advocates): 06/01/04

Giles, Gail. 2002. *Shattering Glass*. Brookfield, CT: Roaring Brook Press. 215p.

The Story: High school senior Young Stewart has been best friends with social power broker Rob Haynes since Rob came as a new student last year. Young likes how confident and controlled Rob is and how Rob seems to understand Young's secret wish to be a writer. Despite his parents' wealth and his father's prestigious job as a doctor, Young is insecure about his place in the school's social strata, so he is grateful that Rob's charisma masks his own lack of self-confidence. Rob also knows Young's darkest secret: that he was molested by a male camp counselor when he was a boy and is frightened that this means he is gay. When Young reveals this secret, Rob is so sensitive and supportive that Young knows he'll do anything for his friend.

Not to say that Rob is lacking in the friend department. Since his arrival, he has replaced former golden boy Lance Ansley as the most popular guy at school, even stealing Lance's beautiful girlfriend, Blair, in the process. Through the sheer power of his charm and personal magnetism, Rob has made his circle of friends—easygoing Young; handsome, smooth-talker Bob; and sweet, dumb-jock Coop—the new in-crowd, effectively shutting Lance and his friends out. But there's one more thing Rob wants to take away from Lance: his bullying victim, pudgy class nerd Simon Glass.

One day after watching Lance give Simon another wedgie in front of the whole school, Rob decides enough is enough. As he explains to Young, there is no power in mocking Glass: "True power would be making the sheep like Simon." Rob decides that he is single-handedly going to make Simon cool, and his crew is going to help. They break the news to Simon in Rob's "office," the locked gym equipment room that Rob mysteriously owns a key to. Simon is agreeable, so they plan a shopping trip for the weekend. As the only son of wealthy, but distant parents, Simon has his own credit card, which the boys give a workout at the mall, buying Simon a new wardrobe and a fresh haircut. Soon, he is taking part in a fitness plan designed by Coop and working on his pickup lines with Bob. Rob even arranges for Simon to become the masked wolverine school mascot at the school games, creating an atmosphere of mystery and suspense around him that only adds to his rising star.

Everything is going according to Rob's plan, but Young is uneasy. He is angry when Simon dares to disagree with Rob about any part of the popularity plan yet equally annoyed when Simon allows Rob to push him around. But Young's attention is soon drawn off Simon when he begins a passionate romance with Ronna, a girl he's had a crush on for the last year, who turns out to like him as much as he likes her.

As Simon's popularity grows, he begins using his technology know-how to do favors for the guys: hacking into the school computer and erasing absences, switching classes and grades, even arranging to take the ACT test for Coop, who's afraid that his bad grades will affect his football scholarship. One night, while Simon and Young are alone hacking into the school records, they discover that Rob has a different last name and that he actually transferred from a small town nearby. Both boys decide to keep quiet about it.

Simon's high status is complete when he is unmasked as the popular wolverine mascot at the homecoming dance. Simon dances with Blair, Rob's girlfriend and homecoming queen, after planting a big, staged kiss on her, all Rob's idea of course. Simon is now unquestionably the most popular guy at school, but Rob wants more. To prove that Simon has become high school royalty, Rob decides that he must be elected senior class "Favorite," a title reserved for the most beloved person in the grade.

Over Christmas break, Young and Simon, still intrigued by Rob's secret name change, discover the reason why Rob moved and changed his name: his father was accused of molesting him and sent to prison. Because both of them owe Rob for different reasons, they vow never to reveal what they know, but Young is somewhat relieved to have something on Rob, since Rob knows so much about Young.

When Simon gets a brand-new Firebird for Christmas, the transformation is complete. Young wonders what happened to the bumbling nerd who tripped over his own feet. Simon is now confident, witty, and smooth. He's even branching out on his own, staging pranks and stunts that Rob hasn't signed off on. Young hates him and wonders what drives Rob to make Simon into a success. He has more reason to hate Simon when Rob asks him, as a personal favor, to break up with Ronna so Simon, who has a crush on her, can take her to the Favorites dance. Rob is convinced that Simon won't get elected Favorite unless he proves that he can get a hot date, so Young reluctantly agrees. But when he tells Ronna the real reason he's breaking up with her, she is furious and hurt that Young would choose sparing Rob's feelings over hers. She accuses him of being a follower and tells him they're through.

Young goes to the Favorites dance alone, and it makes him sick to see how beautiful and happy Ronna looks with Simon. When the results of the election are announced, Simon has been elected Wittiest, and Rob has been elected Favorite. Rob immediately convenes the crew to his office, the equipment room, to find out what went wrong. He had campaigned so hard to make sure everyone would vote for Simon for Favorite, but Simon reveals that he fixed the computer to turn every vote for him into a vote for Rob. Simon, tired of being Rob's pawn, confronts him with the fact that he knows about Rob's father. He also turns on Young, accuses him of being Rob's puppet, and asks him how it feels to have nothing, now that Simon has Ronna. Rob, enraged, begins to beat Simon to death with one of the baseball bats in the equipment room, and Bob joins in. Coop tries to protect Simon and gets his knee bashed in and his football career ruined for his trouble. Young doesn't join in the beating, but his hatred of Simon is so great that he doesn't try to stop it either.

Notes from the beginning of each chapter written by various characters in the story reveal that Rob escapes punishment by running with his mother to Mexico; Coop loses his football scholarship but becomes an elementary school teacher; Bob gets off with a suspended sentence; and Young, who didn't strike a blow, is the only one to serve jail time, since he is the only one to plead guilty.

The Message: You can't control other people's emotions or reactions; you can control only your own. Nothing in life is free; people don't normally do something for nothing. People who appear to be doing so usually have an ulterior motive. There are consequences to every action. Where does group culpability end and individual responsibility begin?

Who's It For?: 8th–12th grade. Besides the actions detailed in the summary, there are references to underage drinking and some strong language. Young and Ronna have sex, though it is not graphically described. The scene where Simon is beaten to death is particularly brutal.

Why It Rocks:
• **Voice:** Young's realistic first-person voice is both conflicted and confident as he tries to figure out how much of his life is his and how much of it belongs to Rob.
• **Plot:** By juxtaposing rising action in the main plotline against telling remarks from various characters that open each chapter dated five years after Simon's death, Giles tells two enormously compelling stories. Readers will finish and then flip the pages to start again on page one to pick up any details they may have missed. Giles foreshadows the grim ending with one of the most memorable first lines in the history of YA literature: "Simon Glass was easy to hate...we each hated him for a different reason, but we didn't realize it until the day we killed him."
• **Pacing:** Slow but steady, with tension building on every page. The postdated remarks that open each chapter may slow down some teens as they put together the clues that tell the story of Simon's untimely demise.
• **Characterization:** Giles does a nice job of developing each secondary character; suave Bob and sweet, but dim Coop are fully realized and are often more sympathetic than Young, who realizes he's selling his soul to the devil that is Rob but can't seem to stop, even when he is forced to give up the love of his life.

Hook It Up With: *Playing in Traffic*, also by Gail Giles, and *Breaking Point* by Alex Flinn.

Read More about It:
Booklist, starred: 03/01/02
Horn Book: 10/01/02
Kirkus Reviews, starred: 02/01/02
Publishers Weekly: 02/11/02
School Library Journal, starred: 04/01/02
V.O.Y.A. (Voice of Youth Advocates): 06/01/02

Klass, David. 2001. *You Don't Know Me.* New York: Farrar, Straus & Giroux. 261p.

The Story: Cynical fourteen-year-old John ("named after a toilet"), whose father left him and his mother when he was a little boy, understands that most things are not what they seem. School is "anti-school" because no real learning happens there, and his friend Billy Beanman is not really his friend, because they are competing for the attention of the same girl, beautiful Gloria from their Algebra class. In band, his tuba is not a tuba but a demented bullfrog because it always croaks at inappropriate moments. Worst of all, his mother, an exhausted factory worker who appears to love him, doesn't seem to notice that her live-in truck-driving boyfriend, "the man who is not my father" (MWNF), hits John when she isn't around.

When Billy is arrested at the mall for stealing an egg roll and then given a suspension at school as well, John sees his chance to get ahead in the race to win Gloria. He asks her to the Friday night basketball game by passing a note during

Algebra, and the next day she tells him she would be happy to go to the game with him. John is so inspired by Gloria's acceptance that he actually answers a question in Algebra and plays his tuba solo correctly in band, which thrills his band teacher, Mr. Steenwilly, who has always told John to come to him if he ever needs anyone to talk to.

The afternoon before the game, John comes home to find the house a mess and an open bottle of whiskey on the table. The MWNF has clearly been drinking, but he appears to have left, so John feels its safe enough to raid the man's sock drawer for some extra money to take out Gloria. When he goes to pick her up, Gloria's father, a former football player known as "Bulldozer," warns him not to get fresh with his "little ducky." They go to the game, and Gloria pays more attention to her social circle than to John. But he gets his chance to shine when there is a sudden riot between the rival spectators and he bravely leads Gloria to safety under the bleachers. After her rescue, Gloria turns amorous and invites John back to her finished basement for a make-out session.

Just as things are getting steamy in Gloria's basement, the Bulldozer starts knocking on the door. He becomes enraged, and John becomes terrified, when they both realize that Gloria has locked the door. The Bulldozer ends up breaking down the door and crashing after John in the dark, while threatening to kill him. John manages to keep his cool and squeeze out the cat door. Unfortunately, he has left behind his shirt, socks, and shoes. After walking home in the cold, John is not in the best shape when his mother's boyfriend attacks him and accuses him of stealing from his sock drawer. The MWNF then locks him into the back of his truck, drives him to a warehouse John doesn't recognize, and forces him to take part in the loading and unloading of stolen televisions. John wonders what new horrors are in store for him now that he knows about the MWNF's illegal activities.

John doesn't wonder long, however. After the televisions have been successfully moved, the MWNF drives John down a deserted road and tells him his mother has left town to take care of her elderly aunt, who is dying. She wanted to take John, but the MWNF convinced her to leave him at home so the two of them could work on their "relationship." But the most chilling news he gives John is that when his mother returns, she and the MWNF are getting married, and there is nothing he can do about it. John is so sore from the illegal loading, and so disheartened by the thought of the upcoming marriage, that he stays home on Monday and just lies in his bed, wondering how he can escape this impossible situation.

When John returns to school, things go from bad to worse. Gloria confronts him in then hallway, blaming him for getting her in trouble with her father. He is so distracted by Gloria that he accidentally speaks his unkind thoughts about his Algebra teacher, who he calls Mrs. Moonface, aloud during class, causing her to run crying from the room. Finally, he completely screws up his tuba solo in front of Mr. Steenwilly's beloved mentor, Professor Kachooski. He is suspended from school for a week for making the comments about Mrs. Moonface, and the MWNF beats him with his belt when he gets home as punishment. He spends the rest of the week making the MWNF's meals and enduring his slaps when he doesn't like the food. John's mother has still not returned from taking care of her ailing aunt, and the situation feels so hopeless that John actually contemplates suicide.

But things start looking up when Violet Hayes, a girl from his band class whom he had never noticed because of his crush on Gloria, comes to his house to ask him to the Holiday dance. He accepts, even though he has no clothes or money. Violet's parents are kind to him when he arrives to pick her up, and Violet lends him her older brother's blazer to wear. John enjoys the dance more than he thought he would, mostly owing to several glasses of spiked punch. When Gloria arrives with her college boyfriend and tries to start an argument, Violet kicks her date and threatens to kick Gloria. John takes Violet home and kisses her goodnight, feeling happier than he has in a long time.

But when John returns home, the MWNF has been drinking and is angry that John didn't make him any dinner before he left on his date. He begins punching John right on the front lawn, but this time John fights back, using a pen from his pocket to rake the MWNF's face. But MWNF is too strong and knocks John down and begins choking him. Just as John is beginning to lose consciousness, Mr. Steenwilly, who has been worried about him and was driving by to check on him, pulls the MWNF off John.

John awakens in a hospital to find his mother leaning over him. She wants to know why John never told her what was going on, and John tells her it was because he was sure she would choose the MWNF over him. She assures him that would have never been the case and is so sincerely upset that John realizes he was wrong. His mother does know him and love him, after all.

The Message: Sometimes people are very different on the inside than they appear to be on the outside. You always have choices, even when you feel like you don't. There are always some adults who can be trusted, and you should seek them out. If you are being hurt or abused, you should always tell someone.

Who's It For?: 8th–12th grade. John's darkly humorous voice helps lighten the book's mood, but the descriptions of the beatings he suffers are still disturbing and may upset some younger readers.

Why It Rocks:
• **Voice:** Klass has penned one of the most original, heartbreakingly funny first-person voices in all of YA literature. John's coping mechanism of looking at his life through a lens of the absurd to avoid dealing with the fact that he is being abused at home is brilliantly executed. Another unusual feature of John's voice is how it often slips into second person, as in his mother being the "you" of the title and the person to whom the whole book is addressed.
• **Plot:** Klass's plot follows a tightly structured pattern where John's life gets better and worse by increments until the chilling, brutal climax where he nearly loses his life. Each chapter expertly balances humor with utter bleakness so that the reader doesn't know whether to laugh or cry.
• **Pacing:** Like a complicated dance step, Klass's pacing is quick, then slow, then quick again, constantly keeping teens on their toes as they wonder which side of the coin John will land on: heads or tails, laughter or tears, life or death.
• **Characterization:** Klass has fun with his secondary characters, giving them outrageous names (Professor Kachooski, His "Bulldozership," Mrs. Moonface) and outsized personalities that add to the upside-down and opposite world John has created to keep his deepest fears at bay.

Hook It Up With: *Dunk* by David Lubar and *Big Mouth and Ugly Girl* by Joyce Carol Oates.

Read More about It:
Booklist: 03/01/01
Horn Book: 07/01/01
Kirkus Reviews: 02/01/01
Publishers Weekly: 03/12/01
School Library Journal, starred: 03/01/01
V.O.Y.A. (Voice of Youth Advocates): 06/01/01

Lynch, Chris. 2005. *Inexcusable.* New York: Simon & Schuster. 165p.

The Story: In a small, dark dorm room, high school senior Keir Sarafian has just been accused of date rape by his tearful friend Gigi Boudakian. He blocks the door and window to prevent her from leaving as he tries to convince both Gigi and the reader that he couldn't have raped Gigi because he is a "good guy" who would never do such a thing. As he argues with Gigi, he mentally reviews his background and specific incidents from senior year that have brought him to this room and this terrible situation.

Keir never knew his mother, who died when he was young. He has been raised by his father, an indulgent, melancholy "quasi-alcoholic" widower who has never quite gotten over the death of his wife; and his two elder sisters, Mary and Fran, who both attend college about three hours away. Keir professes great love for his sisters but saves his highest praise for his father, Ray, who allows Keir to drink with him and is his enthusiastic partner in an ongoing Risk game that hasn't been interrupted since Mary and Fran left for college. Ray often tells Keir what a softhearted "mush" he really is on the inside, and Keir uses his father's opinion of him to defend his idea of himself as a kind, decent person.

But many of Keir's actions belie his belief of himself as a "good guy." Normally a placekicker on his high school football team, Keir is substituted as a cornerback during one of the games, and because of a particularly hard, well-placed hit, he permanently cripples the receiver he tackles. Because of extent of the other boy's injury, an investigation takes place, but Keir is eventually exonerated, since the school decides that the result of the hard hit was an unfortunate accident. Keir uses the investigation findings to defend his choice not to apologize to the boy he injured, because the accident was not his fault. He is defensive when his sisters suggest that he apologize and refuses to admit any wrongdoing. Furthermore, he receives three football scholarship offers after his name is cleared, including a full ride from the college his sisters attend, which he views as further vindication of his actions.

As a result of the football incident, Keir enjoys a level of notoriety at school, where fellow jocks begin calling him "Killer." At first Keir is uncomfortable with the nickname—it doesn't fit with his "good guy" image—but soon all the attention he's receiving assuages his discomfort. He continues to believe himself a "good guy" even after he takes part in a drunken vandalism spree with the football team, during which they break some of the public library's windows and deface a statue in the center of town. When he goes back to view the extensive damage the next day, it doesn't jibe with the picture he has in his head of he and his fellow football players as "lovable rogues," so he convinces himself that another group must have followed after them and done this terrible thing.

Even when captured on tape, Keir doesn't believe he is wrong. He also plays soccer, and as a part of a cruel hazing prank, he and some of the other football players kidnap several of the soccer players after their end-of-the-year banquet and make them skinny-dip in a nearby lake while forcing them to drink whiskey. The soccer players are Keir's teammates, yet he is one of the masked attackers taking part in the dunking and peeing on the unfortunate victims' clothes. One of the football players taped the festivities, and when Keir later sees himself on the video, he is so appalled that he quickly convinces himself that the masked figure may look like him but must be someone else.

Keir is thrilled when his crush, beautiful Gigi Boudakian, agrees to go to the prom with him. He has known Gigi since grade school, and she believes him to be a kind, sincere guy who will respect the fact she has a long-distance boyfriend in the military. Although he does make several halfhearted attempts to grope her, Gigi masterfully eludes them, and they end up having a sweet after-prom breakfast at the local IHOP. The prom date only serves to strengthen Keir's infatuation with Gigi, while Gigi wistfully remarks that Keir seemed much sweeter before everyone started calling him "Killer."

For graduation, Keir tells Ray he would rather have an unlimited use of Ray's cousin Rollo's swanky limousine after the ceremony than a big party. He needs a distraction from the fact that his beloved sisters claimed they couldn't make it back for his graduation because of their exam schedules. The night after graduation, Keir stops by a party that he knows Gigi is attending. He drinks heavily, does some drugs, and happily accepts the chorus of "Killer!" that greets him each time he enters a room. But soon he grows sick of everyone and retreats to the limo, where he is joined shortly by Gigi, who is angry with Carl, her military boyfriend, for standing her up at the party. So when Keir suggests taking a trip to his sisters' dorm three hours away to give them a study break, the spurned Gigi is agreeable and even snuggles up to him on the way there.

At the dorm, Keir is furious to discover that his sisters lied to him about having to study; Mary has left with friends for the weekend, and Fran is out on a date. When she later returns, she is incredulous that Keir has come to confront her. She claims that Keir creates his own reality and that their father supports him in this. The reason that she and Mary didn't want to come to graduation was because Keir had gotten so drunk and behaved so badly at their graduation parties that they wanted nothing to do with him and because he is a spoiled child who refuses to take responsibility for his actions. Keir is shocked by this portrait of himself but heartened when Gigi defends him against Fran.

They leave Fran's dorm, and even though Keir has purposely sent the limo away, he tells Gigi that Rollo must have forgotten them and left. But luckily, he has the key to an empty dorm room used by the campus football team for "visiting friends and family" that he was given when he accepted his scholarship. Gigi is apprehensive but too exhausted to argue because it is now four in the morning. The room has two cots, and Gigi quickly falls asleep on one, unaware that Keir has joined her. She wakes to find him kissing her, and when she makes sounds of protest, he simply kisses her harder and pins her arms above her head. After the rape, Keir spends hours trying to convince Gigi, who was at first hysterical and then ominously silent, that what happened between them wasn't rape. Gigi tells him that "good guys" aren't rapists, and Keir is a rapist. Suddenly he sees himself through her eyes and is horrified. He stops blocking the door and curls up on one of the cots as she leaves, finally seeing himself as he really is and awaiting punishment for his actions.

The Message: "Actions speak louder than words." Everyone is responsible for his or her own actions. Self-delusion is powerful. Be careful in whom you place your trust. Drugs and alcohol remove inhibitions and can lead to destructive behavior.

Who's It For?: 8th–12th grade. Because of content and concept, Lynch's masterfully constructed character study, told by a wonderfully unreliable narrator, is best suited to an older teen audience. The rape is not graphically described, but the horror and pain of the situation are apparent, and there is a great deal of underage drinking and drug use depicted within the text.

Why It Rocks:
• **Voice:** Smooth, cajoling, earnest, and pleading, Keir's unreliable first-person narration is chilling and utterly compelling. Teens will have to decide for themselves if Keir is telling the truth, and the revealing, tension-filled confrontation he has with Fran in the end will decide the issue for many.
• **Plot:** Using flashbacks from the present, claustrophobic room of the rape to the rationalized violent incidents of Keir's recent past provides a sense of movement to what would otherwise be a rich, but more static character study.
• **Pacing:** On first look, this may not seem like a nail-biting suspense novel, but the building tension of wondering whether Keir will ever be able to see himself as he truly is, which readers don't find out until the very last page, is what pushes this story into psychological thriller territory.
• **Characterization:** Although this novel obviously has a very narrowly focused point of view, the conversations Keir has with secondary characters, especially Ray and Gigi, still manage to provide a rich, albeit limited, view into their personalities. Masculine details that Lynch includes about Keir and his father—the ongoing Risk game, the bottomless bottles of beer, the nights at their favorite restaurant, which serves only meat—all serve to subtly underscore the aggressive male nature that Keir keeps trying to deny.

Hook It Up With: *Breathing Underwater* by Alex Flinn.

Read More about It:
Booklist, starred: 09/15/05
Horn Book, starred: 01/01/06
Kirkus Reviews, starred: 10/15/05
Publishers Weekly, starred: 10/17/05
School Library Journal, starred: 11/01/05
Voice of Youth Advocates (V.O.Y.A.): 12/01/05

McNamee, Graham. 2003. *Acceleration.* **New York: Random House. 210p.**

The Story: It is the summer before senior year, and Duncan is stuck with the most boring job ever: assisting in the Toronto Transit Commission's Lost and Found Department. While it does allow him to escape the heat wave everyone else is suffering from aboveground, he is finding the process of assigning lost umbrellas, jackets, and eyeglasses an "expiration" date and weeding out those items that are "past due" for donation to the local YMCA incredibly tedious. But the bleak job suits his mood, which has been dark ever since the Labor Day holiday weekend last year. That was when Duncan tried—and failed—to save a girl named Maya from drowning in dangerous riptides on Lake Ontario. Ever since then, he has suffered from terrible nightmares, where Maya is screaming underwater, begging him for help. His parents tried therapy and medication, but nothing helped, and now Duncan fears that his guilt and regret over the accident will never go away.

While packing up lost books, Duncan comes across a leather journal with no name or address. As he begins to read it, he is disturbed to discover that it is full of descriptions of animal mutilations and arson attempts. As he reads further, he finds that the author is contemplating murder. He's even staked out three women that he sees regularly on the subway, along with the times that they ride and the stops where they get off. Duncan realizes that he has found the journal of a would-be serial killer, but now that he has it, what should he do? He's afraid to turn it in to the police, lest they think it belongs to him. It also occurs to him that the act of finding this man and keeping him from hurting anyone else may finally ease his guilt over Maya's drowning and end his nightmares.

Duncan begins to do research on the man he has dubbed "Roach." He enlists his two best friends, Vinnie and Wayne, to come with him to the air-conditioned public library while he looks up information on serial killers. He finds a book by an FBI profiler that states there are three childhood behaviors that are shared by most serial killers: cruelty to animals, bed-wetting, and the setting of fires. This information frightens Duncan so badly that he decides to take Vinnie, the more serious of his two friends, into his confidence. Vinnie convinces him to take it to the police, but when he does, the bored desk cop is so dismissive that Duncan knows the journal won't be taken seriously. He takes it back and resolves to find Roach himself and then involve the police once he knows exactly who the man is and where he lives.

Duncan asks for Vinnie's help, and his friend reluctantly agrees, even though he doesn't think it is a good idea. "Me and you going after this guy…is like the Hardy Boys meet Hannibal Lecter." Nevertheless, Vinnie uses the directions and locations written about in the journal to create a map of Roach's activities, and discovers that all of the incidents Roach wrote about took place in the same six- to seven-block radius, a working-class neighborhood called Wilson Heights. Meanwhile, Duncan has discovered an old receipt in the journal that indicates Roach received an employee discount at the local mall. Now that they have narrowed down the man's possible home and workplace, they focus their attention on the mall. After deducing that Roach might be a security guard because of his need to have power over others, they follow two likely candidates home but are disappointed when both men end up having families or girlfriends. Duncan is so disheartened that he considers giving up altogether.

Then, they receive a huge break: Roach himself comes to the Lost and Found, looking for his journal. Duncan is shocked to finally see his imaginary nemesis in the flesh, but after pretending to look for the lost journal (it's actually hidden at the bottom of his closet at home), he tells the man he can't find it. Roach leaves, and Duncan tells his boss he's taking lunch, so that he can follow him. After he watches Roach enter a small nondescript house in Wilson Heights, then leave a short while later, he decides to call Wayne for help. Wayne is a semiretired shoplifter and consummate lock picker, and while he's annoyed that Duncan hadn't informed him until now about he and Vinnie's secret project, he agrees to pick the lock on Roach's front door so Duncan can take a look around.

With Wayne's help, Duncan not only gets into the house, but also is able to access the locked basement as well. But they must tread quietly, since they discover Roach's old, deaf grandmother is watching television inside. Duncan explores the basement while Wayne waits outside. He finds animals in jars of formaldehyde, a police scanner, and a small, windowless room that seems to be awaiting a captive, before he hears footfalls on the stairway. He hides in the room, but it's too late; Roach has returned and realized someone is in his sanctuary. Duncan bursts out of the room, brandishing the metal bar used to barricade the door as a weapon. Roach has a knife, and they each get in one blow before Duncan manages to run up the stairs and out of the house. Bleeding badly from a cut on his arm, Duncan races to the subway station, pursued by Roach. Wayne sees him leave but loses him on the side streets. Duncan makes it to the subway platform, but the train doesn't come right away, and Roach has time to catch up. After a short tussle, both of them end up on the tracks; Duncan is able to roll away under the platform edge, while Roach, who is disoriented, is hit and killed by an incoming train.

Duncan survives with 20 stitches, a broken arm, and a concussion. He, Wayne, and Vinnie decide never to tell anyone what really happened. As far as the police know, Duncan's attack was a botched mugging, since he claims he can't really remember what happened. Duncan burns the journal, goes back to work at the Lost and Found, and, after a session of night swimming with Vinnie at the public pool, is relieved to realize that he can no longer hear Maya's underwater screams.

The Message: It's dangerous to take the law into your own hands. Sometimes the hardest person to forgive is yourself.

Who's It For?: 8th–12th grade. The topic is gritty, but not any more so than most of the crime dramas on television that most teens are well versed in and may even watch with their parents. McNamee sprinkles the text with several facts about serial killers, which may prompt older readers to do some research of their own into this fascinating, disturbing topic.

Why It Rocks:
- **Voice:** Duncan's first-person narration makes the fast-moving action that more immediate and compelling. His conversations with Vinnie and Wayne are often humorous and help to offset some of the frightening tension.
- **Plot:** McNamee's premise of a serial killer's journal turning up in the subway Lost and Found is nothing short of genius and sets the stage for a suspenseful thrill

ride that grows only more exciting with the turn of each page. The subplot of Duncan's prolonged grief over the drowning accident sometimes gets in the way of the heart-stopping action, but it will help explain his motivation to the rule-following teen readers who have a hard time understanding his persistent pursuit of the dangerous Roach.

- **Pacing:** Relentless. McNamee never lets up the tension; from the moment Duncan finds the diary, he and the reader are inexorably pulled toward his final meeting with Roach.
- **Characterization:** Duncan is nicely rounded, as are Vinnie and Wayne, who threaten to steal scenes every time they come onto the page. Duncan's parents are excellent examples of caring, working-class people who don't have many material resources but are trying to set a good example for their son.

Hook It Up With: *Tenderness* by Robert Cormier.

Read More about It:
Booklist: 09/15/03
Horn Book: 04/01/04
Kirkus Reviews: 09/15/03
Publishers Weekly, starred: 11/10/03
School Library Journal: 11/01/03
V.O.Y.A. (Voice of Youth Advocates): 12/01/03

Morgenroth, Kate. 2005. *Jude*. New York: Simon & Schuster. 277p.

The Story: Fifteen-year-old Jude has warned his physically abusive, drug-dealing father repeatedly that he'd better stop skimming so much of his product off the top or his suppliers are going to hear about it. But his father, Anthony, doesn't listen, and as he's cutting his latest supply of heroin with baby powder, two armed men break down the door of their shoddy apartment and shoot him. The man who is obviously in charge of the hit tells Jude that he'll let him live, provided he doesn't tell the cops what he saw. Jude agrees, relieved to have escaped his father's fate. After the men leave and Jude calls 911, he tells the police that he didn't see who killed his father, but other witness reports contradict the scenario Jude has constructed.

After the murder, when police are searching the apartment, they discover hidden papers that indicate that Jude, who has never known his mother, is the biological son of District Attorney Anna Grady. An astonished Grady meets Jude at the police station, tells him that his father used to be a cop, and—after a nasty divorce and trial, during which Anthony was convicted of physically abusing Anna—he stole Jude from his crib when he was three weeks old; Anna has had no idea what happened to him until now. She brings him home to a wealth he can't even begin to imagine. He's suddenly gone from a small, dirty apartment to a four-bedroom house with every possible comfort.

Anna's boyfriend and Anthony's old partner, Deputy Commissioner Harry Wichowski, is concerned that the police have found several inconsistencies in Jude's story about his father's murder. Harry promises to cover for Jude and draw the heat off him as long as he tells Harry the truth. Jude decides to tell him that he *did* have something to do with Anthony's death (although he remains vague about exactly how he was involved) to throw suspicion off the real killers, who he's afraid could still come after him.

Anna sends Jude to Benton Academy, a posh private school where his upbringing seems exotic to the privileged, sheltered students who go there. He strikes up a friendship with Nick, a popular student who acts like he's from the projects instead of a million-dollar mansion. Nick wants Jude to hook him up with his friend R.J., who is now a dealer in his old neighborhood, so that he can begin dealing at Benton. After a while, Jude reluctantly agrees, but after setting up the connection, he begins to distance himself from both of them. Anna has decided to run for mayor, and Jude wants to avoid getting in trouble for her sake. He knows he's already been seen by some undercover cops when taking Nick to meet R.J. and is afraid Anna will find out.

When Nick dies at school from an overdose, Jude knows it's only a matter of time before something gets traced back to him. Harry discovers that Anna's rival for mayor has learned about Jude's connections to Nick's drug dealing, and he tells Jude that the only way to keep Anna from losing the election once the media finds out is for Jude to take the fall for Nick's death. Harry wants Jude to lie and say that he gave Nick the drugs, so that Anna can "discover" he is a dealer and turn him in. No one will be able to say that she is soft on drug issues if she is willing to turn in her own son. Harry assures Jude that he will be tried as a minor, do a little time in juvenile detention, and that once the election is over, Harry will make sure Jude gets a new trial and be set free. Jude is frightened, but agrees, even though Harry insists that they not tell Anna the truth, in order to make the situation look real.

Jude endures an arrest, a stay in juvenile detention until the trial (he can't go home because it would be a conflict of interest, since his own mother is preparing a case against him), and Anna's shocked disappointment. Because he pleads not guilty, as Harry had instructed, his defense is a disaster. He is tried as an adult, and receives five years without parole in a state prison. Stunned, he manages to avoid the convicts, who are ominously circling him for 16 days, until his mother's election, which she wins. Anna and Harry come to visit him separately. He tells Anna the truth but is horrified when she doesn't believe him and tells him to let go of this fantasy that Harry set him up. Harry then comes in and tells Jude he never intended to help him, that he just wanted to support Anna's career and that Anna will never believe Jude over Harry. His conscience is clear, though, because he still believes that Jude had something to do with his father's death, and he refuses to listen to Jude's desperate pleas to the contrary now.

Jude does five years of hard time, at first earning a fierce reputation as a brutal fighter, then realizing that he doesn't want to end up like his father and starting an ambitious plan of study. By the time he gets out, he has earned his GED and has graduated from college. He can't get a job better than washing dishes, and his dream of becoming a lawyer is crushed when all ten of the schools he applies to reject him. So he moves on to his next plan: convincing Anna of the truth. He enlists the help of an old classmate from Benton, Davis Marshall. Davis, who is now a journalist, believes that Jude was set up and wants to help so that he can be the one to break the story.

Jude uses his prison know-how to pick the lock of Anna and Harry's house, and then he and Davis scan as many of Harry's personal files as possible to print and review later. With the help of Davis's sister, Lizzie, they pour over the documents, looking for the clue that will prove to Anna that Harry set up Jude. Finally, Lizzie finds the smoking gun—a series of checks written to "cash" for large amounts of money that are spaced out over several years. Jude realizes the connection: the checks coincide with each time he and his father moved. Harry was paying Anthony to stay out of his and Anna's life. Jude and Davis confront Harry and, with the use of a hidden microphone, manage to get him to implicate himself; they threaten to publish the information if he doesn't tell Anna the truth. But Jude is devastated to discover that while his mother believes Harry's confession, she is far more concerned about what this will mean to her congressional bid than about how much Jude has suffered. In the end, they all get what they deserve: Davis wins awards for his articles on Jude's setup, Jude gets accepted to law school, Anna's political career is ruined, and Harry goes to prison for what he's done.

The Message: Not all adults can be trusted, or have the best interests of children at heart. "What can't be cured must be endured." The truth always comes out. "There is no great loss without some small gain."

Who's It For?: 8th–12th grade. This is an excellent example of mystery/thriller genre fiction for older teens. Morgenroth does a nice job of keeping this potentially seedy story mostly clean in terms of language and sexuality. The most graphic part of the book is when Jude is in prison and not only is repeatedly targeted as a victim but also turns into a brutal fistfighter with a reputation for nearly beating his opponents to death—until he learns to curb his anger at the circumstances that brought him to this place.

Why It Rocks:
- **Voice:** Morgenroth's unadorned prose and realistic dialogue are reminiscent of adult mysteries, which comes as no surprise, since she is the author of two adult thrillers. Most teen fans of John Grisham and Scott Turow will recognize and gravitate toward Morgenroth's clean, utilitarian third-person prose.
- **Plot:** The plot twists turn on a dime, and although the prose appears dense, Morgenroth doesn't waste words. Every passage, every turn of phrase (even a long-winded confessional story told to Jude by his elderly, dying cellmate), enriches the plot and is referred to again.
- **Pacing:** Taut. Morgenroth employs short, cliff-hanging chapters that move the action along and heighten the suspense.
- **Characterization:** Jude is a sympathetic, credibly wrought character, who struggles mightily with his temper, his sense of justice, and his burning need for recognition and love from his distant mother. Secondary characters are less well developed, but every character works well in the service to the plot.

Hook It Up With: *The Christopher Killer* by Alane Ferguson.

Read More about It:
Booklist, starred: 11/15/04
Kirkus Reviews: 09/15/04
Publishers Weekly: 11/22/04
School Library Journal, starred: 11/01/04
V.O.Y.A. (Voice of Youth Advocates): 12/01/04

Springer, Nancy. 2006. *The Case of the Missing Marquess: An Enola Holmes Mystery.* **New York: Penguin Group. 216p.**

The Story: In July 1888, 14-year-old Enola Holmes is devastated when her free-spirited, widowed mother seemingly disappears from their country estate on Enola's birthday. When she doesn't return by the next day, Enola sends a wire to her two much older brothers, Mycroft and Sherlock Holmes, in London, to ask for their help. When they arrive, Enola finds them both stuffy and condescending and discovers during their stay the reason they haven't visited Ferndell Hall since their father's funeral, when Enola was four years old. Their mother forbade them to come back after Mycroft suggested that she hand over the running of the estate to him because, as eldest son, he legally owned it. Ever since, she had sent Mycroft bills for imaginary services, such as gardeners, seamstresses, and servants, none of which Enola has ever seen. The brothers surmise that their strong-willed, suffragist-leaning mother had stockpiled the money until she had enough to run away and start a new life free from the constraints of a British male-dominated society.

Enola is left reeling with this new information. She wonders how her mother could abandon her like this and leave her without even a word of farewell. Then she remembers the hand-illustrated book of ciphers her mother left her as a birthday present. Inside, she discovers several secret messages, that instruct her to look in various hiding places around the house, where Enola finds stashes of bank notes. She finds enough money to ensure her own independence and determines to use the money to fund her own expedition to look for her mother. While she longs for the affection and respect of her elder brothers, their chauvinism and obvious distain for the female mind help her decide that she'd be better off on her own than under their dubious care.

By this time, it is five weeks since her mother disappeared. Sherlock has returned to London to continue the investigation of their mother's disappearance, while Mycroft has stayed on and declared that Enola will attend boarding school. Giving every appearance of compliance, Enola makes it nearly to the railway station before she manages to slip away from her driver and make her escape. She has hidden her bicycle behind the church, its basket full of supplies. Since she must travel light, she has also hidden necessary items all over her person, by concealing them in the embarrassing undergarments she has lately been forced to wear to camouflage her skinny frame: a "dress improver" and a "bust enhancer." Enola spends the first day biking toward London, where she decides she has the best chance of finding her mother, knowing that her brothers wouldn't expect her to run toward them instead of away from them. She spends an uncomfortable night in the woods and then rises the next day to discover she is near a town with a train station. She abandons her bicycle, disguises herself in her mother's old black widow's weeds to appear older, and heads into town to catch the next train to London.

In town, she walks right into the middle of another mystery: a young lord, a Marquess, has been kidnapped, and his hysterical mother is enlisting any help she can find. Enola is intrigued and feels a kinship to the boy after seeing his picture in the local paper. Although he is 12, his mother has continued to dress him in velvet and long curls, and from his miserable expression Enola guesses that he would probably do anything—even fake his own kidnapping—to escape his overbearing mother. Enola uses the Holmes name to get herself onto the property, then begins surveying the grounds, looking for the boy's secret hideaway and clues to where he might have gone.

When Enola finds a tree house littered with torn velvet clothing and a mass of shorn hair, she knows her hunch was correct. She tells her idea to the constable in charge of the case, Inspector Lestrade, suggesting that owing to the many pictures of boats in his hideaway, the Marquess may have run off to the London docks to seek service on a ship. She notices she has been overheard by a flamboyant medium named Madame Laelia, whom the Marquess's mother has employed to find her lost son, but wastes no time in beating a hasty exit. Already she has blown her own cover by giving her real last name and must get away before her brother shows up, in order to pursue her agenda of locating her mother.

When Enola arrives in London, she heads for the East End to look for a used clothing store in order to find a new disguise. Having never been to London before, she is shocked by the extreme poverty and filth. As she is walking, she is suddenly attacked by a large man who demands to know the whereabouts of the Marquess. Enola has no idea why this information is being asked of her, but she struggles to escape and nearly gets away but is felled by a blow to the head. When she awakens, she is tied hand and foot in the hull of a docked boat, and sitting across from her, similarly bound, is the missing Marquess.

Enola quickly surmises that she and the Marquess are part of a blackmail plot. The large man's name is Cutter, and by disguising himself as Madame Laelia, he is able to get personal information from wealthy patrons that allows him to orchestrate blackmails and kidnappings. As Madame Laelia, he had overheard Enola's guess about the Marquess's destination and had found the boy right where she said he would be. He had also heard that Enola was related to the famous detective, so he decided to kidnap her as well as the Marquess for ransom.

Enola may be down, but she's not out. She uses the steel ribs of her corset to slice the ropes on her wrists. Then she clobbers Cutter's henchman with a ballast stone and frees the Marquess. They flee the boat, but Cutter sees them and gives chase. They duck into a used-clothing store, where Enola bribes the proprietor into hiding them for the night and outfitting them in fresh clothes the next morning. The Marquess has decided he's had enough adventure and wants to go home, so Enola takes him to Scotland Yard to turn himself in; while there, she catches a glimpse of

Sherlock and overhears how he is now searching for both her and her mother. She slips away before he sees her, giving sketches of Cutter both as himself and as Madame Laelia, to the Marquess, who still doesn't quite know who she is, for the police.

Enola stays in London, using her mother's money to set herself up as Dr. Leslie T. Ragostin, professional "perditorian," or finder of lost loved ones. But because no one would accept a woman in that position, she pretends to be Dr. Leslie's secretary, while really taking the cases herself. She also uses a veiled nun disguise to pass out food and blankets to the unfortunates of London's East End, determined to foil any of her brothers' plans to find her and bring her under their control. She places a cipher in several local papers that only her mother would understand and receives a reply that indicates her mother is doing well in her new life as a member of a wandering Gypsy clan. Happily, Enola has found both her mother and her vocation.

The Message: Girls are just as smart as boys; never underestimate their talents. Trust your instincts. Sometimes the solution to a problem is right in front of you.

Who's It For?: 6th–10th grade. The cover appealing to young people, small size, and short length are deceiving; this is a full-on, authentic Victorian mystery, complete with vocabulary from the time and loads of period detail, some of which is funny (like the descriptions of Enola's despised undergarments) and some of which will be disturbing to readers younger than sixth grade (for example, Enola's description of the hairless "dosses," sick, homeless elderly women who crawl in the gutters begging for food).

Why It Rocks:
•   **Voice:** Enola's spirited first-person narration is amusing and pitch-perfect, balancing her natural smarts with her cloistered innocence.
•   **Plot:** Besides gifting readers with two mysteries to solve for the price of one, Springer also embeds lots of fascinating facts about feminism and classism in Victorian England within this inventive plot that will give curious readers cause to find out more about Enola's world. The series subhead hints at more Enola mysteries to come.
•   **Pacing:** Brisk, after a slow beginning that brings the reader up to speed on Victorian society and mannerisms.
•   **Characterization:** Secondary characters conform to their genre stereotypes, but Enola is fresh and funny, and her precocious voice, which some may find too modern for her Victorian setting, is explained by her unusually liberal upbringing.

Hook It Up With: *Shakespeare's Secret* by Elise Broach.

Read More about It:
Booklist, starred: 12/01/05
Horn Book: 10/01/06
Kirkus Reviews, starred: 12/15/05
Publishers Weekly, starred: 03/06/06
School Library Journal, starred: 02/01/06

Trueman, Terry. 2003. *Inside Out.* **New York: HarperCollins. 177p.**

The Story: Sixteen-year-old Zach is a schizophrenic who hears cruel voices urging him to hurt himself, most often from two frightening characters he has dubbed Dirtbag and Rat. Zach takes medication to control his illness, but it isn't always enough to keep the voices at bay, and he has tried to commit suicide before at Dirtbag and Rat's urging. To help monitor his actions and medication, his mother has begun picking him up every day after school at a local coffee shop, where Zach enjoys his favorite treat, a maple bar, while he waits for his mom to bring his meds.

One day, while Zach is waiting, the coffee shop is robbed at gunpoint by two teenage brothers, Alan and Joey. At first, Zach is confused because he isn't sure if the boys are real or imaginary. He finds out soon enough when the police arrive before the boys can make their getaway, and they herd all of the customers, including Zach, into the back room, where they hold them hostage until they can decide their next move. Zach keeps talking to the two agitated teens out of nervousness and in an attempt to establish what is real and what isn't. Joey, the younger brother, gets very angry at Zach and keeps calling him "retarded," even as Zach patiently tries to explain that he not stupid, just schizophrenic, and that he needs his medication.

The police call the boys on the coffee shop phone and tell them that the charges of kidnapping will be dropped, and they will be tried as juveniles instead of adults, if they let all the hostages go in the next ten minutes. The brothers argue about what to do, while Zach talks to his mother, who has arrived and is waiting outside with the police with his medication. She urges him to hang in there until she can get him his pills. The brothers decide to let the hostages go but don't know if they can trust the police to keep their word. Zach decides to call his psychiatrist, Dr. Curt, and ask him for help. The brothers, anxious to find an adult they can trust, also get on the phone with the doctor, who agrees to come to the scene and look over the police offer for the boys. Dr. Curt also reassures Zach, who is getting more and more upset about the fact that he hasn't taken his meds, which means that Dirtbag and Rat could show up at any time.

Alan and Joey release the other hostages, while Zach agrees to stay until Dr. Curt shows up. Because of his condition, he hasn't felt very fearful of the two brothers and is, in fact, far more frightened of his imaginary enemies than he is of Alan and Joey. While they wait for Dr. Curt, the boys exchange their stories. Alan and Joey reveal that the reason they held up the coffee shop was to get money for their mother, who has cancer and needs expensive treatment. Zach tries to explain his disease, how he tried to take his own life, and how much he needs his medication to make it through his days. None of the boys has a father in their lives. As they are talking, they hear a crash. When Alan sticks his head out of the back room to investigate, there is the sound of gunshot, and he is grazed in the head by a bullet. The police call and claim that it was mistake, but the boys are spooked. In the confusion, Zach grabs Alan's gun, and before he knows it, he is in a standoff with Joey, who points his gun at Zach. Alan tells them both to give it up, since neither gun is loaded—the guns are just for show; the two brothers never intended to kill anyone.

It occurs to Zach that he could just walk out, but he is beginning to feel a bond with these boys. It feels like they are all in this situation together, when Alan encourages Zach not to succumb to his suicidal feelings and explains to his younger brother that Zach is not "retarded," but that his "brain is all upside down and inside out." Zach points out that there is a door to the alley and they could all try and escape that way. He is beginning to feel desperate for his medication, since his head is beginning to pound, and he can clearly hear the voices of Dirtbag and Rat.

The boys make their way to the alley, but when Zach sees a tall, armed figure telling him to halt, he's not sure if it is a police officer or Dirtbag. He begins to hallucinate that his face is on fire and that giant bugs are crawling out of Joey's nose. He collapses and comes to back in the coffee shop. According to Alan, he screamed and passed out as police shot at them. Alan was shot through the hand trying to drag Zach back into the building. Dr. Curt calls and tells the boys that he has the police offer in writing and that it is safe for them to come out. They carefully exit the coffee shop with their hands raised, but Zach nearly gets them all shot when he turns and runs back in to retrieve the one thing he's craved the whole time, even more than his meds: a maple bar. He is reunited with his mother and Dr. Curt, given his meds, and hailed as hero for helping to bring the standoff to a peaceful close.

The last chapter of the book is a simple newspaper article, dated three months after the incident in coffee shop. The article states that the two brothers, according to the deal they made with police, received only nine months in a juvenile detention center. But in a sadly ironic twist, Zach finally killed himself, presumably at the direction of the voices in his head.

The Message: Sometimes your best isn't good enough. Sometimes no matter how hard you try, you become involved in situations that are beyond your control. All you can do when that happens is hang on and hope for the best. You always have choices, even when it appears that there are none.

Who's It For?: 8th–12th grade. The reading level and short length may appeal to younger readers, but the potentially disturbing content—gunplay, frightening phantom voices (Dirtbag and Rat constantly croon, "You need to die die die!" over and over in Zach's head), hostage taking, and suicide—is better suited to older students.

Why It Rocks:
• **Voice:** Zach's convincing first-person narration is laced with the imaginary voices he hears, sometimes spouting nonsense rhyming words, other times instructing him to kill himself. Trueman explains, in "case study" notes that begin each chapter, that Zach's unemotional tone, despite what is happening all around him, is typical for a schizophrenic, who often doesn't know how to feel, since nothing seems real.
• **Plot:** While the idea of obtaining money through illegal means to be used for a noble purpose is not a new plot device, the premise of a schizophrenic trying to find his muddled way through an armed robbery attempt is, and Trueman should be applauded for creating one of the easiest plots on the planet to booktalk. Be prepared for the sad, abrupt ending to shock some readers, especially when it seems that Zach has made his way out of the woods.
• **Pacing:** Blink, and you'll miss it. Trueman doesn't waste time setting up the action—Alan and Joey are robbing the coffee shop by the second paragraph. But she makes up for it by starting each chapter with excerpts from Zach's case history, so

readers get a chance to learn about his condition. A perfect choice for older reluctant readers, in content, reading level, and length.

• **Characterization:** It would have been nice to have more background on Alan and Joey, whose dialogue doesn't move much beyond, "Nobody's gonna hurt you if you just do what we tell you," but Zach's character is fascinating and provides readers with a unique point of view they may never have considered before.

Hook It Up With: *Stuck in Neutral,* also by Terry Trueman, and *Cut* by Patricia McCormick.

Read More about It:
Booklist: 09/01/03
Horn Book: 04/01/04
Kirkus Reviews: 07/15/03
Publishers Weekly: 08/18/03
School Library Journal: 09/01/03
V.O.Y.A. (Voice of Youth Advocates): 10/01/03

Werlin, Nancy. 2006. *The Rules of Survival.* **New York: Penguin Group. 272p.**

The Story: Thirteen-year-old Matthew, 12-year-old Callie, and five-year-old Emmy never know what their volatile, abusive mother, Nikki, will do next. One minute she's showering them with hugs and kisses; the next, she's screaming, breaking dishes, and locking them in their room when she leaves the house. Matt has become accustomed to living in a state of constant fear as he tries to protect his sisters from Nikki's rages. Matt and Callie's biological father, Ben, sends child-support payments, but he is too busy trying to make ends meet as a nurse to visit very often. Their mother's sister, Aunt Bobbie, lives downstairs from them in the three-story Boston townhouse she and Nikki own jointly, but she takes care to stay out of Nikki's way. Matt has never gone to any adult for help, because Nikki's mental and verbal abuse leaves no telling marks, and he worries that even if someone believed him, there's a good chance he and his sisters would be separated in foster care. Matt feels like the only person he can rely on is himself.

Then one hot August night when Matt and Callie have sneaked out of their locked room in search of popsicles at the local store, they witness a stranger named Murdoch defend a young boy who's father is threatening to hit him. Matt immediately becomes obsessed with finding the man, who he is sure will be the person to save him from his mother. After a year of futile searching, Callie methodically goes through an Internet directory until she discovers Murdoch's name and address, which she triumphantly gives to Matt. Before Matt can think of a way to approach the man, however, Nikki happens to see the slip of paper and demands to know what it is. She ends up boldly approaching Murdoch herself and asking him out. To Matt's surprise, the two are soon dating. Murdoch takes a shine to Matt and his sisters, especially little Emmy. For three blissful summer months, Nikki is on her best behavior and Matt relaxes his guard, even though he knows it can't last.

When Nikki dangles Emmy over a patch of slippery rocks during a beach outing simply to get Murdoch's attention, Matt knows the end is near. Sure enough, Murdoch breaks up with Nikki shortly after Labor Day. Nikki punishes him by leaving Matt, Callie, and Emmy on his doorstep, then disappearing for four days. When Nikki finally picks them up, Matt is mortified by his mother's actions, and Murdoch makes it clear that he wants nothing more to do with her.

After the breakup, Nikki shifts into manic mode. She takes them all for pancake "sundaes," then makes them ride every ride at Six Flags, until Matt throws up more than once. That night, as she drives them home, she swings into oncoming traffic until Matt tells her she's the best mother in the world. After this incident, Matt decides its time to get himself and his sisters out of his mother's house in any way possible. He tries asking Ben for help, but the overwhelmed man tearfully refuses, stating he can't afford what it would cost to sue for custody. Disappointed, Matt considers approaching Murdoch again, but his mother, who seems to be able to read his mind, threatens to call Social Services and accuse Murdoch of sexually molesting Matt if he ever tries to contact him again. Matt decides that he must warn Murdoch, but Callie tells him the safest thing for all of them is to forget Murdoch ever existed. As long as Nikki believes that they still care about him, she will do anything she can to hurt him.

Soon after, Nikki brings home a new boyfriend, a big, ponytailed man named Rob, whom Matt and Callie soon discover Nikki has bullied into attacking Murdoch. Matt goes to Murdoch's to see how he is and to warn him about Nikki's threat to accuse him of molestation. When Murdoch hears this, he decides he must do something about the situation and asks for Aunt Bobbie and Ben's phone numbers. Later that day, Aunt Bobbie calls to tell them that Nikki is in the hospital, and that Murdoch beat her up. Matt knows this isn't true, as he was with Murdoch during the time Nikki claims to have been attacked. He reports her lie to the police, but Nikki receives only probation. Murdoch takes out a restraining order on her, and Nikki begins directing all her rage at Matt, who doesn't mind too much because it diverts her attention from Callie and Emmy.

Nikki keeps harassing Murdoch by leaving threatening voice mails and following him in her car. Murdoch dutifully records all the harassment for the police, hoping to goad Nikki into doing something serious enough to get the kids taken away. He stays in contact with Aunt Bobbie and Ben, trying to convince them to sue for joint custody of Matt and his sisters. Ben meets with Matt and tells him he's trying to get a better job and is looking for a bigger apartment so that he can take them in. Nikki finally makes a fatal mistake: she chases Murdoch's neighbor Julie in her car, causing them both to crash. Julie is permanently paralyzed from the accident, and Nikki is sentenced to five weeks in jail awaiting her trial. While she is away, Bobbie and Ben sue for custody and win. Ben moves Callie and Emmy in with him, while Matt stays with Aunt Bobbie to help after Nikki returns home.

When Nikki comes home from jail, she makes life miserable for Matt and Bobbie at the townhouse. She physically attacks Matt as soon as she comes in the door and parties and plays loud music at all hours of the day and night. But the worst is when Matt goes to pick up Emmy from her new school and discovers that Nikki has already taken her. For four long days, the family and police search for her. Finally, Emmy manages to call Matt's cell phone, and from her description of the surroundings, Matt realizes she's somewhere in the South Boston dockyards. He calls Murdoch, then goes in search of her alone. He discovers her in a company trailer, smelling of the alcohol Nikki made her drink to keep her quiet. As he takes out, Nikki appears, taunting him, and Matt realizes he could kill her for what she's done and not feel any remorse. He actually throws her to the ground, before Murdoch shows up and calmly leads Matt and Emmy to his truck. Murdoch never speaks to Nikki, who is raging at him, and that is the last time Matt sees her. He sometimes receives forwarded angry letters from her, but he is no longer frightened of her.

Two years later, Matt is headed to college and has a celebratory dinner with Murdoch when he gets his acceptance. He reveals to Murdoch that he had secretly hoped Murdoch would murder his mother, because he always seemed to Matt to be a man who worked hard to restrain his temper. Murdoch admits that he did kill a man once: his father, who was just like Nikki. But he's glad he arrived in time to keep Matt from making the same terrible mistake.

The Message: Sometimes the only person you can depend on is yourself. Not all adults have the best interest of children at heart. Hating someone hurts you more than it hurts the person you're directing it at. Sometimes you have to make your own luck.

Who's It For?: 8th–12th grade. Nikki is a frightening character, and the physical and mental violence she inflicts on her children will be upsetting and disturbing for some readers. Nikki also does drugs and brings strange men home late at night. Matt often wishes his mother dead and comes close to hurting her himself.

Why It Rocks:
- **Voice:** Werlin writes her story in an unsettling second person; Matt is writing the story of their upbringing as a letter to little Emmy, who is now nine, and address-ing her as "you." This has the often disconcerting (and perhaps intended) effect of making the reader feel as though Matt is addressing him or her, effectively bringing readers further into the story and making them vicariously feel the fear Matt and his sisters are experiencing.
- **Plot:** While Matt's initial meeting of Murdoch and Nikki's eventual courting of Matt's chosen savior feel entirely too staged and convenient, the rest of Werlin's plot is airtight, and like Matt, readers will have no idea when Nikki will strike next.
- **Pacing:** As Matt's dangerous game of cat and mouse with his mother escalates, readers will be held in breathless suspense as they wonder if Matt will find the strength to overcome his paralyzing fear of Nikki.
- **Characterization:** Matt, Callie, and Emmy have compelling, individually developed personalities, especially the strong-willed Emmy, who learns at a very young age how to push her mother's buttons. Aunt Bobbie and Ben serve their purpose but are somewhat one-dimensional. The mysterious Murdoch is never fully understood, although Werlin gifts readers with a big insight into his character by revealing the secret about his father on the last page. Nikki is a monster, but Matt does allude that much of her behavior is a result of mental illness and drug use.

Hook It Up With: *When She Was Good* by Norma Fox Mazer and *When Jeff Comes Home* by Catherine Atkins.

Read More about It:
Booklist, starred: 08/01/06
Horn Book: 09/01/06
Kirkus Reviews, starred: 07/15/06
School Library Journal, starred: 09/01/06
Voice of Youth Advocates (V.O.Y.A.): 10/01/06

CHAPTER 9

DYSTOPIAN DREAMS: TEEN SCI-FI

Introduction

If you think about it, adolescence is just one big science fiction novel. Bodies are beginning to display strange new parts and patterns (some of which don't respond to the operating system's commands), parents seem like aliens (or, at best, from another planet), and high school can resemble an arid, dystopian landscape rife with pitfalls and sandworms with gaping maws—oh wait, that's just the cafeteria lady.

So, if their lives already resemble unhappy or weird dystopias, why would teens want to read about them? According to co-authors Kenneth L. Donelson and Alleen Pac Nilsen, whose textbook *Literature for Today's Young Adults* is in its seventh edition and a staple in most YA literature survey courses, they don't! "To attract young adult readers, dystopian books have to have something extra because, with a few exceptions, young adults are optimistic and imaginative . . . teenagers have not lived long enough to lose their natural curiosity, and they have not been weighed down with adult problems. . . . So even when teenagers read dystopian books, they probably wear rose-colored glasses, feeling grateful for the world as it usually is" (2005: 223).

Whhaaaatt? With all due respect to Donelson and Nilsen, I completely disagree. Come on, how many "optimistic, grateful" teenagers do you know? (Okay, there may be a few in middle school, but they're mostly sixth graders!) Most of the sci-fi titles covered in this chapter have a dystopian setting, and maybe it's just my cynical, jaded self, but I believe that in this post–9/11 world, teens not only want but also need dystopian novels as a place where they deal with their end-of-the-world fears from a safe distance.

As has been the situation since the sun peeked over the horizon for the very first time, we live in dangerous times. And while we entrust our teens with the future and wish them nothing but the best, the truth is the future could very well, like the lunar landscape in M. T. Anderson's brilliant satire *Feed,* "suck." The science fiction in this chapter that deals with such topics as genetic testing, environmental disasters, super safety measures, and the decline of spoken language let teens know that the future will be what they make it. And if they don't want the dystopian landscape of adolescence to go on forever, they'd better start laying the groundwork for a better tomorrow today.

Adlington, L. J. 2005. *The Diary of Pelly D.* **New York: HarperCollins. 282p.**

The Story: On an unnamed planet colonized by humans over 200 years ago, 14-year-old Toni V is the member of a demolition/construction crew responsible for the rebuilding of City Five after a short-term war over water shortages. On this planet humans have devolved to the point of being born with gills, and they use them in addition to lungs to breathe. To maintain peak health, this race must spend part of every day submerged in water, so quality and quantity of water is crucial to their existence. Toni V is from City Three, which suffered the least damage during the war. He was drafted into a work crew and hasn't been home since, but because he whole-heartedly believes the government's postwar slogan, "Back to Work, Back to Normal," he is happy to be of service in the rebuilding effort and doesn't question the hard labor that is expected of him. The work is so exhausting that any free time is spent either swimming or sleeping, which leaves little time leftover for self-reflection or deep thought.

One day while he is breaking up concrete in City Five's main Plaza, Tony V discovers what looks like a diary, hidden and buried in a water can. Even though anything found during excavation is supposed to be reported and turned over, Toni V's mild curiosity is aroused, and he ends up keeping the book. Later that night in his bunk, he begins to read the diary of a spoiled rich girl named Pelly D, and soon he realizes that her journal is an informal record of the events leading up to the war, events that Toni V knows little about and to which he has never really given much thought.

Pelly D seems to have everything. Her father is a lucrative importer of bottled water, her mother is an artist, and she lives in a luxury penthouse (complete with a pool in the living room) with her parents, elder brother, and little sister. She is the self-proclaimed "Queen Bee" at school and expects and receives the admiration, envy, and respect of her classmates. She is as intelligent as she is beautiful, but she sees school only as a social activity.

Pelly D becomes perturbed when current events begin to infringe on her social life. It seems that City One, the first colonized site on the planet, is undergoing a water shortage and is demanding that the government draft citizens from the four other major cities to come help City One build a new irrigation system. This is not an unreasonable request, except for the fact that General Insidian, the leader of City One, is also making claims that his genetic clan, the Atsumisis, are biologically superior to the two other family clans that make up the rest of the population, the Mazzini and the Galrezi. This assertion is causing strife and anger in what has been a peaceful society since its inception.

Pelly D doesn't understand what all the fuss is about. After all, besides the initial Colonists from Earth, everyone on the planet was born from a test tube. Those of the Atsumisi clan have an accidental extra "epigene" in their DNA, as do the Mazzini, except that it lies dormant, while the Galrezi have no epigene at all. Although there have been numerous studies that have proven that the presence of the "epigene" does not make the Atsumisi superior in any way, General Insidian's campaign to make people believe the opposite seems to be working. Those of Atsumisi background are proclaiming their heritage with tattoos on their hands with their clan name, and City

Five is coming under increasing pressure to require mandatory genetic testing of all its citizens. Those of Mazzini and Galrezi heritage are then "compelled" by the government to report for work in City One. The question of testing infuriates many, and soon there are massive demonstrations against the testing, some of which end in violence, a concept that is nearly impossible for Pelly and most of the members of this formerly peaceful society to comprehend.

Pelly D's parents believe in the idea of multiethnicity, and they claim that the genetic testing will never be enforced, but Pelly D notices that more and more people are voluntarily getting the hand stamps to prove they are not Galrezi. While Pelly D publicly distains the popularity of the hand stamps, she is secretly worried when her best friend's family find out they are Mazzini and are forced to move to City One, where they seem to drop off the planet. When her school principal becomes too vocal about the unfairness of the stamps, she also abruptly disappears. Finally, Pelly D's family bows to the pressure of the testing and are horrified to discover that they are all Galrezi, with the exception of Pelly's father, who is noticeably relieved to be Atsumisi.

After that, the situation rapidly goes downhill. Public draft notices appear, commanding those of Galrezi and Mazzini descent to report to work in City One. Students continue to mysteriously disappear from school, genetic testing centers are bombed, and all Galrezi are forced to leave their homes and relocate to a run-down neighborhood of "Artist's Quarters," where their water is strictly rationed. Pelly D's brother hides away on a boat going "Overseas" rather than submit to the draft, and Pelly's father claims he can no longer live with them because of the demands of his work, but Pelly knows it is because he is frightened that their Galrezi stamps will hurt his business. She desperately tries to deny the changes that are happening all around her, but the world that used to revolve around Pelly D is gone.

In the last few pages of her diary, she shares the details of a romantic relationship with a boy named Marek T, someone she would have never considered when she was popular but now has come to love as a fellow Galrezi. Pelly's draft notice comes, and Marek tells her that he believes General Insidian's plan was never to draft more workers, but to wipe out the Galrezi altogether. Pelly can't stand to hear that and continues to believe that everything will work out, even as the Galrezi neighborhoods are systematically emptied and she and Marek T are forced to leave.

Toni V is sad and confused when he finishes Pelly D's diary. He is assigned to help dump some rubble in a landfill outside of City Five, and he resolves to get rid of the diary once and for all because the uncomfortable feelings and questions it raises in him make him feel ill. At the landfill he notices how gray and ashy the ground is and how there are random sparkles in the grass from jewelry that is scattered in with the debris. Suddenly, he wants to know: where did the Galrezi go? And why does nobody seem to care that they are gone? He decides to keep the diary, until he can find someone he trusts to share it with. Until then, he will continue to work on the new Plaza, which will soon bear the name "Plaza Insidian."

The Message: One voice can make a difference. "Those who forget the past are condemned to repeat it." Despite advances in technology and cultural communications, human beings continue to fall into a pattern of intolerance and war.

Who's It For?: 7th–12th grade. Younger readers may have a more difficult time piecing together the complicated politics of Pelly's world, which are initially only briefly mentioned between the airy descriptions of pool parties and water parks.

Why It Rocks:
- **Voice:** Pelly D's breathless, self-absorbed first-person narration contrasts strongly with the pondering, slowly awakening third-person consciousness of Toni V, creating a powerful impression of the vast differences, both socially and economically, between their two worlds.
- **Plot:** The obvious parallels between Pelly D's diary and the events leading up to the Holocaust contain endless potential for classroom discussion. By putting a science fiction spin on an event that has been indelibly burned into the human consciousness, Adlington challenges readers to consider the consequences of the Holocaust in a whole new light.
- **Pacing:** Adlington structures the novel in a way that allows readers to put together the puzzle pieces of Pelly's fate along with Toni V, maintaining both suspense and hope by not revealing the whole truth about Pelly D until the very last page.
- **Characterization:** Because Toni V initially is such a product of government brainwashing, he isn't nearly as compelling a character as the disdainful, proud Pelly D, who clearly boasts about her wealth and status to camouflage her many insecurities and fears about her increasingly perilous future. Teen readers will dig how Adlington slyly combined a typical "mean girl" characterization with such a thought-provoking plot.

Hook It Up With: *Star Split* by Kathryn Lasky and *The Barcode Tattoo* by Suzanne Weyn.

Read More about It:
Booklist, starred: 05/01/05
Horn Book: 07/01/05
Kirkus Reviews: 04/01/05
Publishers Weekly: 05/30/05
School Library Journal: 05/01/05
V.O.Y.A. (Voice of Youth Advocates): 06/01/05

Anderson, M. T. 2002. *Feed.* Cambridge, MA: Candlewick. 237p.

The Story: Titus is a teen who lives in a futuristic society where humans have become vapid and brainwashed consumers, mainly due to the "feed" or computer chip that most of the population has inserted into their brain stems. The feed features virtual instant messaging, enabling people to have entire conversations without opening their mouths, and inundates users with a barrage of targeted advertising created by past buying decisions and sponsored by the giant companies that have taken over every institution, including school.

Titus and his friends are easily bored in an environment where instant gratification is a given and anything can be purchased by simply thinking about it. In their endless pursuit of entertainment, they take off for the moon, a popular spring-break destination. There, Titus meets Violet, an unusually literate girl who eschews plastic clothing for natural wool and is home-schooled by her father, a professor of dead (computer) languages. This is her first trip to the moon, and she is happy to hang with Titus and his friends, who embody the type of "normal" teenage life she craves. Unfortunately, the group is attacked at a club by a socially conscious hacker, who compromises their feeds with a virus that causes them to verbally broadcast messages of imminent doom about the self-centered planet until they fall unconscious.

They wake up in a hospital room, where they must remain "offline" for a period of observation until doctors can be assured they didn't suffer any permanent damage. Titus uses the time to get to know Violet better, and they are soon smitten with each other. After their hospital stay, they are sent back to Earth, a world made up of stacked suburbs (each with its own "sun" and "sky"), oceans so toxic that one must wear a protective suit just to sit on the sand, and filet mignon farms, where genetic science has allowed humankind to do away with cows altogether and simply grow marbled sheets of steaks from bovine DNA.

As Titus spends more time with Violet, he begins to notice their differences. Violet actually listens to the news, takes the time to write her thoughts on paper, and questions the rampant consumerism that is the hallmark of their world. Her family doesn't have much money, which explains why she wasn't fitted for a feed until she was seven. Her father never wanted her to have one, but it became a necessity if she wanted to be able to fit in and compete with her peers. She asks Titus to help her with her latest project, where she attempts to confuse her feed's consumer profile of her by going to the mall and asking about the most outrageous items she can find, then *not* buying them. Titus is amused by the "fight the feed" project and intrigued by Violet's notions of delayed gratification and global responsibility. But he's also confused and frightened by the strength of his feelings for her and all the things she's beginning to make him think about.

When Violet tells Titus that her old, inferior feed, bought on sale by her dad, who couldn't afford the latest model, is beginning to malfunction as a result of the hacker incident, Titus is devastated but unable to show it very well. His communication skills have been seriously hampered by the feed, which encourages him to think and speak in the shortest phrases possible. He tries to show his support by squiring her around in his new "upcar" and taking her to all his friends' big parties. At one party, where a girl is showing off her fashionable new "lesions," surgically created cuts meant to mimic the radioactive sores many people have as a result of the toxic environment, Violet loses it. She begins going off on Titus's friends about their empty lives and upsets herself so much that her feed malfunctions and she falls unconscious. Shaken, Titus rushes Violet to the emergency room, where he is met by Violet's father, who tells him that the damage to her feed is serious. All of her vital bodily functions are wired into the feed, and now that it is failing, it is only a matter of time before one or more of her vital organs quit working as a result of the feed's deterioration. Violet and her father have petitioned the company that made the feed for financial and medical assistance but have been denied because owing to her spotty purchasing history, she is no longer seen as a "good investment."

While Violet is in the hospital, she messages Titus long, sad lists of all the things she wants to do before she dies and huge files of her memories, which she is afraid will soon be lost as her brain is wiped like an old hard drive. Titus can't handle the seriousness of the situation, so he erases the memory files she sends him. When she gets home, she comes over to his house and asks him to go on a camping trip with her to the mountains. He reluctantly agrees, but when she asks him to have sex with her, so she can experience it before she dies, he balks and blurts out that it would be like having sex with a zombie because it feels like she is already dead. They both realize their relationship is over and turn around and go right back home. Violet messages him the next day that she's willing to talk about it if he is, but he ignores the message and goes and plays basketball instead.

Titus spends the rest of the summer partying with his friends, trying to forget about Violet. That fall, her father messages him that the end is near. Titus goes to her house, where she lies in a hospital bed in a vegetative state. Her father messages him images of her body failing and her fear at losing control, and Titus is so distraught that he flees her room, goes home, and does the most mindless thing he can think of, which is to order multiple pairs of khakis through his feed until all his credit is gone. He gets up the courage to go back two days later, this time holding her hand and telling her he will always remember her and, in that way, keep her alive. She continues to stare ahead, unblinking, as he weeps.

The Message: You are what you buy. Question government authority and mainstream media. Feedback vs. feed forward: do we buy materials based on individual need, or do we buy products because mass media and/or huge corporations tell us what products we need?

Who's It For?: 8th–12th grade. Titus and his friends communicate through obscenities (the f-word is dropped frequently) and shorthand slang, like "null," "unit," and "lo-grav," demonstrating how language deteriorates when it is no longer used regularly. Some conservative teens may be turned off by Anderson's creative use of expletives. There is little mention of sex, but drug use (by willfully scrambling the feed) and drinking are implied. Younger readers may not get the full impact of Anderson's message because of the stylized prose and strong employment of irony.

Why It Rocks:
• **Voice:** Titus tells his story in first person, peppered with instant-messaging slang, while in between chapters, Anderson inserts "feed static": snippets of commercials, movie trailers, pop songs, and disturbingly short news sound bytes that hint at a much darker reality than the one Titus is living in, one full of global disasters and riots that an inept American president keeps trying to suppress. The banality of the static contrasts strongly with Violet's bleak situation, making a compelling statement about what is valued and what is not in Titus's world.
• **Plot:** The parallels Anderson draws between his scary vision of the future and our current situation concerning teens, the media, and global politics are clever and profound. In case you haven't noticed, parts of Anderson's future are NOW, and this strongly written satire will hopefully have teens thinking twice before favoring their Trios and Pods over face-to-face human communication.

- **Pacing:** Somewhat slow, this is far more of a character-driven satire than an action-packed, science fiction adventure.
- **Characterization:** Despite the heavy message, Anderson imbues his main characters with a tenderness and humanity that are missing from their materialistic society. Violet, in her messages to Titus, comes across as simultaneously too wise and too naive for this consumer-driven world, while Titus, by the end of the novel, has begun to see the dirty underpinnings of the bright and shiny civilization he believed he lived in.

Hook It Up With: *Brave New World* by Aldous Huxley (of course!) and *Never Let Me Go* by Kazuo Ishiguro.

Read More about It:
Booklist: 10/15/02
Horn Book, starred: 09/01/02
Kirkus Reviews, starred: 09/01/02
Publishers Weekly, starred: 07/22/02
School Library Journal: 09/01/02
V.O.Y.A (Voice of Youth Advocates): 12/01/02

Halam, Ann. 2005. *Siberia: a Novel.* New York: Random House. 262p.

The Story: In 14-year-old Sloe's world, global warming and pollution have ravaged the planet, causing the onset of long, brutally cold winters and short, wet summers that have forced humans to move into huge, indoor, climate-controlled cities. Each city is like its own country, with its own government and system of rule. Some of the cities, like the one Sloe and her mother are from, are strictly monitored and controlled to the point of fascism. When she was four years old, Sloe and Mama were banished from their city and sent to one of the bleak, outdoor Prison Settlements to live. Mama, a biologist, had been convicted of a crime against the government and was now labeled a political prisoner. Her punishment was to give up her profession and spend the rest of her life making nails out of scrap metal for eight hours a day in the workshop of her primitive Settlement hut. If she fulfills her quota of nails, she is given just enough food, water, and heat to keep her and Sloe alive.

When she was little, Sloe didn't understand why they had to move or what happened to her father, also a scientist. Mama doesn't speak about him or their life before. Instead, she distracts Sloe with a shiny white box full of doll-sized test tubes and eye droppers, which she uses to create tiny sparks of life from powdered DNA. Sloe believes the animals her mother makes are "magic," but as she grows older, Mama explains the importance of the white box, which is actually an incubator, and the seeds of life that sleep within it.

Mama explains that all wild mammals are extinct, owing to the extreme temperatures and destruction of their environment. The only animals left are factory animals, genetically grown for food or fur, and the scavengers that feed on human garbage: cats, dogs, rats, and gulls. The little animals that exist in the incubator are called Lindquist kits, after the scientist who discovered their genetic capabilities, and within each kit is entire genetic code of a specific mammal classification. There should be eight classifications, Mama explains, but two were lost, so the incubator contains only seed powders for *Insectivora, Rodentia, Carnivora, Lagomorpha, Artiodactyla,* and *Chiroptera.*

Mama shows Sloe how to "quicken" the kits every now and then to make sure the seed powder is still viable. By mixing the DNA powder with a food formula, Sloe grows six tiny kits, which resemble thumb-sized furry mites with bright black eyes and tiny pink ears. If not taken to the second stage (where a kit is fed until it grows into a real animal), the kits live in the incubator for several days, then hibernate and die, turning into dried cocoons, which are then "harvested" by grinding them back into the powder they were grown from, which is carefully preserved in test tubes. Once, when Sloe was very good, Mama grew one of the kits into a playful ferret Sloe named Nivvy, who was her secret playmate for over a year before he aged and died.

Mama hopes to escape the Settlement someday with Sloe and travel north to another, less repressive city across the frozen sea, where she can use the kits to begin to repopulate the Earth with wild animals again. But before they can make their plans, Sloe is sent to a government boarding school for high school. Mama tells her that if for any reason she isn't there when Sloe returns, that Sloe is the new guardian of the Lindquist kits and must find a way alone to get them to the city across the sea. She also warns her that she must never, ever tell anyone about the kits or they will be taken away and destroyed.

Sloe is disappointed by the New Dawn School, which is not much different from the harsh Prison Settlement, and begins to understand how repressive her world is when she innocently implicates her mother by bragging about Mama's vast scientific knowledge. The principal later tells her that as a result Mama has been relocated to a rehabilitation center, because the teaching of science, even to one's child, is considered extremely dangerous. Devastated, Sloe becomes convinced Mama has been killed because of her; she falls into a group of bad students, and begins drinking and stealing. Soon, she is expelled and sent back to the Prison Settlement to take up her mother's nail commission. At the Settlement, Sloe quickly finds what her mother has carefully hidden for her: the incubator, a map, and a compass, and she escapes, determined to undertake the journey to save the Lindquists on her own.

She starts out but is immediately plunged into a series of frightening adventures. Each time she gets in a bind, however, she is aided by one of the Lindquist kits, which have imprinted upon her as their mother and are determined to keep her from harm. She hops a freight train but is waylaid by a suspicious conductor, who turns her over to the manager of a factory fur farm. The manager locks her up briefly, but she is able to escape with the help of *Insectivora,* who grows into a hedgehog that menaces the attack dogs on her trail and leads her to safety. It is at this point she notices that she is being followed by a man named Yagin, who she recognizes as one of the guards from New Dawn. She wonders why he is tracking her and if he has information about her mother but is too wary after her experience at New Dawn to approach him. Then she joins up with a caravan of Gypsies, who appear to be friendly but end up selling her into slavery at their winter festival. While in the holding pen with other children about to be sold, Sloe grows *Rodentia,* who morphs into a sea of lemmings that chew her an escape hole in the wooden pen. She escapes the fair only to become lost in a blizzard. She makes a temporary shelter and falls into a nearly fatal sleep. She awakes in a cabin, with Yagin nearby. He had tracked her from the fair and saved her from freezing to death.

Yagin explains to Sloe that he is a scientist from her mother's lab who has been forced to go undercover in different government jobs to assist colleagues like her mother who have been imprisoned for their scientific beliefs. He assures her that her mother was rescued and waits for her in the northern city and that he will escort Sloe and the Lindquist kits the rest of the way to safety. Sloe wants to believe him, but she is suspicious of his intense interest in the kits. After a few days, she drugs him with a sleeping draught and escapes on the back of *Artiodactyla,* who has grown into a reindeer. But Yagin tracks her down again, this time with snowmobile-riding government police, and to Sloe's great despair, they shoot and kill the animal she called Toesy. They make a supply stop afterward, and she manages to escape through a broken window in the truck they have locked her in.

From there, she hitches a ride with some Gypsies who give her a lift all the way to the outpost where travelers meet to cross the frozen sea. She rests there a few days and then prepares to cross the ice on her own. For company she grows *Carnivora,* whom she names Nivvy after her beloved childhood pet. Again, just as she is setting out, Yagin shows up with more government police. But Nivvy, who morphs into a menacing tiger, and a patch of rotten ice, which swallows Yagin and his crew, saves her. Before Yagin sinks, he thrusts two test tubes into her hands—powders for the two missing classifications. After this last battle, Sloe makes it across the ice to an old oil rig named Rescue Island, where she is taken in by friendly officials who reunite her with her mother—who is indeed still alive. Mama confirms that Yagin was a scientist in her lab, but he was a double agent, and Sloe was right not to trust him completely. Both of them are happy to have made it across the sea alive, with the hope that all eight mammal classifications may now one day be revived.

The Message: Trust your instincts. Question authority. To survive, we must be willing to evolve, especially when it comes to how we treat our environment. As long as there is life, there is hope.

Who's It For?: 7th–12th grade. Cute animals are killed or die throughout the story, and the way some of the students at New Dawn are punished (solitary confinement, hard labor) may be disturbing to younger readers. At New Dawn, the black-market ring that Sloe becomes involved in includes the trafficking of liquor, so there are also some depictions of underage drinking. The ethics of genetic manipulation also may be an issue for some readers.

Why It Rocks:
• **Voice:** Sloe tells her story in first person from the viewpoint of perhaps a twenty-something looking back. She mentions mistakes that she made and is able to see where she should have chosen a different path. Her voice is rueful, compelling, and frighteningly mature.
• **Plot:** This woefully underappreciated title is a shockingly good sci-fi fairy tale.

What reviewers seem to have missed is that Sloe, as she evades Yagin by growing the different animals to help her on her way, approximates the wise little girl in the Russian fairy tale who throws down magical objects in the path of the witch Baba Yaga, to distract her so that she can escape. Other subplots, such as Sloe's shedding a childhood name of Rosita as she sheds her innocence and her extended stay with the Old World Gypsy tribe, enhance the fairy tale flavor.

• **Pacing:** Meandering. Some teens may lose interest as Sloe slogs through her depression at New Dawn. Still, once she starts on her journey with the Lindquist kits, the action is nonstop.

• **Characterization:** Sloe is a wonderfully flawed character who questions herself every step of the way. Especially harrowing are her scenes with Yagin. Teen readers will go back and forth as much as Sloe as they try to determine whether the slippery double agent is to be trusted with Sloe's greatest secret.

Hook It Up With: The *Fire-Us* trilogy by Jennifer Armstrong and *The Last Book in the Universe* by Rodman Philbrick.

Read More about It:
Booklist: 06/01/05
Horn Book: 04/01/06
Kirkus Reviews: 06/01/05
School Library Journal: 06/15/05
V.O.Y.A. (Voice of Youth Advocates): 06/01/05

Hautman, Pete. 2006. *Rash.* New York: Simon & Schuster. 249p.

The Story: It's 2076, and 16-year-old Bo Marsten lives with his mother and grandfather in the United Safer States of America, where the legal driving age has been raised to 26, SUVs look and run like armored tanks, and calling someone a name could get you thrown in prison. In the future the penal system provides the USSA with most of its workforce, as Bo's family can attest. His dad has been serving time cleaning shrimp at a prison aqua farm for yelling at someone in traffic, while his elder brother got sentenced to three years of roadwork detail after knocking out someone's tooth in a fistfight. In history class, Bo has learned that the USSA became safer when people discovered that if they cut all risk out of their lives, they could live longer. Now, owing to advances in medical science and the utter ban of french fries and alcohol, many people live to be 100.

All contact sports, including football, have been outlawed and are played only in some South American countries. So Bo enjoys running track instead; he just wishes that he didn't have to wear so much safety gear while doing it. His biggest competitor in love and on the track is Karlohs Mink, who not only beats him occasionally but also has been caught flirting with his girlfriend, Maddy. Bo, like most teens his age, takes a mood-altering drug called Levulor, which is supposed to help him maintain his calm and manage his anger, but he fears it is only a matter of time before his anger genes kick in and cause him to kick Karlohs's butt. Like his father and brother before him, Bo is sure his future includes a prison stay.

In computer class, Bo is creating an artificial intelligence (A.I.) named Bork. He is being graded on whether or not Bork can learn to think and reason for himself. At first, he made Bork look like a monkey, with a brain to match, but lately he's been programming some contradictory statements into the A.I. and leaving him alone to let him analyze. Bo is surprised when Bork boots up with a joke. Slowly, the A.I. is gaining a sense of humor and showing signs of sentient life.

Meanwhile, the situation with Karlohs has escalated. Bo tells Karlohs he has a mouth like a dog's anus, and Karlohs retaliates by rubbing his face with hand cream he knows he is allergic to and blaming the resulting rash on Bo. Soon, everyone is exhibiting signs of a psychosomatic rash and blaming Bo. When Bo finds out that Karlohs started the rash business on purpose, he snaps and tries to punch him but is knocked out by a security stun dart before he actually makes contact. But as far as the law is concerned, this is the last straw for Bo. Not only has he "caused the involuntary endangerments of unnamed persons" by giving the whole school hives, but also he has attempted physical violence on another person. Bo is sentenced to three years of food-processing labor at a McDonald's pizza factory in rural Canada.

When Bo first arrives at the prison, he is terrified. Everything is made of steel and concrete, with no padding to be seen, and hungry polar bears roam the fenced perimeter. His roommate is a 300-pound monster named Rhino, and his boss is a sadistic ex–football player named Hammer who doesn't care if any of his charges live or die. He is assigned the duty of pepperoni shooter on the assembly line, and enjoys eating the defective pizzas—until he discovers that this is the sum total of an inmate's diet. Rhino turns out to be a decent guy, except for his explosive gas problem, and soon Bo settles into the normal (if somewhat smelly) routine of prison life.

Bo hasn't been in prison long before he notices a group of big bullies called the Goldshirts, so named because of the special shirts and jeans they wear. He discovers that the Goldshirts are really a highly illegal tackle football team coached by the Hammer, who runs mandatory tryouts every few weeks to recruit fresh meat. Everyone wants to make the team because the Hammer gives them shorter hours and better food. Bo makes the team because of his speed, Rhino because of his bulk. Although he's getting pounded on a daily basis, Bo comes to love the freedom that football represents, the ability to run without pads and to maintain his control without Levulor, which Hammer forbids because it slows the players down.

As a Goldshirt, Bo has access to a computer, where he is surprised to be contacted by his now fully sentient A.I. Bork has gone rouge, creating a human persona complete with a law degree and a bank account. He has been studying the legal system and is sure he can get Bo off on some loophole. Meanwhile, Hammer arranges for the Goldshirts to play another prison team, the Coke Redshirts, coached by one of his old football rivals. Bo knows the game will be violent, but what ensues looks less like a game and more like a barely organized riot. When both teams have too many injured players to continue, Hammer calls it a draw and tells the boys they'll try it again in six weeks when everyone has healed up. Bo is disheartened by the whole experience, which was brutal and discouraging. When he complains to Bork, the A.I. suggests blackmailing Hammer by threatening to make the illegal football team public. Bo doesn't know if he wants to go that far, but before he can decide, Bork calls Hammer, poses as Bo's lawyer, and threatens him with a lawsuit unless he releases Bo early. So Hammer does exactly that: He releases Bo onto the wild tundra, points him in the direction of the next town, and tells him he's home free if he can outrun the bears.

Bo paces himself and jogs 20-plus miles in about three hours, only facing a bear on the final leg of his journey. Fortunately, a tour guide in a "bear buggy" shoots the beast that is pursuing him just as it is about to take a chunk out of his calf. He recovers from his ordeal, flies home, and discovers that after all he's been through, he's . . . bored. Now that he's tasted the excitement of life without padding he can't go back to the Safer States. Bork, who was eventually tracked down and destroyed by the Department of Cybernetics Defense, managed to sock away some money for Bo from a settlement he scored from McDonald's for endangering Bo's safety. This allows Bo to realize what he has only recently discovered is his dream: to go to Argentina and play football, where he may not be safe but at least he'll be free.

The Message: Think carefully before sacrificing personal freedom for safety. Life without highs and lows is no life at all. If you become overly concerned with staying safe, you might miss out on some of the richest experiences life has to offer. Don't be afraid to follow your dreams, ask for what you want, and take what you need.

Who's It For?: 7th–12th grade. Younger readers may not fully understand all of the satirical elements but will still enjoy the action-packed football sequences. There are some over-the-top descriptions of sports violence, but it works well as a foil to Bo's cushioned, pre-prison world. Bo's grandfather, a holdover from a far wilder generation, does engage in some salty language on occasion.

Why It Rocks:
- **Voice:** Bo tells his story in the first person, his tone varying from wry to naive and finally thoughtful and considering as he tries to take what he's learned from prison and use it to decide what to do with his future.
- **Plot:** This biting satire of the U.S. post–9/11 obsession with safety and political correctness is both funny and thoughtful. While the Hammer's gleefully violent football games are obvious metaphors for how life should be experienced—without bumpers on every sharp corner—teen readers will still get the idea that Bo is being bounced from one extreme to another and that he will have to learn how to balance the highs and lows in his life.
- **Pacing:** Fairly measured until Bo gets to prison. The football sequences, paired with Bo's amazing, surreal run from the polar bear, make for some page-turning action, until Bo returns home, where the action coasts down again to a satisfactory ending.
- **Characterization:** Teen readers will empathize with how Bo chafes against the authoritarian bonds of his supersafe lifestyle and relate it to their own adolescent struggles against authority. While Bo's parents make brief appearances hardly worth mentioning, his curmudgeonly Gramps steals every scene he's in with his colorful profanity and outrage at how mediocre the world has become.

Hook It Up With: *Be More Chill* by Ned Vizzini and *Intersteller Pig* by William Sleator

Read More about It:
Booklist, starred: 05/15/06
Horn Book: 05/01/06
Publishers Weekly, starred: 05/08/06
School Library Journal: 08/01/06
Voice of Youth Advocates (V.O.Y.A.): 06/01/06

Lanagan, Margo. 2005. *Black Juice.* **New York: HarperCollins. 201p.**

The Story: These ten speculative short stories feature unusual, otherworldly settings that provide a fascinating milieu for the author's sharply observed examinations of human psychology, sociology, and civilization. In "Singing My Sister Down," a young boy and his family attend his elder sister's public execution/funeral at a tar pit. The boy's sister, Ikky, has been accused of murdering her fiancée, the punishment for which in this seemingly ancient society is to be left at the tar pit to sink and suffocate. The family, sitting safely on mats, surround her with music, food, and flowers as she slowly, sadly descends into the warm, liquid darkness.

In "My Lord's Man," Berry, a loyal steward, joins his master, "Mullord," as he searches for his wild young wife, "Mullady," who has run away from what seems to be a medieval manor. They find Mullady dancing wildly with a band of Gypsies, who are obviously her kin. Berry cannot understand why his master joins the dance instead of punishing Mullady for her indiscretion, but in the end, he must admit to himself that there is something about Mullady that inspires respect, if not love.

The unnamed narrator of "Red Nose Day" is an orphan who has been abused and molested by the adults in an alternative reality, which is made up of hierarchies of circus clowns. He convinces Jelly, another disgruntled clown, who is bitter because he was cut from an audition, to climb a tower with him and shoot down clowns on the street with a high-powered rifle. But when Jelly dons his own white paint and red nose after the killing is through, the orphan, frightened and disgusted, hesitates for only an instant before murdering his partner in crime as well.

The narrator of "Sweet Pippit" is an elephant, part of a domesticated herd that have been trained to work for humans in a rural village. After one of their number goes mad and stampedes through the town, their gentle trainer, Pippit, is blamed and sentenced to death. The devoted elephants travel to the prison where Pippit is being kept and free him just as he is about to be executed. Together, the trainer and his elephants escape into the wilderness, never to return to civilization again.

After the death of his father, Dot, his disabled sister, Ardent, and his mother go to live with the Bard and his many wives deep in the desert wilderness of an alternative African landscape in "House of the Many." The Bard has created his own society that shuns materialism and technology, and he serenades his wives and children with an old, three-key accordion he calls "House of the Three," which he claims is inhabited by three gods who make the music. Dot leaves home at 12, disillusioned after learning that the mystery of the "men's tent" is just the Bard playing accordion as his sons drink alcohol they believe will give them visions. He goes to town, gets a job, and saves his money to buy a "House of the Many," a beautiful new accordion he sees in a shop window. When he returns home as a wealthy young man to visit his mother, he discovers his sister has died and the Bard has become a bitter old man, abandoned by his wives and many sons when he couldn't decide who would be his legal heir. Dot brings his mother back with him to civilization, both ready to embrace all they had left behind when they withdrew to the desert.

In "Wooden Bride," Mattild has second thoughts about completing her "bridal training," a finishing program for young women to teach them how to be proper brides and wives that resembles a huge confirmation ceremony. She dodges the crowds of white-gowned young women and wends her way through town, musing about her reputation of never finishing what she starts and wondering if it will prove true again this time. But in the end, even though she is late, she seeks out the bishop's blessing and the photographer's camera, unsure of her future but pleased she has wholly committed to seeing something through.

In "Earthy Uses" an abused teenage boy is forced by his cruel grandfather to leave their rural mountain cabin in search of what the local mountain folk ironically call "angels," huge winged, horned, rotten-smelling red beasts that seem more demon than heavenly host. The boy's grandmother is dying, and these frightening beasts have been known to grant wishes if given the right offering. The boy calls down an "angel" with a round of cheese, which it promptly eats, then regurgitates as gold. It tells the boy it is too late to save his grandmother's life, but it will sing her into death, which it does loudly, to the grandfather's dismay, then disappears. After the grandmother dies, the boy buries her and discovers the earth is full of ripe potatoes. Combined with the gold, it is enough money and food for him to escape his grandfather's house, granting a wish, after all.

In the not-so-distant, toxic future of "Perpetual Light," college student Daphne is on her way to her grandmother's funeral. As she drives in her hermetically sealed car to the distant outback town, she remembers how her grandmother showed her the secret lives of animals in the bush, made more resistant to the polluted landscape with the use of mechanical parts. After the burial, where she risks exposing her fragile "new age" immune system to the brutal outdoors, Daphne returns to school, thinking about her grandmother's love of nature and about the fate of the real seeds she is attempting to grow, wondering whether or not they, like she, will have the strength to grow in this contaminated world.

The young female narrator of "Yowlinin" was orphaned as a baby by a Yowlinin attack that killed her parents and destroyed her home. Yowlinins—giant, man-eating slugs whose saliva and sweat are poisonous to every living thing—live underground and attack unexpectedly. Those whose families die in the attacks are considered bad-luck "left behinds." Ostracized in her community, the girl survives by stealing and scavenging. When she risks her life by managing to kill a Yowlinin that is threatening to eat the boy she has loved from afar, she dares to hope that he will accept her affections and help her gain respect in the community. But he shuns her like everyone else, so she returns to wilderness alone, resolute not to give her heart away again.

Finally, in "Rite of Spring," a young boy is forced to fulfill his brother's mission of singing in the spring season. The boy's brother, Florius, is considered to be "Deep," or capable of performing the rituals necessary to safeguard their mountain community, while the boy is considered the "thicker" of the two. But now the boy's brother is terribly sick, and the narrator has no choice but to don his brother's ceremonial robe, climb to the top of Bearded Mountain during a screaming blizzard, and chant the words to the spell that will end winter. To his own astonishment, he manages to pull it off, and he returns home in triumph, having gained some much needed self-confidence.

The Message: Life can be brutal and unforgiving, but there is still hope to found, often in the most unlikely of places.

Who's It For?: 9th–12th grade. While this powerful short-story collection by Australian author Lanagan has garnered universal praise, including being named a Printz Award Honor title for 2006, it is not for everyone. Lanagan's writing is challenging and complex, and her habit of dropping readers right into a fully realized world with no warning and forcing them to find their own way out with very few signposts, will be jarring, if not downright uncomfortable, for some readers. There are also incidents of violence and death, as evidenced by the summaries.

Why It Rocks:
• **Voice:** Unnamed narrators, who often begin their tales with little or no explanation of the worlds they inhabit, tell many of Lanagan's stories in first person. Each voice is unique, sometimes invoking a rural twang, other times a futuristic slang, but all are compelling, and occasionally disturbing.
• **Plot:** Each of Lanagan's stories subtly probes the depths of human emotions and encourages the contemplation of the eternal battle of good vs. evil that takes place within us. Although some are just quiet character sketches ("Wooden Bride," "Perpetual Light"), most build to a suspenseful climax. They may need a little explanation at the beginning, but these stories have great potential curricular application, especially among high school AP English students.
• **Pacing:** Lanagan carefully tucks the arguably more quiet stories ("My Lord's Man," "Wooden Bride") in between more plot-driven tales, but make no mistake, this isn't a quick read on any level. The stories take time to get into and are often even better the second time around. Probably not the best choice for reluctant readers.
• **Characterization:** These characters roam unfamiliar landscapes; however, they are still wonderfully, maddeningly human to the core (even the elephants!), and their thoughts, feelings, and emotions will prove instantly recognizable to teen readers.

Hook It Up With: Lanagan's two other utterly original story collections, *White Time* and *Red Spikes*.

Read More about It:
Booklist: 04/15/05
Horn Book, starred: 05/01/05
Kirkus Reviews: 02/01/05
School Library Journal, starred: 03/01/05
V.O.Y.A. (Voice of Youth Advocates): 04/01/05

Oppel, Kenneth. 2004. *Airborn*. New York: HarperCollins. 355p.

The Story: In an alternate past (circa early 1900s) travel by airplanes never becomes popular because of the discovery of a non-flammable gas called hydrium. The public travels across continents and oceans via giant zeppelins. Young Matt Cruse serves as a cabin boy aboard one such ship, a luxury cruiser named the *Aurora*. He has worked on the *Aurora* for three years, ever since the death of his father, who had worked on the same ship as a sail maker. Matt inherited his passion for flying from his father, who died doing the work he loved, and Matt feels that the best way to honor his memory is to wholly commit himself to the ship his father lived and died on. In fact, Matt never feels quite right unless he is airborne, and he believes without a doubt that he is leading the kind of life his father would be proud of.

On a routine return trip to North America from Australia, Matt spies a solitary hot air balloon while he is on watch. He helps bring the pilot in, an unconscious old man named Benjamin Molloy, who was trying to circumnavigate the globe on his own and apparently suffered a heart attack. When Matt speaks to the old man later, Benjamin mentions mysterious winged creatures that he claims to have seen from his balloon. Shortly after, the man dies, and Matt chalks his wild stories up to hallucinations brought on by dehydration and altitude sickness.

A year later, Matt is working on a flight that is traveling to Sydney, and he hopes this is the flight on which Captain Walken will finally promote him from cabin boy to assistant sail maker, partly because he was so instrumental in the rescue of Benjamin Molloy. He is crushed, however, when the Captain tells him that while he would like to promote Matt, he is instead being forced to give the job to the son of one of the *Aurora's* investors, Bruce Lunardi. Matt is bitter about the decision but is distracted from his anger by the intense attentions of Kate de Vries, an upper-class young woman on board this flight with an insatiable curiosity in all things scientific. Kate is constantly testing Matt's knowledge of the *Aurora* and its inner workings. After several tours and conversations, Kate reveals to Matt that Benjamin Molloy was her grandfather, and she has taken this trip (accompanied by her humorless chaperone, Miss Majorie Simpkins) to see if she can find out if the claims he made in his travel journal—of having discovered a new species of flying mammal—could possibly be true. She shows Matt the journal, full of anatomical drawings and observations of these animals—which resemble wild cats with wings instead of forelegs—who rarely land but eat, sleep, and give birth while riding the air currents. If they travel near enough to the coordinates in her grandfather's journal, Kate plans on photographing the beasts in order to prove her grandfather right.

But Matt has more pressing concerns than helping Kate. The *Aurora* is suddenly attacked by sky pirates led by the dread Vikram Szpirglas, a legendary pirate with a reputation for being ruthless. The pirates finish their dirty business and cast off, but a quick brewing storm causes their ship's engines to cut into the *Aurora's* gasbags, and she begins to sink. Luckily, the Captain is able to bring the ship down on a deserted island, but they have been blown far off course, and the pirates have smashed all their radio equipment. The Captain has the passengers camp on the beach and rallies the crew to make repairs. He assigns Matt and Bruce the job of finding fresh-water, and although Matt wants to hate the boy who took his position, he instead finds Bruce sincere and unpretentious.

Kate is thrilled with the unscheduled stop, since she has deduced from her grandfather's sketches and the *Aurora's* last known coordinates that this is the very island over which her grandfather observed the flying cats. She is determined to explore, and Matt is helpless to stop her, even though the Captain has expressly forbidden anyone from leaving the beach. After a few hours of hiking, they find the skeletal remains of one flying cat still clinging to a tree branch, and Kate convinces Matt to return with her tomorrow so she can properly photograph it and dismantle the bones for study. Matt doesn't want to leave the ship, which has been hastily patched and has just enough hydrium left to fly them out the next day, but when Kate threatens to ask Bruce instead, he reluctantly agrees.

The next day, while they are carefully collecting the bones, the sight of a live example of what they have come to call a "cloud cat" surprises Matt and Kate. To Matt's dismay, Kate insists on following the animal to its nest so she can take pictures. But while they are hiking, they are caught in a tropical storm and are forced to take shelter in a cave, where Matt notices the mango scent of hydrium but assumes he actually smells real fruit. When they get back to the beach, the Captain has noted their absence, and Matt is in trouble. But the worse news is that the ship was further damaged by the storm and has lost its remaining hydrium. Luckily, Matt recalls the mango smell in the cave and is able to lead the crew to a natural hydrium vent in the earth. All is forgiven, and Matt is deemed a hero. Using lengths of rubber tubing from the cargo hold, the crew directs the precious gas into the ship, and once more, they ready to depart. But before they can, Kate disappears again, determined to get a photo of the live cloud cat, and Matt and Bruce are sent to find her and bring her safely back so the *Aurora* can leave.

Matt and Bruce predictably find Kate up a tree and agree to help her lay out bait to attract the cat so she can get her picture and they can all get back to the ship as soon as possible. But the cat proves cunning and predatory at close range and ends up stalking Bruce, who is wounded but manages to get away. Kate and Matt, going in the other direction, end up in a worse situation. They have inadvertently stumbled into Szpirglas's secret pirate camp, hidden on the other side of the island from the grounded *Aurora*. They pretend to be clueless castaways from another ship that went down in the storm, but when they try to sneak back to the *Aurora* that night, Szpirglas catches them and figures out who they are. He throws them into a pit with another natural hydrium vent, which Matt and Kate use to fill Kate's pants with gas and fly out.

They manage to meet up with Bruce again in the forest, but when they get back to the ship, they discover that the pirates have gotten there first and imprisoned the passengers and crew. When Matt overhears their plans to murder the entire group in order to keep their pirate paradise a secret, he, Kate, and Bruce execute a daring plan that results in suspenseful chases, drugged food, and a launching of the *Aurora* all on their own. Matt engages in a terrifying battle on top of the ship with Szpirglas, who is determined to kill him and nearly does. But at the last moment, a flock of cloud cats fly over, clipping Szpirglas and causing him to fall to his death. Sadly, Bruce is killed by one of the pirates, but Kate frees the passengers and crew while Matt is fighting for his life, and when the battle is done, the captain gives Matt the helm, since he has earned his right to pilot the *Aurora*.

Six months later, Matt is enrolled in the Sky Academy, getting his officer's training, while Kate is touring museums giving presentations about the new species she's discovered. They meet for lunch, both sensing the unspoken romantic feelings that burn between them. But Matt wants to wait until he has something more to offer Kate as an officer and a gentleman.

The Message: Good always wins over evil. Personal tragedy builds character. Don't be afraid to follow your dream to the ends of the earth if necessary. Always strive to do your best, and you will eventually be rewarded.

Who's It For?: 6th–10th grade. This charming, old-fashioned adventure story contains some cartoony violence, but overall is refreshingly clean and chaste, despite the facts that Szpirglas kills one of the innocent ship's crew with a gunshot to the head, pirates murder Bruce offstage, and Matt and Kate share a quick kiss in the woods as they are fleeing for their lives. Older readers interested in science or engineering will no doubt enjoy reading Oppel's detailed descriptions of the *Aurora's* construction and about what life would have been like aboard a Victorian-era zeppelin.

Why It Rocks:
- **Voice:** Matt's first-person voice is realistically questioning and insecure except when he is discussing one thing: his passion for the great airship and his love of flying. Teens who are equally infatuated with a cause or hobby will recognize and relate to Matt's enthusiastic fervor.
- **Plot:** Equal parts internal musing, as Matt tries to obey his conscience and make his father and Captain Walker proud, and swashbuckling action, including daring shoot-outs on catwalks and desperate hand-to-hand combat on the zeppelin's billowing top and sides. Although there may be one too many convenient coincidences (the deserted island is not only the pirates' hideout but also the same island Kate's grandfather flew over as well as a natural reservoir of hydrium gas!), teens caught up in this inventive alternative history yarn won't notice or care.
- **Pacing:** Oppel maintains suspense with cliff-hanging chapters and crackerjack action sequences that propel the 400-plus-page book forward faster than you can say "Szpirglas!"
- **Characterization:** Rich, despite the plot-driven story. Oppel nicely develops a theme of how personal passion helps shape a teen's identity and future in his depiction of Matt and Kate, doing whatever it takes to fulfill their dreams, while Bruce, forced to do his father's wishes, tries to discover the thing that will give him the same drive and ambition as his two new friends. His tragic death at novel's end adds an especially bittersweet poignancy to Oppel's message.

Hook It Up With: *Skybreaker,* the sequel to *Airborn,* and *The Sterkarm Handshake* by Susan Price.

Read More about It:
Booklist: 06/01/04
Horn Book: 10/01/04
Kirkus Reviews: 05/15/04

Publishers Weekly: 04/26/04
School Library Journal, starred: 07/01/04
V.O.Y.A. (Voice of Youth Advocates): 06/01/04

Pfeffer, Susan Beth. 2006. *Life as We Knew It.* New York: Harcourt. 352p.

The Story: The spring of her sophomore year, Miranda's biggest concerns are getting her license, taking up ice-skating lessons, and keeping the peace between her two best friends, Megan and Sammie, who have been at odds since Megan became a born-again Christian. So when Miranda begins hearing about the asteroid that is supposed to hit the moon that May, she is mildly interested but far more concerned with what is going on in her own life.

When the collision happens, however, it is far more serious than astronomers had predicted. The moon has been pushed out of its regular orbit, causing the tides to go crazy and magna to erupt from volcanoes that have long been considered dead. Big cities on both American coasts are washed away by tsunamis and pounding rains. There are flash floods, violent thunderstorms, and earthquakes worldwide. Untold numbers of people have perished. While the people of Miranda's small town in Pennsylvania don't experience any of these disasters firsthand, they see the results of these events in the form of lost electricity and phone service and astronomical gas prices. The grocery stores are ransacked and not restocked, because there is no gas to fuel supply trucks. Businesses close, postal delivery stops, and families leave town in droves, in the hope that the situation elsewhere is not as grim. By the beginning of June, the schools are more than half empty, so administrators cancel finals and send the students home for the summer.

At home, Miranda is fighting with her mother, who seems to be preparing for the very worst. Right after the collision, Mom went out and stocked the house from top to bottom with canned goods, preserved foods, and such supplies as blankets, candles, matches, and batteries. Miranda, who can't believe that the government won't be able to straighten this mess out by the end of the summer, finds her mother's efforts a little extreme. But she is glad that her elder brother, Matt, is safely home from college and that her younger brother, Jonny, seems okay with the end of the world as long as he can still play baseball. After noticing how obsessive her mother has become with rationing the canned goods, Miranda goes to Matt for the truth on how bad things really are, and he spells it out for her: Mom doesn't know how long this will last and is counting on Miranda's visiting their dad and his wife in the Midwest and Jonny's going to baseball camp, so she will have fewer mouths to feed. She is already skipping meals herself to conserve food. When Miranda hears this she is shocked to realize how serious this situation has become.

Over the summer, Miranda pursues as normal of a life as possible under the circumstances. There is record heat, so she goes swimming in the local pond most days and strikes up a romance with a fellow swimmer, Dan. Jonny goes to baseball camp, about which Mom is happy to discover is next to a farm that will provide the boys with fresh food and milk in exchange for work. When Mom asks Miranda and Matt to cut down to two meals a day and fast one day a week to conserve food, Miranda becomes resentful and angry when she recalls that her mother waited until Jonny left to make these requests. Deep inside she is terrified that her mother believes that Jonny is the only one who is young and hardy enough to survive if this situation continues.

By mid-July, the temperature suddenly drops. The ash from all the active volcanoes has finally begun to spread throughout the atmosphere, blocking the sun's heat and light. Droughts, famines, and early frosts are predicted as crops die from the lack of sunlight. Miranda's trip to her dad's is cancelled. Instead he will pick up Jonny from baseball camp; then he and his pregnant wife, Lisa, will spend a few days at home before starting their journey west to reunite with Lisa's parent's. Dad's visit is wonderful, and he brings them extra food and blankets. When he leaves, Miranda has a hard time letting go, knowing there is no way to keep in contact with him and that this may be the last time she ever sees him. She is further dispirited by the news that her friend Sammie and sometime boyfriend Dan also are making plans to leave town and that Megan has stopped eating in order to show God her willingness to die for him. All of these things make Miranda feel closer to her mom than she has in a long time.

In September school resumes but with such a lack of resources that Miranda decides to study at home. The air quality continues to worsen, and already there has been a killing frost. Matt and Jonny spend their days chopping wood for the winter. There are no more fuel deliveries, and the natural gas runs out in October. Miranda's family is luckier than most because they have a wood-burning stove on the sunporch. When Mom sprains her ankle, Miranda must assume all the responsibility of cooking the meals and hand-washing the laundry in ash-gray cold water. When the tempera-ture drops below freezing, they close off the rest of the house and move into the sunporch. Matt covers all the windows with plywood to conserve heat, and as the days continue to darken, Miranda feels like her world is becoming smaller and smaller.

The winter months are hungry and cold for the family. When the snow begins to fall, it is an added source of water, but the drifts are so deep that it's impossible to chop wood. Everyone is losing weight, and they are all down to one meal a day. But Mom insists that they keep up with their studies, and there are still lively games of poker, Scrabble, and chess. Christmas is hallmarked by neighbors who brave the snow to come caroling but don't expect to be invited in, because no one wants anyone else to see how much food they have left. Mom allows a small feast for Christmas, includ-ing linguine with canned sauce and lime Jell-O. After New Year's, tragedy strikes when everyone in the house comes down with a deadly flu except Miranda. She works desperately to keep her family comfortable, but just when things are looking up, the woodstove clogs and nearly asphyxiates them in their sleep. Still, Miranda manages to pull them through, and they slowly begin to recover.

Through February, Jonny and Mom continue to regain strength and are heart-ened by short bursts of electricity, which seems to indicate that things may be improving. Mom is able to get reception on the radio for the first time in months, and though it is the same old disaster news, at least it makes them feel less lonely. But by the beginning of March, they are down to their last ten days' worth of food, and

Miranda begins to believe she will starve to death. She resolves to make one last trip into town, hoping to find some help. But by the time she struggles there through the snow, the post office is closed and there are no signs of life. So it feels like a miracle when she discovers that the town hall is open and relief efforts have arrived in the form of food that is being distributed free to any family who asks for it. The worst is finally over.

The Message: Never give up, even when things seem bleakest. Suffering builds character. Love knows no bounds. Personal sacrifice can be liberating.

Who's It For?: 7th–12th grade. There is little language or sexual situations, other than Mom's warning to Miranda that she simply cannot have sex with Dan, because an unplanned pregnancy under these circumstances would be catastrophic. The violence is of the natural disaster variety and mostly kept at a distance. There is one disturbing incident where Miranda is told that Megan succeeded in starving herself to death and Megan's mother committed suicide when she found out.

Why It Rocks:
• **Voice:** Miranda's first-person voice is narrated through the pages of a journal she starts shortly before the asteroid collision, and like *The Diary of Anne Frank,* it paints a poignant, bittersweet portrait of a young life bursting with potential that is being impeded by extreme circumstances.
• **Plot:** This is a deftly layered story that goes far beyond your typical disaster drama, with nuanced subplots concerning Mom's romantic relationship with a local doctor who ends up dying of the flu, the family's involvement with a female neighbor who provides them with valuable resources just when they need them the most, and Miranda's preoccupation with her friend Becky, who died of cancer last year and whose presence still haunts Miranda's dreams.
• **Pacing:** Thoughtful, with a several incidents of rising action along the way that ratchet up the suspense of whether Miranda and her family will live or die.
• **Characterization:** Although there is a large cast of interesting characters that make an appearance in Miranda's journal, it is the narrator herself when the reader will find most compelling as she grows from a typical teen who resents her brother's good fortune to a compassionate, sacrificial young woman who would give her life so that her family might survive.

Hook It Up With: *Z for Zachariah* by Robert C. O'Brien and *How I Live Now* by Meg Rosoff.

Read More about It:
Booklist, starred: 09/01/06
Horn Book: 11/01/06
Kirkus Reviews: 09/15/06
Publishers Weekly, starred: 10/16/06
School Library Journal: 10/01/06
V.O.Y.A. (Voice of Youth Advocates): 10/01/06

Reeve, Philip. 2003. *Mortal Engines.* New York: HarperCollins. 310p.

The Story: In the future, millennia after the global explosion that wiped out most of the ancients in what is known as the "Sixty-Second War," all cities exist on caterpillar tracks, hunting and running one another down in order to absorb the loser's resources in the form of metal, fuel, and human bodies. The largest, strongest cities fare the best, and this principle is known as Municipal Darwinism.

Fifteen-year-old Tom Natsworthy is a Third Class Apprentice in the Guild of Historians, one of the four Guilds (Engineers, Merchants, and Navigators) responsible for the operation of the traction city of London. An orphan, he spends his days dreaming about his hero, Thaddeus Valentine, the dashing Head Historian who is more Indiana Jones than Albert Einstein. So he is thrilled when he gets to meet the man himself while on salvage duty, picking through the pieces of a recently "devoured" city to see if there is anything that would be of interest to the Guild. Valentine introduces Tom to his daughter, Kate, who happens to be along with him. As they peruse the piles, Valentine is suddenly accosted by a teenage girl with a horribly scarred face who tries to stab him. Tom sees his chance to make an impression and wrests the knife away from her, then gives chase when she runs away. She heads for the nearest rail and, to Tom's horror, leaps over but not before telling Tom that her name is Hester Shaw and that his hero, Valentine, is the one who scarred her face. Valentine soon arrives, and Tom tells him what the girl said. Before he knows it, Valentine has heaved him over the rail after Hester. He wakes up in the dirt, alone on the bare earth with Hester, who is as happy to have had her assassination thwarted as Tom is about being tossed overboard by his hero. They begin to walk toward London, which is now miles away in the distance, and Hester tells Tom her story.

Her mother worked as a scavenger and seller of "Old Tech," pieces of equipment that date back to before the Sixty Second War and are worth a great deal to Historians. Hester claims that her mother found a piece of Old Tech that Valentine wanted; when she wouldn't sell, he murdered her and her husband for it, then tried to kill Hester as well but succeeded only in slicing her face. After her parents' death, Hester was informally adopted by a half-human, half-machine Stalker named Grike who cared for her until she was old enough to come to London and seek her revenge on Valentine. What she doesn't know is that the Lord Mayor Crome of London has struck a deal with Grike after he heard of Hester's attempt on Valentine's life. He has promised Grike his heart's desire—to have Hester resurrected into a Stalker like himself so that they will never be separated again—if he locates Hester and Tom and kills them both.

Unaware of Grike's mission, Tom and Hester continue to follow London's tracks, meeting up with a number of unsavory traveling companions, including a small-town mayor who tries to sell them as slaves, and a semimad, violent suburban pirate named Peavy whose recklessness makes them fear for their lives. At one point, Grike does find and confront them, but Tom saves Hester from his iron-clawed hands by running a sword through his machinery and ending his stalking for good.

Back in London, Kate has become suspicious of her father's activities. She eavesdrops on Valentine and the Lord Mayor Crome and hears them mention something called MEDUSA. This starts her on a trail of investigation and intrigue, where she finally discovers that MEDUSA is the name of a top-secret atomic weapon that London's engineers have resurrected from pieces of Old Tech and plan to use to destroy the Shield Wall, an ancient structure that protects a static society that chooses to live its life in one place. London hopes to be the first city to ravage this new "hunting ground" after leveling the wall with MEDUSA. Kate also discovers that MEDUSA's "brain" is a piece of Old Tech recovered by a scavenger named Shaw— Hester's mother. Suddenly, Hester's assassination attempt makes terrible sense. Kate is floored by her father's betrayal and vows to do whatever she can to stop the engineers from going forward with their evil plan.

After Grike's demise, Hester and Tom finally end up in the care of Anna Fang, a balloon aviatrix who also happens to be a spy for the Anti-Traction League, a group of rebels opposing Municipal Darwinism and advocating for a static lifestyle. Anna takes them to the city of Batmunkh Gompa, beyond the Shield Wall. They have learned what the Engineers intend to do, and she and the rest of the League plan on launching their warrior fleet of airships against London should it level Medusa against the Wall. But Valentine has sabotaged by the fleet by setting fire to it, and before making his escape, he also kills Anna. Tom and Hester escape in Anna's airship and head for London, both now bent on Valentine's destruction.

When Valentine returns to London, Kate confronts him with what she knows. He admits what he has done but says he did it for her. Tom and Hester arrive in London, and Tom drops Hester off to complete her revenge as he circles the city, ready to pick her up as soon as her bloody business is finished. However, she is intercepted by guards, who take her to Valentine and the Lord Mayor just as they are aiming MEDUSA at the Shield Wall. Valentine, seeing Hester, runs at her with his sword, intending to kill her once and for all, but Kate, in an attempt to stop her father, throws herself in front of his weapon and is fatally wounded. Her body falls on MEDUSA's controls, causing the weapon to malfunction. Tom lands the airship in time to pick up Hester, and they are the only ones to escape with their lives as MEDUSA explodes, destroying London, including Valentine, who is cradling his dying daughter. Hester and Tom aim the airship toward a safe port, where they can begin to heal from their arduous journey and further explore the romantic relationship that is growing between them.

The Message: Some ideas are better left unexplored. Humankind will never lose its capacity for war and violence. We must learn from the past if we are to create a better future. Looking back is just as important as moving ahead. Power corrupts. Love can form between the most unlikely partners and in the most unlikely places.

Who's It For?: 8th–12th grade. Sophisticated younger readers well versed in science fiction or fantasy may also enjoy it, but the complex world building and themes of warring societal systems might stymie them. There are also several violent, graphically depicted death scenes, including those of Grike, Anna Fang, and Kate.

Why It Rocks:
- **Voice:** Third person, from various points of view, including those of Tom, Hester, Grike, Kate, and Valentine. Reeve flits in and out of characters' heads rapidly through chapter changes, adding to the breathless pace toward the utterly destructive climax.

- **Plot:** Tight as a drum and wholly original. Similar in "steam-punk" technology to Oppel's Printz Award-winning *Airborn*, *Mortal Engines's* concepts of Municipal Darwinism, Anti-Traction activists, "Old Tech," and "pirate" suburbs are at once inventive and familiar.
- **Pacing:** Quick but deliberate, with key pieces of information revealed slowly through long investigations by different characters. As each new part of the mystery of MEDUSA comes to light, however, tension builds, and readers won't be able to resist rushing to find out who will live and who will die in the final showdown.
- **Characterization:** All the characters, even secondary ones, are richly depicted, full of passion, anger, self-righteousness, and pathos. Tom loses his naïveté, Hester learns what it means to be loved; Grike transcends his metal bonds to follow his heart; Kate becomes an active participant in her life, rather than simply a passive observer; and Valentine discovers that, in the end, he is a coward. This novel solidly delivers on both exciting action sequences and meaningful character development.

Hook It Up With: *Shade's Children* by Garth Nix and *The Copper Elephant* by Adam Rapp.

Read More about It:
Booklist: 11/01/03
Horn Book: 11/01/03
Kirkus Reviews: 10/15/03
Publishers Weekly, starred: 10/27/03
School Library Journal, starred: 12/01/03
V.O.Y.A. (Voice of Youth Advocates): 12/01/03

Westerfeld, Scott. 2005. *Uglies.* New York: Simon & Schuster. 425p.

The Story: In Tally Youngblood's world, everyone wants to be Pretty. When teenagers turn 16, they undergo a cosmetic operation to make them generically gorgeous, the purpose being to end racial discrimination and strife, since everyone looks essentially the same. Children, or "Littlies" are raised by "Middle Pretties" (who age into "Late Pretties" before reaching the "Crumbly" stage) until they reach adolescence. Termed "Uglies," they then move into dorms, where they attend school and await their operations. Once they have their operations, the former Uglies, now Pretty, move into New Pretty Town (separated from Uglyville by a river), where they lounge, gossip, try on clothes all day, and party all night, admiring one another's stunning features.

Tally is only two months away from her operation when she meets Shay, another young Ugly who also enjoys hoverboarding (air surfing on magnetically powered boards that draw their energy from metal) and pranking Pretties over in New Pretty Town. Shay isn't as enamored as Tally with the idea of becoming Pretty and tries to convince her new friend that while Pretties may be beautiful, their empty lives seem pretty boring. Tally doesn't buy it, but she does let Shay talk her into hoverboarding at night to the Rusty Ruins, the remains of a city that used to be populated by "Rusties," the old race of humans who fought wars over physical differences and ruined the environment with their factories and pollution.

At the Ruins, Shay reveals that she had a specific reason for bringing Tally there. Shay knows a boy named David, a member of a renegade group called the Smoke, who doesn't believe all the Pretty propaganda. He comes to the Ruins occasionally to guide runaways who wish to escape the confines of Pretty society. Shay has decided to join the Smoke, and she wants Tally to come with her. But Tally is quick to turn her down. There is nothing she wants more than to become Pretty, and she's not about to jeopardize that because of a silly whim of Shay's. The girls return to Uglyville that night, and Tally hopes that Shay will give up her crazy idea. But six days before their operations, Shay tells Tally she's leaving for good. She gives Tally a set of coded directions to the Smoke if she ever changes her mind, then takes off on her hoverboard, to Tally's great dismay.

The day of her operation, Tally is told there's a problem, and instead of being taken to the hospital, she ends up in Special Circumstances, the law-and-order branch of Pretty society. Tally is taken to meet Dr. Cable, a high-ranking Special. Specials are Pretty but in a feral, cruel way, intended to frighten and intimidate. Dr. Cable knows Shay ran away, and she knows about the Smoke. She wants Tally to follow Shay, discover the location of the Smoke, and then alert Special Circumstances, so they can break up the rebellious Ugly resistance. When Tally refuses, Dr. Cable tells her if she doesn't, she will never be allowed to go through the Pretty operation. After a few days of soul searching, Tally reluctantly agrees. Dr. Cable supplies her with everything she needs for the journey, including a heart pendant with tracking device. Once Tally is in the Smoke, she is to activate the device, which will lead Special Circumstances right to her.

Tally spends a frustrating and frightening two weeks in the wild trying to decipher Shay's cryptic directions, and when she finally arrives at the Smokies' meeting place, she is dirty and tired. At first, she is shocked at the Smokies' rough ways, how they burn wood and hunt for their own food instead of rehydrating a bag of freeze-dried SpagBol (spaghetti Bolognese). But the longer she spends with the them, the harder it becomes to activate the pendant that will summon the Specials, especially after she meets David. Unlike Tally, he was raised in the wild by doctor parents who rejected the ideas behind the Pretty operation. She becomes entranced by the natural beauty of the woods, by the deep sleep that comes from hard work, and by David's unusual viewpoint. She even begins to fall in love with David, though she knows Shay likes him, but it's when David introduces Tally to his parents that her resolve to become Pretty finally crumbles.

David's parents were doctors in the same city Tally came from. They left because they discovered that during the operation not only were physical features altered but mental capacity as well. New Pretties were given tiny brain lesions that kept them flighty and thoughtless—peaceful but boring and unquestioning of higher authority. David's parents wanted to start a new society where people thought for themselves and rejected the Pretty standard. After the meeting with his parents, David tells Tally how much she means to him and kisses her. It is then that Tally knows she must destroy the pendant, which she does by throwing it on a bonfire.

Unfortunately, Dr. Cable knew Tally might waver, so she rigged the pendant to send a signal if it was damaged in any way. The next day, the Specials arrive to destroy the Smoke. Tally tries to run away but is captured with several others, one of which is Shay. Her friend accuses her of both stealing David and being a spy, which Tally denies until a Special comes and cuts her bonds so she can be taken to Dr. Cable. She eludes both Dr. Cable and her guards and manages to escape on a hoverboard. She coincidently meets up with David in the woods, and they resolve to go back to the city to rescue David's parents, who they believe were among the captured.

With the help of some Ugly groupies who have heard of the legend of the Smoke, Tally and David infiltrate the halls of Special Circumstances, where they manage to free seven of the Smoke captives, including David's mother, Maddy, and Shay, who has been turned Pretty and, more disturbingly, has no memory of Tally's betrayal. David's father is dead, a casualty of Dr. Cable's experimentation to erase his knowledge of the Pretty brain lesions. The freed captives gather at the Rusty Ruins, where Maddy, using supplies pilfered from the city, tries to discover a cure for the brain lesions. She finally creates some pills that she believes will reverse the process, but Shay, the only Pretty among them, refuses to take them. That's when Tally volunteers to go back to the city and undergo the operation for the sole purpose of testing the drug. She writes a letter to herself that gives Maddy permission to give her the drug, because as a Pretty she's not likely to remember her promise. Then she and Shay ride a hoverboard back to New Pretty Town, where Tally turns herself in.

The Message: Pretty is as pretty does. Physical attractiveness is relative, and there's often no telling what someone will find attractive about someone else. Trustworthiness and loyalty are more important qualities in a person than the way he or she looks. Sometimes in a misguided effort to do the right thing, organizations or governments go too far in the other direction.

Who's It For?: 6th–10th grade. This relatively clean read can go young; while there is some violence and death, especially when the Specials are rounding up the Smokies, there is very little discussion of sex outside of some kissing, and no strong language. Westerfeld's solid, yet highly accessible writing will get his messages of environmental conservation and the dangers of buying into physical beauty across even to a young YA reader.

Why It Rocks:
•   **Voice:** Westerfeld peppers his third-person narrative with fun slang of the future like "tricky," 'bubbly," and "bogus-making," expressions that will sound both vaguely familiar and slightly exotic to today's teens (while evoking the 1980s for some adult readers!).
•   **Plot:** Polished and crisp, this high-concept plot is cinematic in scope; many of the breathless hoverboard action sequences read like they are playing out across the big screen.
•   **Pacing:** Despite the original paperback's impressive length of 400-plus-pages, this story *moves*. Westerfeld keeps readers so occupied with their concern for Tally and the residents of the Smoke that it's hard to believe he could ratchet the suspense any higher. But he does, masterfully, when he reveals the conspiracy to keep Pretties sweet and malleable. So totally bubbly-making!

- **Characterization:** Tally's inner conflict at being forced to betray a whole movement in order to gain a shallow facade is nicely executed, as is David's youthful idealism. Dr. Cable is just a ruthless villain, while Shay's character mostly helps move the plot along; but keep an eye on her—she comes back with a roar in subsequent sequels.

Hook It Up With: the two other books in the *Uglies* trilogy, *Pretties* and *Specials*, and *Black Hole* by Charles Burns (for older readers).

Read More about It:
Booklist, starred: 03/15/05
Kirkus Reviews, starred: 02/15/05
Publishers Weekly: 03/21/05
School Library Journal, starred: 03/01/05
Voice of Youth Advocates (V.O.Y.A.): 06/01/05

Zahn, Timothy. 2003. *Dragon and Thief.* **New York: Tor. 254p.**

The Story: Fourteen-year-old Jack is an orphan, a small-time space thief. His partner in crime, Uncle Virgil, taught him everything he knows. Unfortunately, Uncle Virge died a year ago in an accident, and since then Jack has gone straight, using Uncle Virgil's ship, the *Essenay,* to take on legitimate freelance transport jobs. However, Uncle Virge's cantankerous personality still exists in the *Essenay's* operating program, since he imprinted the ship's interface with his speech and vocal mannerisms before he died.

Recently, Jack accepted a transport job from a huge space corporation named Braxton Universis. He transported ten sealed crates to their correct destination, but when Jack arrived, he discovered that one of the crates was empty. Jack was forced to run when he couldn't produce the missing cargo, and now Braxton Universis has a warrant out for his arrest. He and "Uncle Virge" have been hiding out on the uninhabited planet of Iota Klestis until they can decide what to do next.

On Iota Klestis, Jack witnesses a battle in the sky between two ships and watches as one crash-lands not far from where the *Essenay* is hidden. When he goes to see if he can find anything of value, he is attacked or, rather, embraced by Draycos, a member of an alien race of dragonlike poet-warriors that depend on a symbiotic host for survival. Draycos is the only survivor of the crash, but he will disappear forever if he doesn't find another host before six hours go by. So when he sees Jack, he has no choice but to leap on him and assume his two dimensional symbiotic form, which makes Jack look like he is sporting a life-size, full-color dragon tattoo.

Jack is understandably shocked, so quickly and calmly, Draycos explains who and what he is. Draycos's people, the K'da, and their host race, the Shontine, have been fleeing their mortal enemies, the Valahgua for two long years. They thought they had outrun their pursuers, but just as they were about to land on Iota Klestis, they discovered that their enemy had somehow arrived ahead of them. Using a terrible laser weapon called simply the Death, which kills everything within the range of its purple beam, the Valahgua killed most of the crew of Draycos's ship, causing it to crash. Draycos is afraid that the Valahgua may have made an alliance with a species in Jack's galaxy, in which case, because of the sheer invincibility of the Death, everyone in the galaxy is in great danger. In addition, Draycos's ship was merely an advance team. The rest of the K'da and Shontine refugees will arrive on Iota Klestis in the next six months, and now that the Valahgua know their destination, they are horribly vulnerable to attack unless Draycos finds a way to warn them. Draycos proposes a plan: if Jack will agree to be his host and help him find a way to warn his kinsmen, Draycos will help him discover what happened to the lost cargo and clear his name.

Jack reluctantly agrees. They travel back to the warehouse where he delivered the cargo. Using Draycos's flattening abilities, they are able to break into one of the boxes Jack carried, and they discover a container that used to be full of dry ice, which clearly evaporated over the course of Jack's journey. Jack realizes he was framed the same moment he discovers that breaking the lock on the box has set off a silent alarm and guards are descending on them. They escape the warehouse, and Jack sees the *Essenay* take off in the distance. He tells Draycos that whenever there is trouble, he and "Uncle Virge" agree in advance to meet at a predetermined rendezvous spot when the coast is clear. They are headed for an airstrip to hire a shuttle to "Uncle Virge" when their pursuers catch up to them. Draycos stays hidden while they drug Jack unconscious and have him loaded onto a ship.

After three days, Jack awakens to a disembodied voice demanding to know the whereabouts of his uncle. The voice, which Jack calls Snake Voice, confirms Jack's suspicions that he had been framed in order to make him vulnerable to the threats of this mysterious captor. Snake Voice wanted to hire Uncle Virgil to carry off a heist, not knowing that Jack has been secretly concealing his death in order to avoid losing the *Essenay*. Snake Voice reluctantly allows Jack to accept the job on the condition that Uncle Virge will be his partner on the job and with the understanding that if he runs, they will hunt him down and kill him. His instructions are to break into the purser's safe on the luxury ship *Star of Wonder*, steal a mysterious silver cylinder within, and replace it with a fake. He will be watched, and Snake Voice will contact him when the job is done.

Snake Voice has arranged for Jack to have his own room aboard the *Star of Wonder*, where he and Draycos begin to plan. Using a smoke bomb for distraction, and Draycos's two-dimensional powers, they make the switch. Jack has surmised from clues Draycos has gathered and his own observations that Snake Voice is probably part of Braxton Universis, and is using Jack as a pawn in a high-stakes game of cat and mouse with another corporate power. So he and Draycos decide to double-cross Snake Voice and go directly to the man on board who owns the cylinder, however, when Jack does, he gets a surprise—the man he confronts IS Cornelius Braxton. Between the two of them, they figure out that Snake Voice is Braxton's chairman of the board, Arthur Neverlin, who is obviously staging a company coup, and that the cylinder contained Braxton's DNA samples for rejuvenation treatments, which Neverlin had replaced with poison. Neverlin's goons, undercover in Braxton's service, realize what's up and take both Braxton and Jack to an unguarded airlock, where they intend to heave them into open space. Jack manages to shoot a two-dimensional Draycos out his sleeve; Draycos then cuts the light cables and overwhelms the goons in the dark. In return, Braxton has the charges against Jack dropped and his name cleared. He also arranges for Jack to meet "Uncle Virge" at the rendezvous spot, and on their way, Jack pledges to uphold his end of his bargain with Draycos—their next adventure will be solving the mystery of the Valahgua ambush.

The Message: Sometimes you have to bend the rules when trying to do the right thing. Honesty is the best policy, except when it isn't. It takes time and experience to develop a strong sense of right and wrong.

Who's It For?: 6th–10th grade. Although there is some violence and death, these scenes are not graphically depicted and are necessary to the story. Both Jack and Draycos struggle with the ethics and morality of their illegal actions, weighing them against the greater good they are trying to achieve, in a way that is clear and accessible to middle school students.

Why It Rocks:
• **Voice:** The story is told in the third person, mostly from Jack's point of view and occasionally from Draycos's. Zahn maintains crisp, snappy dialogue that establishes the characters' personalities early on and reveals their quirks and strengths as the plot unfolds.
• **Plot:** Definitely action-oriented, with enough galactic detail to keep readers expecting a *Star Wars* type of adventure happy.
• **Pacing:** Quick and smooth. Other than his finely tuned dialogue, Zahn's prose is utilitarian and efficient, meant to keep the plot briskly rolling along.
• **Characterization:** Surprisingly deep for such a plot-driven adventure story. The poet side of Draycos's warrior-poet nature is clearly Eastern in respect to spirituality, and he struggles with the necessity for violence to protect those he loves. Jack is distraught by the fact that he must go back to a life of crime because of circumstances beyond his control, and in each dicey situation he and Draycos are thrown into, he agonizes over what it is the right thing to do. An excellent introduction for younger teens to the concept of the gray area between black and white.

Hook It Up With: the other books in Zahn's *Dragonback Adventures* (*Dragon and Soldier, Dragon and Slave*) and the *Pit Dragon Chronicles* (*Dragon's Blood, Heart's Blood, A Sending of Dragons*) by Jane Yolen.

Read More about It:
Booklist: 02/15/03
Kirkus Reviews: 01/01/03
Publishers Weekly: 02/03/03
Voice of Youth Advocates (V.O.Y.A.): 08/01/03

CHAPTER 10

GRADUATING HOGWARTS: POST-HARRY POTTER FANTASY FOR TEENS

INTRODUCTION

For the foreseeable future, most fantasy novels aimed at teens will fall into two categories: BHP (Before Harry Potter) or AHP (After Harry Potter). Ever since the boy wizard captured the imagination of young readers all over the world, a deluge of hopeful pubescent voices have been pleading with YA librarians to fork over anything they have to see them through the dry spell until the next installment. Fortunately, this is not a difficult request to fulfill, because publishers, wild about Harry and the sheer amount of money his name has generated for the Scholastic empire, are responding by printing loads of Potter-esque fantasy, some of it better than others, but all of it in multiple volumes, series, or trilogies.

This is wonderful for teens, but not so great for librarians. First of all, we're the ones who have to wade through all these 500- to 800-page fantasy opuses to decide which ones are worthy of including in our collections and recommending to readers. Plus, by the time we get to the last book in a trilogy, we've completely forgotten the complicated plot of the first one. Lucky for you, dear reader, you own *Reading Rants*, which contains the plot summaries for first volumes of several highly praised and very long fantasy multivolume works, including *Abarat*, *The Amulet of Samarkand*, *A Great and Terrible Beauty*, and *The Wee Free Men*, among others. Now you will be able to quickly avail yourself of the pertinent plot points of Bartimaeus's first adventures when quizzed by a discerning teen fantasy reader who wants to know how the djinni has evolved since his initial escapades.

The following books are excellent recommendations for teens who have graduated from Hogwarts and are looking for something similar or are wishing to dive further into the fantasy genre. Once they tear through these titles, you're on your own. But don't worry: If you wait long enough, another sequel is bound to come along!

Barker, Clive. 2002. *Abarat*. New York: HarperCollins. 388p.

The Story: Just as three otherworldly women named Joephi, Diamanda, and Mespa navigate stormy waters on a mysterious mission in another dimension, Candy Quackenbush, a teenager in this one, has decided she's had enough—enough of her small-minded hometown, Chickentown, Minnesota, and enough of her alcoholic, abusive father. After one last dictatorial outburst from her unimaginative teacher, Candy simply walks out of school without a backward glance.

Candy ends up in a grassy field outside of town, standing below a tumbledown structure that resembles an old lighthouse. It is there that she stumbles on John Mischief, a friendly eight-headed fellow who introduces her to his other seven heads (all siblings, also named John), informs her that he is on the run from a villain named Mendelson Shape, and tells her she can save them both from this monster if she climbs the old lighthouse and "lights the light." Shape, a shambling, menacing skeletal figure, soon shows up and starts after Mischief. While Mischief distracts him, Candy drops an ornate metal ball into an inverted pyramid that stands at the top of the tower, and suddenly, impossibly, a giant sea begins to flow across the field. After a fierce tussle with Shape that nearly kills her, Candy rejoins Mischief on the ground, and he tells her of his homeland, the 25 islands of Abarat, where each island is ruled by an Hour of the day. Abarat exists in this approaching ocean, which is actually a living entity called the Sea of Izabella. Candy begs to go with Mischief, and he reluctantly agrees, giving her the object Shape is after to hold onto for safekeeping: a mysterious key that is desperately wanted by Shape's master, the evil Christopher Carrion. Then, Mischief draws a pistol, shoots the ball from the pyramid, and the waters begin to recede, carrying Mischief and Candy away from Shape and toward Abarat.

For Candy, it is the beginning of a delirious, dreamy adventure that feels strangely familiar. She and Mischief are carried through the waters to the island of Yebba Dim Day (8:00 PM) by sea skippers, friendly aquatic beings who are fond of card games. There, she is separated from Mischief because of his several outstanding arrest warrants (he is a master thief-for-hire) and ends up alone on the streets of the island, which is shaped like a giant head and full of outrageous beings that appear to be half human and half beast. She is taken in by a friendly woman with gills, named Izarith, who offers her dry clothes. In exchange, Candy gives her dollar bills from her world and discovers that the people of Abarat know what America is but consider it a myth, calling it the Hereafter.

Candy is disturbed when she notices an enormous mechanical bug spying on her. She tries to smash it, but it gets away, leaving Candy feeling vulnerable to attack. She is right to be afraid: the bug spy comes from Christopher Carrion, Shape's master and the Lord of Midnight. He rules the island of 12:00 AM would like to bring all of Abarat under his dark command. He is furious that Shape didn't return with the Key and, after hearing his story, becomes convinced that Candy has it. Carrion needs the Key to free the ancient evil beings called Requiax, which he hopes will help him in his quest to conquer Abarat.

Meanwhile, Candy meets Samuel Klepp, author of *Klepp's Almenak*, a guide to the 25 islands of Abarat, of which the the 25th island is Time Out of Time. Klepp tells Candy about Rojo Pixler, a business baron who is slowly sucking the magic out of

Abarat with his commercialism. He and Carrion are waging a quiet war over the land and soul of Abarat, but neither is well liked. When Klepp takes Candy to the top of Yebba Dim Day to show her the rest of the archipelago, they are greeted by the terrifying sight of Shape astride a giant moth. He swoops down and snatches Candy.

Candy's life hangs in the balance as she is flung from one close call to the next. After Shape's moth is shot down near the island of Ninnyhammer (10:00 PM) by Pixler's goons, Pixler offers her shelter from Carrion, mainly because he wants her to take his products back to the Hereafter; but Candy, suspicious of his motives, runs away into Ninnyhammer's forests. She is briefly captured by the evil wizard Kaspar Wolfswinkel, who tries to ransom her to Otto Houlihan, Carrion's second in command. Candy escapes Wolfswinkel by appealing to his sweet but beaten-down slave, a creature named Malingo who turns on his former master and breaks his magic staff. Malingo and Candy can escape in a glyph, a flying machine spoken into solidity by the chanting of magical phrases.

The glyph is pulled into the orbit of the 25th island, and as it crashes, Candy suddenly finds herself in a time before she was born. She is greeted by the three sisters of fate, Joephi, Diamanda, and Mespa, who show her beautiful visions from the past and future, then inform her they have brought her here to prepare her for a future where she will do great things for Abarat but not without also facing great danger. When she comes to, she and Malingo escape the terrifying guards of the island, a violent pair called the Fugit Brothers, by stealing a small boat and sailing away. Meanwhile, Carrion plots and stews in his dark tower, muttering only one word over and over: "Candy!" An appendix includes informative excerpts from *Klepp's Almenak*.

The Message: Believe in yourself. If you don't like something, change it. You have control over what happens in your life. Standardization is often the death of individuality and uniqueness.

Who's It For?: 7th–12th grade. Barker has lavishly illustrated this book himself with over of 100 full-color paintings, but while most are whimsical, some are dark and may be frightening to younger readers. The portrait of a gray-skinned Carrion, wearing a contraption that allows him to breathe in the liquid of his own nightmares, especially gave me the creeps. There is really no sexuality or language but some violence, especially on the part of Carrion and Shape and in Candy's abusive home life.

Why It Rocks:
• **Voice:** The limited third-person point of view narration mostly moves back and forth from Candy and Carrion, with a few departures in order for Barker to introduce characters who are featured more in the next volume. Much of the story's leavening humor comes from snappy, crisp dialogue between Candy and the various creatures she meets.
• **Plot:** Occasionally meandering, but Barker picks up many of these dropped threads in the sequel; this is a planned four-book series. There are numerous subplots, which limited space won't allow me to address, including the introduction of a heroic dragon-slaying team and background on Christopher Carrion's failed romance, which

is presumably why he became so evil. Anything readers don't understand will probably be made clear in the movie—Disney has already purchased movie, theme park, and multimedia rights to Barker's fantasy opus.

• **Pacing:** Uneven. Sometimes the action rushes along; sometimes Candy pauses to have long side discussions with another character who invariably shares some important information with her about the strange land in which she has found herself. Most of these bits come into play in the next book, so readers need to pay close attention and not just skip to the next action sequence.

• **Characterization:** This is where Barker shines. Each character he introduces (and there are a lot!) maintains his or her own unique personality, even if the reader gets to know the individual only for a few pages. While Candy herself is a bit of an "Everygirl," John Mischief, Malingo, Wolfswinkel, and Carrion are wonderfully rounded and flawed. The real star of the show, however, is Barker's impressive artwork, which alone is well worth the price of admission to this Seussian circus.

Hook It Up With: *The Sandman* graphic novel series by Neil Gaiman and *Sabriel* by Garth Nix.

Read More about It:
Booklist, starred: 09/01/02
Horn Book: Fall 2003
Kirkus Reviews: 09/01/02
Publishers Weekly: 06/24/02
School Library Journal: 10/01/02
Voice of Youth Advocates (V.O.Y.A.): 10/01/02

Bray, Libba. 2003. *A Great and Terrible Beauty.* New York: Random House. 403p.

The Story: In 1895, after 16-year-old Gemma Doyle's mother is fatally stabbed in the Bombay marketplace, her upper-class family loses no time in sending her to a proper finishing school in London named Spence, in order to learn the social graces necessary to land a wealthy husband. Gemma, who was raised in India, has always wanted to move back to England but is sickened by the fact that her wish has been granted only through her beloved mother's death. She is also haunted by her last interaction with her mother, a petty argument that led Gemma to leave her in the crowded marketplace, and perhaps vulnerable to attack by the Indian man whose body was found next to hers.

Since her mother's death, Gemma has been suffering from frightening, uncontrollable visions, one of which suggests that her mother's death wasn't murder but suicide. At Spence, she is assigned to room with mousy Ann Bradshaw, a scholarship student and the butt of mean jokes by popular Felicity and beautiful Pippa. When Gemma stands up for Ann, she earns Felicity's grudging admiration and is soon initiated into her inner circle, which Gemma insists must also include Ann. Gemma is uneasy when she notices a caped figure following her; soon he reveals himself to be the younger brother of the man who died next to her mother. His name is Kartik, and he orders her to resist the visions or worse will happen to her. But the visions won't stop. One even leads Gemma to the discovery of an old diary belonging to a girl named Mary Dodd.

Mary also went to Spence and had visions. But she was able to control and use them to open a portal into a magical dimension called the Realms, where she and her best friend, Sarah, slipped off the constraints of Victorian society and practiced magic. Gemma doesn't fully understand Mary's writings, but she is curious. She is even more intrigued after their art teacher, Miss Moore, tells the class about an ancient organization of women called The Order that was said to practice magic in the caves near Spence and believed in a world between worlds called the Realms. Gemma shares Mary's diary with Felicity, Pippa, and Ann, and the girls decide to create their own Order.

Soon they are sneaking out to meet in the caves at night to drink stolen wine and share their darkest secrets. Gemma feels responsible for her mother's death; Ann cuts herself to ease the pain of being an outsider; Pippa has epilepsy, which, if widely known, could ruin any marriage prospects; and Felicity's mother has left the family to live with her artist lover. When they jokingly try to open the portal to the Realms one night by following Mary's instructions, they are shocked when they succeed. The place is even more beautiful than they had imagined, with any wish instantly granted. Ann is made beautiful; Pippa, who is being married off to a man twice her age by her parents in the real world, basks in the attention of a fabled knight in shining armor; while Felicity learns self-sufficiency at the side of an Athena-like goddess who teaches her to hunt. But Gemma is the happiest of all because she is reunited with her mother, who explains the mystery of her death and the meaning of the Order and the Realms.

Gemma's mother, Virginia, was a member of the Order, and Aman, Kartik's brother, who also died, was a member of the Order's guardian organization, the Rakshana. She did indeed kill herself in order to escape a fate worse than death at the hands of an evil being named Circe, who rules the Realm's Winterlands. Gemma's mother raised her in India to keep her away from Circe's power. Virginia warns her to be careful how she wields the power of the Realms, because even though Gemma has the ability to raise the Order again, she must be cautious of Circe, who could take Gemma's power as her own.

The girls are delighted with their secret world and visit it almost daily. But as Gemma begins to probe more deeply into the life of Mary, she is disturbed to discover that Mary was actually her mother, Virginia, and Circe is what is left of Mary's best friend, Sarah. Sarah wanted more power before the elders of the Order thought she was ready and convinced Mary to help make a human sacrifice to a dark spirit. This very act shut Circe into the Realms until Gemma appeared, opening the portal again and setting Sarah, now Circe, free to slake her thirst for power in the real world.

Back at Spence, Pippa is finally being forced to marry her aged fiancée. She begs for one more chance to experience freedom in the Realms, but when the girls arrive, they are confronted by Circe. The meadow shrivels, the sky grows dark, and they are forced to leave Pippa behind in order to save themselves. In the cave, Pippa collapses into an epileptic fit and falls into a coma. Gemma returns to the Realms alone to look for Pippa after the danger has passed, but Pippa would rather stay in the Realms forever with her knight than be forced into a loveless marriage. Gemma returns to the real world to learn that Pippa has died. Both Felicity and Ann are shaken by the news, but it just stiffens Gemma's resolve to raise the fallen Order and bring the Realms and Circe under control. But to do that, she will have to face down Kartik and the rest of the Rakshana, who are just as convinced that the Realms are too dangerous and should remain closed forever. It is especially difficult for Gemma to think about going up against Kartik, since she seems to be falling in love with him.

The Message: Life is a balance of both light and dark; you can't have one without the other. It can be difficult to escape society's expectations of you when you belong to a certain class or gender. Stay true to yourself no matter what mixed messages you may receive from the world around you.

Who's It For?: 8th–12th grade. Gemma has some steamy sexual dreams about Kartik, and near the end of the story, Felicity, who has grown jealous of Gemma's control over the portal, convinces the others girls to strip, hunt down a deer in the woods, and brutally kill it as a sacrifice to gain entrance into the Realms without Gemma. This novel is a full-on Victorian Gothic revival, replete with sexual repression, supernatural beasties, and spirit summonings. It will be enjoyed most by teens old enough to understand Bray's themes of female oppression and her luscious period vocabulary, which pays homage to Victorian ghost and horror stories of yore.

Why It Rocks:
• **Voice:** Gemma's first-person narration is by turns brave and insecure, courageous yet conscience stricken. Although she sometimes feels wiser than her years, her sharp caustic wit and lively dialogue with her friends will quickly charm older female teen readers and draw them into the story.
• **Plot:** Occasionally muddy, especially when it comes to the world building of the Realms, which is far more atmospheric than concrete. But Bray does a beautiful job of comparing and contrasting the freedom of the Realms with the constraints of Victorian society, which is the book's strongest aspect. There are many subplots, involving Gemma and her relationships with her family and her connections with Kartik and the Rakshana, that are expanded upon in the sequels of this planned trilogy.
• **Pacing:** A slow-burning build to Gemma's first but certainly not last confrontation with Circe that is laced with horror and suspense at every twist of the plot. Despite its length, teens won't be able to put it down.
• **Characterization:** Some of Gemma's friends seem stock (beautiful, shallow Pippa, plain, smart Ann); however, Gemma herself is a wonderfully round character, full of contradictions, and none of the girls remains unchanged by story's end. An especially well-drawn secondary character is art teacher, Miss Moore, whose voice of reason and sympathetic ear help develop Gemma's character.

Hook It Up With: *The Minister's Daughter* by Julie Hearn and *Twilight* by Stephanie Meyer.

Read More about It:
Booklist: 11/15/03
Horn Book: 10/01/04
Kirkus Reviews: 11/15/03
Publishers Weekly, starred: 12/08/03
School Library Journal: 02/01/04
V.O.Y.A.(Voice of Youth Advocates): 04/01/04

**Delaney, Joseph. 2005. *The Last Apprentice, Book 1: Revenge of the Witch.*
Illustrated by Patrick Arrasmith. New York: HarperCollins. 343p.**

The Story: Twelve-year-old Tom is the seventh son of a seventh son, which makes
him ideally suited to becoming an apprentice to the local Spook, a man who performs
the unique service of ridding the countryside of boggarts, ghosts, and witches. His
Mam, a midwife and healer, encourages him in his new position, though Tom is
already dreading the homesickness and loneliness that are sure to come along with
the job. Everyone has need of the Spook's services now and again, though no one
seeks him out as a friend, since his ways are strange and the deeds he performs
frightening.

Soon Tom is learning the basics of his new master's trade back at the Spook's
house, a weird and not altogether comfortable place where the cooking and cleaning
are done by an invisible tamed boggart and the garden contains three witches. Two of
the witches are dead and buried head first just to be safe, but the third one, named
Mother Malkin, is so evil the Spook warns Tom to stay far away at all times. Tom
learns the different types of boggarts (hairy, hall knocker, and stone chucker) and
witches (malevolent, benign, falsely accused, and unaware) and that professional
spooks rely more on common sense and intuition than on magic. The Spook also
warns him to be careful of girls with pointy shoes, a warning he fails to heed when he
promises to help out Alice, the niece of a local witch named Bony Lizzie.

Alice chases away some bullies who are bothering Tom and in exchange asks
Tom to do her a favor in the future. Tom agrees without thinking and then goes home
for a few days to visit his Mam and strengthen his resolve to continue his apprenticeship. When he returns, the Spook has left on urgent witch business, and Tom is on
his own when Alice calls in her favor. She wants him to take some cakes and drop
them into Mother Malkin's pit. Mother Malkin is the grandmother of Bony Lizzie,
and the family wants to relieve her suffering with a little treat. Tom reluctantly
agrees, but he notices that after he has dropped the second cake into the pit, the bars
that cover the top are bent. The cakes have clearly made Mother Malkin stronger, and
now Tom is afraid she will escape the pit before the Spook returns to help.

Tom asks the house boggart for help, and the spirit shows him a book in the
Spook's library that chronicles how the Spook initially trapped Mother Malkin using
a silver chain. The journal is of little comfort—it describes Mother Malkin as a child-
eating witch who drinks the blood of her victims. The Spook was forced to cage

instead of kill her, because she is so powerful that she could raise herself from the dead by possessing another's body.

That night a frightened but determined Tom goes in search of Mother Malkin, who has indeed escaped the pit. He encounters her on the banks of a river, on her way to Bony Lizzie's. After a brief tussle, Tom manages to knock Mother Malkin into the river with one of the Spook's staffs. The running water and the rowan wood of the staff serve to weaken the witch, who slips under the water and drowns. Tom continues to Bony Lizzie's house, where he has a feeling the witch has kidnapped a village child for Mother Malkin to feed on. He manages to rescue the child, with Alice's help, who is ashamed of what she has done. When the Spook returns and hears what has happened, he warns Tom that Mother Malkin is far more dangerous dead than alive and will be looking for a body to possess in order to get her revenge on the one who killed her.

Soon after, Bony Lizzie uses Alice to lure Tom into a grave, where he is almost buried alive, but again Alice helps him at the last moment, and this time the Spook manages to trap Lizzie instead. Although he is suspicious of Alice, the Spook sends her back home with Tom, to see if Tom's no-nonsense Mam can set her straight. They're there but a few days when Tom senses that Mother Malkin is near. Terrified that she may possess one of his family members, he begins closely monitoring everyone for signs of possession—the dizziness of a person who is newly possessed, and the short bursts of rage a possessed person displays as the evil spirit begins to express itself. He arms himself with iron shavings and salt, the only things he knows that help repel evil.

When Mother Malkin finally shows herself, it is through Snout, the local pig slaughterer who is at the farm helping with the fall slaughter. Using Snout's body, Mother Malkin threatens Tom's brother's wife and baby, but before she can cause any real harm, Alice distracts her with a kick to the stomach while Tom throws the iron and salt on her. Defeated, she leaves Snout's body as a shapeless creeping mass, but before she can escape, the frenzied pigs eat her. Again, Alice has helped save Tom's life, but he still isn't sure she can be trusted. The Spook leaves it up to him to decide her fate, whether she will be allowed to go live with non-witchy relatives or be sentenced to a pit in the Spook's garden. Tom lets her go free, hoping he won't live to regret his decision.

The Message: "There is nothing to fear but fear itself." The things that frighten us most are usually far scarier in our imaginations than in real life. Education and commonsense are more valuable than magic and tricks. Don't be afraid to ask for help if you need it. Never trust a girl in pointy shoes!

Who's It For?: 6th–10th grade. It isn't often that I run across a perfect "scary" book for middle schoolers. It has to be scary enough to satisfy their taste for horror but not so frightening that the story keeps them up at night. *Revenge of the Witch* is one such treasure. That doesn't mean there isn't some very grisly stuff here: blood-drinking, bone-crushing, child-killing monsters and witches and long-dead ghosts of hanged soldiers and murderous husbands who refuse to move on. But the medieval, pastoral setting, the Spook's matter-of-fact tone, and the somewhat comforting employment of traditional folk cures (iron filings and rock salt) will help distance younger readers from their fright.

Why It Rocks:
* **Voice:** The story is told in Tom's first-person voice, simple and spare, infused with a curiosity and dread about the new life on which he is about to embark.
* **Plot:** This is old-fashioned, 'round-the-campfire storytelling reminiscent of the original Grimm's fairy tales, the dark versions where witches didn't hesitate to cook children in ovens and the devil ran free to make unsavory bargains with men. Tom's handwritten journal is appended, complete with a map of the countryside and his notes on binding boggarts and recognizing possession.
* **Pacing:** Each new chapter begins with wonderfully creepy black-and-white woodcut illustrations by Patrick Arrasmith and ends in a cliffhanger. Delaney ratchets up the suspense once the Spook reveals that Mother Malkin is actually more powerful dead than alive and Tom's just killed her!
* **Characterization:** Solid. Tom is a recognizable preteen, wanting to please his parents but also learning his own way. The Spook's commonsense manner and strong work ethic make a nice counterbalance to the chaotic world of specters he is teaching Tom to tame. Alice will keep readers guessing as to her motives and is a good foil to Tom's steadfastness.

Hook It Up With: *Coraline* by Neil Gaiman and *The Ranger's Apprentice, Book One: The Ruins of Gorlan* by John Flanagan.

Read More about It:
Booklist, starred: 08/01/05
Horn Book, starred: 11/01/05
Kirkus Reviews: 08/01/05
Publishers Weekly, starred: 10/10/05
School Library Journal: 11/01/05
V.O.Y.A. (Voice of Youth Advocates): 10/01/05

Fisher, Catherine. 2004. *The Oracle Prophecies, Book 1: The Oracle Betrayed.* New York: HarperCollins. 341p.

The Story: In a Mediterranean civilization that shares characteristics of both ancient Greek and Egyptian cultures, ruthless royal politics force a shy young woman to conquer her fears in order to play a vital role in the naming of a new ruler. Mirany is a member of the Nine, a group of priestesses who serve the god, a being that appears to his people both in scorpion and human form known as the Archon. The priestess Hermia, who holds the highest position as Speaker-for-the-God, rules the Nine. Mirany holds the title of Bearer-of-the-God, the most vulnerable of the positions, since she is responsible for carrying the god in the form of a poisonous scorpion in a wide brass bowl during rituals.

It has not rained for many months, and the current Archon, an old man, has declared that he will sacrifice himself in order to bring rain. The people do not mourn his passing, because they believe that within nine days of his death, his reincarnated soul will pass into the body of an innocent ten-year-old boy, who will become the new Archon. Mirany is in charge of carrying the scorpion that will sting the Archon to death. Only she and Hermia are present when the old man calmly places his hand in the bowl with the scorpion, but the moment Hermia turns away, the man thrusts a scrap of paper into Mirany's hand with the instruction to keep it secret and stay alive. Stunned, Mirany takes the note and reads it later in her room. The note says that the Speaker is corrupt and is not listening to the true voice of the god; instead, she tells the people whatever will most personally benefit her and her consort, the head of the army, General Argelin. Now, the Speaker will choose a new Archon that she and Argelin can control, and it is up to Mirany to find the true Archon. To aid her, she is to look up a musician named Oblek, who will help her in her quest.

Oblek, a cantankerous old man, is being held with the rest of the old Archon's servants and staff, to await his burial. The law says that the ruler's entire household is to be killed and buried with him. Using the strength of her position, Mirany springs Oblek from jail, with the reluctant help of a scribe named Seth, who has his own problems. Seth is a minor archivist in the City of the Dead, the vast necropolis that houses all the tombs of past Archons. He has made a deal with the notorious tomb robber named Jackal to lead the thief to an especially rich intact tomb. In exchange, the man will use his black-market connections to make sure Seth's ailing little sister has fresh water delivered every day.

When Oblek, Mirany, and Seth are safely back at Seth's house, Mirany tells them about the note and conspiracy to place a puppet Archon on the throne. Oblek, close friends with the last Archon, confirms her story by telling them how the Archon made the mistake of questioning Argelin's heavy taxes and discounting Hermia's pronouncements, so they forced him to kill himself by telling the people only his death would bring rain. Mirany leaves Oblek with Seth to go to the mouth of the Oracle, a deep fissure in the earth where Hermia receives her messages from the god. There, she hears the real voice of the god telling her that the new Archon lives in a small desert village called Alectro. Mirany cannot go look for the boy, because she must attend the old Archon's funeral, a nine-day affair that calls for the priestesses to wait on his dead body as it travels through the Nine Houses, where it will be made ready for burial.

Seth reluctantly agrees to go to Alectro with Oblek, though he is worried about putting off his meeting with the Jackal until he returns from the quest. The two, after much trouble and threats on their lives, manage to secure the true Archon, a boy named Alexos who is mostly just thrilled to see his old friend Oblek again. Mirany hides Oblek and Alexos on the rocky hillside below her window after overhearing Hermia and Argelin talking. Somehow they have discovered the plot to put someone other than their choice on the throne, and Hermia knows Mirany is involved. When Hermia drops all pretense with Mirany and demands to know where she has hidden the boy, the god enters Mirany's body and speaks through her, accusing Hermia of betraying him. Hermia is enraged and tells Mirany that her days are numbered. Meanwhile, Seth hides Oblek and Alexos in the City of the Dead, where they are cared for by Kreon, an old albino man who has lived in the tunnels as long as anyone can remember and claims to be kin to the god, the shadow brother who lives underground. Hermia declares Mirany a traitor to the god and the Oracle, saying that her sentence is to be buried alive. Seth meets with the Jackal as planned, but instead of leading him to the treasure he wants, he takes the Jackal to the tomb where Mirany is trapped and promises him that when Alexos is Archon, he will be given a position of power. Once the tomb is sprung and Mirany is saved, everyone splits up and makes their way aboveground and to the Ninth House, where the new Archon is about to be named.

Alexos manages to join the line of the boys being considered, and a masked Speaker, who is not Hermia but the mysterious Rain Goddess, companion to the god, chooses him. Argelin tries to raise the people against him, but Alexos demonstrates his power by making a ruby scorpion pin come alive and finally causing the rain to fall. The grateful people accept him as Archon, but it is not the last time Argelin or Hermia will question his rule.

The Message: Power corrupts. It isn't easy to establish a trust based entirely on faith. There are often many shades of gray between what is right and what is wrong. The means justify the end. Sometimes it is permissible to do many small "wrongs" in order to ensure a big "right."

Who's It For?: 6th–12th grade. There is some ritual violence, including the Archon's death and Mirany's burial. When Oblek and Seth go searching for Alexos, they encounter a village of cutthroats and thieves who would murder them for the clothes on their back and are willing to sell their own children. Alexos himself is an abused child, even though the god inhabits his body. Oblek is an admitted drunk. But the palace politics, with all the literal and figurative backstabbing (Oblek attempts to assassinate Argelin but fails) are probably the most ruthless aspect of the novel.

Why It Rocks:
• **Voice:** A third-person narration, with the viewpoint mostly shared between Mirany and Seth. Each chapter begins with a short first-person prologue marked with a scorpion, which the reader comes to understand is the mysterious voice of the god.
• **Plot:** Along with the suspenseful and politically charged plot, Fisher's building of a Greco-Egyptian world is flawless, from the brass masks the Nine wear, reminiscent of Greek theater masks, to the Archon's elaborate funeral proceedings, like those afforded the pharaohs. The chapters are artfully ordered and themed according to which "House" the Archon's body is in on its way to the tomb.
• **Pacing:** Many of the chapters end in nail-biting cliffhangers that constantly leave Mirany's and Alexos's fate in doubt. This is not a predictable story; in fact, Fisher lays so many pitfalls for her protagonists that it is only when Argelin admits Alexos is his lord on the last page that readers will know for sure the right boy will take the throne.
• **Characterization:** By novel's end, each character has been changed by his or her encounter with the god. Mirany gains faith, Seth learns honesty and responsibility for others, and Oblek learns selflessness. Most teens will easily be able to relate to one or all of these sympathetic, realistically flawed characters.

Hook It Up With: the other volumes of *The Oracle Prophecies* (*Sphere of Secrets, Day of the Scarab*) and *The Singer of All Songs: Chanters of Tremaris, Book One* by Kate Constable.

Read More about It:
Booklist: 02/15/04
Horn Book: 10/01/04
Kirkus Reviews, starred: 02/01/04
Publishers Weekly, starred: 01/19/04
School Library Journal: 03/01/04
V.O.Y.A. (Voice of Youth Advocates): 04/01/04

Horowitz, Anthony. 2005. *Raven's Gate.* New York: Scholastic. 254p.

The Story: Fourteen-year-old Matt Freeman has been in and out of trouble since his parents died, when he was eight. Now he has been involved in a burglary in which a guard was stabbed, and the aunt who took him in has washed her hands of him. Instead of being sentenced to a youth detention center, he is chosen to take part in a government program that sends juvenile offenders to England's rural areas to do farmwork in the fresh air.

Matt's new foster "mother" is Jayne Deverill, a sharp, cruel older woman who has no patience for teenagers. She takes him to her home, Hive Hall, a dreary, sodden place in a tiny village called Lesser Malling. There, he is set to work, but it's not long before he senses something very wrong about the place. First, there are the disquieting dreams of four other teens calling out to him from a great distance whom he can never seem to reach. Then, there is the strange fact that when he runs errands for Mrs. Deverill in Lesser Malling, all of the odd, disfigured inhabitants seem to know who he is. Finally, fed up with the cruel old woman and the weird village, he tries to run away one night, but every road leads back to Mrs. Deverill's front yard.

Giving up in frustration, Matt explores the nearby forest, where he finds an abandoned nuclear power plant and encounters local hunter Tom Burgess, who appears to be the only normal person in Lesser Malling. Tom warns him that Mrs. Deverill and the people of the village are up to no good, and he will tell Matt the whole story and help him escape if he comes to Tom's house tomorrow. He also gives Matt a key talisman that resists the enchantment that causes each road to end at Hive Hall. But when Matt arrives at Tom's farm the next day, the house is ransacked, the man is dead, and the only clue to his murder is the phrase "Raven's Gate" scrawled on the wall.

Matt tries to alert the police, but Mrs. Deverill and the other villagers create a masterful cover-up and warn Matt against trying to escape. He doesn't give up but instead uses the talisman to ride his bike into Greater Malling, where he meets local reporter Richard Cole and tries telling him his bizarre tale. The man doesn't believe Matt, and before he knows it, Mrs. Deverill has shown up to escort him home in her car. Matt despairs of ever getting away, especially when a concerned detective who handled his case comes to check on him but mysteriously loses control of his car on the way home and is killed. In desperation, he follows Mrs. Deverill one night and witnesses what appears to be an occult meeting of all the Lesser Malling villagers at the abandoned power plant.

When Matt accidentally trips an alarm and alerts the coven to his presence, Mrs. Deverill raises a pair of demon dogs out of thin air that chase him through the woods. He falls into a bog but is saved by Richard Cole, who was intrigued by Matt's story after all and came driving by to look at the power plant. Cole takes Matt back to his apartment, where Matt tells him his life story, including a secret few people know: eight-year-old Matt saw his parents' death before it happened and has had flashes of precognition all of his life. Furthermore, he believes that the people of Lesser Malling are witches and are plotting something shady at the abandoned power plant.

Cole is skeptical, but the next day he arranges meetings with Michael Marsh, the government scientist who designed and built Omega One, the closed power plant, and Professor Dravid, a historian who works for the Natural History Museum in London. While Marsh assures them that there is no way the plant could ever function again and that their doubts are unfounded, Professor Dravid, when he hears they are looking for any information about "Raven's Gate," shares frightening information that confirms all of Matt's fears. Dravid is a member of the Nexus, a secret society whose one purpose is to keep a group of ancient evil beings called the Old Ones from ever finding their way into this world. Raven's Gate is an ancient site where the Old Ones could enter with help from their followers in this dimension. Dravid believes that the residents of Lesser Malling are practicing black magic in order to open the Gate and intend to use Matt as their human sacrifice. According to legend, five children originally vanquished the Old Ones, and Professor Dravid also believes that Matt is the first of a new five who will help keep the Old Ones in check.

Suddenly, Matt understands his strange dreams about four others calling him. But before he or Richard Cole can process this new information, Professor Dravid is murdered by an invisible assassin and the dinosaur fossils in the museum where they are meeting spring to unbelievable, terrifying life and begin attacking Matt and Cole. Matt manages to escape, only to be captured and drugged by Mrs. Deverill. He wakes in the power plant on a sacrificial slab as the coven gathers to open the gate. He is relieved to see Cole nearby, alive but also trapped. The group is lead by Marsh, who has secretly been supplying the plant with radioactive material in order to harness nuclear energy to help the coven open the Gate.

Just as Marsh is about to stab Matt, the boy's sleeping power suddenly surges through him. He frees himself and Cole, and they escape the building just as a monstrous hand begins to come through the shimmering portal in the floor. Marsh is thrilled that his plan is working, but the energy raised is too great, and the reactor explodes, killing everyone in the coven and falling back in on the Old Ones, again sealing the Gate shut. Matt and Cole get back to Cole's apartment safely, where a Mr. Fabian, another member of the Nexus, meets them. He informs them that the Nexus has arranged for Cole to be Matt's guardian and that the organization will provide both of them with whatever they need materially, because they believe that Matt is one of the fabled five and the war against the Old Ones is just beginning.

The Message: Good always prevails over evil. Situations and people aren't always what they seem. If you can keep your head while being attacked by reanimated dinosaur bones, you can survive just about anything.

Who's It For?: 7th–12th grade, although reviewers vary widely on this one. The several gruesome deaths, including the slashing of Professor Dravid's throat and the horrible (but deserving) demise of Mrs. Deverill in a clear blue vat of radioactive acid, kick this one into seventh grade and above, but the gore isn't dwelt on, so recommend to younger readers if you think your audience can handle it.

Why It Rocks:
- **Voice:** The novel is written in omniscent third person, mostly from Matt's point of view. Horowitz's prose is industrious and not too detailed, intended to get the job done as the author moves on with the crackerjack plot.
- **Plot:** Tight and incredibly exciting, this marvelous plot rockets along at smoldering pace without giving short shrift to any of Horowitz's imaginative story elements. Come on, you have to give it up for an author who combines witchcraft with nuclear energy. Outstanding!
- **Pacing:** Just understand that you'll need to have the rest of the series on hand, because readers are going to easily tear through this one in a single sitting.
- **Characterization:** Matt is a sympathetic character rounded by his genuine anguish over his parents' deaths and both his desire to and fear of uncovering his hidden talents. Secondary characters are stereotypical, but Mrs. Deverill is a wonderfully wicked, if somewhat one-note, villain.

Hook It Up With: the rest of the *Gatekeeper* series by Anthony Horowitz and *The Supernaturalist* by Eoin Colfer.

Read More about It:
Booklist, starred: 07/01/05
Horn Book: 10/01/05
Publishers Weekly: 06/20/05
School Library Journal: 07/01/05
V.O.Y.A. (Voice of Youth Advocates): 10/01/05

Pattou, Edith. 2003. *East.* **New York: Harcourt. 498p.**

The Story: A sumptuous retelling of the Norwegian fairy tale "East of the Sun and West of the Moon," *East* is the story of a young girl in 16th-century Norway who pits herself against the iron will of the evil Troll Queen in order to win the heart of the man she loves. Rose is the youngest in her family of eight siblings and has always been her mother's greatest trial because of her habit of wandering off. Her mother, a deeply superstitious woman, believes this is because Rose was a "North-born," born pointed toward the direction of travelers and troublemakers. The one exception to Rose's adventurous personality is her talent for sewing and weaving, a hobby usually attributed to hearth and home-oriented Eastborns.

When Rose is a teenager, the family falls on hard times. Her father, a mapmaker by trade, has never been a successful farmer, and after a few years of bad weather, he unable to pay their rent. Just as they are about to be evicted, Rose's elder sister, Sara, becomes very sick. As the family tries to decide what to do, they are visited by a huge white bear. The animal, speaking with great difficulty, offers them riches and Sara's health if they will give him Rose. He gives them seven days to decide, then leaves. Rose, reluctant to leave her family but eager for adventure, agrees to go with the bear when he returns.

The bear takes Rose far away to a wondrous castle carved into the base of a mountain. It is filled with every comfort known to humans, including a beautiful loom for Rose to weave on. As the days pass, Rose begs the bear to tell her why she has been brought to this place, but his only reply is that she will come to no harm. Shortly after she comes to stay, Rose notices that every night after she goes to sleep, she is visited by an invisible presence that climbs into bed with her. She suspects it is the white bear "without his fur," but he never speaks or touches her, and she feels powerless to speak to him or light a lamp. Instead, she weaves a soft nightshirt of the bear's shed fur and leaves it on the bed for the stranger to find.

What Rose doesn't know is that the white bear is a prince enchanted by the Troll Queen who wants him for her husband. She stole him from his parents when he was very small, and her father, the King, punished her by turning him into a white bear for 150 years. To break the enchantment, the bear must get a maiden to live with him of her free will for a year without once seeing his human form, which he changes back into at night. At the end of the sentence, if the bear is unable to meet the set terms, the Troll Queen would be allowed to take him as her husband. It is she who has set him up in the mountain castle with every luxury to wait out his sentence.

Back at the farm, the family has prospered. The farm's landlord, a man named Soren, has become enchanted with Father's old maps and offers to set him up in business again. He also brings a doctor for Sara. Meanwhile, Rose has become so homesick that she asks the bear for permission to visit her family. He allows her to return home for one month, but warns her to tell no one about her life in the mountain. She agrees, but while she is home, her mother overhears Rose tell her brother, Neddy, about the nighttime visits. So she gives her daughter a candle and flint as she prepares to leave, in the hope that she will use it to see who is in her bed.

Rose returns to the mountain, and as the days and months pass, she becomes closer to the bear, telling him stories and playing him music. He still won't tell her why she is there, and finally Rose can't stand not knowing who he is any longer. She lights her mother's candle in the middle of the night and sees lying beside her a handsome young man with golden hair. The wax from the candle drips and wakes him. The instant he sees her, the castle disappears and the two find themselves alone in the snow. He barely has time to explain the enchantment and that the Troll Queen lives "east of the sun and west of the moon" before they hear the sounds of her sleigh. Then he is gone.

Rose is devastated by what she has done and resolves to find and rescue him. She begins an epic journey across arctic lands, aided on her way by a kindly mother and daughter named Sofi and Estelle, a drunken Viking named Thor, and finally, an Inuit shaman woman named Malmo. It is Malmo who guides her to the legendary ice bridge that connects the land of men to the land of trolls. Rose hikes through extreme cold and snow to the Queen's ice palace. There, she poses as one of the many human slaves the trolls keep to gain entrance, and soon she discovers that she has arrived in the midst of preparation for the Queen's wedding to the human man Rose knows as the white bear.

Rose creates a mask and gloves that mimic the hard white skin of the trolls so that she can attend the wedding in disguise. The Queen has drugged the prince into forgetting his past, but he is slowly regaining his memory and begins to remember his life with Rose as the white bear. At the wedding, he asks the Queen to take part in a tradition from his country—to wash an article of his clothing to show her allegiance to him. She agrees, and he hands her his old nightshirt stained with candle wax. Although she scrubs and scrubs, she is unable to get it out. Rose steps out of the crowd and offers to try. The Queen realizes who she is, despite her mask, and allows her to try, confident that she will fail also. Rose, who knows what the substance is, uses heated water and washes the garment clean. The Queen is enraged and strikes out with a bolt of fire, which causes her ice castle to collapse. The prince shelters Rose, and they both survive, making their way back to the land of men with a few other human survivors. Eventually, Rose is reunited with her family, the white bear remembers who he was (a French prince named Charles), and they marry, living happily ever after.

The Message: Believe in yourself and follow your heart. Your intuition rarely leads you astray. Nothing is stronger than the love of family. Everything worth doing is worth doing well. "Nothing ventured, nothing gained."

Who's It For?: 6th–12th grade. This title can go young because there is no sex or strong language and little violence. Thor the Viking is a heavy drinker who becomes verbally abusive as the result of too much ale, but the only truly disturbing scene is when Rose discovers the "killing field," the icy plain where the trolls leave their human slaves to freeze to death after they can no longer work.

Why It Rocks:
•   **Voice:** Pattou tells her reimagined tale through multiple first-person voices, including Rose; Father; Rose's brother, Neddy; the White Bear; and the Troll Queen, giving the traditional story a new richness by providing many different perspectives of familiar events.
•   **Plot:** Pattou stayed true to the bones of the original tale while fleshing it out with real historical detail that is utterly fascinating. In her author note, Pattou lists the areas she had to research in the writing of *East*: "weaving, compasses, mapmaking and its history, seamanship, Scandinavian languages, Norway in the sixteenth century, the Inuit people, Norse mythology, everything to do with the Arctic, and of course, polar bears." Readers not only get a romantic adventure but also receive the added bonus of learning how to use both a Viking compass and an Inuit story knife!
•   **Pacing:** Very quick for such a long novel. The short chapters that switch perspective with each chapter change keep the story moving at a fast clip.
•   **Characterization:** Pattou keeps each voice fresh and distinct as each character is changed by lessons of love and magic. Every reader will be able to find a character with which to identify within these pages, whether it is the headstrong Rose, practical Neddy, or the lonely, lovelorn white bear.

Hook It Up With: *Zel* by Donna Jo Napoli and *Daughter of the Forest* by Juliet Marillier.

Read More about It:
Booklist, starred: 09/01/03
Horn Book: 04/01/04
Publishers Weekly: 07/28/03
School Library Journal, starred: 12/01/03
V.O.Y.A. (Voice of Youth Advocates): 12/01/03

Pratchett, Terry. 2003. *The Wee Free Men.* **New York: HarperCollins. 263p.**

The Story: Nine-year-old Tiffany Aching comes from a long line of Achings who have farmed on the Chalk, a series of rolling hills perfect for sheep herding, forever. Her family lives and works on Home Farm, rented from the Baron, the village lord. Tiffany is proud of her family's history and especially of her Granny Aching, who died two short years ago but was renowned throughout the countryside for her wisdom and strength. Tiffany has decided lately that she would like to become a witch in Granny Aching's memory because although no one ever labeled her as such, Tiffany knows Granny had a special gift when it came to working with animals and the land. When her sticky little brother, Wentworth, is almost snatched off the riverbank by a fabled monster known as Jenny Greenteeth, Tiffany senses trouble of the supernatural sort and heads to the village to look for answers. She visit the tents of the traveling teachers, who sell education just like any other ware, and it is there that she encounters Miss Tick. Miss Tick is a real practicing witch who quickly disabuses Tiffany of all the myths she believes to be true about witches. For instance, real witches never use magic unless absolutely necessary, broomstick riding is cold and impractical, and often the most important tool a witch can carry is a piece of string. Miss Tick is impressed with Tiffany's commonsense but worried to hear about the appearance of Jenny Greenteeth. Apparently, the monster's presence heralds a colliding of worlds that is liable to loose much worse creatures on the people of the Chalk if action isn't taken to stop it. Miss Tick tells Tiffany to sit tight while she flies for reinforcements, leaving her talking toad to advise Tiffany should matters become worse in her absence.

Tiffany thoughtfully goes back to the farm and her chores, wondering if there is anything she can do to help stop the collision. She's not there long before her mother comes home to announce that Wentworth has gone missing. While the whole village is out looking, Tiffany is left to watch the farm. Shaken, she tries to go about her chores but discovers that they have mysteriously been done for her. When she orders who or what has been doing her chores to show themselves, she is confronted by hundreds of tiny blue men with red hair and braided beards called the Nac Mac Feegles, or the Wee Free Men.

These pictsies are tiny, absolutely fearless warriors with Scottish accents, proud of their reputation for "stealin' an' drinkin' an' fightin.'" Their hidden clan had a close bond with Granny Aching, and since her death they have been searching for the person who will inherit Granny's witch or "hag" mantle. They need to find this person because they too have sensed the collision between the worlds and need the help of a "bigjob" human to help fight it. Tiffany, who understands immediately that these are the creatures to help her find Wentworth, pretends that she is the new hag, though she has no idea what they are talking about. When she tells them about Wentworth, they seem to think that he has been stolen away by the evil Queen of the Fairies, whose world is the one threatening to collide with this one. Tiffany leaves a note for her parents, then leaves with the Feegles, armed only with an iron skillet and the talking toad.

The Feegles take her to meet the "kelda," their mother and eldest member of the clan. She tells Tiffany that Wentworth was indeed taken by the Queen and that to get him back, she will have to find the "place where time doesn't fit," which is the doorway to the Queen's world. Tiffany finds the transparent door among a set of ancient standing stones on the Chalk. Once she and the Feegles go through, they find themselves in a cold and strangely unfinished world where even the trees and grass look half formed. The Feegles explain that the Queen doesn't have the power to make the world more real, so she butts up against other worlds and sends her monster minions in to steal what she needs to furnish this dismal place. Time also moves slower here, and if they can't escape, their own world will have aged and passed them by while they stay the same.

Shortly after they enter, they are attacked by a pack of frightening "grimhounds" and shapeless "dromes," dream-spinning creatures that trap their prey within a dream of their own making. If a person eats anything in the dream, he or she is trapped forever and becomes the food of the drome. The Feegles use a high-pitched bagpipe to chase away the dogs and manage to drag Tiffany back into reality when she becomes trapped in a drome. Once released, she is surprised to discover the Baron's son, Roland, wandering in the woods. He mysteriously disappeared from Tiffany's village a year ago, and now Tiffany understands he was another victim of kidnapping by the Queen. She convinces Roland to help her find her brother by promising to help him escape, a promise she is beginning to doubt she can keep.

They eventually find Wentworth on a rock surrounded by candy, but before Tiffany can rescue him, the Queen appears and her smooth talk almost lulls Tiffany into leaving him again. But she quickly recovers her wits and smashes the Queen with the skillet. At this point, Tiffany, Wentworth, the Feegles, and Roland enter a frightening and confusing dreamscape controlled by the Queen. They tumble through several settings, including a hot summer field, a ship at sea, and a raging storm. Throughout it all, Tiffany tries to separate what is real from what isn't. She sees a vision of Granny encouraging her and suddenly understands that the key to the defeating the Queen is "to wake up. Waking up is harder. I have woken up and I am real. . . . You cannot fool me anymore."

Suddenly flush with the power of her realization, Tiffany pushes the vanquished Queen back into her world with a warning to stay put. And just like that, she and all her friends are returned to the hills of the Chalk, safe. Miss Tick has returned with fellow witches Miss Ogg and Mistress Weatherwax a bit too late to help, but when the powerful Mistress Weatherwax hears about Tiffany's adventure, she promises Tiffany a witch apprenticeship when she is a bit older and grants her an invisible witch's hat to wear in the meantime.

The Message: Be observant. Be an active participant in your life. Never give up, even in the face of great adversity. What doesn't kill you makes you stronger. If you're not always sure of yourself, "fake it 'til you make it."

Who's It For?: 6th–12th grade. Don't let the age of the protagonist fool you. Tiffany may be only nine years old, but the clever dialogue, time-twisty dream sequences, and themes of love and loss can and will appeal to older teens as much as younger ones. While there are danger and intrigue in the world of the Queen, there is only offstage death and little violence (unless you count Tiffany's deadly aim with the skillet).

Why It Rocks:
• **Voice:** Pratchett tells his novel in third person, mostly from Tiffany's practical point-of-view, flavored with the outrageous Scottish burr of the Feegles (Wee Free Men) that simply begs to be read aloud. Before you know it, you'll be shoutin', "Aye, crivens!" next time you're cut off in traffic.
• **Plot:** There are many fun and interesting details and subplots to this novel that had to be dropped in the interest of space, including Tiffany's flashbacks of dramatic episodes in Granny Aching's life where she performed heroic deeds or meted out justice and humorous insights into the chaotic lives of the Nac Mac Feegles, including their fear of lawyers and love of strong drink. Fans of the prolific Pratchett will note the novel takes place in his familiar Discworld.
• **Pacing:** Fairly quick in the first half of the book, but once Tiffany crosses over into the land of Fairy, the potentially confusing dream sequences and Tiffany's longer internal dialogues slow the action quite a bit. This is the point where more reluctant readers may become mired down.
• **Characterization:** Girl power all the way, from tough-talking Granny and no-nonsense Tiffany to the matriarchal Kelda, who rules her drunken sons with a tiny iron fist. Serious Tiffany does learn how to be more flexible and also when to push the envelope, Granny-style.

Hook It Up With: the other books in the *Tiffany Aching Adventure* series (*A Hat Full of Sky, Wintersmith*) and the *Septimus Heap* series by Angie Sage (*Magyk, Flyte,* and *Physik*).

Read More about It:
Booklist: 04/15/03
Horn Book: 10/01/03
Kirkus Reviews, starred: 04/15/03
Publishers Weekly, starred: 05/12/03
School Library Journal, starred: 05/01/03
V.O.Y.A. (Voice of Youth Advocates): 08/01/03

Shinn, Sharon. 2004. *The Safe-Keeper's Secret.* New York: Penguin Group. 222p.

The Story: Late at night, in the small medieval village of Tambleham, a mysterious rider leaves a baby at the doorstep of a local wise woman named Damiana, the village safe-keeper. Her trade is listening to and keeping the secrets, some trivial, some serious, of the villagers she serves. When the rider comes, she herself is giving birth to her first and only child. Her sister, Angeline, the safe-keeper in the neighboring town, is helping her sister with her labor and is the one to answer the door. She accepts the baby from the richly dressed rider, who reveals that he himself is safe-keeper to the king. He whispers the secret of the baby's lineage to Angeline, who promises to tell only Damiana. The next day, his body is found on the road. He has committed suicide to protect the identity and location of the baby. Damiana takes the baby and raises it along with her true child. The villagers gossip that the baby is an illegitimate heir to the king, but Damiana, true to her calling, says nothing more about the matter.

As the two children, Reed and Fiona, grow up as brother and sister, both wonder about the identity of their respective fathers. Reed has heard the talk that he is the king's bastard, while Fiona only knows that her mother has reasoned that her father's identity isn't important because Fiona has so many other loving adults around her that function as her family. These include her aunt, Angeline, and her mother's closest friend, Thomas, a truth-teller by trade. His job is telling people the truths that are hard for their friends and family to tell them, and to serve as a traveling source of news as he moves from village to village. Fiona has never liked Thomas much because since she was a little girl, he has insisted that it is not her fate to grow up to be a safe-keeper like her mother, for she is too passionate to passively listen to a wrong without trying to right it. Another adult instrumental in Fiona's life is Isadora, the kingdom's dream-maker. While the kingdom has many safe-keepers and truth-tellers, there is only one dream-maker at any one time, usually an older woman who has experienced much personal tragedy but whose very presence makes other people's wishes come true.

When Fiona and Reed are 15, they spend the summer with Angeline, Fiona learning more herb lore at her aunt's side, while Reed, who can't seem to maintain an interest in any one subject for longer than a season, is apprenticed to Damiana's friend Robert Bayliss, a kind and wealthy merchant. Robert's frail wife, Victoria, has been sickly since their engagement, when she was swept away in a boating accident and never fully recovered from her ordeal. Near the end of the summer, Robert reveals to Fiona that he and Victoria are unable to have children because of her frailty and that Reed has become like a son to him. Meanwhile, Thomas visits Angeline's with the news that King Marcus, who refuses to name his only child, Princess Lirabel, as his heir because she is a woman, has just had a new baby boy by his latest wife, but Thomas and other truth-tellers are quite sure that the king is not the baby's true father.

When it is time for Fiona and Reed to go home to Damiana, Angeline reveals a sad truth: their mother is dying, and she sent them away for the summer so they wouldn't have to witness it. Devastated, Fiona and Reed rush home to tend to their mother in her final days. Before her death, Damiana reveals the identity of her father to Fiona, telling her she will know when the time is right to share that information with Reed, her closest friend and confidante. After their mother dies, Fiona begins service as Tambleham's safe-keeper, while Reed continues to flit from trade to trade, mastering many but sticking with nothing.

Over the next few years, Fiona excels at safe-keeping, although she often meddles behind the scenes in order to help people, as Thomas had always warned she would. When she and Reed are 18, the king visits Tambleham, looking for a bastard son he has heard lives there. He has long since driven away the woman who bore him the child that was not his own, and he still refuses to name his daughter heir. To Reed's surprise, Fiona steps forward and tells her secret: that she was the baby brought by the rider and that Reed is actually Damiana's true son. Thomas finishes her announcement with one of his own: Reed's father is Robert. Damiana and he had had a brief affair when he believed Victoria was lost, and Damiana never told so as not to bring shame to his family.

The king is finally persuaded to name Lirabel as his heir, and the new queen tells Fiona she would like her to join her at the palace so they can get to know each other. It is Reed who will continue as safe-keeper, since it is his legacy as his mother's true child. Just before Fiona travels to court, she is visited by a middle-aged noblewoman named Melinda, who tells her that she asked Isadora to give her life meaning because she had suffered so much, starting with when she was forced to give away her only child, a bastard of the king, when it was an infant. Fiona realizes that not only has the dream-maker power passed from Isadora to this woman, but also that Melinda is her own true mother.

The Message: Some secrets are meant to be kept, while others are meant to be told, and it is important to understand the difference. The truth has many sides, depending on who is doing the telling. Magic doesn't have to be supernatural; everyday life with a loving extended family is a type of magic in and of itself. "Be it ever so humble, there's no place like home."

Who's It For?: 7th–10th grade and could have gone even younger were it not for one terrible secret told to Fiona by a village woman: that the woman's teenage daughter is carrying her husband's child. Other than the question of nonmarital birth (Fiona is ridiculed by another child for being a "bastard"), that is the only sexual content that mars an otherwise cozy and domestic fireside fantasy rich in the detail of everyday medieval life and rituals.

Why It Rocks:
• **Voice:** The third-person narration is told from Fiona's point of view in a close, confidential tone that is nicely suited to the topic of the text.
• **Plot:** Lyrically written in the tradition of Robin McKinley and Meredith Ann Pierce, the gently told plot focuses on the ordinary "magic" of daily life, with all its tangled truths, mysterious secrets, and hopeful dreams. Even the chronological order of the story follows the seasons, emphasizing the "everyday magic" of nature.
• **Pacing:** The setting is homey and sweet, but the shock and dramatic unveiling of different secrets throughout the story add the necessary spice that keeps readers moving through this deliberately paced and artfully plotted novel.
• **Characterization:** Rich and warm, with especially well-drawn portraits of all

the secondary characters. Most readers will come away from this story wishing for a wise, witchy Aunt Angeline of their own! In addition, both Fiona and Reed learn and grow from the secrets they have learned about themselves and the secrets they have been trusted to keep.

Hook It Up With: Shinn's two companion novels to this one, *The Truth-Teller's Tale* and *The Dream-Maker's Magic; Spindle's End* by Robin McKinley; and *Juniper* by Monica Furlong.

Read More about It:
Booklist: 04/15/04
Horn Book: 10/01/04
Kirkus Reviews, starred: 05/01/04
School Library Journal: 06/01/04
V.O.Y.A. (Voice of Youth Advocates): 06/01/04

Stroud, Jonathan. 2003. *The Bartimaeus Trilogy, Book. 1: The Amulet of Samarkand.* New York: Miramax. 462p.

The Story: In an alternate version of London, where magicians make up the Parliament, the prime minister is the top wizard, and the non-magical "commoners" are beginning to chafe against their spell-casting superiors, 12-year-old Nathaniel is in over his head. Apprenticed to a sour, minor government magician named Arthur Underwood, Nathaniel has lived with Underwood and his wife since he was 5 years old and sold into apprenticeship by his birth parents. When he was 10, a rising star of the British magical government, Simon Lovelace, publicly humiliated him. Lovelace hung Nathaniel upside down in midair and had him spanked because he had dared to talk back to him. Nathaniel swore one day he would become a powerful magician and get revenge on Lovelace, and he began studying furiously in secret, acquiring, summoning, and conjuring skills far beyond what someone his age should know. Using a "scrying" glass to spy on Lovelace, Nathaniel happened to witness the ambitious magician illegally purchase a powerful magical object, the famous Amulet of Samarkand. Now, he has summoned a 5,000-year-old djinni named Bartimaeus to aid him in a dangerous mission: steal the amulet and expose Lovelace as a thief.

Bartimaeus, like all other djinnis, demons, imps, horlas, and afrits, are vulnerable to the summonings of human magicians. Bound by incantations, pentacles, and spells, they are made to do the bidding of the person who has summoned them, be it the building of a city, the waging of war, or the spanking of a small boy. These shape-changing spirits, invisible to commoners, who are denied the special lenses that allow magicians to see them, are the basis of all the ruling magician class's power. Bartimaeus, a mid-level djinni whose personality is a cross between Obi Wan Kenobi and Monty Python, is not pleased to have to do the bidding of such a small, scrawny magician, and he's even more upset when he hears that he must steal something of such value from such a powerful magician as Lovelace.

The balance of power shifts, though, when Bartimaeus, purely by chance, happens to overhear the fact that "Nathaniel" is indeed his new master's birth name. In this world, magicians keep their birth names a deep secret because the knowledge of someone's birth name is a source of great power to anyone who knows it. If a demon ever discovers the name of its master, it is able to turn any spell cast upon it right back at the spell caster. When Bartimaeus begins to use Nathaniel's name to deflect his commands, Nathaniel works a time-sensitive charm on an old tobacco tin that will imprison Bartimaeus within its close quarters if Nathaniel gets hurt or goes missing.

After much grumbling and trouble, Bartimaeus secures the amulet, and Nathaniel hides it in his clueless master's study for safekeeping. Bartimaeus continues to spy on Lovelace and discovers that he is plotting something big that involves an upcoming magicians' conference and the amulet, which he is desperate to get back. He also gets into a tangle with two of his old enemies, the demons Farqual and Jabor, who are in Lovelace's service, but not before he is also able to learn that Lovelace hired an assassin to steal the amulet from the government official who was in charge of watching over it, murdering the man in the process. As Nathaniel ponders how he can best use this information to expose Lovelace, his own master discovers that he has been performing summonings on his own, furiously takes away all of his magical tools, and locks him in his room.

Meanwhile, Lovelace has arrived at the Underwood home, demanding the amulet back. His servants Farqual and Jabor have informed him that a djinni named Bartimaeus stole it, and he has tracked Bartimaeus to this very house. Underwood, completely baffled, orders Lovelace out but reconsiders when Lovelace threatens him with his greater power. Nathaniel, freed by Bartimaeus and suffering from a painful conscience, walks into Underwood's study and announces he is the one at fault, just as Lovelace triumphantly finds his prize. Lovelace smirks and orders Jabor to kill them both and burn the house to the ground. Bartimaeus is able to save Nathaniel, but Underwood and his wife, who was the only person who ever showed Nathaniel any kindness, are killed. Nathaniel is devastated but even more determined to bring down Lovelace.

Nathaniel and Bartimaeus spend the night in an abandoned building, only to discover from the next day's morning paper that Nathaniel has been implicated as the one who started the Underwood fire. But they also happen upon the date and location of Lovelace's upcoming conference, to which he has invited all the members of Parliament, including the prime minister himself, Rupert Devereaux. Nathaniel and Bartimaeus make their way to the countryside from the city, hijacking a grocery van and disguising themselves as the drivers to get into Heddleman Hall, the great mansion where Lovelace's conference is to take place. The two, not without some trouble, manage to join everyone else as they begin to gather in a great central meeting hall.

While Bartimaeus was initially casing the Hall, he discovered Lovelace's plan. Lovelace intends to call up a demon so deadly that it can easily destroy everyone in the room, except himself, since the amulet protects him. Once he has no other competition, he will appoint himself the new prime minister. Lovelace begins to address the group, but before Nathaniel can approach him, he blows an ancient summoning horn and a giant portal opens in the middle of the room. A tremendous being begins to come through, utterly huge and translucent. When the other magicians realize that Lovelace is staging a coup, they try to battle the demon, but its power is so great that it reverses all of their spells.

Nathaniel tries to grab the amulet away from Lovelace, who shoves him aside and orders the demon, Ramuthra, to destroy Nathaniel first. But Bartimaeus, assuming the shape of Lovelace's girlfriend, distracts him so that Nathaniel can make another grab at the amulet, this one successful. In short order, Lovelace is swallowed by his own demon and Nathaniel chants a counter summon, sending Ramuthra back to the void, and humbly hands the amulet to the prime minister; thus normalcy is restored. Nathaniel is rewarded with an auspicious apprenticeship under the Minister of Security, while Bartimaeus is happily discharged from service. But tensions are still brewing between the commoners and the magicians as Britain continues to use demons to wage war against other countries and maintain law in its own and the commoners begin to raise a Resistance movement intended to bring down the magical class system once and for all.

The Message: Be careful for what you wish for. It just might come true. Humility is a valuable quality. Know your limits in order to maintain control of a situation instead of allowing an overwhelming situation to control you. Power corrupts.

Who's It For?: 6th–12th grade. Underwood and his wife's killings take place offstage, as do other deaths and/or murders that are mentioned. Younger readers may not understand all the historical and literary references Bartimaeus makes, but that won't keep them from enjoying the engaging plot.

Why It Rocks:
• **Voice:** The story is told in alternating chapters between Bartimaeus's first-person narration and Nathaniel's third-person point of view. While Nathaniel's chapters are compelling, it is Bartimaeus's verbose and witty voice that will ultimately charm readers. Keeping his audience apprised of his archaic references through a series of riotously funny footnotes, B. is one of the most well-written, well-traveled, and well-read voices in YA literature today (in both the fantasy AND realistic realms).
• **Plot:** Definitely of the Harry Potter school, with wizard training and apprenticeships, but Stroud adds an additional intriguing political layer that becomes more apparent in subsequent sequels.
• **Pacing:** Stroud builds tension nicely as Nathaniel gets closer and closer to his goal of utterly destroying Lovelace, but he allows Bartimaeus ample space to show off his considerable shape-changing powers. Two especially memorable scenes include an investigative foray into a magic shop that goes terribly wrong and a daring escape from a seemingly impossible trap set by some of the government magicians.
• **Characterization:** While Bartimaeus is the shining sun that the rest of the characters stand in the shadow of, Stroud also does a wonderful job of developing Nathaniel's character by showing how his natural boyish wonder is leached away and

replaced by jealousy and a dark hunger for power as a result of his loveless raising and training.

Hook It Up With: the other two books in the *Bartimaeus Trilogy, The Golem's Eye* and *Ptolemy's Gate;* and Megan Whelan Turner's *The Thief* and its sequels, *The Queen of Attolia* and *The King of Attolia.*

Read More about It:
Booklist, starred: 09/01/03
Horn Book: 04/01/04
Kirkus Reviews: 10/01/03
Publishers Weekly, starred: 07/21/03
School Library Journal: 01/01/04
V.O.Y.A. (Voice of Youth Advocates): 12/01/03

Wooding, Chris. 2005. *Poison.* New York: Scholastic. 273p.

The Story: Sixteen-year-old Poison has straight black hair, "shocking" violet eyes, and a sharp tongue. She lives in the village of Gull, deep in the Black Marshes, with her father, stepmother, and little sister, Azalea, the only person she loves. Poison has always had a contrary attitude, but her cynicism has been deepened by daily warfare with her stepmother and the gloomy surroundings in which she spends her days. Her only friend is another village outsider, an old storyteller named Fleet. She often scoffs at his stories, but Fleet tells her that life and story are one and that the same rules apply; they are just more numerous and complicated. Poison will come to find this to be true when her own adventure is initiated by a tragic event: Azalea is stolen from her crib by an evil phaerie and replaced by a dull, dark-eyed changeling.

Fleet advises her to keep the changeling in the hope that someday the phaeries will return her own sister, but Poison refuses, instead vowing to go all the way to the Phaerie King to get her sister back. The next day, she hitches a ride out of Gull with a gruff peddler named Bram, who takes her to Shieldtown, where she secures directions to a "passing place" between the Realm of Man and the Realm of Phaerie from a shady character named Lamprey. Poison is dismayed to discover that the Phaerie gate is guarded by Maeb, the Bone Witch, a fanged, warty creature who is both blind and deaf but whose strong sense of smell is enough to locate intruders for her cooking pot. The witch does catch Poison, but Maeb's timid housekeeper, a girl named Peppercorn, and her clever cat, Andersen, along with Bram, work with Poison to plan a daring attack that ends with Maeb, not Poison, in the cooking pot.

The small group enters the Realm of Phaerie, where they meet a froglike creature, named Myrrk, who uses a fire to signal for the Phaerie King's coach to take them to the palace. Myrrk reminds Poison that there are rules to be followed if she wants her sister back, and when she asks too many questions, he tells her she must find the mysterious Hierophant if she wants answers. When they get to the palace, they are met by Scriddle, the King's secretary, and Aelthar, the Phaerie King. Aelthar tells Poison that if she goes to the castle of the spider woman Lady Asinastra and steals her two-pronged dagger and brings it back to him, he will return her sister. After a horrifying experience that includes facing giant man-eating spiders and a terrifying audience with Asinastra herself, Poison does just that. But she overhears Aelthar tell Scriddle to kill them all because he has more important business he must attend to with the Hierophant. Aelthar and the rulers of other Realms are anxiously waiting for the Hierophant to finish his latest work, because from what Poison can gather, he exerts total control over what happens in the Realms with his pen and paper.

Furious at the betrayal, Poison and company escape Scriddle by piggybacking on Aelthar's magic as he spirits away to the Hierophant's castle. There, Poison is surprised to see Fleet waiting for them in the Hierophant's vast library. He reveals that he is an Antiquarian, a "biographer of the Realms." His job is to collect stories "and, where necessary, help them along." The endless library they are in holds millions of stories, from the dawn of time until the present, though lately Fleet has been watching and assisting Poison's story. Poison is confused at how her life can be both her life and a story, so Fleet takes her to meet the Hierophant, creator of all stories.

When Poison meets the Hierophant, he confirms her worst suspicions: her whole life is a fiction spun by the Hierophant, and she is just character in his story. Poison can't bear the fact that she is essentially a puppet, and she sinks into a deep depression. She sleeps for days, only to awaken and discover everyone, even Fleet and Aelthar, are sick and wasting away. Bram finally urges her to take control of her story, of which they are all a part, before they lose their lives. As soon as she recovers, the Realms are again thrown into turmoil when the Hierophant is murdered.

A complicated murder plot involving an ambitious Scriddle and the Hierophant's duplicitous wife (where they not only kill the Hierophant but also try to murder Poison) results in Poison's finally realizing that this is her life story as well as the story of how she becomes the new Hierophant. Her whole journey into Phaerie, even her sister's kidnapping, was a test to see if she was capable of mastering her own story and creating others. She discovers her sister was returned home; ironically, it is now Poison who will never see Gull again. She bids a fond farewell to Bram, who elects to stay in the Realm of Man, and begins her new calling with the writing of her own story, tended by Fleet, Peppercorn, and Andersen.

The Message: Don't take no for an answer. If you want something, you can find a way to get it. You are in charge of your story and of creating the kinds of experiences you want to have. Stories are an inherent part of our lives, and they help us recognize problems common to all humankind—and their solutions.

Who's It For?: 7th–12th grade. This is a gruesome fantasy, full of chills, thrills, and gore. The Bone Witch gets cooked in her own pot, after her fearsome dogs are poisoned and skinned, while later Poison nearly becomes spider chow and, in a truly terrifying climax near the end, is stabbed repeatedly by Scriddle, who wants to become the Hierophant himself. The meta-fiction angle may confound some younger readers, but Wooding does an admirable job of explaining how Poison comes to be the author of not only her own story but also all human- and phaerie-kind.

Why It Rocks:
• **Voice:** The third-person narrative is from Poison's point of view, ripe with lush descriptions of other worldy creatures and settings.
• **Plot:** Completely and cleverly archetypical. Savvy readers will realize before Poison does that she is on the exact type of adventure quest that she despises in all of Fleet's stories: a personal journey of heroism where she must overcome obstacles and stave off monsters to win the day.
• **Pacing:** Occasionally meandering, and some readers who fail to understand that Poison is following familiar fairy-tale footsteps may wonder where this is all headed (at around page 100, Poison is still dodging the Bone Witch.) But all is made clear soon enough, and the suspenseful ending more than makes up for a few slow spots in getting there.
• **Characterization:** What makes Poison endearing is that despite the fact she is adamantly sullen and cynical, beneath it all beats a heart that yearns to do the right thing—just like almost every teenager you know. All of the secondary characters also are nicely developed, but the biggest scene stealer is the intrepid Andersen (clearly named after a certain famous fairy-tale author), breathing kitty sighs of frustration when the dense humans can't seem to understand which way he is leading them.

Hook It Up With: *Tithe* by Holly Black and *I Am the Messenger* by Markus Zusak.

Read More about It:
Booklist: 08/01/05
Horn Book: 04/01/06
Kirkus Reviews, starred: 09/01/05
Publishers Weekly: 11/28/05
School Library Journal: 09/01/05
V.O.Y.A. (Voice of Youth Advocates): 12/01/05

TITLE INDEX

30 Days of Night 127
33 Snowfish 114

A Bad Boy Can Be Good for a Girl 41
Abarat 234
Absolutely, Positively Not 61
Acceleration 189
Adam Canfield of the Slash 97
Airborn 218
Al Capone Does My Shirts 80
America: a novel 105

Bartimaeus Trilogy, The, Book One: The
    Amulet of Samarkand 254
Becoming Chloe 55
Beet Fields, The 113
Bermudez Triangle, The 58
Better Than Running at Night 27
Black Juice 215
Bloody Jack 157
Born Blue 111
Boy Meets Boy 63
Boyfriend List, The 29
Breath 162
Bucking the Sarge 3

Case of the Missing Marquess, The 194
Crank 106

Deep 43
Diary of Pelly D, The 204
Doing It 102
Dragon and Thief 229

Earth, My Butt, and Other Big Round Things,
    The 31

East 246
Eight Seconds 48
Empress of the World 68
Eyes of the Emperor 165

Fables: Legends in Exile 141
Feed 206
Full Service 15
Funny Little Monkey 2
Fray 138

Gender Blender 87
Geography Club 53
Girls for Breakfast 18
Godless 7
Great and Terrible Beauty, A 236

Hard Love 71
How to Disappear Completely and Never Be
    Found 89

Inexcusable 186
Inside Out 197
Interman, The 129

Jude 191

Kissing Kate 66
Kite Rider, The 154

Last Apprentice, The 239
Last Dance on Holladay Street 146
Life As We Knew It 221
Looking for Alaska 5

Mabel Riley: A Reliable Record of Humdrum,
    Peril, and Romance 85

Milkweed 168
Millions 76
Minister's Daughter, The 151
Montmorency: Thief, Liar, Gentleman? 171
Mortal Engines 224
My Heartbeat 50

No Laughter Here
Northern Light, A 148
Nothing to Lose 178

One of Those Hideous Books Where the
    Mother Dies 38
Oracle Prophecies, The: Book One: The Oracle
    Betrayed 241
Out of Order 9

Poison 257
Private Peaceful 159

Queen Bee 122

Rag and Bone Shop, The 176
Rash 212
Raven's Gate 244
Rock Star, Superstar 10
Rose 131
Rules of Survival, The 199

Runaways: Pride and Joy 134

Safe-Keeper's Secret, The 252
Saving Francesca 33
Schwa Was Here, The 92
Selina's Big Score 120
Shakespeare's Secret 78
Shattering Glass 181
Siberia: a novel 209
So B. It 94
Spiderman: Blue 124
Stained 108

Target 110
Things Not Seen 83
This Lullaby 22
Three Clams and an Oyster 12
Tribes 14

Uglies 226

Wee Free Men, The 249
Whale Talk 104
Who Am I Without Him? 24

Y: The Last Man—Unmanned 136
Year of Secret Assignments, The 36
You Don't Know Me 183

AUTHOR INDEX

Adlington, L.J. 204
Anderson, M.T. 206
Auseon, Andrew 2

Barker, Clive 234
Boyce, Frank Cottrell 76
Bray, Libba 236
Broach, Elise 78
Burgess, Melvin 102

Carbone, Elisa 146
Choldenko, Gennifer 80
Clements, Andrew 83
Clugston-Major, Chynna 122
Cooke, Darwyn 120
Cormier, Robert 176
Crutcher, Chris 104
Curtis, Christopher Paul 3

Delaney, Joseph 239
Dessen, Sarah 22
Donnelly, Jennifer 148

Ferris, Jean 48
Fisher, Catherine 241
Flake, Sharon G. 24
Flinn, Alex 178
Frank, E.R. 105
Frank, Hilary 27
Freymann-Weyr, Garret 50

Giles, Gail 181
Green, John 5

Halam, Ann 209
Hartinger, Brent 53

Hautman, Pete 7, 212
Hearn, Julie 151
Hopkins, Ellen 106
Horowitz, Anthony 244
Hyde, Catherine Ryan 55

Jacobson, Jennifer Richard 108
Jenkins, A.M. 9
Jocelyn, Marthe 85
Johnson, Kathleen Jeffrie 110
Johnson, Maureen 58

Klass, David 183

Lanagan, Margo 215
Larochelle, David 61
Levithan, David. 63
Lockhart, E. 29
Loeb, Jeph 124
Lynch, Chris 186

Mackler, Carolyn 31
Marchetta, Melina 33
McCaughrean, Geraldine 154
McNamee, Graham 189
Meyer, L.A. 157
Moline, Karl 138
Morgenroth, Kate 191
Moriarty, Jaclyn 36
Morpungo, Michael 159
Myracle, Lauren 66

Napoli, Donna Jo 162
Nelson, Blake 10, 87
Nickerson, Sara 89
Niles, Steve 127
Nolan, Han 111

Oppel, Kenneth 218
Owens, Andy 138

Parker, Jeff 129
Pattou, Edith 246
Paulsen, Gary 113
Pfeffer, Susan Beth 221
Powell, Randy 12
Pratchett, Terry 249

Rapp, Adam 114
Reeve, Philip 224
Ryan, Sara 68

Sale, Tim 124
Salisbury, Graham 165
Shinn, Sharon 252
Shusterman, Neal 92
Slade, Arthur 14
Smith, Jeff 131
Spinelli, Jerry 168
Springer, Nancy 194
Sones, Sonya 38
Stone, Tanya Lee 41

Stroud, Jonathan 254

Templesmith, Ben 127
Trueman, Terry 197

Updale, Eleanor 171

Vance, Susanna 43
Vaughn, Brian K. 134, 136
Vess, Charles 131

Weaver, Will 15
Weeks, Sarah 94
Werlin, Nancy 199
Westerfeld, Scott 226
Whedon, Joss 138
Williams-Garcia, Rita 116
Willingham, Bill 141
Winerip, Michael 97
Wooding, Chris 257
Wittlinger, Ellen 71

Yoo, David 18

Zahn, Timothy 229

ABOUT THE AUTHOR

Jennifer Hubert is the Middle School/Coordinating Librarian at Little Red School House and Elisabeth Irwin High School in New York City's historic Greenwich Village and the author of "Reading Rants! Out of the Ordinary Teen Booklists," which has been an online presence since 1998. She reviews young adult literature for Amazon.com, *Booklist, Time Out New York Kids,* and *V.O.Y.A.,* and has served on A.L.A.'s Best Books for Young Adults and Michael L. Printz Award committees. Jennifer teaches workshops on young adult literature to teachers and librarians all over the United States and has also taught young adult literature at Queens College in Jamaica, New York. When not reading or writing, she enjoys quilting and watching far too many reality television shows. She lives in Kew Gardens, Queens, with her husband, Philip, and her very high maintenance tabby, Molly.